Williamson County Tennessee

Marriage Records

1800-1850

By:
Wilena Roberts Bejach
and
Lillian Johnson Gardiner

This volume was reproduced from
An 1957 edition located in the
Publisher's private library,
Greenville, South Carolina

All rights reserved. No part of this publication
may be reproduced, stored in a retrieval system,
transmitted in any form, posted on to the web
in any form or by any means without the
prior written permission of the publisher.

Please direct all correspondence and orders to:

www.southernhistoricalpress.com
or
SOUTHERN HISTORICAL PRESS, Inc.
PO BOX 1267
375 West Broad Street
Greenville, SC   29601
southernhistoricalpress@gmail.com

Originally published: Memphis, TN. 1957
Reprinted by:
Southern Historical Press, Inc.
Greenville, SC
ISBN #0-89308-909-5
All rights Reserved.
Printed in the United States of America

PREFACE

Williamson County was created from Davidson, October 26, 1799, three years after Tennessee became a State. The County was named for General Hugh Williamson of North Carolina - the county seat for his friend, Dr. Benjamin Franklin. Only Maury County (1807) has been cut from Williamson. Hunters and explorers went into this territory as early as 1784, but permanent settlement was begun shortly before 1800.

The first recorded marriage is: John Moore to Nancy Rodgers - Feb. 3, 1800. The records from this date until January 1804 are reported to have been destroyed. From this time on, however, they seem to be complete. Over 5000 marriages are contained in this book which were copied from the original bonds and licenses. They include grooms' and brides' names, bondsmen, date of marriage and person performing marriage, where given, or date license was secured.

It is well-known that in the early days, due to bad roads, distances from the court-house, weather, etc., clergymen or justices of the peace who performed the ceremonies did not always record the rites solemnized by them. Hence, we often find the bond but not the return by the official.

As everyone knows who has tried to decipher the script of old documents, many are faded, illegible, torn, or otherwise difficult or impossible to read. The clerk copied the groom's signature or wrote it as it sounded to him. Many people in our early days did not have the advantages of "schooling", as is shown by the many who signed with their mark (X). Use your imagination - check all names that may sound or look like yours; for there were as many ways to spell a name as there were clerks, or people copying same.

The marriages are arranged alphabetically by grooms' names, with a complete index to brides' names. You can refer quickly to more than 10,000 names of persons living in one of Tennessee's early and strategically located counties from which many of the western migrations began. These families came to Williamson County from Virginia, North and South Carolina, Kentucky, Georgia, Maryland and Pennsylvania. It is interesting to note that in this 50 year period more than one generation often appears.

We offer sincere thanks to Mrs. W. A. Duke for tedious hours spent "copying" at the court-house. We appreciate the encouragement given us by Mrs. Hermione Embry, head of the Genealogical Section of the Tennessee State Library; also, we thank Mrs. S. L. Dunham, Miss Margaret Bell, Miss Lois Bejach and Adam B. Lanning, III who sketched the cover design. And special thanks are due our patient and helpful husbands, Judge Lois Dilliard Bejach and Mr. Laurence Gardiner.

> Lillian Johnson Gardiner
> Wilena Roberts Bejach
> January 1957

WILLIAMSON COUNTY, TENNESSEE

MARRIACES

1804 - 1850

-A-

Adams, Addison F. to Amanda Jane Hall   April 2, 1840 by John Landrum
    Bondsman: E. C. Eggleston

Adams, Benjamin to Martha Bailey   Sept. 5th, 1833 by Michael Finney, J.P.
    Bondsman: Darrington Garrett

Adams, Benjamin to Mary Aldridge   Dec. 23, 1839 by E. C. White, M. G.
    Bondsman: C. C. Church

Adams, Benjamin to Elizabeth Chapman   Dec. 3rd, 1845
    Bondsman: Wiley B. White

Adams, Benjamin (X) to Elizabeth Caldwell   April 19, 1846 by Thos. P rowell
    Bondsman: Franklin B. Haynes

Adams, Daniel to Susanna Fielder   Apr. 10, 1811 (bond)
    Bondsman: James Wisenor   Witness: Wm. P . Harrison

Adams, David to Betsey Fielder   Sept. 11, 1816 by J. G. Barnes, J. P.
    Bondsman: Henry McClur   Test: Ann Hardeman

Adams, George W. to Mary D. Adams   Feb. 22d, 1831   (bond)
    Bondsman: Frederick Halfacre

Adams, George W. to Jane H. Orms   Nov. 27, 1832 by Jabez Owen, J. P.
    Bondsman: Robert A. Pearce

Adams, Hiram to Martha W. Key   Dec.4th, 1844 by Benj. T. Weakley, M. G.
    Bondsman: James Williams, Jr.

Adams, James (X) to Charlotte Ingram   Feb. 9, 1832   (bond)
    Bondsman: Samuel X Adams

Adams, James W. to Susan Magness   March 4, 1822 by H. Adams, J. P.
    Bondsman: William C. C. Gambill

Adams, Joseph to Elizabeth S. Curry   Jan. 29, 1822 by Thos. Nelson
    Bondsman: David House

Adams, Nathan H. to Amanda Daizey   June 10, 1828 by Thos. D. Porter, M. G.
    Bondsman: Wm. Ditto

Adams, Samuel (X) to Diana Yates February 25, 1833 (bond)
    Bondsman: Joshua (X) Yates

Adams, William to Amey Gilbert April 23, 1825 (bond)
    Bondsman: Lewis J. Johnston

Adams, William (X) to Elinor Paschal Aug. 25, 1828 by John M. Holland
    Bondsman: James W. Adams

Aden, Harvey E. to Louisa Brown July 2nd, 1829 by Donald White
    Bondsman: Sidney B. Aden

Aden, Sidney B. to Delila Brown June 25, 1829 by Mallachi Henly, J.P.
    Bondsman: Harvey C. Aden

Aikin, Arthur S. to Nancy J. Mays Feb. 15, 1842 by H. B. North
    Bondsman: Samuel S. Campbell

Akin, Francis M. to Eliza Ann Witt Dec. 13, 1848 by H. B. North, M. G.
    Bondsman: Joseph Satterfield

Akin, George to Mary Lacy Dec. 15, 1833 by Geo. Shannon, J. P.
    Bondsman: Gustavus Holland

Aldridge, Jackson (X) to Nancy Jane Peach Dec. 27, 1847 by S.S.P.A. Knott
    Bondsman: Jesse Burns

Alexander, Alfred to Rebecca Kirby Jan. 27, 1827 (bond)
    Bondsman: William Alexander

Alexander, Ebenezer C. to Nancy C. Roberts Nov. 21st, 1825 (bond)
    Bondsman: Robert S. Montgomery

Alexander, Franklin to Rachael Seaton (Leaton) October 10, 1832 by Wm. Moor
    Bondsman: John A. Moore

Alexander, Hail W. to Marina Adams August 12th, 1835 (bond)
    Bondsman: Joshua H. Parham

Alexander, James to Edith Akin Dec. 29, 1815 by J. Pope, M.G.
    Bondsman: Sam Akin

Alexander, James F. to Sarah Jane Inman June 29, 1848 by A. K. Cunningham
    Bondsman: William (X) Brown

Alexander, James J. to Mary Jane Ballow June 9, 1841 by M. L. Andrews, M.G.
    Bondsman: Mark L. Andrews

Alexander, James R. to Ann P. Shelburn Aug. 2, 1822 by Joel Anderson
    Bondsman: Lewis Corzine

Alexander, Jesse W. to Phebe Williams Jan. 12, 1823 by Joel Anderson
    Bondsman: J. R. Alexander

Alexander, John to Henrietta Williams Feb. 25, 1821 by Joel Anderson
    Bondsman: James Williams

Alexander, John to Rebecca Williams April 28, 1842 by M. L. Andrews, M.G.
    Bondsman: Jas. S. Williams

Alexander, John C. to Mary W. Sparkman Dec. 16, 1845 by W. H. Baldridge, M.G.
    Bondsman: William W. Campbell

Alexander, Joseph to Sally Ridge Jan 25th, 1814 (bond)
    Bondsman: William Burris

Alexander, Nathaniel (X) to Ann Thackey Sept. 20, 1821 by Wm. Dunnegan, J.P.
    Bondsman: Daniel X Wright Test: Elisha L. Hall

Alexander, R. J. to Harriett J. Landrum Sept. 21, 1840 by Jno. Crick, J.P.
    Bondsman: Barnet Jackson Witness present: Blount Jordan

Alexander, Randolph to Elizabeth Sharber Feb. 7th, 1828 by Thos. Potts, M.G.
    Bondsman: Willie Potts

Alexander, Sidney (S.R.) to Rosena S. Dodson Sept. 23, 1840 by H.B. North, M.G.
    Bondsman: J. P. Bond

Alexander, Spencer A. to Susan H. Seaton Sept. 8, 1836 by J. S. Bartlett, J.P.
    Bondsman: John Seaton

Alexander, William to Betsey Norman Aug. 5, 1811 (bond)
    Bondsman: Robert Norman

Alexander, Zebulun to Mary Anne Whaly Feb. 1, 1816 by Tristram Patton, J.P.
    Bondsman: Wm. Whaly

Alford, Andrew (A his mark) to Polly Atkinson May 27, 1828 by H. Bailey, J.P.
    Bondsman: Balaam Hay

Alford, Edward to Margaret Irvin Aug. 4, 1831 by Isaac Jones, M. G.
    Bondsman: Christopher Irvin

Alford, George W. to Polly Hill Feb. 21st, 1825 (bond)
    Bondsman: Henry T. Bowles

Alford, Thomas to Mary Irvin Aug. 28, 1841 by J. B. Boyd, J. P.
    Bondsman: James X Irvin Witness present: Chesley Williams

Allen, Andrew A. F. to Susan H. Johnston April 25, 1833 by Thos. L. Douglass
    Bondsman: Abner N. White

Allen, Andrew S. to Elizabeth Ann Allen Jan. 1st, 1845 by M. L. Andrews, M.G.
    Bondsman: Benjamin T. Hutson

Allen, Benjamin F. to Martha Jordan Aug. 25, 1841 by Benjamin F. Weakley, M.G.
    Bondsman: Archer J. Wood

Allen, Charles M. to Sophronia M. Allen Dec. 22nd, 1836 by H. B. North, M.G.
    Bondsman: (none given)

Allen, Charles M. to Lucy Jane Betty Oct. 8, 1843 by M. L. Andrews, M.G.
    Bondsman: Samuel P. Allen

Allen, David to Susan Brooks Nov. 5, 1831 by John Alkinson, V.D.M.
    Bondsman: William H. Thweatt

Allen, David J. to Mary Sinder (Sincler) Dec. 22, 1836 by John Alkinson, V.D.M.
    Bondsman: Samuel Smith, Jr.

Allen, Edward H. to Nancy T. Allen Dec. 22, 1835 (bond)
    Bondsman: Samuel P. Allen

Allen, Edward H. to Sarah C. Jones Nov. 23, 1842 by Joseph Carle
    Bondsman: Zebulon M. Pilloway (Pillowry)

Allen, George to Betsey Beasley Jan. 20, 1824 (bond)
    Bondsman: Jones R. Coleman

Allen, George W. to Sarah Ann Ingram Sept. 13, 1843 (bond)
    Bondsman: Miles R. Hudson

Allen, Gideon to Elvira K. Vaughan Nov. 2, 1836 by William Lanier, J.P.
    Bondsman: Sylvanus W. Smithson, Jr.

Allen, Grandison to Nancy Rodgers Nov. 30th, 1829 (bond)
    Bondsman: Jones B. Coleman

Allen, Grant I. to Nancy Allen January 13, 1831 by Wm. Allison, J.P.
    Bondsman: Henry Bailey

Allen, Henry to Winny Standley Sept. 25, 1813 (bond)
    Bondsman: Wm. Heaton

Allen, Henry to Nancy Flippin Sept. 15, 1824 by John Alkinson, V.D.M.
    Bondsman: S. Cayce

Allen, Henry to Margaret S. Mallory Feb. 2, 1845 by J. N. Cunningham, M.G.
    Bondsman: Robert A. McLemore

Allen, James to Nancy Fitzgerald Oct. 8, 1834 by James King
    Bondsman: John Southall

Allen, James H. to Catherine Adams Nov. 11, 1841 by R.B.B. Cannon, J.P.
    Bondsman: Samuel P. Chaplain

Allen, John to Martha Freeman Oct. 28, 1810 by N. Scales
    Bondsman: Matthew McGaugh Witness: N. P. Hardeman

Allen, John to Mary Guinn Dec. 25, 1836 by J. A. Holland, J.P.
    Bondsman: None given.

Allen, John to Emeline Gibson Jan. 31, 1838 by M. L. Andrews, M.G.
    Bondsman: Joseph Gibson

Allen, John A. to Elizabeth Walker July 20, 1842 by H. B. North, M.G.
    Bondsman: Zebulon M. Pellowry

Allen, John H. to Lucinda Meadow March 22, 1832 (bond)
    Bondsman: Arthur S. Denton

Allen, John W. to Mahala Howlett April 5, 1821 by Levin Edney, M.G.
    Bondsman: Benjamin Russell Howland, Att'y in fact. (Letter found
              with license and bond from John W. Allen appointing
              B. R. Howland as his attorney in fact. Witnessed by:
              David C. Waters and Lewis C. Allen.)

Allen, Joseph B. M. to (not given) Dec. 19, 1839 by Jesse Cox, M.G.
    Bondsman: Benjamin B. Russell

Allen, Lewis C. to Rebecca Whitfield Oct 11, 1823 by Levin Edney, M. G.
    Bondsman: Jeter Perkins

Allen, Nelson to Mary Owen Oct. 22, 1840 (bond)
    Bondsman: Washington C. McCutchen

Allen, Pleasant H. to Elizabeth Knight Dec. 23rd, 1818
    Bondsman: Robert M. Carter

Allen, Samuel to Lavinia H. Pinkston March 19, 1835 by M. L. Andrews, M.G.
    Bondsman: Richard Yarbrough

Allen, Samuel S. to Jane (June) C. Andrews June 23, 1836 by Justin William, M.G.
    Bondsman: Jas. Hogan, Jr.

Allen, Sanford to Amanda Hall Jan. 14, 1846 by Acton Young, M. G.
    Bondsman: Berryman Allen

Allen, Shadrack S. to Eliza Ann Owen May 8, 1839 by W. C. Lowe, M. G.
    Bondsman: William H. Theweatt

Allen, Theophilus N. to Elizabeth M. K. Allen Nov. 18, 1845 by Henry B. North
    Bondsman: Patrick H. Southall

Allen, Theophilus N. to Mary Ann Blackburn Dec. 26, 1850 by M. L. Andrews, M.G.
    Bondsman: Samuel P. Allen

Allen, Valentine to Betsey Peay Dec. 17, 1823 (bond)
    Bondsman: Ree Joyce

Allen, William to Susannah Chitwood Oct. 15, 1816 by Lewis Edney, M. G.
    Bondsman: David Squier

Allen, William C. to Tenesse Allen Aug. 26, 1849 by Ellis E. Cook, J. P.
    Bondsman: Robert B. Allen

Allen, William C. to Mary D. Buchanan Sept. 25, 1849 by Wm. Watson
    Bondsman: Erasmus C. Ashworth

Allen, William F. to Sarah Ann Ford Jan. 5, 1837 by Jesse Cox, M. G.
    Bondsman: (None given)

Allen, William H. to Caroline Brown March 7, 1826 by John Alkinson, V.D.M.
    Bondsman: (None given)

Allen, William I. to Mary A. Jackson   Sept. 30th, 1837 by Jas. King
    Bondsman: (None given)

Allen, William J. Catharine McCoy   Dec. 31, 1842 by Joseph Carle, M. G.
    Bondsman: James X F. Jackson

Allen, Zechariah to Elizabeth S. Brooks   Nov. 5, 1843 by R. M. McDaniel, J. P.
    Bondsman: Luke L. Smith

Allison, James P. to Margaret W. C.Davidson   Sept. 19, 1832 by Wm. Allison, J.P
    Bondsman: Thos. Davidson

Allison, John to Naoma Gillespie   Oct. 12, 1814 by D. Brown, D. M.
    Bondsmen: John Wilson and Thos. Ridley

Allison, Thomas to Nancy Ogilvie   Oct. 26, 1811 (bond)
    Bondsman: Wm. House

Allison, William to Charity Upshire (Upshare)   Dec. 3, 1808
    Bondsman: Arch Potter

Allmon, Nathan J. to Ann Matilda Ray   Oct. 29, 1845 by John Richardson
    Bondsman: J. G. Mansker

Almond, Richard to Elizabeth Hill   Aug. 3, 1829 by H. B. Hyde, J. P.
    Bondsman: Johnson Wood, Jr.

Almond, William to Mary Dean   Oct. 8, 1835 by T. D. Porter
    Bondsman: Franklin Coleman

Alston, Augustine to Eliza B. Scales   May 29, 1834 by H. B. Hyde, J. P.
    Bondsman: Sam'l M. Copeland

Alston, Hardaway to Rebecca Bradley   Jan. 5, 1821 by H. Adams, J. P.
    Bondsman: M. Bostick

Alston, James to Nancy Swansey   Nov. 26, 1816 by David Shannon, J. P.
    Bondsman: Esaiaz (?) Kaigler

Alston, John to Ann M. Tulloss   Nov. 7, 1844 by M. L. Andrews, M. G.
    Bondsman: James M. Peebles

Alston, Thomas E. to Joanna J. Palmon   Dec. 20, 1848 (bond)
    Bondsman: Candor Sanford

Alston, Solomon G. to Mary E. S. Peebles   Nov. 26th, 1841 by Benjamin F. Weakley
    Bondsman: John Alston

Alston, William I. to Martha Ridley   Oct. 13, 1842 by B. D. Neal, M. G.
    Bondsman: John Alston

Alston, William J. to Elizabeth Jane Bell   Dec. 29, 1850 by Wm. A. Whitsett,M.3
    Bondsman: Joseph Hunter

Alsup, Drury to Tabitha Brown   Jan. 27, 1806 (bond)
    Bondsmen: Joseph Roberts   Test: John Hardeman

Alsup, Robert A. to Louise Smith Feb. 3, 1808 (bond)
    Bondsman: John Alsup Test: A. Potter

Amis, William to Polly Anderson March 26, 1822 (bond)
    Bondsman: F. B. Carter Witness present: Thos Hardeman

Amis, William to Elizabeth Bugg May 28, 1839 (bond)
    Bondsman: William Anderson

Amos, Jonathan to Nancy Boyd Dec. 21st, 1825 by Joel Anderson
    Bondsman: John Boyd

Amos, Latney to Susan Walker April 12, 1835 by John Landrum
    Bondsman: Drury Nance

Anderson, Abraham to Betsey Merchant Mar. 5, 1813 (bond)
    Bondsman: Azariah Anderson

Anderson, Azariah (X) to Elizabeth Glover May 13, 1824 (bond)
    Bondsman: William K. Layne Witness present: Elisha L. Hall

Anderson, Branch H. to Milly Toone May 14th, 1821 by Berry Nolen, J. P.
    Bondsman: Holland L. White

Anderson, David to Harriett Brantley Aug. 16, 1820 by Henry Petty, M. G.
    Bondsman: Ely Dodson

Anderson, David P. to Mary Cooper July 17, 1808 (bond)
    Bondsman: Silas Stephens Test: N. P. Hardeman

Anderson, George W. to Catharine Brown Oct. 22, 1837 by J. J. Bingham
    Bondsman: None given

Anderson, Henry M. to Mariah Alexander Nov. 2nd, 1833 (bond)
    Bondsman: Thomas J. Inman

Anderson, James to Henrietta N. Anderson April 30, 1835 by Andrew Craig, M.G.
    Bondsman: David Campbell

Anderson, James to Parthenia Bostick Nov. 16, 1845 by Benj. F. Weakley, M.G.
    Bondsman: Beverly (?) B. Toon

Anderson, Joel to Susan S. Priest Oct. 15, 1846 by M. L. Andrews, M. G.
    Bondsman: M. L. Andrews (Mark)

Anderson, John to Elizabeth Nall Dec. 21, 1839 (bond)
    Bondsman: Hugh Brown

Anderson, John N. to Catherine Dowdy Feb. 25, 1823 by Lewis Loyd, J. P.
    Bondsman: A. A. Edney

Anderson, Robert to Rebecca Wilkins July 14, 1809 (bond)
    Bondsman: Robert Wilkins Witness: Wm. P. Harrison

Anderson, Stanfield to Drucilla Skinner Oct. 21st, 1847 by Lycurgus McCall, J.P
    Bondsman: J. C. Bigger Witness present: Chesley Williams

Anderson, Thomas to Nancy Hartly Sept. 16, 1816 by James Wilson
    Bondsman: Wilson White Test: Ann Hardeman

Anderson, Thomas to Sarah A. Wiley Aug. 22nd, 1827 by M. L. Andrews, J. P.
    Bondsman: John C. Wylie Witness present: J. W. McCown, D. C.

Anderson, Thomas to Annis (Annie) R. Alston Aug. 15, 1829 (bond)
    Bondsman: James Alston

Anderson, Thomas M. to Minerva Ann Tennessee Wall Feb. 9, 1832 by Daniel White
    Bondsman: John N. Anderson

Anderson, Thomas P. to Mary Frances Cowles Oct. 16, 1850 by J. M. Macpherson
    Bondsman: Jesse G. Core (Gore)

Anderson, William to Elizabeth Thompson Mar. 24, 1817 (bond)
    Bondsman: Thos. Craig Test: Robert Davis

Anderson, William to Sally Robinson Dec. 13, 1827 by David Kinnard, J. P.
    Bondsman: James Robinson

Anderson, William to Sally White Dec. 20th, 1827 by Andrew Craig, M. G.
    Bondsman: John Marshall

Anderson, William D. to Nancy Chadwell Jan. 1, 1849 (bond)
    Bondsman: Samuel Waters

Anderson, William P. to Anna Brown Jan. 24th, 1831 by F. Ivy, J. P.
    Bondsman: John X Montgomery

Andrews, Ananias to Sally McCrady April 3, 1808
    Bondsman: James Neil Test: A. Potter

Andrews, Andrew L. to Elizabeth H. Andrews Dec. 26, 1816 by A. Mebane, J. P.
    Bondsman: Eli McGan

Andrews, Ephraim B. to Elizabeth L. South (?) Nov. 4, 1835 by H. C. Horton
    Bondsman: Thos. N. Figures

Andrews, Ephraim B. to Lucy R. Padgett Sept. 27, 1842 by Acton Young, M.G.
    Bondsman: Knacy H. Locke

Andrews, Ephraim F. to Sarah J. Bizzell Nov. 8th, 1849 by A. Burns, M. G.
    Bondsman: W. Y. Burnett

Andrews, Ephraim M. to Nancy H. Pinkston July 10, 1822 by H. Adams, J. P.
    Bondsman: James B. Bond

Andrews, George Jr. to Winnifred E. Matthews Jan. 6, 1825 by M. L. Andrews, M.G.
    Bondsman: M. L. Andrews

Andrews, George S. to Margaret J. Shelton Feb. 12, 1846 by Acton Young, M. G.
    Bondsman: Jas. Hogan, Jr.

Andrews, George Stanfield to Frances Rogers Dec. 12, 1849 by Robert Davis, M.G.
    Bondsman: Jas. Hogan, Jr.

9.

Andrews, Henry to Elizabeth Williams Feb. 14, 1818 (bond)
    Bondsman: Goodwin Taylor Test: Robert Davis

Andrews, John to Minerva Matthews Sept. 20, 1840 by Robert Davis, M.G.
    Bondsman: Loving H. Wolridge

Andrews, John T. to Madaline Andrews Nov. 25, 1840 by Robert L. Andrews
    Bondsman: Sam Henderson

Andrews, Jones to Lucy Lanier (Laneer) Sept. 26, 1816 by Thos. Wilson, J.P.
    Bondsman: Ephraim Bugg

Andrews, Joseph to Sarah E. Barnes Dec. 27, 1838 by T.L. Douglass, M.G.
    Bondsman: Solomon Barnes

Andrews, Lemuel to Caroline A. Dean March 8, 1849 (bond)
    Bondsman: Ephraim F. Andrews

Andrews, Mark M. to Sarah P. L. Andrews Dec. 15, 1835 (bond)
    Bondsman: N. L. Locke

Andrews, Richard L. to Caroline Andrews Oct. 30, 1833 by Thos. L. Douglass
    Bondsman: Gilbert Marshall

Andrews, Robert L. to Mary D. Horton March 25, 1835 by M. L. Andrews, M.G.
    Bondsman: Richard L. Andrews

Andrews, Samuel to Kitty Dunnagan May 23, 1812 (bond)
    Bondsman: John McSwine Test: Wm. P. Harrison

Andrews, Stith H. to Mariah S. A. Andrews Dec. 21, 1840 (bond)
    Bondsman: Octavius C. Hatcher (signed O.C.)

Andrews, Tapley to Nancy Ragsdale Feb. 13, 1909 (bond)
    Bondsman: Robt. Ragsdale Test: A. Patton

Andrews, William to Nancy Grimes Feb. 23, 1813 by J. R. Trotter, J.P.
    Bondsman: Samuel Joslin

Andrews, William to Elisabeth Stephens Nov. 22, 1816 by Garner McConnico, M.G.
    Bondsman: Ephraim Young

Andrews, William to Mary P. Matthews Dec. 24, 1833 by Thos. D. Porter
    Bondsman: Clarbourne H. Kinnard

Andrews, William B. to Tennessee Tucker Oct. 23, 1849 by Z. W. Calhoun, M.G.
    Bondsman: None given (This and following license found. May be same.

Andrews, William V. to Tennessee Tucker Oct. 25, 1849 by J. Hendricks, J. P.
    Bondsman: John R. Bigger

Anglen, Zephaniah to Elizabeth Cole Sept. 9, 1828 by Thos. Potts, M.G.
    Bondsman: Elisha Hendrix Witness present: J. W. McCown

Anglin, James (X) to Polly Ann Hendrise Nov. 16, 1836 by Lewis Magee, J.P.
    Bondsman: John (X) Hendrise

Anglin, Jonathan to Matilda Turman Dec. 14, 1829 by Daniel White, M. G.
    Bondsman: Wiley White

Angling, Philip to Betsey Watkins Oct. 25, 1832 by James P. Brown, J.P.
    Bondsman: John X Hutchenson Wit. present: Will Hardeman

Ansley, Charles P. to Elizabeth P. Thompson Feb. 16, 1830 by Wm. Moor, J.P.
    Bondsman: J. W. Greer

Anthony, John G. to Mahala D. German March 2, 1830 (bond)
    Bondsman: William B. Hobson

Appleby, Hezekiah to Margaret Herrin Dec. 2, 1819 by D. Brown, Pastor
    Bondsman: David McCurdy

Arendell, William (X) to Minthy Edwards Feb. 19, 1821 (bond)
    Bondsman: William E. Owen Witnesses: M. L. Bond, Elisha L. Hall

Armstrong, George to Ann L. Baugh Oct 10, 1850 by H. B. North, M.G.
    Bondsman: Wm. A. Baugh

Armstrong, George W. to Eliza Jane McGavock Sept. 16, 1847 by Jas. Marshall
    Bondsman: Samuel E. McCutchen

Armstrong, James to Mary Mebane August 28, 1833 (bond)
    Bondsman: Alex F. McKinney

Armstrong, John to Nancy Benthal July 28, 1807 (bond)
    Bondsman: Thomas Benthal

Armstrong, John M. to Elizabeth Briant July 29, 1813 (bond)
    Bondsman: John M. Walker Witness: Thos. J. Hardeman

Armstrong, Nathaniel to Caty Derresberry Sept. 5, 1807 (bond)
    Bondsman: Adam Derresberry Witness: N. P. Hardeman

Armstrong, Thomas to Matilda Gunter Nov. 14, 1822 by Jas. A.M.T. Howard, J.P.
    Bondsman: William McFadden

Armstrong, William to Elizabeth Starks Sept. 10, 1811 (bond)
    Bondsman: Richard Orton

Armstrong, William to Martha Oldham Jan. 23, 1830 (bond)
    Bondsman: Henry B. Cowles

Armstrong, William to Elizabeth Leigh Nov. 2, 1836 (bond)
    Bondsman: William Bowers

Armstrong, William H. to Malvina Durch Oct. 12, 1835 (bond)
    Bondsman: Asberry X Tarkington

Arnold, James E. to Nancy Jackson Aug. 23, 1838 by Sam B. Robison, J.P.
    Bondsman: Edward C. Eggleston Witness present: Sam B. Robison

Arnold, John to Nancy Hogan Sept. 10, 1818 by Frank Jackson, J.P.
    Bondsman: None given

11.

Arnold, Osborn to Lamisa Winrow Jan. 23, 1838 by Sam B. Robison, J.P.
        Bondsman: W. K. Ransom

Arnold, Turney to Marion Gwinn Apr. 14, 1822 by Jonathan Norman, J.P.
        Bondsman: Winfield Pope

Arnold, William (X) to Mintha Edwards June 28, 1819 (bond)
        Bondsman: William Johnson

Ashworth, Erasmus C. to Nancy Walker March 11, 1845 by Gilbert Marshall, J.P.
        Bondsman: George Sweeny

Asure (Asine?), John to Nancy Morgan Dec. 17, 1808 (bond)
        Bondsman: Daniel Sumner   Test: A. Potter

Asure, Samuel to Betsey Armstrong Aug. 21, 1806 (bond)
        Bondsman: Amos Asure   Witness: N. P. Hardeman

Atkinson, Arthur to Cassa Breese Aug. 11, 1813 by David Mason
        Bondsman: Abram Hill   Witness: N. P. Hardeman

Atkinson, Dossey to Mary Ann Patton Dec. 18, 1832 (1833?) by Robert Hardin, M.
        Bondsman: Elisha C. Williams

Atkinson, Jesse B. to Margaret Patton Oct. 27, 1831 by Robert Hardin, M.G.
        Bondsman: Wm. T. North

Atkinson, John, Jr. to Sally Staten July 26, 1836 by H. C. White, J.P.
        Bondsman: Andrew J. Toon

Atkinson, John H. to Mary P. Hall Feb. 20, 1823 (bond)
        Bondsman: Edward Hall

Atkinson, Richard D. to Elizabeth Harford June 28, 1824 (bond)
        Bondsman: John Corlett

Atkinson, Robert W. to Elizabeth Ann Powell Feb. 22, 1845 by J.B. Boyd, J.P.
        Bondsman: James M. Whitfield

Atkinson, Stephen B. to Rachel Mihale (?) Corzine Nov. 7, 1844 (bond)
        Bondsman: Jesse M. Corzine Witness present: C. Williams

Atkinson, Thomas to Lucinda Lambert Mar. 10, 1824 by Abner Hill, E.C.C.
        Bondsman: Thomas Rolland

Atkinson, Tilman F. to Mary White June 27, 1822 (bond)
        Bondsman: Thos. S. Spencer

Atkinson, Tilman F. to Harriet Pipskin Jan. 15, 1835 by Rev. Jas. King, M.G.
        Bondsman: L. B. McConnico

Atkinson, William to Mary C. Hobbs Oct. 2, 1832 by Wm. Rucker, J.P.
        Bondsman: James Chandler

Attinson, John to Sally Short Nov. 2, 1815 (bond) (Note found: "Sir, I am
        Bondsman: Samuel Attinson (resident of Williamson County having
                                  (neither parent or gardeen but of full age to act for my-
                                  (self. Please issue License for purpose of my entering
                                  (marriage with John Atkinson Sally X Short Test: Jese A.

Avery, Orlando to Mary A. Criddle   Feb. 4, 1850 by M.L. Andrews, M.G.
    Bondsman: Young G. Cannon

-B-

Badger, Felix H. to Catharine S. Smith   Oct. 2, 1823 by Tho. L. Douglass
    Bondsman: Thomas L. Robinson

Bagly, Clark H. to Mary Thompson   Nov. 7, 1830 by Tristram Patton, J.P.
    Bondsman: William Sanders

Bailey, Albert H. to Louisa Ann Figures   June 28, 1839 by Thos. L. Douglass
    Bondsman: John J. Watson

Bailey, Alexander to Elizabeth Davis   Oct. 30, 1805 (bond)
    Bondsman: William Bailey   Witness: N. P. Harrison

Bailey, Charles to Polly Old   May 17, 1808 (bond)
    Bondsman: R.P. Currin   Test: A. Potter

Bailey, Henry T. (X) to Mary Ann Price   July 20, 1846 by S.S. Atkman (?), J.P.
    Bondsman: James A. (X) Wallis
    Letter found with bond: "Personally appeared before me, Hugh Thomson
    an acting justice for said county Polly Bailey and makes oath that
    her son Henry T. Bailey is of mixed blood and beyound the third gen-
    eration. Polly X Bailey Test: William L. Neely Hugh Thomson, J.P."

Bailey, John to Catherine Ragans   March 7, 1821 by C. McDaniel
    Bondsmen: John X Bailey   Isaac X Rhodes

Bailey, John R. (X) to Susan M. Peach   July 25, 1847 by W. Anderson, J.P.
    Bondsmen: John A. X Wallace

Bailey, Joseph S. to Sarah B. Fore   Jan. 6, 1831 by Geo. Shannon, J.P.
    Bondsman: None given

Bailey, Philip to Ann C. Johnson   April 24, 1834 by M. Fenney, J.P.
    Bondsman: Darrington Garrett

Baird, John (X) to Elizabeth Bradford   Sept. 28, 1839 by R. White, J.P.
    Bondsman: Thomas X Harris

Baird, John to Nancy Hutchison   Aug. 15, 1839 by R. White, J.P.
    Bondsman: Philip X Anglin

Baird, William (X) to Mary McGee   Dec. 26, 1844 by Jas. A. Cunningham, J.P.
    Bondsman: William McGee

Baker, Abraham (Abram) to Rebecca Phillips   Apr. 30, 1812
    Bondsman: Owen Hines Witnesses: N. P. Hardeman W. R. Nunn

Baker, German to Mary Kirzer   Dec. 24, 1828 by A. B. Rozell, M. G.
    Bondsman: Thos. Hardeman

Baker, Giles (X) to Martha Mullen   Feb. 26, 1835 by Wm. Edmondson, J.P.
    Bondsman: Alfred E. Conner

Baker, James to Sally Skelly   Nov. 10, 1818 by John K. Campbell
    Bondsman: John X Baker

Baker, John to Elizabeth Derriberry   Nov. 26, 1811 (bond)
    Bondsman: Daniel Dereberry   Witness: Wm. P. Harrison

Baker, Richard W. of Murfreesboro - Letter written to Thomas Hardeman authorizing N. Cannon's signature to marriage bond. Letter from Harpeth, Dec. 23, 1828. Bride's name not given on any bond or license.

Baldridge, William H. to Unity Brogden   Nov. 4, 1844 (bond)
    Bondsman: Parson M. Brogden

Baldwin, Aaron to Henritta Tally   March 2, 1811 (bond)
    Bondsman: Wm. Francis   Witness: Wm. P. Harrison

Ballance, Joshua to Marjory Roberts   Dec. 29, 1808 (bond)
    Bondsman: Thos. Garrett   Test: A. Potter

Ballard, John to Oney (Denny) Pope   Feb. 24, 1827 (bond)
    Bondsman: Jonathan Cor or Cox (Illegible)

Ballow, Leonard G. to Helen Mary McCown   Feb. 26, 1836 by Robert Davis, M.G.
    Bondsman: None given

Ballow, Robert S. to Martha Ann Temple   Sept. 9, 1840 by W.B. Carpenter
    Bondsman: Perry M. Neal

Banks, James M. (W.?) to Louisianna D. Cash   June 3, 1820 by Geo. Blackburn, M.(
    Bondsman: D. C. Kinnard

Banks, Madison C. to Susan C. Bugg   Oct. 5, 1842 by James B. Porter
    Bondsman: Jas. Hogan, Jr.

Banks, Thomas C. to Elizabeth F. Morton   Aug. 9, 1848 by Wm. J. Barber, M.G.
    Bondsman: John B. McEwen

Barclift, John H. to Lucy Ann McRay (Lucy M. Ray (?)   Aug. 11, 1837 by
    Bondsman (None given)   R. C. Goodwin in M. E. Church

Barclift, Samuel to Nancy A. Davis   Oct 30, 1839 (bond)
    Bondsman: Thomas Barclift

Barfield, Eli to Tabetha Webber   May 23, 1814 (bond)
    Bondsman: John Jones

Barfield, Lewis to Rosanna Bateman   Feb. 11, 1825 (bond)
    Bondsman: John L. McEwen

Barfoot, Jonathan to Nanny White   May 2, 1812 (bond)
    Bondsman: James Norton   Witness: Wm. P. Harrison

Barham, Newsom to Mary Bond   Nov. 23, 1837 by Wm. R. Horton, M. G.
    Bondsman: None given

Barham, William P. to Narcissa T. Toon   Sept. 7, 1845 by W. Anderson, J.P.
    Bondsman: George R. Long

Barker, Alexander to Margaret Dotson (Dodson ?) Oct. 5, 1820 (bond)
    Bondsman: Thomas Dotson Teste: Elisha L. Hall

Barker, David D. to Betsey Spencer June 6, 1807 (bond)
    Bondsman: David Squier

Barker, Richard B. to Margaret W. Patton Sept. 7 (1?), 1836 by M.L. Andrews
    Bondsman: H. G. Barker

Barker, William to Ellen Dotson Oct 2, 1834 by Jas. King
    Bondsman: Ely Dodson

Barker, Wilson to Hannah Bailey Dec. 15, 1814 (bond)
    Bondsman: Frederick Avery Witness: N. P. Hardeman

Barksdale, William to Nancy Lester Oct 14, 1813 (bond)
    Bondsman: Thomas Mabry

Barnes, Andrew J. to Mary Robinson Feb. 17, 1842 by B.B. Toon, J.P.
    Bondsman: John B. Barnes

Barnes, Ansalam (Ansylum) to Miram Leak June 26, 1816 (bond)
    Bondsman: Thos. P. Carsey

Barnes, Bolin C. to Emily Nolen Jan. 23, 1834 by T.D. Porter
    Bondsman: John King

Barnes, Horatio (X), to Polly Phillips April 20, 1820 by H. Burne
    Bondsman: Josias Jackson Witness: Jno. P. McCutchan

Barnes, James to Celia Region Nov. 4, 1840 by H. B. North, M.G.
    Bondsmen: William P. Henderson, James X Barnes

Barnes, Jeremiah to Marilla Lagooch Aug. 8, 1816 by G. Hunt, J.P.
    Bondsman: Daniel R. Gooch

Barnes, Jesse to Elizabeth Fly Oct 17, 1824 by Thomas Nelson, J.P.
    Bondsman: John Briley

Barnes, Joel to Sarah Ann Ballow June 12, 1844 by Thos. I. Nolen, J.P.
    Bondsman: Benjamin X Housden

Barnes, John to Mary Addeline Nevills Nov. 18, 1844 (bond)
    Bondsman: William Merritt

Barnes, John B. to Louisa Layne Sept. 2, 1847 by Wm. Carter, J.P.
    Bondsman: George P. Brimm

Barnes, John H. to Mary Holliday Aug. 10, 1848 by John Hay
    Bondsman: Alfred Sanders

Barnes, Peter to Mary Peay March 11, 1819 by T. Barnes, J.P.
    Bondsman: John L. Fielder

Barnes, Robert S. to Mary E. Edmiston Dec. 10, 1835 by T.D. Porter
    Bondsman: William Edmondson

15.

Barnes, Samuel H. to Sarah H. Howel   Dec. 23, 1830 by Jabez Owen, J.P.
    Bondsman: Joel H. Still

Barnes, Solomon M. to Edney Haethcock (?) March 13, 1839 by Thomas L. Douglass
    Bondsman: Samuel P. Allen

Barnes, Solomon M. to Lurana Heathcock   June 14, 1842 by John Z Wren, J.P.
    Bondsman: Joel Wren

Barnes, Valentine T. (X) to Louiza H. Hamer   Jan. 13, 1842 by N.R. Owen, J.P.
    Bondsman: Lander Hamer

Barnes, Wiley to Sarah Hargrave   April 3, 1822 by Levin Edney, M.G.
    Bondsman: Samuel Clark

Barnett, Elias to Nancy Taylor   June 30, 1824   (bond)
    Bondsman: Winfield Pope

Barnett, George W. to Eliza Patton July 6, 1820 by Jno. Hamilton, M.G.
    Bondsman: William H. Hamilton   Witness: Jno. P. McCutchan

Barnett, James P. to Peggy Gibson   Sept. 10, 1810   (bond)
    Bondsman: Thomas Barnett   Wit: Wm. P. Harrison

Barnett, John to Mary Patterson   July 9, 1821   (bond)
    Bondsman: William Taylor

Barnet, Thomas to Penelope Ogilvie   June 14, 1815   (bond)
    Bondsman: Morris L. Bond

Barnett, William R.D. to Jane C. Wilson   July 24, 1828 by M.L. Andrews, J.P.
    Bondsman: J.M. Patton   Witness present: J.W. McCown

Barr, Joseph A. to Lucy Pognor (?)   Feb. 27, 1830   (bond)
    Bondsman: Stephen S. Pognor

Bartlett, Henry (X) to Nancy Thweatt   March 15, 1847 by John Z Men (?) J.P.
    Bondsman: Samuel X Coleman

Bartlett, Joseph S. to Amanda F. Zacry   March 11, 1828   (bond)
    Bondsman: Joseph M. X Porter   Witness present: Will Hardeman

Bass, Ambrose H. A. to Rebica Yeargan   Nov. 5, 1850 by B.R. Gant, Minister
    Bondsman: W. B. House   Witness present: J. P. Rankin

Bass, Thomas to Ann Maria Shines or Shinn   Nov. 8, 1817   (bond)
    Bondsman: Thos. B. Jones and Thomas L. Bass

Bass, William to America R. Elam   Nov. 23, 1831 by Lewis Heath, J.P.
    Bondsman: Bennett F. Elam

Bateman, Andrew D. to Nancy L. Hall   March 12, 1827   (bond)
    Bondsman: L. S. Bateman   Witness present: Joshua W. McCown

Bateman, Jonathan T. to Sally M. S. McGavock   March 28, 1830 by Andrew Craig, M.C
    Bondsman: Jas. McGavock   Witness present: Jno. G. Hay

Bateman, Simeon to Penny Brady Nov. 4, 1807 (bond)
    Bondsman: Allen McClure Test: Peter Hardeman

Bateman, Thomas to Ann Barclift July 24, 1828 by Wm. Moor, J.P.
    Bondsman: Reuben Overman

Bateman, William to Elizabeth Pearse Dec. 11, 1817 (bond)
    Bondsman: Wm. R. Wood Test: Robert Davis

Bateman, William J. to Sarah Jane Wright Jan. 12, 1847 by M.L. Andrews, M.G.
    Bondsman: Oscar H. McGavock

Bates, David to Elizabeth Akridge Feb. 23, 1812 (bond)
    Bondsman: John Avery

Bates, Robert to Jane Marlin May 12, 1827 (bond)
    Bondsmen: Robert X Bates, George Marling

Batey, James (X) to Nancy Davis April 8, 1840 by B M. Joie, J.P.
    Bondsman: Samuel X Davis

Batty, Henry to Frances Hutson Jan. 12, 1837 by H. B. Hyde, J.P.
    Bondsman: None given

Baucom, Avery K. to Nancy Blythe May 13, 1829 by Wm. Craig
    Bondsman: Josiah X Baucom

Baucom, Edmund B. (X) to Rachael Blythe April 22, 1829 by Wm. Craig
    Bondsman: Avery H. Baucom Witness present: Thos. Hardeman

Baucom, William A. to Catharine H. Hemphill Dec. 22, 1846 (bond)
    Bondsman: James F. Graham

Baucom, Willis to Elizabeth Wilson Dec. 17, 1823 by W. R. Nunn, J.P.
    Bondsman: B. B. Lanier

Baucom, Wilson (X) to Crissy Creek Feb. 9, 1821 by Edward Ragsdale, J.P.
    Bondsman: John Christopher Wit.: Elisha L. Hall

Baugh, Daniel to Elizabeth Armstrong Dec. 19, 1822 by Thos. L. Douglass
    Bondsman: P. Reese

Baugh, James (X) to Eliza Neelly Oct. 21, 1840 by Jacob Critz, J.P.
    Bondsman: Obediah Jones

Baugh, John to Martha E. Trotter June 27, 1826 by Thos. L. Douglass
    Bondsman: None given

Baugh, Philip W. to Elizabeth Lemons Nov. 10, 1831 by Jas. King, M.G.
    Bondsman: Boling C. North

Baugh, Robert to Malinda Montgomery Feb. 11, 1830 by Andrew Craig, M.G.
    Bondsman: Thos. E. Wooldridge

Baugh, William to Amarillar Pope March 9, 1828 by Thos. L. Douglass
    Bondsmen: William Pope, Mordecai C. H. Puryear

Baugh, William (X) to Hannah E. Church Aug. 21, 1848 by Jesse Cox, M.G.
    Bondsman: John Baugh

Baughman, Christian to Lurena or Raney Floyd June 25, 1813 (bond)
    Bondsman: Isaac C. Oakes Witness: N. P. Hardeman

Baxter, William to Eleanor Cowen Nov. 14, 1832 (bond)
    Bondsman: Ezekiel Baxter

Beale, Livingston C. to Mary M. Reynolds Oct. 3, 1847 (bond)
    Bondsman: Jacob H. Cowley

Beale, Livingston C. to Martha M. Reynolds Oct. 15, 1847 (bond)
    Bondsman: C. P. Logan Witness present: Chesley Williams
        (Above two bonds on file. May be same bride.)

Beale, Richard H. to Mary A. V. Moon Jan. 10, 1850 by M.L. Andrews, M.G.
    Bondsman: Joshua J. Toon

Beard, Aaron P. to Mahala Green Oct. 18, 1849 by J. Hendricks
    Bondsman: John White

Beard, Andrew to Nancy Edwards Aug. 17, 1831 by Andrew McCrady
    Bondsman: Andrew X Beard and John Alderson

Beard, Bird Near (X) to Sarah Kennedy Aug. 11, 1824 by Wm. Dunnegan, J.P.
    Bondsman: Enos S. Corzine

Beard, Charles to Nancy Roberts July 19, 1825 by John Nelson
    Bondsmen: Chas. **Baird**, Daniel H. Hamer

Beard, George to Matilda Nail June 8, 1806 (bond)
    Bondsman: William Legate

Beard, George T. P. to Tabitha Green July 19, 1850 by J. Hendricks, J.P.
    Bondsman: William C. Hendricks

Beard, Moses (X) to Mary Morton June 23, 1831 by Daniel White, M.G.
    Bondsman: Davis Bradford

Beard, Thomas L. to Mahala Shaw July 19, 1835 (bond)
    Bondsman: William H. Bugg

Beard, William to Celia Edwards April 9, 1836 by S.W. McKinn, J.P.
    Bondsman: David N. McManus

Beard, William to Nancy Bradford Oct 25, 1849 by J. Hendricks, J.P.
    Bondsman: Zachariah Green

Beasley, Andrew (X) to Martha J. Meacham Sept. 16, 1846 by J.J. Bingham, J.P.
    Bondsman: William T. Allen

Beasley, Charles to Delilah Owen March 5, 1810 (bond)
    Bondsman: John Owen Wit: Wm. P. Harrison

Beasley, Daniel to Julia Ezell Nov. 1, 1820 (bond)
    Bondsman: William Beasley

Beasley, Hilliard to Ibby Griffin March 23, 1836 by S.S. Newman, J.P.
    Bondsman: None given

Beasley, James A. to Amanda J. Adams Dec. 3, 1846 by J.J. Bingham, J.P.
    Bondsman: Wm. D. Frantham

Beasley, John B. to Altamyra Graham May 23, 1833 by S.S. Harkness
    Bondsman: Arthur S. Denton

Beasley, John P. to Polly Bates March 17, 1825 (bond)
    Bondsman: James Short

Beasley, John W. to Nancy Coatney Dec. 22, 1805 (bond)
    Bondsman: George Wrenn

Beasley, Littleberry to Rebecca Thompson July 18, 1839 by Thos. Powell, J.P.
    Bondsmen: Little B. Beasley (as signed), James H. Wilkins

Beasley, Littleberry to Macharina Thurman Nov. 21, 1850 (bond)
    Bondsman: Joseph R. Hunter

Beasley, Nehemiah Courtney to Judith B. Womack Oct 11, 1832 by Jas. King
    Bondsman: Asbury M. Kelley

Beasley, Thomas to Tabitha Allen Oct. 16, 1828 (bond)
    Bondsmen: Thomas X Beasley and Charles D. Ivey

Beasley, Wiley to Polly Johnston April 16, 1829 by Robt. Davis, M.G.
    Bondsman: Boswell X Drake Witness present: Will Hardeman

Beasley, Wiley E. to Elizabeth Fox Sept. 23, 1842 by Thos. Prowell, J.P.
    Bondsman: Michael Cody

Beasley, William to Barbary Denton April 29, 1818 (bond)
    Bondsman: James B. Beasley

Beasley, William to Mary Johnson Feb. 12, 1829 by Thos. D. Porter
    Bondsman: John Johnson

Beasley, Wyatt W. to Sarah Neelly April 23, 1846 by G. W. Barker
    Bondsman: John Baugh

Beasley, Zachariah to Nancy Adams Sept. 2, 1825 (bond)
    Bondsman: Green X Mitchell

Beasley, Zechariah to Sarah McNabb April 13, 1836 by James W. Rea, M.G.
    Bondsman: None given

Beaty, David (X) to Mary Hutson July 5, 1841 by J. B. Boyd, J.P.
    Bondsman: James R. Cherry

Beaty, James to Fanny Preast Nov. 4, 1813 (bond)
    Bondsman: James McCombs

Beaty, John to Joannah Moore May 27, 1807 (bond)
    Bondsman: Basil Berry Wit.: N. P. Hardeman

19.

Beatty, John (X) to Elizabeth Pinkston   Feb. 5, 1838 by M.L. Andrews
    Bondsman: Isaac W. Drake (date given is of bond, not marriage).

Beech, Americus to Harriet E. Pointer   Jan. 16, 1849 by A.N. Cunningham, M.G.
    Bondsman: John L. McEwen

Beech, Constantine to Addeline V. Beech   Oct. 16, 1849 by J. Hendricks, J.P.
    Bondsman: John Haffner (Groom signed "Beach").

Beech, James D. to Sarah E. Wilkinson   Jan. 31, 1849 by Wm. M. Wright, J.P.
    Bondsman: Jacob Sweeney

Beech, Jonathan to Sarah W. Hughes   Nov. 30, 1848 by M.L. Andrews, M.G.
    Bondsman: George Sweeney

Beech, Lodwick B. to Sarah Williams   Feb. 5, 1845 by M.L. Andrews, M.G.
    Bondsman: Lemuel Farmer

Beech, Patrick B. to Nancy W. Houston (Huston)   Dec. 11, 1823 by Geo. Shannon
    Bondsman: John Collier

Beeman, Philo to Martha C. Campbell   Feb. 21, 1820 (bond)
    Bondsman: James C. Hill

Belcher, Daniel to Catharine Baker   Jan. 12, 1838 by Thos. Prowell, J.P.
    Bondsman: Newberry H. Belcher

Belcher, John (X) to Martha Coleman   Jan. 12, 1812 (bond)
    Bondsman: Grief X B. Hawkins

Bell, David to Elizabeth Edminston   April 7, 1814 (bond)
    Bondsman: Robert McCutcheon

Bell, David A. to Sarah Ann Hamer   Dec. 24, 1843 by W.B. Carpenter
    Bondsman: Turner S. Foster

Bell, Hugh M. to Elizabeth L. Sanford   March 4, 1830 by Abner McDowell
    Bondsman: Joseph Sanford

Bell, James to Jane Hemphill   Dec. 7, 1820 by G. Hunt
    Bondsman: Robert Johnston

Bell, James F. to Nancy Wall   Dec. 23, 1830 by A.B. Morton
    Bondsman: Ezekiel Wall

Bell, James N. to Sally A. Moore   July 26, 1832 by Wm. Little, J.P.
    Bondsman: Joseph X Corzine

Bell, James N. to Nancy Marchant   Nov. 5, 1837 by Sam B. Robinson, J.P.
    Bondsman: (none given)

Bell, Jobe to Elizabeth Bostick   April 4, 1816 by N. Scales, J.P.
    Bondsman: Thomas Shumate

Bell, Joel to Sarah Ann Bugg   June 15, 1848 by B.R. Gant, M.G.
    Bondsman: J. N. Oslin

Bell, John to Sally Quinn Jan. 14, 1820 by Wm. Anthony, J.P.
    Bondsman: Enoch X Quinn Teste: Jno. P. McCutchan

Bell, Joseph to Sally Shumate May 19, 1808 (bond)
    Bondsman: Dan'l Shumate Test: N.P. Hardeman

Bell, Robert R. to Polly Carlisle July 16, 1822 by G. Hunt
    Bondsman: Daniel Carmac

Bell, Thomas to Caty Dooley Nov. 6, 1805 (bond)
    Bondsman: William Dooley Witness: N. P. Harrison

Bellerfant, John to Jane Scales April 8, 1819 by Horatio Burns
    Bondsman: Joseph Bellerfant

Bellerfant, Joseph to Sally Turner April 9, 1819 (bond)
    Bondsman: Alex Johnston Wit: Thos Hardeman, Jr.

Bennet, Alexander to Rebekah Yarborough Oct 1, 1808 (bond)
    Bondsman: H. L. Fennel Test: N. P. Hardeman

Bennett, Cooper M. to Anne Miller March 18, 1815 (bond)
    Bondsman: John Miller

Bennett, Drury to Elizabeth Manier Dec. 10, 1811 (bond)
    Bondsman: Cooper Bennett

Bennett, George to Polly Rounswall Oct 6, 1813 (bond)
    Bondsman: Lewis Stephens

Bennett, George W. to Elizabeth Garner Sept. 7, 1824 by Thomas Nelson
    Bondsman: Jacob Chrisman

Bennett, John D. to Elizabeth Terrell May 29, 1820 (bond)
    Bondsman: Chas. A. Dabney Wit: Thos. Hardeman

Bennett, John D. to Elizabeth H. McGee Aug. 10, 1842 by Thos. L. Douglass
    Bondsman: Wm. Harrison

Bennett, Joseph A. to Martha S. McGee March 29, 1843 by Monroe Short, J.P.
    Bondsman: Andrew Stuart

Bennett, Newman S. to Cessey O.F. McGee March 26, 1838 by M.L. Andrews, M.G.
    Bondsman: Joseph L. Dean

Bennett, Richard C. to Mary R. Hughes March 16, 1841 by M.L. Andrews, M.G.
    Bondsman: Henry C. Reynolds

Bennett, Stephen to Sarah C. Brown Dec. 18, 1849 by W. Burns, M.G.
    Bondsman: David B. Hairgrove Wit. present: Chesley Williams

Bennett, Thomas A. to Mary H. Johnson Jan. 9, 1850 by B.R. Gant, M.G.
    Bondsman: William H. Owen

Bennett, Walter to Jincy Reynolds Aug. 22, 1808 (bond)
    Bondsman: John Witherspoon Test: A. Potter

Bennett, Walter W. to Mary M. Short   Oct. 10, 1847 by Jas. Marshall, M.G.
    Bondsman: Barnett R. Hughes

Benson, James to Sency Winsett   April 7, 1816 by N. Scales, J. P.
    Bondsman: Stringer Potts   Test: N. P. Hardeman

Benton, Jesse to Polly Childrep (Childres ?) (bond)
    Bondsman: Metcalf Degraffenried

Benton, Samuel to Mary Hunter   March 21, 1808 (bond)
    Bondsman: Archibald Potter

Berkley, John to Polley Bradley   June 6, 1811 (bond)
    Bondsman: Archibald Potter   Wit: Wm. P. Harrison

Berry, Adam H. to Eliza Anderson   Aug. 15, 1824 by W. R. Nunn, J.P.
    Bondsman: Daniel German

Berry, Leonard to Nancy Brooks   Jan. 3, 1819 by John K. Campbell
    Bondsman: Taylor Jones

Berry, Leonard to Rebecca Short   Dec. 6, 1828 (bond)
    Bondsman: William Burns

Berry, Richard to Julia G. Moor   Dec. 11, 1833 (bond)
    Bondsman: Wesley Jackson

Berry, Robert to Rebecca Hulme   Jan. 22, 1824 by Levin Edney, M.G.
    Bondsman: William X Spencer

Berry, Thomas to Charity Tarkington   May 23, 1827 by Wm. Moor, J.P.
    Bondsman: William Spencer

Berryman, James to Mary Atkinson   July 6, 1833 (bond)
    Bondsman: William Ragsdale

Berryman, William J. to Narcissa Woolridge   Feb. 26, 1829 by Thos. Douglass
    Bondsman: Josiah J. Woodridge

Berson, Solomon W. to Lucinda S. Van Pelt   Feb. 1, 1837 by T. Fanning, Elder
    Bondsman: None given   (C. of Christ)

Best, Joseph to Nancy Phelps   Nov. 22, 1820 by Levin Edney, M.G.
    Bondsman: Jessee Phelps

Bethel, Lemuel H. to Elizabeth Buchannan   Dec. 11, 1833 by S.B. McConnico, J.P.
    Bondsman: William Anderson

Bethel, Rufus K. to Elizabeth C. Morton   Jan. 13, 1840 (bond)
    Bondsman: Willie Harmon

Betty, John D. to Isabella Hill   Sept. 19, 1838 by James W. Rea, M.G.
    Bondsman: Alexander W. Gray

Betty, William H. to Mary Covington   Nov. 29, 1832 by Robert Pate, J.P.
    Bondsman: Charles M. Scott

Beverage, Thomas (X) to Ann Ratcliffe   Oct. 29, 1829 by H.C. Horton, M.G.
    Bondsman: John B. Anderson

Bibb, Thomas to Mirah Fielder   Nov. 28, 1815 (bond)
    Bondsman: Frederick Owen

Biggars, James to Mariah Robertson   Feb. 24, 1824 by H. Bailey
    Bondsman: John H. Price

Bigger, Andrew J. C. to Malinda W. Hartley   Dec. 25, 1839 by G.J. Wall, J.P.
    Bondsman: James W. Whitehead

Biggers, Joseph to Polly Robinson   Aug. 23, 1817 by Sam Shelburne, J.P.
    Bondsman: Alexr. Robinson   Test: Robert Davis

Biggers, Robert to Elizabeth P. Price   Feb. 19, 1840 by Pet Owen, J.P.
    Bondsman: William T. Price

Binam, Elijah to Methilda Henderson   Sept. 8, 1819 by E. Ragsdale, J.P.
    Bondsman: Elijah Binam by Jno. Goodmarker and Edward Ragsdale
    Witnesses: Thos. Hardeman and T. H. Lewis

Bingham, Franklin M. to Elizabeth Ann Haley   Dec. 22, 1836 by James W. Rea, M.G.
    Bondsman: Wm. E. Hughes

Bingham, James J. to Emilia Haley   Oct. 3, 1827 by John Atkinson, V.D.M.
    Bondsman: Thomas Hughes   Witness present: J.W. McCown, D.C.

Bingham, William to Nancy Haley   July 8, 1829 by John Atkinson V.D.M.
    Bondsman: Nicholas P. Stone

Bird, Hugh to Susan Crane   Oct. 13, 1829 (bond)
    Bondsmen: Hugh L. Bird, Reuben Dollar, John Crawford

Bird, John to Tabby Taylor   April 14, 1812 (bond)
    Bondsman: Luke Patterson   Wit: Wm. P. Harrison

Bird, Moses to Peggy Potts   Jan. 19, 1816 by Wm. Dunnesan, M.G.
    Bondsman: Henry Potts   Test: Thos. H. Perkins

Bird (Byrd), Richard to Bersheba Butt   April 30, 1847
    Bondsman: Wiley B. White   (Groom signed "Byrd")

Bishop, James P. (X) to Palina E. Wills   Dec. 23, 1847 by Hiram Perkins, M.G.
    Bondsman: Raleigh M. Jackson

Bittick, John R. to Cintha Reatraw (Rentrow ?)   Dec. 21, 1814 (bond)
    Bondsman: Robert McCracken   Wit: N. P. Hardeman

Bittick, Samuel F. to Elizabeth Goodrum   Aug. 19, 1824 by G. Barnes, J.P.
    Bondsman: Jacob Page

Bittick, William D. to Martha Ann Still   Jan. 1, 1850 by B.R. Gant, M.G.
    Bondsman: John H. Carmichael

Bizzel, Isaac to Zilpah Musgrave   Feb. 19, 1817 (bond)
    Bondsman: Henry Oliver   Test: Robert Davis

Bizzell, William to Elizabeth Kirk Sept. 17, 1814 (bond)
  Bondsman: Glen Owen

Black, Alexander to Tabitha Dodson Nov. 18, 1809 (bond)
  Bondsman: A. Clark

Black, Henderson to Nicy Bazzell March 21, 1826 (bond)
  Bondsman: None given

Black, Isaac C. to Elizabeth Jane Cody Feb. 19, 1835 by Robert Davis, M.G.
  Bondsman: John H. Black

Black, John to Orpeth Simpson Dec. 31, 1807 (bond)
  Bondsman: Joseph Jackson

Black, Levi to Anna Crouse Aug. 26, 1828 (bond)
  Bondsmen: Levi X Black and William Hendrix

Black, Lunsford P. to Anna Eliza Carden June 18, 1850 by A.N. Cunningham, M.G.
  Bondsman: Joseph B. Palmer

Black, Mark to Susan Brice Oct. 8, 1807 (bond)
  Bondsman: William Bowls (?)

Black, Thomas H. (X) to Patsey Adaline Howell Nov. 28, 1849 by M.L. Andrews
  Bondsman: P. Giles

Black, William to Fanny Hill Dec. 30, 1806 (bond)
  Bondsman: Willie Brown

Blackamore, James A. to Evelina Hadley April 9, 1828 by Wm. Hamer (?) V.D.M.
  Bondsman: Richard Alexander

Blackburn, Alexander S. H. to Melissa Ann Williams May 19, 1847 by R.C. Gar-
  Bondsman: Hezekiah Oden   (rison, V.D.M.)

Blackburn, Andrew D. to Mary Ann Mitchum April 1, 1824 by John N. Blackburn, M.
  Bondsman: Hugh D. King

Blackburn, Bluford to Elizabeth Gray March 6, 1828 by Joel Anderson, J.P.
  Bondsmen: Bluford X Blackburn and William H. Carson

Blackburn, Gabriel C. to Mary Butter Nov. 16, 1840 by Daniel Baugh, J.P.
  Bondsman: John McAlpin

Blackburn, Moses B.G. to Diana B. Allen Oct. 25, 1848 by M.L. Andrews, M.G.
  Bondsman: William A. Blackburn

Blackburn, William to Nancy Hassell Oct. 7, 1819 by Geo. Blackburn, D.M.
  Bondsman: John T. Hamilton

Blackman, Albert M. (W?) to Elizabeth H. Andrews Apr. 8, 1835 by Thos.L.Dougla
  Bondsman: George R. Cox

Blackman, Benjamin B. to Elizabeth Ford May 16, 1832 (bond)
  Bondsman: Felix G. Gunter

Blackman, Elijah to Margaret Rutledge Aug. 31, 1807 (bond)
    Bondsmen: Alex Rutledge and William Rutledge

Blackshaw, Elijah to Diana McMahan April 10, 1822 (bond)
    Bondsman: Benjamin White

Blackshaw, James to Susan Littleton Apr. 11, 1820 by P. Russell, J.P.
    Bondsman: George Glasscock

Blackshaw, Jesse to Matilda Truett Nov. 11, 1820 by G. Hunt
    Bondsman: John Edmiston

Blackshire, Ezekiel to Isbel Dobson May 17, 1814 (bond)
    Bondsman: none given Witness: Wm. Stone

Blair, James H. to Sarah Ann Jones July 10, 1845 by Wm. A. Whitsett
    Bondsman: John B. McEwen

Blair, Thomas L. to Jane Carson Feb. 22, 1821 by Geo. Blackburn, V.D.M.
    Bondsman: William S. Hamilton

Blair, Thomas W. to Catharine C. Neely July 10, 1837 by H.B. North, M.G.
    Bondsman: none given

Blake, Samuel S. to Elizabeth Tweatt July 29, 1824 (bond)
    Bondsman: Jeremiah Terry Wit.: Elisha L. Hall

Blakeley, William to Nancy Dobdon or Dodson (illegible) Nov. 5, 1806 (bond)
    Bondsman: Robert Neelly

Blanton, Lemuel to Martha Nicholson July 20, 1839 by Thos. L. Douglass
    Bondsman: James W. Crawford

Blanton, William H. to Matilda Nicholson Jan. 20, 1830 (bond)
    Bondsman: Harmon W. Smith

Blessing, Jacob (X) to Ally Ballard Jan. 3, 1839 by J. Landrum, B.M.
    Bondsman: Green B. Mangrum Witness present: Sam B. Robinson

Bloodworth, Edwin to Delila Griffin April 8, 1811 (bond)
    Bondsmen: John and Wm. Porter and Chas. Franklin Wit: W.P. Harrison

Boatswright, Thomas to Clarissa Wade July 13, 1812 (bond)
    Bondsman: Edmund Lawrence

Bobbitt, John to Martha Glenn March 3, 1836 by Thos. D. Porter, M.G.
    Bondsman: none given

Bobbitt, Thomas to Elizabeth Walker Feb. 3, 1842 by Benjamin F. Weakley, M.G.
    Bondsman: Daniel Glenn

Boehms, William G.D. to Susan A.G. Aug. 15, 1849 by F.S. Petway
    Bondsman: F. S. Woldridge

Boleng (Boling - Boleny), James to Charlotte Barton Feb. 2, 1807 (bond)
    Bondsman: Richard Orton, Samuel Dobbins, Jon. McCracklin

25.

Bolerjack, John to Sarah S. Polk   Jan. 25, 1848 by A.S. McFerrin, J.P.
    Bondsman: Andrew X Polk

Bolerjack, Vincent (X) to Nancy Haley   Nov. 13, 1845 by J.B. Johnson, J.P.
    Bondsman: Thomas Burch

Bolling, William S. to Mary M. Hill   Dec. 13, 1838 by A.H. Dashiell, M.G.
    Bondsman: William Park

Bolton, James (X) to Sarah Malone   March 6, 1841 by Jas. C. Owen, J.P.
    Bondsman: William McAlpin

Bolton, James (X) to Ellen Esties   July 16, 1846 by R.M. McDonald, J.P.
    Bondsman: George White

Bolton, John (X) to Elizabeth McAlpin   Aug. 8, 1839 by John P. McKay
    Bondsman: Thomas X Lawrence

Bolton, William (X) to Amanda Jane Shelton   Nov. 29, 1845 (bond)
    Bondsman: Joseph A. Hall

Bomer, William to Margaret B. Ricketts   Aug. 7, 1827 by George Tilman
    Bondsman Thomas X Ricketts Witness present: J. W. McCown

Bomer, William I. or J. to Elizabeth Terry   Aug. 14, 1816 by Donnalson P atton
    Bondsman: Angus McPhail and James Jordan

Bond, James to Sarah Chapman   April 8, 1827 (bond)
    Bondsman: Moses Steele

Bond, James W. to Mary Nolen   Dec. 17, 1845 by L. B. Johnson, J.P.
    Bondsmen: J. W. Vaughn and James Wisenor

Bond, John to Sarah Hunter   Sept. 21, 1808 (bond)
    Bondsman: Wm. Voohress

Bond, John to Polly Anderson   June 19th, 1823 (bond)
    Bondsman: B. H. Anderson

Bond, John P. to Nancy M. Garrett   Dec. 8, 1840 by W.H. Baldridge, M.G.
    Bondsman: John D. Bond

Bond, Morris L. to Joan E.C. Hunter (Juan?) July 3, 1844 by J.C. Anderson, M.
    Bondsman: Samuel T. Hunter

Bond, Nathaniel (X) to America Shelton, July 8, 1846 by John Nichols, J. P.
    Bondsman: Robert C. Mayfield (May be Bonds or Bands)

Bond, Nathaniel (X) to Elizabeth Malone   Oct. 19, 1850 (bond)
    Bondsman: Joel X Lockett

Bond, Page to Jane Holland   May 26, 1818 (bond)
    Bondsman: M. L. Bond Wit: Thos. Hardeman

Bond, Thomas B to Eliza H. A. Thomason   Jan. 21, 1829 (bond)
    Bondsman: Ray S. Orton

Bond, Thomas B. to Barbara A. McLemore Feb. 2, 1841 (bond)
    Bondsman: John T. Word

Bond, Thomas J. to Sarah B. Warren May 27, 1830 by Robert Hardin, M.G.
    Bondsman: John Herron

B ond, William to Nancy Dabney Dec. 21, 1808 (bond)
    Bondsman: Charles Dabney Test: A. Potter

Bond, William W. to Catherine Chapman March 2, 1820 by Robert Davis, Minister
    Bondsman: D. C. Kinnard

Bone, Andrew M. to Lucinda Moore May 30, 1811 (bond)
    Bondsman: Ephraim Moore

Bone, Young Ewen to Dorchas Stephenson June 1, 1815 (bond)
    Bondsmen: Young X E. Bone and James Stephenson

Booker, Peter R. to Susannah Gray April 16, 1806 (bond)
    Bondsman: R. P. Currin

Booker, Peter R. to Mary T. Garland Nov. 11, 1847 by R.C. Garrison, V.D.M.
    Bondsman: Isaac Roscoe Porter

Booker, Samuel to Mary Adeline Judkins June 1, 1826 by Thos. L. Douglass
    Bondsman: None given

Boon, John to Matilda Durham Jan. 18, 1827 by A.W. Morton
    Bondsman Elijah Mayfield

Boon, Josiah to Sarah J. Wells May 30, 1849 by Lycurgus McCall J.P.
    Bondsman: John A. McCaul

Boroughs, Francis (Also Burroughs) to Emelia Hill June 14, 1811 (bond)
    Bondsman: Jonathan Wood

Bostick, Absolem to Mary G. Patton Sept. 24, 1829 by Thos. D. Porter, M.G.
    Bondsman: John Bostick, Jr.

Bostick, James A. to Nancy W. King Aug. 23, 1826 by Francis A. Owen
    Bondsman: none given

Bostick, James A. to Margaret Tremmer (?) Nov. 8, 1848 by Benj. F. Weakley, M.
    Bondsman: W. Lafayette McConnico

Bostick, James H. to Louisa E. King Dec. 24, 1850 by Thos. W. Roscoe, M.G.
    Bondsman: Jordan H. Scott

Bostick, John to Polly Hyde Dec. 15, 1815 (bond)
    Bondsman: Absolem Bostick

Bowers, Malachi (X) to Nancy Ellen Hobbs Feb. 22, 1843 by G.W. Parker, J.P.
    Bondsman: Franklin McCrory

Bowles, Thomas to Nancy Hill Jan. 11, 1821 by T. Hunt
    Bondsman: Benjamin Hill

Bowman, Samuel to Elizabeth Hyde Oct. 28, 1819 by Nich's Scales
    Bondsman: H. B. Hyde

Bowman, William H. to Elizabeth M. Maury Sept. 20, 1843 by J.S. Edgar
    Bondsman: D. Hardeman

Boxley, Harrison to Peggy A. Maury (bond)
    Bondsman: George L. Neely

Boxley, Harrison I. to Nancy Ellen Cloud Dec. 24, 1839 by Robt. A. Hill, J.P.
    Bondsman: Miles White

Boyd, Armistead to Polly Cook Dec. 28, 1808 (bond)
    Bondsman: Henry Cook

Boyd, George to Martha A. Walker Feb. 20, 1821 (bond)
    Bondsman: Samuel T. Edwards

Boyd, George W. to Mary C. Wiggins Jan. 13, 1843 by W.J. Tucker, J.P.
    Bondsman: William Boyd

Boyd, James W. to Mary Ann Collins July 7, 1832 by Thos. L. Douglass
    Bondsman: Samuel Pratt

Boyd, John to Nancy Graham Aug. 31, 1828 by Wm. Carson, J.P.
    Bondsman: Brinson (?) Smith

Boyd, John C. to Caroline K. Collins March 10, 1827 by T.L. Douglass
    Bondsman: Henry H. Swisher

Boyd, John R. to Nancy Wood Dec. 23, 1816 by N. Scales
    Bondsman: Thompson Wood

Boyd, Marcus to Eliza H. Hamilton Feb. 15, 1825 (bond)
    Bondman: John S. Russwurm

Boyd, Nathan A. to America Wood April 4, 1844 by A.P. McFerrin, J.P.
    Bondsman: John S. Pickering

Boyd, Robert S. to Elizabeth Banks Dec. 12, 1844 by M.L. Andrews, M.G.
    Bondsman: Haman Critz

Boyd, William A. to Christener H. L. Wall Nov. 30, 1836 by John Alkinson, V.D.M.
    Bondsman: Moses E. Farmer

Boyker, Williamson (X) to Elizabeth Fry June 16, 1805 (bond)
    Bondsman: James Neely (Probably Boykin)

Boykin, Williamson to Malinda Malone Sept. 10, 1815 (bond)
    Bondsman: Fames X Fry

Braden, James (X) to Jane Corzin Aug. 30, 1820 by Eleazar Hardeman
    Bondsman: Thomas X Berry

Braden, William (X) to Rebecca Hampton Nov. 22, 1820 by Eleazar Hardeman
    Bondsman: Elisha L. Hall and Thomas X Berry

Bradford, Davis to Jane Beard Oct. 2, 1828 by Thos. Prowell, J.P.
    Bondsman: Byrd N. X Beard

Bradford, Thomas (X) to Eve Harris March 14, 1834 (bond)
    Bondsman: Henry W. Harpending

Bradford, Willie to Roma Ingram Aug. 18, 1841 by R. White, J.P.
    Bondsman: Davis Bradford

Bradley, Charles G. to Ann Nevills Jan. 18, 1843 by Benjamin F. Weakley, M.G.
    Bondsman: Stephen Elliott

Bradley, George (X) to Polly Oxford May 24, 1807 (bond)
    Bondsman: Samuel Oxford Test: Peter Hardeman

Bradley, John to Ann E. Childress July 22, 1841 by Rev. Robert A. Lapsley
    Bondsman: George T. Thomas

Bradley, Leland I. to Mary E. Perkins Sept. 8, 1836 by Matt Marshall
    Bondsman: Charles D. Parrish

Bradley, Thomas H. to Jane E. Watson Sept. 8, 1838 by Thos. L. Douglass
    Bondsman: Wm. M. Turner

Brady, John to Polly Chamberlain (lin?) March 14, 1805 (bond)
    Bondsman: James Brady

Bragg, Henry J. to Dolly E. Joice Dec. 17, 1846 by Robt. L. Andrews
    Bondsman: John T. Sanford

Bragg, John to Caty Campbell April 5, 1814 (bond)
    Bondsman: Nicholas Witness: William H. Stone

Bramlett, Lansford M. to Mary Crockett, Sept. 14, 1848 by A.N. Cunningham, M.G.
    Bondsman: Simon Venable

Bramlett, Longsford M. to Sarah Slater June 29, 1815 (bond)
    Bondsman: Jas. Patterson

Brandon, John to Holly Tucker Sept. 19, 1834 by S.B. McConnico, J.P.
    Bondsman: Henry X Tucker

Brandon, Thomas H. to Salinda Taylor Dec. 6, 1836 by S.B. Robinson, J.P.
    Bondsman: Jefferson Taylor

Brantley, John to Hannah Allen April 6, 1837 by H. B. North, M.G.
    Bondsman: None given

Brantly, Blake to Margaret Dotson June 25, 1822 by John Holland, M.G.
    Bondsman: Presly Dotson

Bratten, Robert to Matilda Hulme Dec. 12, 1816 by Garner McConnico, M.G.
    Bondsman: Adam H. Berry

Breathitt, Edward to Paulina P. Eaton July 25, 1815 (bond)
    Bondsman: David Mason

Brechean, Ezeriah to Delinda Harper   July 4, 1833 (bond)
    Bondsman: John McAnelly

Breechun, William to Sarah Tucker   Sept. 11, 1833 by Geo. Shannon, J.P.
    Bondsman: Willie J. Harris

Breeding, William to Elizabeth Patterson   Aug. 20, 1818 (bond)
    Bondsman: Wm. Patterson   Witness: Tho. Hardeman, Jr.

Brent, Thomas to Jenny McWherter (McWheter)   Jan. 5, 1808 (bond)
    Bondsman: Solomon Brent   Test: A. Potter

Brewer, John to Martha F. Orman   Sept. 16, 1847 by M.B. Molloy (?) G.M.
    Bondsman: William M. Pope

Briant, Owen (See Bryant)

Brice, Anderson to Alzada McLaughlin   July 11, 1850 by J. Hendricks, J.P.
    Bondsman: Wiley B. White

Brickle, Henry B. to Elizabeth P. Smith   Jan. 10, 1839 by A.H. Dashiell, M.G.
    Bondsman: Samuel N. Stephens

Bridges, James C. to Sarah Blake   Dec. 25, 1821 by Samuel Wells, J.P.
    Bondsman: Jno. W. Bridges

Bridges, James C. to Jane Gordon   Jan. 20, 1834 (bond)
    Bondsman: Samuel B. Bridges

Bridges, James R. to Eliza F. Moore   Nov. 19, 1843 by A.N. Cunningham, M.G.
    Bondsman: Joseph R. Hunter

Bridges, John W. to Sleaty Blake   Dec. 25, 1821 by Sam'l Wells, J.P.
    Bondsman: James C. Bridges

Bridges, Terry to Rachel Mairs   June 11, 1808 (bond)
    Bondsman: Thos. Goff   Test: A. Potter

Bridges, William D. to Nancy Morris   July 10, 1805 (bond)
    Bondsman: John McCollum and John Alsup

Briggs, Isaac W. to Dorothy M. Bennett   Jan. 3, 1832 by Joseph Carle
    Bondsman: James Kennedy

Briggs, John H. to Martha W. Durden   Nov. 23, 1847 by L.B. Johnson, J.P.
    Bondsman: Miles C. X Taylor

Bright, George W. to Ann B. Sharp   June 5, 1828 by Thos. D. Porter, M.G.
    Bondsman: E. T. Collins

Bright, George W. to Marion G. Watson   April 9, 1833 by M.L. Andrews, M.G.
    Bondsman: William P. Sharp

Briley, Joshua to Nancy Howell   March 27, 1811 (bond)
    Bondsman: Thomas Mason   Witness: Wm. P. Harrison

Brim, John to Polly McClellan May 16, 1811 by Nick Scales
    Bondsman: Rep. O. Childrep

Brim, Joseph A. to Jane Osburn Jan. 6, 1831 by J.T.D. Porter
    Bondsman: Cowden McCord

Brimm, Bradford to Levicy Henderson Aug. 28, 1821 by Edward Ragsdale, J.P.
    Bondsman: Luke Bynum (Groom may be Bradford Bynum)

Brimm, John C. to Seniza C. Holloway Nov. 22, 1832 by T.D. Porter
    Bondsman: Eli M. Corzine

Brimm, Pleasant R. to Sarah E. Christopher Dec. 19, 1838 (bond)
    Bondsman: William Roberts

Brimm, Robert W. to Ann M. Tatum April 2, 1846 by Wm. Carter, J.P.
    Bondsman: John B. Barnes

Brimm, Thomas S. to Sarah Johnston Nov. 7, 1827 by H. Bailey, J.P.
    Bondsman: Robert McClellan

Brisby, David to Louisa Joyce Dec. 16, 1824 by Jas. Reid, J.P.
    Bondsman: John Brisby

Brittain, Philip to Kitty Smith May 7, 1820 by J. Farrington
    Bondsman: Samuel X Winstead

Broadnax, John P. to Jane Sharp March 10, 1813 (bond)
    Bondsman: David Dunn

Brock, James to Martha Jordan April 22, 1840 by John Rushing, M.G.
    Bondsman: Blount Jordan

Brock, Thomas G. to Ellinor Smith Oct. 24, 1818 (bond)
    Bondsman: Samuel Winstead Witness: Tho. Hardeman, Jr., Thos. Miller,

Brogdon, James J. to Mary Ann Sires Dec. 21, 1848 by B.R. Gant, M.G.
    Bondsman: Doctor T. Brogdon

Brooks, Elijah G. to Elizabeth A. Holland Jan. 19, 1848 by R.M. McDaniel, J.P.
    Bondsman: R. M. McDaniel

Brooks, George A. to Martha Berry Dec. 18, 1840 by Joseph Carle
    Bondsman: Joseph L. Berry

Brooks, George A. to Sarah A.E. Burgess Aug. 16, 1843 by J.J. Bingham, J.P.
    Bondsman: Clint Jones

Brooks, James to Ferrely Stephens Jan. 24, 1814 (bond)
    Bondsman: Enoch Bateman

Brooks, James to Mary McMurray Nov. 26, 1846 by Wm. A. Whitsitt, Baptist Min.
    Bondsman: Robert M. McDaniel

Brooks, James to Elizabeth Brooks Dec. 18, 1850 by M.L. Andrews, M.G.
    Bondsman: Jas. M. Whitfield

Brooks, John to Sally Williams   April 11, 1823 by William Lacy, M.G.
    Bondsman: Thomas X Brooks

Brooks, Joseph to Polly Atkinson   April 24, 1823 by William Lacy, M.G.
    Bondsman: William Lacy (illegible) Wit. present: J.W. McCown

Brooks, Joseph F. to Frances Taylor   Sept. 1, 1842 by E.W. Hendrix, M.G.
    Bondsman: John G. Cromer

Brooks, Matthew to Nicey Gray   Sept. 22, 1827 (bond)
    Bondsman: Samuel H. Adams

Brooks, Price W. to Lewe or Leue Bateman   Oct. 13, 1814 (bond)
    Bondsman: Christopher E. McEwen

Brooks, Price W. to Catherine Stephens   Jan. 6, 1823 by C.E. McEwen, J.P.
    Bondsman: Enoch Bateman

Brooks, Robert C. to Sarah C. Sudbury (Seedbury?)   July 24, 1837 by G. Marshall
    Bondsman: none given

Brooks, Samuel C. to Elizabeth C. Hailey   Aug. 26, 1819 by Henry Petty, M.G.
    Bondsman: Wm. Wallace

Brooks, William W. to Martha Jane Allen   July 11, 1847 by J.P. McKay, J.P.
    Bondsman: Stephen Bradley

Brothers, Jackson C. to Margaret W. McCutchen   May 11, 1842 by Robt. A. Lapsley
    Bondsman: Felix G. Reese

Brown, Aaron to Susan Stockett   Dec. 9, 1821 by Thos. L. Douglass
    Bondsman: C.E. McEwen (bond signed May 29, 1821)

Brown, Alexander to Charollotta Cloyd   Feb. 5, 1828 by Jno. C. Hicks
    Bondsman: Frederick Ezell (Hicks from M.E. Church)

Brown, Arthur (X) to Sarah Moon   Dec. 20, 1830 by Wm. Moor, J.P.
    Bondsman: Thos. S. Wyatt

Brown, Arthur (X) to Catharine Oden   Feb. 14, 1838 by John Thompson, J.P.
    Bondsman: Charles Henry Weber

Brown, Benjamin F. to Catharine A. Hunter   March 27, 1839 by James C. Ander-
    Bondsman: Wm.S. Campbell   (son, "Teacher of Christian Religion")

Brown, Cornelius (X) to Sally White   Nov. 15, 1817 (bond)
    Bondsman: Lewis X Brown Test: Robert Davis

Brown, Elijah (X) to Love Ritter   March 4, 1817 (bond)
    Bondsman: William Cullum   Test: Robert Davis

Brown, Elisha to Polly Martin   June 15, 1820 by Horatio Burns
    Bondsman: James X Prisley

Brown, Enoch to Fanny Cloyd   Aug. 22, 1832 by Levin Edney
    Bondsman: Alexander Brown

Brown, Ephraim to Susannah Crouch May 6, 1823 by John Witherspoon
    Bondsman: Daniel Perkins

Brown, George C. (X) to Sarah Ann Hargrove April 2, 1844 by Wm.W. Boyd, J.P.
    Bondsman: James Hargrove

Brown, James to Judy Walker Jan. 4, 1809 (bond)
    Bondsman: John Walker Test: A. Potter

Brown, James (X) to Dorcas McCrady Feb. 16, 1825 by Wm. Dunnegan, J.P.
    Bondsman: Alexander Thompson

Brown, James (X) to Charlotte McDaniel April 28, 1833 by Wright Stanley, J.P.
    Bondsman: Willis R. Dortch Wit. present: J.W.M.E. Stewart

Brown, James M. to Jane Thompson April 18, 1846 by S.S.P.A. Knott
    Bondsman: James H. X Little

Brown, James Richard to Nancy Nobles Dec. 19, 1810 (bond)
    Bondsman: Samuel Cox and Richard Brown

Brown, Jessee to Milley H. Williams July 11, 1814 (bond)
    Bondsman: Edwin Hickman Witness: William H. Stone

Brown, John (X) to Mary Robertson Dec. 12, 1820 (bond)
    Bondsman: Henry Brown Witness: Elisha L. Hall

Brown, John to Mary Jane Barfield Nov. 16, 1824 by J.N. Blackburn, M.G.
    Bondsman: John L. McEwen

Brown, John to Jane Irvin Oct 13, 1825 by M.L. Andrews, J.P.
    Bondsman: Andrew Irvin

Brown, John to Mary F. Montgomery April 28, 1832 (bond)
    Bondsman: Thos. S. Blair

Brown, John J. to Elizabeth H. Carson Feb. 22, 1832 by A.B. Lawrence
    Bondsman: none given (license only, on file)

Brown, John J. to Elizabeth H. Carson Feb. 21, 1833 (bond)
    Bondsman: Henry J. Walker (Bond for above. Note date discrepancy)

Brown, Luther to Sara Garrett Feb. 24, 1819 by Levin Edney, M.G.
    Bondsman: E. Brown

Brown, Merritt R. to Mary A. Hunter May 12, 1831 by Andrew Craig, M.G.
    Bondsman: Milton P. Ewing

Brown, Peter to Comfort Beard Dec. 11, 1815 (bond)
    Bondsman: Peter X Brown and Moses X Beard

Brown, Philip to Elizabeth J. Hill June 18, 1849 by M.L. Andrews, M.G.
    Bondsman: Ephraim Y. (or J.) Andrews

Brown, Pleasant W. to Martha Jane Warren Dec. 16, 1845 by C.B. Horn, M.G.
    Bondsman: John C. Lawrence

Brown, Ruffin to Mary P. Sudbury   Aug. 17, 1837 by Gilbert Marshall, J.P.
    Bondsman: None given

Brown, Samuel to Eleanor H. White   July 15, 1835 (bond)
    Bondsman: George R. X Robinson

Brown, Spencer to Catherine Venatta   April 28, 1831 by Nich's Scales
    Bondsman: Willis Nichols

Brown, Thomas (X) to Nancy W. Davis   March 3, 1823 by Wm. Dunnegan, J.P.
    Bondsman: Henry W. Davis

Brown, Thomas to Margaret Hunter   May 1, 1838 by Wm. Horten, E.C.C.
    Bondsman: Benjamin F. Brown   (Horton may be "Hooten")

Brown, William (X) to Rebecca Jane Housden   Sept. 14, 1845 by J.A. Cunningham
    Bondsman: Thomas X Brown

Brown, William to Rachel Couley   May 18, 1848 by Wm.A. Whitsitt, Minister
    Bondsman: John M. Winstead

Brown, William L. to Eliza Hightower   Aug. 15, 1816 by George Blackburn
    Bondsman: Harry Cage and John Bell

Brown, William M. to Catharine J.A. Clemm   Sept. 18, 1828 by Thos.L. Douglass
    Bondsman: Wm. P. Campbell

Brown, William R. to Mary F. Roberts   Dec. 1, 1830 by G. Hunt
    Bondsman: William Roberts

Brown, Willie to Peggy Wisner   Oct. 8, 1807 (bond)
    Bondsman: Drury Alsup

Brown, Zedekiah (a free man of color) to Mary Bone (free woman of color)
    Bondsman: Henry Brown   (Sept. 2, 1836)

Browning, Lwen ? to Lucinda Hightower   Sept. 15, 1825 by Wm. Humer, V.D.M.
    Bondsman: G.W. Gwin, H.R.W. Hill   Wit. present: John McCord

Brownley, Isaac to Parthenia Burch   July 22, 1837 by F.B. Carter, J.P.
    Bondsman: none given

Bruce, William to Nancy Parker   Oct. 17, 1822 by Edward Ragsdale, J.P.
    Bondsman: James B. Ragsdale   (rites celebrated by candlelight)

Bruce, William C. to Charlotte F. Griffin   Nov. 22, 1840 by Robt. Davis, M.G.
    Bondsman: none given   (license only)

Brunsfield, Dennard to Ailsey Lewis   April 8, 1831 by Jas. S. Williams, M.G.
    Bondsman: Thos. Prick (h) ett

Bryan, William D. (X) to Polly Cannon   Oct. 29, 1831 by G.L. Nolen, J.P.
    Bondsman: James Bradley

Bryan, William P. to Elizabeth A. Oliver   Jan. 4, 1830 by Levin Edney, M.G.
    Bondsman: William Cummins

Bryant, Archibald H. to Mary Cartright Feb. 7, 1834 (bond)
    Bondsman: Jefferson Jones Wit. present: J.A.M.E. Stewart

Bryant, Lewis (X) to Rebecca Martin March 27, 1828 by Lemuel Manire, J.P.
    Bondsman: Argel X Filyaio? Wit. present: J.W. McCown

Bryant, Owen to Elizabeth Hutson Oct. 11, 1825 (bond)
    Bondsman: Randolph Alexander (groom signed Briant)

Bryant, Thomas J. (X) to Harriet Newcomb Sept. 28, 1846 by Daniel Baugh, J.P.
    Bondsman: James H. X Little

Bryant, William P. to Olly Bateman Oct. 5, 1818 (bond)
    Bondsman: Thomas B. Garrett

Bynum, Bradford (See Brimm)

Buchanan, David (X) to Selina J. Harper Jan. 4, 1849 (bond)
    Bondsman: William Whitby

Buchanan, James (X) to Sarah Ann H. White May 9, 1844 by Thos.H. Roberts, J.P.
    Bondsman: Ellis E. Cook

Buchanan, James M. to Mary M. Hughes Nov. 16, 1847 by R.D. Jordan
    Bondsman: Jno. Buchanan

Buchanan, John S. to Elizabeth A. Vaughn Oct. 31, 1827 (bond)
    Bondsman: John Petway

Buchanan, Joseph to Martha Edmiston Jan. 20, 1836 by T.D. Porter
    Bondsman: Robert S. Barnes

Buchanan, Robert to Sally Hampton Oct. 12, 1807 by N. Scales
    Bondsman: James Hampton

Buchanan, Robert S. to Harriett S. Bateman Feb. 8, 1838 by Jesse Cox, M.G.
    Bondsman: William Bateman

Buchanan, Thomas to Rebecca Jane Shannon Nov. 5, 1846 by Jesse Cox, M.G.
    Bondsman: Daniel J. Sample

Buchanan, John W. to Obedience Turnage June 17, 1824 by J. Farrington
    Bondsman: Samuel Harkness

Buck, Elias to Hannah Kincaid Oct. 30, 1827 by M.L. Andrews, J.P.
    Bondsman: Wm. Amis

Buck, John B. to Parmelia Wilburn Aug. 17, 1836 by Matt Marshall
    Bondsman: Chas. D. Parrish

Buck, William to Jane Vaughan July 26, 1838 by George Long, J.P.
    Bondsman: Robert X Hawkins

Buckingham, James M. to Elizabeth F. Townlin (Tomlin?) June 29, 1845 by Thos.
  George W. Maupin (groom made mark)   (H. Roberts, J.P.

Buckingham, William J. to Viney Prince   Jan. 10, 1847 by Wm. Y. Carter, J.P.
    Bondsman: James W. (X) Griffith

Buckley, James W. to Sally Downie   Nov. 20, 1820 by H. Adams, J.P.
    Bondsman: William X Mizell   Test: Elisha L. Hall

Buford, Andrew J. to Susan S. Buford   March 7, 1838 by James King
    Bondsman: Samuel S. Graham

Buford, Gabriel to Mary W. Wall   Oct. 23, 1814   (bond)
    Bondsman: Edward Ragsdale

Buford, Gabriel to Elizabeth Thompson   Dec. 18, 1822 by Geo. Blackburn, V.D.M.
    Bondsman: Edw'd Buford

Buford, Gabriel to Amanda W. Buford   Aug. 10, 1829   (bond)
    Bondsman: Lawrence O. Bryan

Buford, James to Polly Giddens   Oct. 6, 1812   (bond)
    Bondsman: Edward Buford

Buford, Nicholas C. to Elizabeth W. Brandon   March 6, 1838 by T.L. Douglass
    Bondsman: Christopher C. McEwen

Buford, Robert J. to Mary W. Buford   Feb. 6, 1833   (bond)
    Bondsman: Joseph J. Pugh

Buford, Spencer to Mary McClellan   Nov. 12, 1835 by Rev. James King
    Bondsman: Charles C. Hardy

Buford, Thomas to Elizabeth Buford   Nov. 18, 1834 by Rev. Jas. King
    Bondsman: Charles C. Hardy

Buford, William C. to Harriet A. Buford   May 25, 1837 by Jas. King
    Bondsman: none given

Buford, William W. to Eleanor R. Pointer   Nov. 24, 1840 by Jas. King, M.G.
    Bondsman: John T. Word

Bugg, Benjamin N. to Annis Tucker   Mar. 9, 1835 by A.J. Blackburn, M.G. (In
    Bondsman: John Dowdy   (Methodist Church)

Bugg, Ephraim to Patsey Lanier   April 18, 1814   (bond)
    Bondsman: David Pinkston

Bugg, John V. to Mary E. Pinkston   Nov. 1, 1849 by R.C. Owen, J.P.
    Bondsman: John Bigger

Bugg, William H. to Martha McCord   Sept. 16, 1835 by James King, M.G.
    Bondsman: James B. Porter, Jr.

Bullington, Albert to Mary E. Hays   Nov. 1, 1838 by W.D.F. Sawrie, M.G.
    Bondsman: Perry M. Neal   ("Solemnized in evening")

Bullock, Amos to Rachel Tompkins   Jan 9, 1805   (bond)
    Bondsman: Richard Hay

Bullock, John H. to Mary Wooldridge   July 6, 1834 by Robt. Davis, M.G.
    Bondsman: Smith H. Sample

Bullock, Nathan to Sarah Hays   April 22, 1806 (bond)
    Bondsman: Abe Mayfield

Bulls, Barnabas to Elizabeth Deens   Aug. 18, 1813 (bond)
    Bondsman: William Gurley

Bumpass, John G. to Verlinda J. Taliafero   Dec. 14, 1837 by Wm. B. Carpenter
    Bondsman: none given

Bumpass, Thomas P. to Mary Jane Woodruff   Dec. 22, 1836 by C. McDaniel, J.P.
    Bondsman: Howell S. Woodruff

Bunham, Newton E. to Polly Gamble   Sept. 13, 1820 by C. McDaniel, J.P.
    Bondsman: Alson E. Linton   Witness: E.L. Wall

Burch, Anderson (X) to Eliza McNabb   April 30, 1840 by P.P. Neely, M.P.
    Bondsman: Thomas H. Goodrum

Burch, Edmund to Nancy L. Broughton   Sept. 10, 1828 by C. McDaniel, J.P.
    Bondsman: Larkin Burch

Burch, James to Mary Teresa Wilkes   Aug. 24, 1835 by Wm. Moor, J.P.
    Bondsman: William Moor

Burch, Jesse to Sarah Easteys   Jan. 9, 1840 by Wm. Johnson, J.P.
    Bondsman: Thomas H. Goodrum

Burch, John to Susan A. Grimm   July 11, 1848 by John Hay, J.P.
    Bondsman: John X Sadler

Burch, John L. to Susan Barnes   Aug. 24, 1847 by W. Anderson, J.P.
    Bondsman: J. Burch

Burch, Lemuel (X) to Quinny Griggs   Dec. 11, 1823 by Geo. Shannon, J.P.
    Bondsman: Rhodham X Griggs

Burford, John M. to Polly Berry   Feb. 21, 1818 (bond)
    Bondsman: Edward Smith   Wit.: Robert Davis

Burge, Epaphroditus to Elizabeth Grimmer   March 23, 1824 (bond)
    Bondsmen: E. W. Burge and R. A. Irion   Wit. present: E.L. Hall

Burge, Henry A. to Eliza Tuning? (illegible)   Nov. 29, 1820 (bond)
    Bondsman: Henry W. Watson

Burge, John (X) to Nancy Stephens   Dec. 18, 1833 (bond)
    Bondsman: Andrew Crockett

Burge, John W. to Lucinda Winsett   Dec. 15, 1835 by Jesse Cox, M.G.
    Bondsman: Benjamin Stevens

Burge, Thomas to Sarah Buck   Oct 19, 1837 by R.W. Robinson, J.P.
    Bondsman: none given

Burge, William W. (X) to Margaret S. Alexander Dec. 24, 1846 by Wm. Carter
    Bondsman: William Whitby

Burgess, Davis H. to Elizabeth Baker Sept. 21, 1849 by B.R. Gant, M.G.
    Bondsman: Wm. H. S. Hill

Burgess, John to Matilda Wilkinson Jan. 20, 1820 by Robert Davis, E.M.C.
    Bondsman: Wm. Johnson (groom signed "Burggs)

Burke, Franklin A. to Mary L. Owen Dec. 23, 1845 (bond)
    Bondsman: F. A. Burke

Burke, Hiram (X) to Susanna Burnett Spet. 9, 1825 (bond)
    Bondsman: Thos. A. Thompson Wit. present: J.W. McCown

Burke, John to Mary Whitley April 12, 1838 by R.B.B. Cannon, J.P.
    Bondsman: Franklin A. Burke

Burke, John R. to Polly W. Mitchell Dec. 14, 1818 (bond)
    Bondsman: Yancy Powers

Burke, Samuel to Peggy Waters Sept. 1, 1821 by Thos. Wilson
    Bondsman: Henry McClure

Burke, William A. to Nancy J. Warren May 15, 1842 by Thos. H. Roberts
    Bondsman: Jas. Hogan, Jr.

Burkett, William to Betsey Gibson July 25, 1826 by Thomas Prowell, J.P.
    Bondsman: none given

Burkett, William S. to Rachel Norris Mar. 15, 1827 by Thos. Truwett?, J.P.
    Bondsman: Thos. Prowell

Burkitt, James (X) to Jane R. Wilson Dec. 23, 1827 by Wm. Carson, J.P.
    Bondsman: Robert Calhoun Wit. present: Joshua W. McCown

Burnam, Joshua (X) to Hanna McPherson Jan. 4, 1816 by C. McDaniel
    Bondsman: George X Davis "his security"

Burnes, George to Nancy C. Butt Aug. 8, 1839 (bond)
    John A. Wilkins

Burnes, Jese to Nancy Hickman Feby. 11, 1816 (bond)
    Bondsman: William Watson

Burnes, William to Susan Cowan Jan. 12, 1850 (bond)
    Bondsman: Joseph D. Hunter

Burnett, John J. (X) to Julia Ann Hampton Sept. 1846 by John Nichols, J.P.
    Bondsman: Thomas A. Wilkes

Burnett, Josephus to Molinda Ann Short Jan. 15, 1846 by N.L. Andrews, M.G.
    Bondsman: Patrick Gibson

Burnett, Richard to Mary Ann Coleman Sept. 14, 1821 by Tristram Patton, J.P.
    Bondsman: Tristram Patton

Burnett, William W. to Elizabeth E. Bowden Nov. 30, 1848 by James King
    Bondsman: Carter H. Witt

Burnham, Ira E. (X) to Elizabeth McLain April 21, 1828 (bond)
    Bondsman: John H. White Wit. present: J.W. McCown, D. Clk.

Burnham, Ira E. to Sally White Jan. 26, 1830 by F. Ivy, J.P.
    Bondsman: Cornelius X Brown (White in one place)

Burnham, William (X) to Cynthia Reed Feb. 8, 1838 by C. McDaniel, J.P.
    Bondsman: Robert A. Reed

Burns, George to Elizabeth Peach July 31, 1811 (bond)
    Bondsman: Daniel McCollum Witness: Wm. P. Harrison

Burns, James to Masa Osteen Mar. 31, 1812 (bond)
    Bondsman: James Wrenn Witness: Wm. P. Harrison

Burns, James to Mary H. Gautt Oct. 28, 1819 by Wm. Potts
    Bondsman: James Gautt (Gantt?)

Burns, James to Flora Church July 28, 1834 (bond)
    Bondsman: Gassaway Peach

Burns, William to Keturah N. Rucker Sept. 22, 1825 by Finch P. Scruggs, M.G.
    Bondsman: Wm. Rucker Witness present: John McCord

Burns, William to Sally Wilkins March 11, 1829 by Thomas Prowell, J.P.
    Bondsman: John Gordon

Burr, William to Mary E. Hill Nov. 6, 1850 by Adam S. Riggs, M.G.
    Bondsman: Adam S. Riggs

Burroughs, Francis (see Boroughs)

Burroughs, Michael to Polly Walke Aug. 6, 1812 (bond)
    Bondsman: James Rogers

Burrow, John (X) to Nancy Hill April 6, 1818 (bond)
    Bondsman: John Campbell Witness: Thomas Hardeman, Jr.

Burton, John Henry to Rebecca Robbins Aug. 13, 1816 by Sims Well?
    Bondsman: John Robbins

Burton, Peter to Elizabeth Gee June 24, 1830 by Joel Anderson, M.G.
    Bondsman: Lewis Corzine

Butter, Edmund (X) to Permelia Ann Ensley Jan. 6, 1830 (bond)
    Thomas X J. Davis   (Butters may be Butlers)

Butter, James H. (X) to Eliza Stanley Jan. 22, 1835 by Wm. Roach, J.P.
    Bondsman: Jas. M. Butter

Butter, Thomas to Sarah E. Harper Aug. 19, 1841 by Daniel Baugh, J.P.
    Bondsman: Matthew Figures ("Not to be published" on back of bond)

Butter, James M. to Caroline Phelps March 20, 1836 by Wm. Roach
    Bondsman: Richard Hudson

Butt, James to Nancy Carlile   Jan. 12, 1826 by G. Hunt
    Bondsman: none given

Butt, Nathaniel to Rebecca Cook   Jan. 8, 1829 by M. Herby?, J.P.
    Bondsman: James W. Butt

Buttery, Emory to Adeline Doton?   May 2, 1837 by C. McDaniel, J.P.
    Bondsman: none given

Buttry, Mason F. to Amanda Griggs   Aug. 9, 1843 by J.A. Cunningham, J.P.
    Bondsman: Thomas J. Griggs

Butts, Swearengin (X) to Sarah Stephens   Feb. 16, 1825 by James Scott, M.G.
    Bondsman: Andrew Montgomery

Buyers, to Casy Overton   Aug. 21, 1815 (bond)
    Bondsman: Tristram Patton

Byars, Anderson to Mary Ann Mincy   June 14, 1847 by L. McCall, J.P.
    Bondsman: Richard R. Mincy

Byers, Abijah to Margaret Hill   Nov. 16, 1843 (bond)
    Bondsman: Francis N. Cloud

Byers, Alexander (X) to Elizabeth Goodwin   May 9, 1845 (bond)
    Bondsman: Griffin T. Skinner

Byers, David P. to Lavinia Hill   March 28, 1825 (bond)
    Bondsman: David P. Hill

Byers, Francis W. to Charlotte Williams   Dec. 22, 1830 by Jno. Rea, M.G.
    Bondsman: Alexander Porter

Byers, John M. to Eliza A.M. Bingham   Sept. 23, 1847 by Jas. Marshall, M.G.
    Bondsman: George W. Parham

Byers, Samuel A. to Susan McCowen   Dec. 29, 1842 by J. H. Mann, M.G.
    Bondsman Samuel H. Powers

Byrd, James S. to Sarah Ann Buck   Dec. 22, 1837 by Reuben White, J.P.
    Bondsman: none given

Byrd, Richard to Sina Ousburn   Oct. 20, 1830 by F. Ivy, J.P.
    Bondsman: Lemuel Burch

Byrn, William B. to Sarah C. Hunt   Jan. 26, 1843 by R.W. Ramsey
    Bondsman: J. A. Knose?

Byrns, Asberry to Anna Smith   April 17, 1811 (bond)
    Bondsman: Weak Smith Witness: Wm. P. Harrison

-C-

Cage, Wilson to Mary Crockett   Oct. 1, 1828 by Wm. Humer, D.M.
    Bondsman: Wm. Smith

Caldwell, Andrew B. to Nancy Ann Waller   Dec. 1, 1840 by A.H. Dashiel, M.G.
    Bondsman: Granville Cameron

Caldwell, Andrew B. to Rachel E. Parrish   March 14, 1843 by Rev. L.P Giddings
    Bondsman: James W. Beal

Caldwell, Charles to Drucilla Haynes   Jan. 21, 1828 by Robt. Davis, M.G.
    Bondsman: Josiah Gorham

Caldwell, Robert to Sarah Grimes   Feb. 15, 1810 (bond)
    Bondsman: John Compton

Caldwell, William to Mary McCutchen   (bond)
    Bondsman: Wm. Edmiston   Test: Robert Davis

Calhoon, James A. to Nancy Oslin   Oct. 16, 1834 by Wm. Rucker, J.P.
    Bondsman: George Calhoun

Calhoon, Wilson to Piety Ogilvie   Sept. 20, 1805 (bond)
    Bondsman: Geo. E. Tulin   Test: Peter Hardeman

Calhoon, Wilson C. to Martha Jackson   Nov. 6, 1842 by J. B. Boyd, J.P.
    Bondsman: Wilson C. Calhoon   Witness: Chesley Williams

Calhoon, Zaccheus C. to Mary J. Burke   July 24, 1834 by Wm. Rucker, J.P.
    Bondsman: William S. Neal

Calhoun, Robert W. to Eleanor C. Wilson   Dec. 29, 1835 by A.A. Wilson, J.P.
    Bondsman: Samuel Scales

Call, Thomas to Holly Putman   March 25, 1835 by J. Landrum
    Bondsman: Thomas X Call and William L.W. X Putman

Calvert, Robert to Nancy Porter   July 12, 1808 (bond)
    Bondsman: Robert Porter (Letter by Robt. Porter saying he agreed
                             to witness "match intended".)

Camden, Marbell J. to Virginia M. Clark   Aug. 3, 1848 by M.W. Ray, M.G. of M.E.
    Bondsman: John L. Morton   Witness present: Chesley Williams

Cameron, Donald to Elizabeth Ann Mayfield   Oct. 3, 1841 by Robt. Davis, Minister
    Bondsman: Perry M. Neal

Cameron, Donald to Mary S. McClellan   May 6, 1846 (bond)
    Bondsman: Donald Cameron and James W. Beal

Cameron, John to Artemisia Parker   Sept. 28, 1844 (bond)
    Bondsman: Lemuel B. McConnico

Camp, Joseph W. to Margaret N. Sharpe   Aug. 21, 1824 (bond)
    Bondsman: Peter Perkins

41.

Camp, Orville C. to Mary C. Baird   Sept. 21, 1837 by Levin Edney, Minister in
    Bondsman: none given   (Methodist Church

Campbell, Daniel to Elizabeth Cummins   Feb. 13, 1833 by J. W. Rea, M.G.
    Bondsman: Robert Orr

Campbell, David to Sina H. Hamilton   Jan. 28, 1819 by Geo. Blackburn
    Bondsman: Elijah Hamilton

Campbell, David to Frances A Park   Oct. 20, 1836 (bond)
    Bondsman: Nicholas C. Buford

Campbell, David to Ann Duff   Feb. 13, 1848 by M.L. Andrews, M.G.
    Bondsman: J. R. Hunter

Campbell, Duncan to Polly Akins   May 27, 1818 (bond)
    Bondsman: William X Floyd

Campbell, Duncan to Nancy C. Anderson   July 24, 1827 (bond)
    Bondsman: John A. Wilkins

Campbell, Edward to Rachel Dobbins   July 29, 1813 (bond)
    Bondsman: Gilbert Brown   Witness: Thos. J. Hardeman

Campbell, Edward to Martha Robinson   March 13, 1821 (bond)
    Bondsman: Robert S. Williams   Witness: Elisha L. Hall

Campbell, Hiram to Polly Hilburn   Feb. 22, 1816 by Wm. Dunnesan, J.P.
    Bondsman: John Copeland

Campbell, James to Elizabeth Garrett   Oct. 6, 1816 by Jno. Witherspoon
    Bondsman: Ralph McFadden

Campbell, James P. to Susan Wiley   Oct. 1, 1836 (bond)
    Bondsman: Thomas E. Woldridge

Campbell, John to Mary Edgar   Feb. 17, 1823 (bond)
    Bondsman: Jonathan X Steepleton

Campbell, John (X) to Elizabeth Bennett   Apr. 24, 1828 by Joel Anderson, M.G.
    Bondsman: Spencer X Epps

Campbell, John to Rebecca B. Ridley   Dec. 4, 1850 (bond)
    Bondsman: David Campbell

Campbell, John X. to Nancy Robbins   Feb. 2, 1808 (bond)
    Bondsman: John Witherspoon   Witness: A. Potter

Campbell, John S. (or L.) to Jenet Orr   Jan. 10, 1808 (bond)
    Bondsman: Wm. Hulme   Test: A. Potter

Campbell, Neal to Elizabeth C. Wilkins   May 18, 1824 by Wm. Dunnegan, J.P.
    Bondsman: Alexander Campbell

Campbell, Richard, Jr. to Frances Neely (Nelly?)   Dec. 12, 1819 by W.Dunnegan
    Bondsman: John Copeland

Campbell, Robert to Martha E. Reeves Sept. 8, 1842 by G.W. Sneed, M.G.
    Bondsman: Joseph P. Sneed Witness: J.A.M.E. Stewart

Campbell, Robert H. to Mary A.C. McCrory Nov. 7, 1844 by W.B. Carpenter
    Bondsman: Jas. Hogan, Jr.

Campbell, Thomas to Eliza Hill Jan. 5, 1821 by Henry Petty M.G.
    Bondsman: Light McCrory

Campbell, William P. to Susan A. Nicholson Oct 22, 1829 by Wm. Hume, V.D.M.
    Bondsman: John Marshall

Campbell, William S. to Margaret M. Campbell Jan. 4, 1849 by G.B. Ferguson
    Bondsman: Andrew Campbell

Cannon, James (X) to Polly Childress (Childreps?) May 25, 1823 by Geo. Shannon
    Bondsman: Silas Stephens

Cannon, Robert to Elizabeth Scales Nov. 25, 1822 by W.R. Nunn, J.P.
    Bondsman: Jeremiah Field

Cannon, Thompson to Elizabeth Kinnard July 20, 1811 (bond)
    Bondsman: Robert Cannon

Cannon, William P. to Agatha S. Perkins July 28, 1842 by Benj. F. Weakley, M.G.
    Bondsman: Peter A. Perkins

Cantrell, William to Sally Gillaspie July 19, 1826 by Wm. Hume, V.D.M.
    Bondsman: none given

Capell, John to Elizabeth Freeman Dec. 2, 1809 (bond)
    Bondsman: John Fitzpatrick

Capelman, Arthur L. to Mary Jane Sharber Mar. 16, 1842 by E.W. Hendrix, M.G.
    Bondsman: Samuel R. Rankins

Caperton, John to Sally M. Hailey Feb. 15, 1819 by Donaldson Potter, M.G.
    Bondsman: William A. Kirk

Caperton, John H. to Margaret J. Wells Sept. 18, 1846 by M.B. Molloy, M.G.
    Bondsman: William J. Wells

Caperton, Samuel to Amelia H. Haley July 3, 1819 by Henry Petty, M.G.
    Bondsman: Wm. W. Hailey

Caperton, Thompson to Mary Ann Cowsert Dec. 23, 1841 by Jas. King, M.G.
    Bondsman: Wm. Caperton

Caperton, Thomas H. to Nancy Jones Nov. 17, 1838 (bond)
    Bondsman: Thomas H. Briggs

Capps, Henry to Anna Fly June 10, 1818 (bond)
    Bondsman: John Cochran

Capps, William to Lucy Fly Oct. 12, 1815 by G. Garnes
    Bondsman: Luke Pryor

Caps, Benjamin to Nancy Scurlock   Nov. 1, 1824 (bond)
    Bondsmen: Benjamin X Caps and H.R.W. Hill

Carey, Thomas (X) to Sally Homble (Hamble?) Oct. 2, 1828 (bond)
    Bondsman: Samuel W. Thompson

Carl, Jacob B. to Jane B. Stewart April 24, 1825 by Robert Davis, M.G.
    Bondsman: Wilkins Oldham

Carl, Jonathan to Sally Oldham Sept. 14, 1832 (bond)
    Bondsman: John A. Wilkins

Carlton, Jeptha B. to Cilicia M. Wilks May 25, 1840 by J.R. Pearcy
    Bondsman: Gideon Cole

Carlton, Peter J. to Eleanor Yates Oct. 25, 1837 by J. Richardson, J.P.
    Bondsman: none given

Carlton, Thomas B. to Jane Putman Sept. 17, 1833 (bond)
    Bondsman: William D. Taylor

Carlton, Wade H. to Sarah Putman Nov. 13, 1829 (bond)
    Bondsman: Thomas Carlton

Carmac, Daniel to Thursey Herbert Dec. 2, 1823 (bond)
    Bondsman: Herbert Owen

Carmichael, Thomas to Eliza Jane Kidd Dec. 23, 1840 by J.M. Green, J.P.
    Bondsman: James Wisenor

Carnchan, Andrew to Sarah Helten Feb. 5, 1808 (bond)
    Bondsman: John Carnchan and Thos. Dave Stephens

Carothers, Andrew to Polly Stanley July 23, 1817 (bond)
    Bondsman: John Rutherford

Carothers, James to Penelope H. Barfield Sept. 30, 1818 (bond)
    Bondsman: John L. McEwen

Carothers, James to Parmelia S. Noble Oct 22, 1843 by M.L. Andrews, M.G.
    Bondsman: Thomas J. Cook

Carothers, James D. to Mary L. Boyd July 11, 1837 by Thomas L. Douglass
    Bondsman: none given

Carothers, James R. to Isadora M. Carsey Feb. 24, 1849 by M.L. Andrews, M.G.
    Bondsman: G. B. Barker

Carothers, John to Polly Carothers May 29, 1809 (bond)
    Bondsman: Robt. Carothers

Carothers, Robert to Martha S. Whitsitt Feb. 28, 1843 by Jesse Cox, M.G.
    Bondsman: Truman W. Jordan

Carothers, Robert B. to Margaret J. Crockett Sept. 9, 1846 by A.N. Cunningham
    Bondsman: Wm. Hill, Jr.

Carothers, Robert B. to Priscilla R. Hodge   Oct 25, 1849 by M.L. Andrews, M.G.
    Bondsman: Jas. McEwen

Carothers, William to Sally Carothers   Feb. 6, 1808 (bond)
    Bondsman: Robert Carothers

Carothers, William B. to Martha S. Whitsitt   May 10, 1843 by Jesse Cox, M.G.
    Bondsman: Robert B. Carothers

Carpenter, John to Penny McAfee   May 21, 1808 (bond)
    Bondsman: Wm. C. Collins   Test: Anne Hardeman

Carr, Hugh to Harriet Nolen   Oct 14, 1839 by Stephen Nolen
    Bondsman: Henry X H. Gray

Carr, John to Polly Orr   Aug. 14, 1810 (bond)
    Bondsman: Jas. Orr

Carrol, James to Nancy Luty   Jan. 5, 1818 (bond)
    Bondsman: David Craig

Carroll, Wm. to Lockey Walton   Dec. 27, 1825 (bond)
    Bondsman: John Tignor

Carsey, Thomas P. to Louisa M. Davis   Sept. 24, 1846 by L.B. Johnson, J.P.
    Bondsman: Wm. M. House

Carson, James to Ellendar Taylor   June 18, 1813 (bond)
    Bondsman: Joe Gibson

Carson, Jesse to Nancy Gillaspie   Mar. 23, 1830 by J. Norman, J.P.
    Bondsman: Robt. W. Calhoon   Wit. present: John G. Hay

Carson, John (X) to Patsey Webb   Jan. 2, 1824 by W.R. Nunn, J.P.
    Bondsman: Moses T. Span

Carson, John B. to Elizabeth C. Walker   Apr. 21, 1831 by Rev. James H. Shields
    Bondsman: John Moore

Carson, Joseph to Rebecca Wilson   Nov. 30, 1808 (bond)
    Bondsman: James Wilson   Test: A. Potter

Carson, Norflet D. to Martha Ann Bridges   April 11, 1839 by W.A. Scott, M.G.
    Bondsman: Augustus (Aug.) Bass

Carson, Robert to Jane Burgep (Burges)   Feb. 8, 1825 by M.L. Andrews, J.P.
    Bondsman: John Thompson

Carson, Samuel to Sally Bradley   Oct. 16, 1811 (bond)
    Bondsman: Terry Bradley

Carson, William H. to Mary Goff   Sept. 10, 1828 (bond)
    Bondsman: William Goff

Carson, William M. to Almyra T. Wilson   Jan. 1, 1827 (bond)
    Bondsman: Bailey Hardeman and Jas. H. Wilson

Carson, Willis to Peggy Burges (Burses) Dec. 19, 1811 (bond)
    Bondsman: James Burges

Carson, Willis to Zilpha A. Fenny Oct. 29, 1846 by Wm. W. Hendrix, M.G.
    Bondsman: Enoch B. Kelley

Carter, Alexander C. to Milly Staggs Dec. 7, 1827 by Thos. Douglass, M.G.
    Bondsman: Wm. M. Wilson

Carter, Brackstone to Levithey Morton Nov. 25, 1821 by H. Adams, J.P.
    Bondsman: H. B. X Hyde

Carter, Coleman F. to Ruth Radford Oct. 12, 1840
    Bondsman: Wm. D. Ferguson (Note on back of license: "Oct. 13, 1840.
        The within license was obtained without the consent of
        Ruth Radford and therefore I wish to return it to the
        Clerk of the County Court." Coleman J. Carter.
        Witnesses: Pettus Shelburne and Henry Walker.

Carter, Fountain B. to Polly A. Atkinson June 28, 1823 by John Atkinson, V.D.M.
    Bondsman: Thomas A. Thompson

Carter, James to Eliza Jane Morris March 4, 1845 (bond)
    Bondsman: McNairy Waller

Carter, John C. to Florence R. Otey April 20, 1845 by Jas. H. Otey, Bishop
    Bondsman: Richard Alexander   (of Tennessee.

Carter, Richard to Sally Winrow Aug. 23, 1809 (bond)
    Bondsman: Henry Winrow

Carter, Samuel J. to Eliza Staggs Jan. 5, 1826 by Thos. L. Douglass
    Bondsman: none given

Carter, Theodorich to Mary Wilburn Jan. 27, 1831 by James Erwin
    Bondsman: Thomas Hardeman

Carter, Vincent (X) to Elizabeth Murphy July 17, 1839 by Joseph W. Burnett, J.P.
    Bondsman: John McNabb

Cartright, Isaac to Lucretia M. McPherson Aug. 23, 1842 by W.B. Carpenter
    Bondsman: John Wilson

Cartright, James to Sarah Jane Whitus June 17, 1849 by John P. McKay, J.P.
    Bondsman: James X Cartright and George X Bolton

Cartright, Robert to Elizabeth Warson? Oct. 1, 1808 (bond)
    Bondsman: Clayton Talbolt Test: A. Potter

Cartwright, John (X) to Alley Wilkinson March 12, 1838 by H. McNish, J.P.
    Bondsman: Horatio McNish

Cartwright, Albert R. to Priscilla B. Gideon May 5, 1835 by Henry B. North, M.G.
    Bondsman: none given (license only)

Cartwright, Charles W. to Susanna C. Morin? Dec. 18, 1834 by Levin Edney, M.G.
    Bondsman: Seth S. Davis

Cartwright, Daniel to Polly Haley   July 15, 1807 (bond)
    Bondsman: Lemuel Jones

Cartwright, Daniel (X) to Sally Murphy   Oct. 27, 1819 by C. McDaniel
    Bondsman: John White

Cartwright, Enoch (X) to Hannah Ragins   Feb. 4, 1818 (bond)
    Bondsman: John X Cartwright

Cartwright, Henry (X) to Polly Wilkinson   April 3, 1828 by Robt. McCutchen, J.P.
    Bondsman: L. A. Millett   Wit. present: Will Hardeman

Cartwright, Thomas D. to Cynthia Ann Modlin   Jan. 1, 1840 by Wm. Moor, J.P.
    Bondsmen: Thomas D. X Cartwright and Thos. S. Wyatt

Case, James to Nancy Owens   July 16, 1805 (bond)
    Bondsman: Harrison Boyd

Casey, Hiram to Sally Fox   Aug. 2, 1821 by Wm. Dunnegan, J.P.
    Bondsman: James X T. Sedan   Wit: Thos. Ballow

Casey, Willis (X) to Hannah Inman   Dec. 31, 1822 by Wm. Dunnegan, J.P.
    Bondsman: Irey X Casey

Cash, Thomas W. to Virginia Dudley   Aug. 29, 1830 by Jas. H. Otey, Rector
    Bondsman: John G. Hay   (St. Paul's Episcopal Church

Caskey, George to Jane C. Wiley   Aug. 17, 1847 by M.B. Molloy, M.G.
    Bondsman: John J. Stephenson

Castleman, Ahab to Nancy Fielder   Jan. 28, 1836 by Wm. Edmondson, J.P.
    Bondsman: Waller Cummins

Castleman, Abraham to Sally Hicks   Feb. 13, 1813 (bond)
    Bondsman: Reddick Counsell

Castry, Moses D. to Frances C. Cattery   Oct. 6, 1841 by Thos. E. Kirkpatrick, MG
    Bondsman: Thomas Cattery

Catchum, William H. to Mary Roach   Dec. 30, 1823 by Wm. Dunnegan, J.P.
    Bondsman: James Gee   (Groom signed "Ketchum")

Cater, Moses E. to Mary J. Porter   March 4, 1834 by Levin Edney, M.G.
    Bondsman: William D. Taylor   (May be Cates)

Cates, John N. to Jane Ferguson   June 13, 1830 by Andrew McCrady, J.P.
    Bondsman: Elijah Cates

Cates, William to Matilda Roberson   Nov. 30, 1843 (bond)
    Bondsman: William Bomar

Cathel, Jonathan to Mary Crow   Jan. 7, 1819 by D. Brown, Pastor
    Bondsman: James Crow

47.

Cathey, Josiah to Martha Ann Gunter   Aug. 11, 1836 by M.L. Andrews, M.G.
    Bondsman: none given

Cathey, William to Lucinda Walker   July 3, 1844 by Jeremiah Stephens, M.G.
    Bondsman: James X Walker

Cattrey (Cathey) William to Margaret Calhoun   March 12, 1835 by J. Wall, J.P.
    Bondsman: William Holden

Caudle, John to Mary Jane Harper   Nov. 8, 1837 by Jacob Critz, J.P.
    Bondsman: none given

Cavendar, Harrison to Julisey Cavendar   Aug. 28, 1845 by Wm. F. Carter, J.P.
    Bondsman: James X Cavender

Cavender, James to Rebecca Cavender   Feb. 16, 1823 by Joel Anderson, J.P.
    Bondsman: James Cavender and J. B. Cavender

Cavender, James S. (X) to Tincy Jackson   Oct. 12, 1834 by John Hughes, J.P.
    Bondsman: Henry W. Sweeney

Cavender, James S. (X) to Nancy A. Underwood   April 20, 1848 by J.M. Burns, J.P.
    Bondsman: Patrick X Cavender

Cavender, Silas to Rachel Cox   Jan. 30, 1823 by Joel Anderson
    Bondsman: Daniel Crenshaw, Jr.

Cavender, Stephen to Sally L. Short   Feb. 18, 1819 by John Alkinson, Minister
    Bondsman: Elisha Walker

Cavendar, William to Mary Scruggs   June 2, 1847 by H. Thomson, J.P.
    Bondsman: Edward A. Truit

Cavin, Samuel (X) to Betsey Haynes   Dec. 8, 1829 (bond)
    Bondsman: Nathaniel G. Murphy

Cayce, Fleming to Cyntha Little   Nov. 13, 1816 by Henry Petty, M.G.
    Bondsman: Andrew Carothers   (groom signed "Flemmin")

Cayce, John B. to Prumett or Pruett E. Carter   Dec. 14, 1839 (bond)
    Bondsman: John B. "Casey" and William A. Gilliam

Cayce, Marshall to Nancy Ann Reese   Oct. 8, 1846 by M.B. Molloy, M.G.
    Bondsman: James Orman

Cayce, Matthew C. to Eliza A. Cameron   Sept. 15, 1832 by James B. Porter
    Bondsman: Wm. W. Parker

Cayce, Thomas to Hannah Standley   Oct. 14, 1815 (License & Bond Filed)
    Bondsman: Sam Steele

Cayce, William to Sarah Cayce   Feb. 3, 1824 by John Alkinson, V.D.M.
    Bondsman: Wm. E. Anderson

Chamberlain, Willis (X) to Keziah Sawyers   Dec. 26, 1822 by C. McDaniel, J.P.
    Bondsman: David X Ferrell

Chamberlin, Samuel to Polly Housden May 6, 1841 by R.B.B. Cannon, J.P.
    Bondsman: Asa X Harper

Chambers, John to Anne McKey Jan. 14, 1807 (bond)
    Bondsman: Wm. Stephenson

Chambers, John C. to Elizabeth S. Collier Feb. 10, 1834
    Bondsman: Thomas X Chambers and John P. Chambers

Chambers, John P. to Elizabeth Jones July 28, 1824 by Geo. Shannon, J.P.
    Bondsman: Henson X Sanders

Chambers, William to Rhoda Cannady (or Kennedy) June 29, 1813
    Bondsman: John Kennedy

Champ, Sutherlin to Jane Copeland Oct. 1, 1817 (bond)
    Bondsman: Daniel J. Humphreys   Test: Robert Davis

Chandler, Isaac (X) to Sally Taylor Feb. 19, 1821 by H. Adams, J.P.
    Bondsman: Isaiah Atkinson

Chandler, Isaac to Matilda Quarles Aug. 9, 1837 by William Lanier, J.P.
    Bondsman: none given

Chandler, James M. to Jane C. Price Dec. 5, 1832 by Wm. Rucker, J.P.
    Bondsman: James Price

Chaney, Wilkins T. to Letitia Burgess Feb. 1, 1838 by Robert Davis, M.G.
    Bondsman: Ely Dodson

Chany, Archabald (X) to Inda O'Briant Sept. 23, 1850 (bond)
    Bondsman: Knacy L. Tanner

Chapel, Elias to Mary F. Wilson June 22, 1842 by Christian G. Miller, M.G.
    Bondsman: Jacob H. Crowley

Chaplain, Samuel P. to Matilda Jane Adams Nov. 11, 1841 by R.B.B. Cannon, J.P.
    Bondsman: John A. Roach

Chapman, Nelson to Sarah Sumners June 13, 1807 (bond)
    Bondsman: Joseph Sumners

Chapman, Robert to Elizabeth Elam Aug. 16, 1824 (bond)
    Bondsman: John X Rainey

Chapman, Thomas to Dorothy Plumley Aug. 30, 1825 by H. Bailey, J.P.
    Bondsman: George White

Chapman, Thomas N. to Catherine Wall Oct. 1, 1835 by J. Wall, J.P.
    Bondsman: Lycurgus McCall

Charter, John N. to Harriet Hall Oct. 30, 1823 by Geo. Blackburn, V.D.M.
    Bondsman: John F. Smith

Charter, Robert to Martha Ann Whitfield June 7, 1827 by John P. Hicks,
    Bondsman: Basel B. Saterfield   (L.D.M.E.P. Church.

Cheairs, John W. to Susan T. Pointer May 1, 1838 by Robert Hardin, M.G.
    Bondsman: Wm. A. Sanford

Cheairs, Martin T. to Martha A. Bond Sept. 11, 1837 by H. B. North, M.G.
    Bondsman: none given

Cheatham, John to Elizabeth Amis March 4, 1820 (bond)
    Bondsman: John L. Douglass

Cheatham, Thomas to Faney Gentry Aug. 24, 1818 (bond)
    Bondsman: Samuel C. Brooks Witness: Wm. Wallis

Cherry, James R. (X) to Mary Russell Aug. 12, 1840 by John Landrum, B.M.
    Bondsman: Daniel D. Russell Witness present: Chesley Williams

Cherry, William N. (X) to Elizabeth Whitby April 5, 1843 by Wm. F. Carter, J.P.
    Bondsman: Charles Stevens

Childress, Alexander to Onah Key March 23, 1820 (bond)
    Bondsman: Garner Hayes

Childress, Alexander M to Rebecca Taylor Aug. 6, 1835 (bond)
    Bondsman: D. Hardeman

Childress, Anderson to Mary W. Lansom Dec. 14, 1820 by Geo. Blackburn, V.D.M.
    Bondsman: Russell Dance

Childress, Edwin C.(T?) to Angelina Barnett Dec. 23, 1841 by Jas. King, M.G.
    Bondsman: Josephus Barnet

Childress, Joel G. to Mary A. Edney May 13, 1824 by Levin Edney, M.G.
    Bondsman: Daniel P. Perkins

Childress, John B. to Martha Chrisman Oct. 7, 1846 by James M. Green, J.P.
    Bondsman: E.S.B. Gocey

Childress, Nelson to Annis Harris Nov. 1, 1823 by Thos. L. Douglass
    Bondsman: Thos. Hardeman

Childress, Preston S. to Louisa P. Edwards Dec. 31, 1833 by H.B. Nash
    Bondsman: Wm. M. Blackwell

Childress, William G. to Mary Berkley Dec. 31, 1818 (bond)
    Bondsman: David Mason

Childrey (Childress?) (X), John to Elizabeth Lester April 26, 1838 by
    Bondsman: John X Wallace   (Gilbert Marshall, J.P.)

Childrey (Childress?) (X), William J. to Jane Montgomery Oct. 7, 1840 by
    Bondsman: Preston S. Childress   (A. Short, J.P.)

Childs, Calvin J. to Mary Ann Duff April 7, 1846 (bond)
    Bondsman: James M. Singleton

Christley, John to Frances Barnes April 9, 1850 by H. B. North, M.G.
    Bondsman: Frederick Christley

Chrisman, Aaron W. to Matilda Pate   Jan. 18, 1837 by William Lanier, J.P.
    Bondsman: none given

Chrisman, Alfred to Sophia Rozell   April 1, 1828 by A.W. Martin, J.P.
    Bondsman: Fielden Ezell

Chrisman, Alfred to Julia Farmer Featherston   July 4, 1843 by Robt. G. Irvine
    Bondsman: Wm. Smith

Chrisman, David to Mary Evans, Jan. 6, 1839 by John Wall, J.P.
    Bondsman: Eli McGan?

Chrisman, George W. to Amelia Allen   Feb. 20, 1830   (bond)
    Bondsman: John C. Corlett

Chrisman, George W. to Jane Sprott   Dec. 14, 1836 by H. C. Horton, M.G.
    Bondsman: Samuel Sprott

Chrisman, Harvy to Amanda Slone (Stone?)   Aug. 15, 1841 by Jas. M. Green, J.P.
    Bondsman: Turner S. Green

Chrisman, Jacob to Matilda McFarlan   Oct. 16, 1828   (bond)
    Bondsman: Henry Williams

Chrisman, James H. to Mary Jane Liggett   Aug. 17, 1841 by J.N. Wall, J.P.
    Bondsman: Elisha Farrar

Chrisman, Marcus S. to Tabitha Calhoun   Dec. 29, 1839 by R. White
    Bondsman: Wm. S. Hatcher

Chrisman, Silas to Jane E. Smith   Sept. 20, 1836 by Wm. Lanier, J.P.
    Bondsman: Samuel W. Smith

Chrisman, Thomas to Martha Dodge   Jan. 7, 1828   (bond)
    Bondsman: Alfred Christman

Christmas, Henry to Matilda C.G.L. Denson   April 11, 1827   (bond)
    Bondsman: William J. Denson

Christmas, Richard to Mary E. Smith   Sept. 12, 1832 by Jas. H. Otey, Rector
    Bondsman: Atkins W. McLemore   (St. Paul's Episcopal Church

Christopher, James to Lourana White   Oct. 8, 1840 by William Davis, M.G.
    Bondsman: Young Nicholson

Christopher, William B. to Betsey Nicholson   Dec. 13, 1823   (bond)
    Bondsman: James R. Davis

Chriswell, Abel (X) to Frances White   Sept. 11, 1836 by William Lanier, J.P.
    Bondsman: Thomas Jones

Chriswell, Laben to Polly White   July 26, 1825 by Jas. Reid, J.P.
    Bondsman: Thomas White

Chriswell, William C. to Martha Ann Hartley   Sept. 26, 1839 by J. Wall, J.P.
    Bondsman: Lycurgus McCall

Chumbly, Thomas (X) to Caroline M. Sherman Aug. 24, 1843 by G.W. Barker, J.P.
    Bondsman: John J. X Chumbly

Church, James M. to Susan A. Satterfield July 9, 1846 by Thos. Prowell, J.P.
    Bondsman: William Edgar

Church, John T. to Oney Sewell April 20, 1838 by Thos. Prowell, J.P.
    Bondsman: Charles Wakefield

Church, Samuel to Elizabeth Campbell Jan. 28, 1836 by S.S. Newman, J.P.
    Bondsman: Gassaway Peach

Church, Thomas to Cynthia Wakefield Sept. 23, 1840 by Thos. Prowell, J.P.
    Bondsman: Milas Fox

Church, Thomas A. to Nancy Jane Beasley Nov. 11, 1846 by Thos. Prowell, J.P.
    Bondsman: William Peach

Clagett, William G. to Theodosia Whitfield July 21, 1835 by Wm. Roach
    Bondsman: Elijah Walker

Claibourne, Micajah G.S. to Livinia T. C. Cannon Oct. 19, 1848 by C.D. Elliott
    Bondsman: John S. McEwen, Jr.

Clanton, H. L. to Branchy Dilliard July 2, 1807 (bond)
    Bondsman: Henry Clanton

Clardy, Albert to Matilda Wells Feb. 26, 1837 by James W. Rea, M.G.
    Bondsman: none given

Clark, Alexander R. to Lucy Young Aug. 14, 1833 by Tristram Patton, J.P.
    Bondsman: Isham Lamb

Clark, Henry (X) to Elizabeth Ham Jan. 7, 1817 (bond)
    Bondsman: Davis Ham

Clark, James W. to Caroline Williams Nov. 25, 1843 by J.B. Boyd, J.P.
    Bondsman: Robert C. Ivie

Clark, John to Patsey Moore July 23, 1807 (bond)
    Bondsman: Bazil Berry

Clark, John to Sally Rains Aug. 13, 1808 (bond)
    Bondsman: John McCanless

Clark, John (X) to Polly Morgan June 15, 1820 (bond)
    Bondsman: William X Hogan

Clark, Joseph to Nancy Dean Sept. 3, 1825 by W.R. Nunn, J.P.
    Bondsman: Robert Clark

Clark, Moses to Mary Roper June 18, 1830 by Robert Davis, M.G.
    Bondsman: Jonathan McCurdy and W. T. Clark

Clark, Robert to Mary York Feb. 13, 1816 by W. Smith
    Bondsmen: Jeremiah X Pope and Wm. Peebles

Clark, Samuel to Judy Mays Feb. 24, 1820 by J. Farrington
    Bondsman: Edward Cochren

Clark, William to Ann B. Scales April 24, 1827 (bond)
    Bondsman: A.P. Hughes

Clark, William L. to Dicey W. Manley April 22, 1829 (bond)
    Bondsman: William Moore

Clarke, Bowling (X) to Charlotte Willett Mar. 11, 1819 by Jno. Alkinson, M.G.
    Bondsman: Jno. McCutchan

Claud, Eldridge to Nancy K. McGavock Nov. 17, 1831 by Andrew Craig, M.G.
    Bondsman: Alexander Brown

Claxton, Dawson (X) to Micha Mays Dec. 18, 1832 by Daniel Baugh, J.P.
    Bondsman: Wm. B. Barker

Claxton, Dawson (X) to Narcissa Ferguson Nov. 2, 1843 by G.W. Barker, J.P.
    Bondsman: Thomas Beasley

Clay, Green (X) to Emily Halfacre Feb. 1, 1849 by G.W. Pollard, J.P.
    Bondsman: William M. X Williams

Clay, James L. to Barbary Halfacre May 12, 1818 (bond)
    Bondsman: Francis X Gunter

Clay, James L. to Rebecah Shaw June 6, 1818 (bond)
    Bondsman: George Long

Clay, James L. to Martha Jane Gilbert Oct. 1, 1847 by G.W. Barker, J.P.
    Bondsman: Oscar Reams

Clay, James S. to Amelia Russell June 13, 1842 by Jacob Critz, J.P. ("Not
    Bondsman: William B. Patton   to be advertised til next week."

Clay, James S. to Nancy Terry Dec. 27, 1846 (bond)
    Bondsman: Franklin B. Haynes

Clay, Mark to Fanny Smith July 20, 1814 (bond)
    Bondsman: John Clay

Clay, Monroe J. to Caroline Wells Feb. 8, 1849 by Wm. M. Wright, J.P.
    Bondsman: H. H. Yates

Clay, Thomas J. to Luraney S. Alston Aug. 31, 1844 (bond)
    Bondsman: John Alston

Clay, Woody (Wooddey) to Sally Sarmons July 12, 1814 (bond)
    Bondsman: John B. Crafton Witness: William H. Stone

Claybrooke, John S. to Mary Ann Perkins April 24, 1834 by T.L. Douglass
    Bondsman: Watkins Harris

Clayton, Robert to Ruth Morris June 18, 1805 (bond)
    Bondsman: Terry Bridges

Clayton, Stephen to Nancy Hill Nov. 15, 1808 (bond)
    Bondsman: James Holbert

Clemons, Hargis to Mary E. Blackburn Oct. 11, 1849 by Richard Steele, J.P.
    Bondsman: Benjamin F. Wells

Cliffe, Daniel to Virginia C. Whitfield Nov. 15, 1842 by Robert Davis, M.G.
    Bondsman: Jas. Hogan, Jr.

Cloud, Edward to Angelina B. McConnico Mar. 11, 1841 by M.L. Andrews, M.G.
    Bondsman: Robert A. Hill

Cloud, Eldridge (See Claud, Eldridge)

Cloud, Francis N. to Sarah Jane Temple Sept. 15, 1844 by Stokley A. Davis, J.P.
    Bondsman: Harrison Boxley

Clouston, Edward G. to Cena McCabe March 13, 1823 by Geo. Blackburn, M.G.
    Bondsman: B. L. Tappan Witness present: W. M. McCown

Clow, John J. to Theodocid Whitfield Dec. 11, 1833 (bond)
    Bondsman: Thomas J. White

Clynard, Alexander (X) to Martha Ann Brumley Nov. 19, 1820 by Eleazar Hardeman
    Bondsman: James X Braden   Teste: Elisha L. Hall

Coale, James (Cook?) to Priscilla Heeman Dec. 13, 1818 (bond)
    Bondsman: Charles Legate

Coale, James to Jane York June 24, 1819 by Joel Anderson
    Bondsman: James P. Barnett

Cochran, John to Rebecca Fly Jan. 19, 1818 (bond)
    Bondsman: James Wisener

Cochran, Robert to Jane Allen Feb. 7, 1822 by Tristram Patton, J.P.
    Bondsman: James Cochran

Cochran, Thomas R. to Sarah A. Jones Sept. 20, 1836 by J.A. Holland, J.P.
    Bondsman: John Waters

Cochran, Thomas R. to Debby Jones Oct. 14, 1840 by N. R. Owen, J.P.
    Bondsman: Braxton R. Powell

Cochran, Thomas R. to Almira Waller Dec. 9, 1848 by Wm. A. Whitsett, Minister
    Bondsman: William C. Burke

Cochran, William to Sally Cordd (very indistinct) June 20, 1807 (bond)
    Bondsman: John Garner

Cocker, Jacob to Jane Stone May 21, 1826 by G.S. Nolen, J.P.
    Bondsman: none given

Cokerham, John to Annis Prowell Dec. 21, 1811 (bond)
    Bondsman: Daniel Campbell

Coggin, Daniel to Margaret Carson May 24, 1831 by L. Manire, J.P.
    Bondsman: James W. Carson

Cole, Andrew to Sally Crafton Sept. 22, 1812 (bond)
    Bondsman: Wm. Goforth

Cole, Dixon to Sally Tucker Dec. 3, 1811 (bond)
    Bondsman: William Tucker

Cole, Gideon to Nancy White Dec. 20, 1833 (bond)
    Bondsman: Samuel Jackson

Cole, Hiram (X) to Polly Lammons (Sammons) Sept. 10, 1818 (bond)
    Bondsman: William X Montgomery Witness: Thos. Wilson

Cole, Isham to Nelly Reed Dec. 26, 1806 (bond)
    Bondsman: John Reed

Cole, John Smith (colored) to Esther McClary "a girl of color" Apr. 2, 1846
    Bondsman: Moses X Summers. John made mark too. (by E.Scales, J.P.

Cole, Joseph to Nancy Sammons Oct. 23, 1812 (bond)
    Bondsman: Jas. Dyal

Cole, Samuel to Polly Deal April 14, 1807 (bond)
    Bondsman: William Harder

Cole, Thomas to Ruth White Aug. 19, 1830 by M.L. Norvell
    Bondsman: Jno. R. Mulherrin

Cole, William R. to Roseana McGee (bond)
    BondsmanL Thos. N. Figures

Coleman, Jackson (X) to Julia Ann Jones June 28, 1840 by M.L. Andrews, M.G.
    Bondsman: John C. Wilkes

Coleman, James A. (X) to Sarah A. Denton Jan. 16, 1832 (bond)
    Bondsman: John H. Allen Witness present: John C. Hay

Coleman, James M. (X) to Elizabeth Thweatt Dec. 24, 1846 by G.W. Barker, J.P.
    Bondsman: John McDaniel

Coleman, Daniel T. to Rosanna Stephens March 17, 1823 (bond)
    Bondsman: Moses X Priest

Coleman, George W. (X) to Dorothy Debuam? May 7, 1845 by Jas. M. Green, J.P.
    Bondsman: Abram X McLemore

Coleman, Jones to Mary Allen July 8, 1824 (bond)
    Bondsman: Matthew Allen

Coleman, Jones R. to Asenette Hill March 27, 1841 by James W. Rea, M.G.
    Bondsman: Samuel P. Allen

Coleman, Joseph to Anna White Aug. 16, 1826 by H. C. Horton, Sr.
    Bondsman: none given

Coleman, Joshua T. to Mary E.S. Neal Nov. 25, 1830 by T.D. Porter
    Bondsman: Jordan Coleman

Coleman, Mark Jackson (X) to Louisa Jane Crocker Jan. 28, 1847 by Wm.Whitsitt
    Bondsman: Harding X Lambs

Coleman, Samuel A.C. (X) to Elizabeth J. West April 23, 1844 by G.W. Barker
    Bondsman: Thomas Clifft

Coleman, Thomas (X) to Eliza Barker Aug. 18, 1831 by Tristram Patton, J.P.
    Bondsman: Eli Dodson

Coleman, Thomas (X) to Elizabeth Hutchens Feb. 13, 1833 by Thos. D. Porter
    Bondsman: Thomas X Tucker

Coleman, William A to Lucinda M. Morton Dec. 8, 1835 by T.D. Porter
    Bondsman: Wilfred Coleman

Coleman, William A. (X) to Frances Williams June 7, 1839 by S. Green, J.P.
    Bondsman: Thomas Bennett

Coleman, William H. to Telitha C. Hart May 28, 1844 by M.L. Andrews, M.G.
    Bondsman: Marquis S. Haley

Coleman, William W. to Mary R. Johnson July 23, 1832 by A.L.P..Green, M.G.
    Bondsmen: A.F. Berry and Marshall Pinkard
    (Letter with bond addressed to Thos. Hardeman Esq. Clerk of Wmson,Co.
                                          "Williamsport, July 21, 1832
    Sir: Mr. A. F. Berry is authorized by me to set my name to a Bond
    for License to solemnize the rites of matrimony between myself and
    Miss Mary R. Johnson of your county. You will do me the favor to
    let Mr. Berry have the License and oblige, Yours Respectfully,
                                          Wm. W. Coleman"

Coleman, Zachariah (X) to Latitia Brack Mar. 21, 1832 by William Rucker, J.P.
    Bondsman Francis B. Epps

Colier, Charles (X) to Mary J. Meadows Feb. 9, 1832 (bond)
    Bondsman: John H. Allen

Collier, Dabney C. to Isabella White Sept. 27, 1836 (bond)
    Bondsman: William T. Collier

Collier, James to Elizabeth C. Wray July 11, 1844 by J. Richardson, J.P.
    Bondsman: Dorrington Garrett

Collier, John (X) to Rebecca Hood Dec. 7, 1839 by Geo. G. Boyd, J.P.
    Bondsman: James X Hood

Collier, John (X) to Amanda V. Hood Apr. 7, 1850 by Geo. Andrews
    Bondsman: Thos. A. Graham

Collins, Daniel F. to Mary A. D. Owen Sept. 21, 1843 by Jesse Cox, M.G.
    Bondsman: John D. Ferguson

Collins, Erastus to Martha North Dec. 13, 1817 (bond)
    Bondsman: Elijah Maury Test: Robert Davis

Collins, Erastus T. to Ellen D. Mowry (Maury?) May 13, 1835 (bond)
    Bondsman: Wm. Johnson

Collins, John S. to Virginia W. Duffy   Dec. 24, 1840 by Robt. Davis, M.G.
    Bondsman: James C. Bailey

Collins, John W. to Frances T. Gray, Nov. 29, 1848 by M.L. Andrews, M.G.
    Bondsman: James E. Collins

Collins, Joshua to Rebecca Tucker   June 30, 1825 by M.L. Andrews, J. P.
    Bondsman: Thomas Gillaspie

Collins, Patrick to Harriet Hailey   Feb. 29, 1822 by Jno. Alkinson, V.D.M.
    Bondsman: Michael Doyle

Collins, Bhomas (X) to Nancy Tucker   Sept. 8, 1830 by Isaac Jones
    Bondsman: Josiah Gillespie

Collins, William to Patsey McAfee   March 19, 1808   (bond)
    Bondsman: Benjamin White

Collum, Cloud to Celia P. Patterson   July 19, 1804 by Tristram Patton, J.P.
    Bondsman: none given

Coltart, John to Christiana Bostick   Oct. 27, 1833   (bond)
    Bondsman: N. P. Edmiston by Jno. Coltart

Combs, Henry (X) to Judith Smith   May 20, 1815   (bond)
    Bondsman: Abraham X Smith

Combs, Henry (X) to Elizabeth Hammons   June 27, 1836 by Lewis Magee, J.P.
    Bondsman: Henry M. Hutton?

Comes, George to Casander Hutcherson   Feb. 9, 1841 by Pet Owen, J.P.
    Bondsman: George W. Hutcherson

Comes, James G. to Elizabeth S. Harris   Aug. 2, 1846 by J.R. Pearcy, J.P.
    Bondsman: Banister Royster

Commander, Caleb to Matilda Long   April 9, 1827   (bond)
    Bondsman: John Dillin

Compton, James W. to Catharine R. Gosey   Jan. 18, 1849 by Green J. Simmons,
    Bondsman: Allen Cotton, Jr.   (Minister of Methodist Church

Comstock, Clark M. to Mary Elizabeth Tull?   July 2, 1835 by T.D. Porter
    Bondsman: James G. Guy

Condon, James to Ann Chowning   Nov. 8, 1825 by J. Whitsitt
    Bondsman: H.R.W. Hill

Condon, Robert V to Eleanor White   May 3, 1829 by James Whitsitt
    Bondsman: John Armstrong

Connelly (Connally), John to Polly Cavannaugh   Nov. 28, 1807
    Bondsman: James Berry

Connelly, William to Jane Castleman   Sept. 4, 1814   (bond)
    Bondsman: Barnabus McVey

Conner, Alfred to Sidney Baker March 7, 1823 (bond)
    Bondsman: Isaac X Rhodes

Cook, Anderson to Sinderilla Atkinson Aug. 4, 1836 by James J. Rea, M.G.
    Bondsman: John J. Short

Cook, Andrew to Judith T. Bumpass Sept. 22, 1836 by James W. Williams, M.G.
    Bondsman: James Hogan, Jr.

Cook, Daniel to Julianah Chambers April 1, 1814 (bond)
    Bondsman: William Linster

Cook, Ellis E. to Harriett Hampton Nov. 28, 1833 by Gilbert Marshall, J.P.
    Bondsman: Thomas Wilson

Cook, Ellis E. to Elizabeth H. Hogan June 18, 1848 by W. Burns, M.G.
    Bondsman: F. B. Haynes

Cook, Henry to Marthy Sheppard July 30, 1823 (bond)
    Bondsman: Henry Cook, Jr. and Daniel P. Perkins

Cook, James (See Coale, James)

Cook, John C. to Emily M. Stanley Oct. 30, 1850 by Wm. A. Whitsitt, Minister
    Bondsman: Burnett H. Sadler

Cook, John T. to Gracy Shute Oct. 15, 1827 (bond)
    Bondsman: R. H. Campbell

Cook, Joseph to Elizabeth Ragsdale March 22, 1840 by L.S. White, M.G.
    Bondsman: Edward O.D. Moore

Cook, Josiah to Sarah L. or S. Toone April 12, 1838 by James King, M.G.
    Bondsman: Benjamin F. Holland

Cook, Lewis to Elizabeth Moore April 14, 1836 by M. Johnston, J.P.
    Bondsman: none given

Cook, Lewis to Margaret J. Owen March 1, 1838 by Jesse Cox, M.G.
    Bondsman: Johnson Vaughn

Cook, Marcus to Amelia Ann Swanson Jan. 14, 1835 by John W. Hanner?
    Bondsman: none given

Cook, Thomas I. to Volantia Carothers Aug. 25, 1836 by R.C. Howell
    Bondsman: David W. Peeler

Cook, William C. to Elizabeth Putnam Sept. 27, 1831 by L. Manire, J.P.
    Bondsman: Zachariah Little

Cook, Willis H. to Margaret McPherson Dec. 29, 1846 (bond)
    Bondsman: John W. X Young

Cooke, Claibourne to Frances T. Gillispie Nov. 17, 1836 by M.L. Andrews, M.G.
    Bondsman: E. R. Parrish

Cooke, John W. to Nancy Duke Jan. 21, 1819 (bond)
    Bondsman: Thomas Hardeman

Cooke, Pendleton R. to Elizabeth Cartright Oct. 24, 1833 by Wm. Moor, J.P.
    Bondsman: Brinkley X House

Cooper, Jacob to Dynitia Harris Aug. 2, 1828 (bond)
    Bondsman: James W. Demon

Cooper, James J. to Isabella E. Dickson Jan. 21, 1836 by M. Johnson, J.P.
    Bondsman: Alfred Waller

Cooper, Job to Elizabeth C. Landrum May 25, 1821 by Franc Jackson, J.P.
    Bondsman: George C. Cooper

Cooper, John to Nancy Love Aug. 24, 1808 (bond)
    Bondsman: John Maxwell

Cooper, Jonathan to Elizabeth Duffill Sept. 9, 1809 (bond)
    Bondsman: Jonathan Cooper Witness: Wm. P. Harrison

Cooper, Thomas to Eliza C. Walton Oct. 25, 1822 by S. Hunt
    Bondsman: Daniel German

Cooper, William to Elizabeth Lunn Oct. 5, 1816 (bond)
    Bondsman: James Blythe

Cooper, William H. to Elizabeth A. Hall Feb. 13, 1843 by J.R. Pearcy, J.P.
    Bondsman: James Jackson

Cooper, William H. to Sarah Field April 22, 1844 (bond)
    Bondsman: William J. Lockridge

Coore, William to Nancy Bizzel Sept. 12, 1818 (bond)
    Bondsman: Jonathan Coore Witness: Thos. Hardeman, Jr.

Copeland, Samuel M. to Mary V. Martin Dec. 24, 1835 by T.D. Porter
    Bondsman: Thomas Mayfield Sconce

Copeland, James C. to Mary Tait July 10, 1835 (bond)
    Bondsman: Samuel M. Copeland

Corbitt, Josiah to Lucinda P. Whitehead Dec. 21, 1837 by B.W. Bird, J.P.
    Bondsman: none given

Cordell, Sterling to Margaret Christly Dec. 23, 1830 by Daniel Baugh, J.P.
    Bondsman: Mastin Clay

Core, James H. to Mary Baugh Aug. 28, 1832 by Thos. L. Douglass
    Bondsman: Elisha North

Core, Jesse G. to Elizabeth K. Blythe Jan. 12, 1847 (bond)
    Bondsman: Thomas A. Graham

Core, Jonathan to Debotha Carrel March 15, 1817 (bond)
    Bondsman: Wm. Core Test: Robert Davis

Corhein, Aaron to Elizabeth Ann Yarbrough March 6, 1812 (bond)
    Bondsman: George Andrews

Corlett, James to Elizabeth Whailey July 4, 1816 by James Miller, J.P.
    Bondsman: Robert Corlett

Corlett, John C. to Polly Ann Chrisman Feb. 25, 1830 by A. B. Morton, J.P.
    Bondsman: G. W. Chrisman

Corlett, Joseph to Ruth Chrisman Sept. 4, 1832 by J. Wall, J.P.
    Bondsman: Benjamin Blackman

Corn ?, to Mary Carter Oct. 27, 1840 by W. H. Baldridge, M.G.
    Bondsman: Hiram McGan

Corzein, Joseph H. (X) to Elizabeth A. Moore Oct. 20, 1828 (bond)
    Bondsman: Joseph A. X Brimm

Corzine, Eli M. to Elizabeth M. Johnson Dec. 6, 1834 (bond)
    Bondsman: Sylvanus W. Smithson

Corzine, Lewis to Jane Burton Dec. 29, 1825 by Andrew Craig, M.G.
    Bondsman: John W. Crunk

Corzine, Lewis to Nancy Cayce Sept. 30, 1835 by Joel Anderson
    Bondsman: William Anderson

Corzine, Lewis to Jane R. White Sept. 6, 1838 by T. Fanning, M.G.
    Bondsman: Eben S. Crocker

Corzine, Ruse to Elizabeth Owen March 29, 1827 by Andrew Craig, M.G.
    Bondsman: Andrew Craig

Corzine, Shelby to Sally Kinnard Sept. 4, 1813 (bond)
    Bondsman: Geo. Bennett

Cosbey, Lewis to Mary Brewer March 20, 1836 by Wm. Edmondson, J.P.
    Bondsman: William C. Hunt

Cotton, Charles to Betsey Lyons Feb. 3, 1806 (bond)
    Bondsman: Charles Cotton

Cotton, Henry to Susan Denton July 27, 1824 (bond)
    Bondsman: William Beasley

Cotton, John S. to Eliza G. Huggins Oct. 20, 1846 by J.J. Bingham, J.P.
    Bondsman: James S. Rodgers

Cotton, Thomas Knight to Polly Gocey Feb. 11, 1830 by Robert Davis, M.G.
    Bondsman: William McCrory

Couch, James P. to Margaret Parker Sept. 26, 1839 by R.W. Robinson, J.P.
    Bondsman: Eleazor Stewart (Stewart at top of bond - error?

Coughanon, David to Malinda Irvin Dec. 2, 1834 by John Allison, J.P.
    Bondsman: Jinkins D. Scanlon

Couldwell, John M. to Matilda Fields   Mar. 17, 1842 by J.W. Haynes, M.G.
    Bondsmen: John M. Couldwell by James M. Haines & J.M. Haines
        (Letter attached: "L.B. McConnico Sir I have requested
        James M. Haines to apply to you for marriage license. I
        hereby authorize him to place my signature to a Bond
        for same. Yours respectfully, J.M. Couldwell
        March 12, 1842.

Coursey, Charles to Matilda Manier   Nov. 22, 1832 by L. Manire, J.P.
    Bondsman: John A. Manier or Manire

Coursey, Chesley to Elizabeth Hogan   Jan. 7, 1841 by E.W. Hendrix, M.G.
    Bondsman: Eldridge X Smotherman?

Coursey, James R. to Malinda Manire   Jan. 30, 1833 by L. Manire, J.P.
    Bondsman: Jas. W. Carson

Courtney, Robert to Eliza J. Haynes   Dec. 3, 1835 by Wiley Burge, M.G.
    Bondsman: William Hollowell

Covington, DeLaFayette to Elizabeth Ransom   Sept. 13, 1838 by C.G. Porter, J.P.
    Bondsman: John Covington

Covington, James C. to Mary M. Orton   Dec. 21, 1843 by M.L. Andrews, M.G.
    Bondsman: Wm. B. Orton

Covington, John to Susan Pate   Jan. 2, 1840 by H.B. Hyde, J.P.
    Bondsman: Stephen D. Turner

Covington, Wm. L to Margaret W. Demumbren   Dec. 16, 1837 by Sam B. Robinson, J.P.
    Bondsman: none given

Covington, William J. to Minerva P. Pate   Oct. 13, 1836 by H.B. Hyde, J.P.
    Bondsman: Benjamin W. Haley

Cowan, John to America Johnston   (bond date: Oct. 10, 1832)
    Bondsman: William Baxter   (Mar. date thus: Oct., 1832.)

Cowan, Joseph to Jane Cowan Graham   Aug. 30, 1804 by Tristram Patton, J.P.
    Bondsman: none given

Cowles, John to Mary King   March 25, 1830 by Thos. D. Porter
    Bondsman: Henry B. Cowles   Wit. present: Jno. Hay

Cowley, Jacob H. to Frances A. Beale   Jan. 20, 1848 by Rufus Ledbetter
    Bondsman: A.W. Woldridge

Cowsart, James to Rebecca Rowland   June 3, 1819 by T. Farrington
    Bondsman: Thos. S. Blair

Cowsert, Anderson A. to Mary A. Stephenson   Jan. 20, 1842 by Wm. Davis, M.G.
    Bondsman: James W. Crawford

Cowsert, Benjamin T. to Mary E. Reams   Sept. 30, 1847 by M.B. Molloy, M.G.
    Bondsman: William M. Pope

Cox, Edward to Mary Ann Sledge   Dec. 24, 1845 (bond)
    Bondsman: Dooly Pate

Cox, George R. to Elizabeth P. Reynolds   Nov. 1, 1837 by Jesse Cox, M.G.
    Bondsman: none given

Cox, James to Ferrily Allen   Mar. 8, 1807 (bond)
    Bondsmen: James Cox, Richard Orton, Benjamin White, Peter Estes,
        John Gee.

Cox, James to Susan A. Reynolds   Aug. 14, 1845 by Jas. King
    Bondsman: Samuel S. House

Cox, James R. to Catharine M. Couley   Sept. 26, 1850 by J.M. Macpherson
    Bondsman: James A. X Moore

Cox, Jessee to Elizabeth Brown   Jan. 18, 1816 by Timothy Shaw
    Bondsman: Joseph Ledbetter

Cox, John to Martha B. Allen   Feb. 9, 1838 by Jesse Cox, M.G.
    Bondsman: James P. Stevens

Cox, Samuel to Clotilda Darden   March 14, 1805 (bond)
    Bondsman: John Cook   Test: John Hardeman

Cox, Samuel to Polly Reynolds   July 20, 1814 (bond)
    Bondsman: Richard Orton   Witness: William H. Stone

Cox, Samuel to Barbary Hammond   Jan. 17, 1830 by John Hughes, J.P.
    Bondsman: Will Hardeman

Cozart, John W. to Mary Jordan   Feb. 27, 1843 by John Richardson, J.P.
    Bondsman: Elijah J. Russell

Craddock, Matthew R. to Martha Williamson   Jan. 21, 1830 by Robt. Davis, M.G.
    Bondsman: Henry Ellbeck

Crafton, Alphonso I. to Nancy Ann Cromer   July 25, 1844 by C. Williams, J.P.
    Bondsman: Henry Cromer   Witness present: Chesley Williams

Crafton, Dennis M. to Mary S. Shelburne   Oct. 4, 1827 by Andrew Craig, M.G.
    Bondsman: Andrew Montgomery

Crafton, George F. to Clarissa H. Russell   April 10, 1823 by Thos. L. Douglass
    Bondsman: A. Montgomery

Crafton, John W. to Rebecca W. Neal   June 26, 1845 by W. Burns, M.G.
    Bondsman: Robert W. Brim

Crafton, Richard L. to Malissa J. Edmondson   Dec. 16, 1830 by Andrew Craig, M.G.
    Bondsman: D. M. Crafton

Craig, Andrew to Jemima Crafton   Oct. 23, 1810 (bond)
    Bondsman: Daniel Wilkes

Craig, Andrew to Martha D. Hardeman   April 21, 1835 by Joel Anderson, M.G.
    Bondsman: William Anderson

Craig, James to Jane Alexander Nov. 4, 1823 by Anorme? Craig, M.G.
    Bondsman: Dennis M. Crafton

Craig, James B. to Mary Ann Neal Jan. 16, 1840 by J.R. Pearcy, J.P.
    Bondsman: Daniel D. Russell

Craig, Owen T. to Sarah M. Reams Nov. 6, 1850 by M.L. Andrews, M.G.
    Bondsman: P. H. Achey?

Craig, Thomas to Jane Thompson May 25, 1816 (bond and License)
    Bondsman: Wm. Montgomery

Craig, Uriah to Mary Ann Tillett Jan. 3, 1839 by Robert Davis, M.G.
    Bondsman Martin Clay

Craig, William W. to Mary A. Hamilton Oct. 17, 1844 by Jesse Cox, M.G.
    Bondsman: Joel A. Anderson

Craighead, Thomas B. to Tennessee V. Johnston June 11, 1846 by A.L.P. Green
    Bondsman: P.G. Stivers? Perkins

Crane, Columbus A. to Martha A.E. Robinson Sept. 20, 1850 by J.C. Corlett, J.P.
    Bondsman: Evans Hargrove

Crane, Thomas W. to Nancy R. Andrews Nov. 26, 1846 by M.L. Andrews, M.G.
    Bondsman: William D. Andrews

Crank, Robert to Rosannah Clynard Feb. 6, 1821 by Eleazar Hardeman
    Bondsman: Alexander X Clynard

Crawford, James W. to Martha Jane Patton March 6, 1845 by M.L. Andrews, M.G.
    Bondsman: Moses A. Dunlap

Crawford, John to Elizabeth Rutherford Feb. 25, 1808 (bond)
    Bondsman: Charles A. Dabney

Crawley, William C. to Jane Atkinson Sept. 14, 1838 by James King, M.G.
    Bondsman: Thomas Boxley

Crayton, Gloud? to Mary Hiles Dec. 3, 1806 by N. Scales
    Bondsman: none given

Creasey, John to Nancy Hill Feb. 10, 1807 (bond)
    Bondsman: Henry Bateman

Creek, Edmund (X) to Josephine Andrews Jan. 4, 1829 by J. Wall, J.P.
    Bondsman: Wm. X Creek

Creek, George to Sally Glass Nov. 6, 1811 (bond)
    Bondsman: Wm. Power

Creek, Luke to Elizabeth Sampson Nov. 29, 1821 by W.M. Hogan, J.P.
    Bondsman: William Wilson

Creek, Newton C. to Cyntha Pope Nov. 28, 1832 by R. Ransom, J.P.
    Bondsman: George Hopkins

Creek, William to Elizabeth Ragsdale   April 20, 1820 by Thos. Wilson
    Bondsman: Wilson X Baucom

Crenshaw, Chester (X) to Sarah Crenshaw Nov. 15, 1831 by Wm. Moor, J.P.
    Bondsman: Willie Gee

Crenshaw, Daniel to Amanda Moore Dec. 29, 1824 (bond)
    Bondsman: James A. Rodgers

Crenshaw, Daniel to Ruth Anderson June 20, 1829 by Richard Tanner, J.P.
    Bondsman: Wm. H. Wells

Crenshaw, James to Eliza Winslow April 8, 1811 (bond)
    Bondsman: Joseph W. Ellis

Crenshaw, Oliver to Elizabeth Crawford July 11, 1814 (bond)
    Bondsman: William W. Gilleray

Crenshaw, William to Eliza R.B. Davis Oct. 13, 1831 by Joel Anderson, M.G.
    Bondsman: Wm. P. Campbell

Crews, Joseph to Serissicy? S. Johnson Jan. 2, 1838 by W. H. Meadows, J.P.
    Bondsman: McAlpin X Johnson

Crews, Thomas to Charlotte Meadow Jan. 2, 1838 by Jas. W. Rea, M.G.
    Bondsman: McAlpin X Johnson

Crichlow, Henry S. to Martha Ann Williamson Feb. 9, 1832 by Wm. Allison, J.P.
    Bondsman: John M. Currin

Crichlow, John B. to Martha J. Long Dec. 21, 1843 by R. G. Irvine, M.G.
    Bondsman: Thomas S. Williamson

Crichlow, Joseph E. to Harriet S. Moore Dec. 14, 1836 by Wm. B. Carpenter
    Bondsman: Thos. B. Smith

Crick, Felix G. to Ruthy Pope March 28, 1832 by John Patterson
    Bondsman: Felix X G. Crick and Joseph X Webb

Crick, Felix G. (X) to Susan Putman March 19, 1839 by Sam B. Robinson, J.P.
    Bondsman: Wm. H. Crick

Crick, John to Nancy Landrum Sept. 20, 1825 (bond)
    Bondsman: Bennet Hargrove

Crick, Jonathan (X) to Sarah Mitton (Milton?) Nov. 27, 1848 by Lucurgus McCall
    Bondsman: Daniel X Martin

Crick, Mark L. to Janetta Putman Jan. 17, 1839 by Sam Robinson, J.P.
    Bondsman: Alfred X Hutson

Criddle, Smith to Lucy Whitfield Sept. 4, 1832 by Levin Edney M.G. (date of
    Bondsman: Smith Criddle by B.W. Drake, Blount W. Drake (bond only)
        (Letter attached authorizing Drake to secure bond.)

Crisman, Isaac to Barbara Halfacre Aug. 11, 1822 by Jno. N. Blackburn, M.G.
    Bondsman: Jacob Halfacre

Critchlow, Henry to Sally G. Roper   June 24, 1845 by W.B. Carpenter
    Bondsman: Sutherland   (Henry signes "Crichlow")

Crittenden, James to Narcissa Staggs   Apr. 7, 1831 by Robt. Davis, M.G.
    Bondsman: Thos. Hardeman

Crittenden, John to Sarah Harrel   Dec. 29, 1818 by Sam Moore, J.P.
    Bondsman: Jesse Walton   Witness: Thos. H. Hardeman, Jr.

Critz, Jacob to Lila T. Drake   July 25, 1825 (bond)
    Bondsman: Searcy D. Sharp

Crocker, Eben L. to Dicey Adelia White   June 25, 1835 by Jas. King, M.G.
    Bondsman: Watkins Harris

Crocker, James M. to Manerva Francis   July 6, 1832 by Geo. Shannon, J.P.
    Bondsman: James M. X Crocker and William Edmondson

Crockett, Andrew, Jr. to Nancy D. Scales   Jan. 30, 1834 by Thos. D. Porter
    Bondsman: Robert Sayers

Crockett, Benjamin F. to Ann M. D. Stephens   Feb. 14, 1828 by T.D. Porter, M.G.
    Bondsman: Peter J. Walker

Crockett, Benjamin F. to Martha T. Gooch   Oct. 13, 1836 by Thos. D. Porter
    Bondsman: Wm. T. Merrett

Crockett, John to Elizabeth M. Crockett   Feb. 3, 1836 by T.D. Porter
    Bondsman: Benjamin F. Crockett

Crockett, John H. to Mary M. Bell   Sept. 8, 1836 by Robt. A. Lapsley
    Bondsman: Thos. P. Buchanan

Crockett, Joseph to Polly Crockett   Dec. 11, 1812 (bond)
    Bondsman: John H. Crockett

Crockett, Joseph to Sarah Ann Robinson   Dec. 12, 1844 by M.L. Andrews, M.G.
    Bondsman: Edwin P. Gaines

Crook, Richard M. to Mary C. Stanley   July 15, 1838 by J.M. MacPherson
    Bondsman: Perry M. Neal

Crosen, John to Viny Wells   Sept. 21, 1818 (bond)
    Bondsman: William X Bramtel   Witness: Thos. Miller, Jr.

Crosley, Levi to Martha Barns (Barus?)   Dec. 30, 1824 by Thos. S. King, J.P.
    Bondsman: James Park

Crouch (Cranck?) Charles W. to Lucretia Nash   June 6, 1827 (bond)
    Bondsman: Neal Hopkins

Crouch, John E. to Elizabeth D. Midgett   Nov. 1, 1842 by W.B. Carpenter
    Bondsman: Jas. Hogan, Jr.

Crouch, James to Louisa Garrett   Feb. 3, 1835 (bond) (no license)
    Bondsmen: James Crouch, Jacob Garrett, J.E. Crouch (Letter found:
        "Feb. 3, 1835 Mr. Thos. Hardeman Sir plese to let the
        barer of this note Jacob Garrett have my lisins for Louise
        Garrett and assine my name to the bond .. James Crouch"

Crouch, William H. to E. H. Stone (initials only) Dec. 5, 1832 by Joel An-
    Bondsman: P. W. Crouch   derson

Croucher, Larkin to Julia Pratt May 29, 1812 (bond)
    Bondsman: John Pratt

Croucher, William to Elizabeth Shute (Sheete?) Nov. 11, 1819 by Henry Petty
    Bondsman: William Crutcher? and John P. Perkins

Crouse, Harrison (X) to Malinda Alford Aug. 13, 1828 by A.W. Morton, J.P.
    Bondsman: Joseph X Alford

Crouse, Jacob to Didimoah Weaver June 7, 1819 (bond)
    Bondsman: Absolom Crouse

Crouse, Samuel to Nancy Howard Oct. 16, 1822 by Lewis Loyd, J.P.
    Bondsman: Absolem Weaver

Crow, Isaac to Elizabeth Tinsley Nov. 28, 1827 by Wm. Craig, M.G.
    Bondsman: Thomas Crow

Crow, James to Narcissa Bright April 23, 1819 (bond)
    Bondsman: William Bright

Crow, Thomas A. to Louise Bugg Jan. 16, 1829 (bond)
    Bondsman: Davis Humphreys

Crowder, Richard B. to Henrietta M. Clardy Feb. 8, 1849 by W.B. Carpenter
    Bondsman: Charles W. Crowder

Crowder, Robert (X) to Isabela Pinkerton July 14, 1807 (bond)
    Bondsman: Joseph Pinkerton

Crowder, Stephen to Milley Davis May 5, 1809 (bond)
    Bondsman: Robert Crowder

Crump, Fendale to Martha Pope April 15, 1815 (bond)
    Bondsman: Alexander Clark

Crump, John Q. to Elizabeth Stanley Dec. 24, 1837 by Robert Davis, M.G.
    Bondsman: none given

Crump, John O. to Mary T. Kinnard June 3, 1841 by M. L. Andrews, M.G.
    Bondsman: John B. Watson

Crunk, John W. to Jurusha Corzine June 28, 1821 (bond)
    Bondsman: Lewis Corzine

Crunk, Joseph H. to Ascennatta M. Corzine May 13, 1847 by Wm. Y. Carter, J.P.
    Bondsman: George Brimm

Crunk, Nicholas S. to Lavinia S. Pratt Feb. 12, 1833 by M.L. Andrews, M.G.
    Bondsman: John Williams

Crunk, Richard to Nancy L. Hardeman July 16, 1835 by Andrew Craig, M.G.
    Bondsman: Isaac W. D. West

Crutcher, D. R. to Nancy P. Scruggs   June 10, 1847 by M.L. Andrews, M.G.
    Bondsman: Azariah L. Kimbro

Crutcher, John to Jane McCracken   Dec. 4, 1810 (bond)
    Bondsman: Wm. P. Harrison

Crutcher, Lee H. to Melita Ann Garrett   March 10, 1847 (bond)
    Bondsman: D. R. Crutcher

Crutcher, Robert M. to Margaret S. Hodge   Dec. 24, 1840 by M.L. Andrews, M.G.
    Bondsman: David M. Odil

Crutcher, Samuel to Catharine P. Blackwell   Feb. 28, 1843 (bond)
    Bondsman: Jas. Hogan, Jr.

Crutcher, Thomas S. to Nancy H. Carothers   Sept. 10, 1846 by M.L. Andrews, M.G.
    Bondsman: Peter A. Perkins

Crutcher, William H. to Charity S.P. Evans   March 11, 1839 (bond)
    Bondsman: Wm. Crutcher (Same name as groom - cousin? perhaps?)

Cuddy, Lee to Elizabeth Vinegarden   June 11, 1813 (bond)
    Bondsman: John Vinegarden

Culbertson, Benjamin to Anna Elliott   Aug. 23, 1810 by N. Scales
    Bondsman: Jno. Elliott

Culbertson, Samuel (X) to Mourning Cyrus   Jan. 6, 1831 by Jas. S. Williams
    Bondsman: Bennett Sires

Cullipher, William to Elizabeth Phelps   Feb. 14, 1820 (bond)
    Bondsman: Bernard Richardson

Cullum, Simpson H. (X) to Adeline Clark   Aug. 8, 1843 (bond)
    Bondsman: William S. Cullum Witness present: Chesley Williams

Cullum, Thomas J. to Casandrew Morris   May 9, 1843 by J. Dyer, J.P.
    Bondsman: Bird Palmer

Cullum, William H. to Hicksy Simmons   Oct. 8, 1817 (bond)
    Bondsman: Castor Freeman

Cummins, Samuel to Rachael Dobbins   Feb. 21, 1805 (bond)
    Bondsman: Wm. Locke

Cummins, Samuel to Dorothy B. Holt   Sept. 4, 1828 by Thos. S. King, J.P.
    Bondsman: R. T. Currin

Cummins, Waller to Martha Hunter   Jan. 22, 1835 by Joseph Calahan, M. G.
    Bondsman: Wm. Edmondson

Cummins, William to Elizabeth Jane Mayberry   Dec. 18, 1843 by M.L. Andrews
    Bondsman: Morris L. Bond

Cundiff, Wiley to Mary E. Orman   Dec. 28, 1846 (bond)
    Bondsman: Alexander S. H. Blackburn

Cunningham, Francis M. (W?) to Sarah Maberry   July 11, 1829 (bond)
    Bondsman: Ezekiel Mayberry

Cunningham, James to Josephine Aden   Sept. 30, 1833 (bond)
    Bondsman: George W. Graham

Cunningham, John D. to Elizabeth J. West   Jan. 11, 1840 by J.C. Anderson, M.G.
    Bondsman: Mack DeGraffenreid

Cunningham, John P. to Sophia Merrin   Jan. 13, 1822 (bond)
    Bondsman: James H. Wilson (groom made mark)

Cunningham, Joseph to Mary Louisa Payne   Oct. 23, 1845 by J. Bridges, J.P.
    Bondsman: Thomas P. Coursey

Cunningham, Thomas P. (X) to Jane Stanfield   Mar. 25, 1835 by Wm. Edmondson
    Bondsman: Thomas J. X Moreen

Cunningham, Thompson to Bethenia S. Bennett   Jan. 26, 1836 by Joel Anderson
    Bondsman: Jobe Mayberry

Curl, William H. (X) to Nancy Jane Rea   Dec. 20, 1840 by M.L. Andrews, M.G.
    Bondsman: John Farmer

Currey, Moses to Joanna Osteen   May 31, 1812 (bond)
    Bondsman: William Osteen

Currin, David M. to Laetitia J. Watson   Dec. 16, 1845 by Sam Sherwell,
    Bondsman: R. P. Currin, Jr.   (minister Episcopal church

Currin, John M. to Elizabeth M. Reese   June 16, 1837 by Thos. L. Douglass
    Bondsman: none given

Currin, Jonathan to Elizabeth Jenkins   Dec. 14, 1813 (bond)
    Bondsman: M. DeGrafenreed

Currin, Robert T. to Elizabeth H. Primm   Jan. 14, 1830 by German Baker
    Bondsman: Boyd M. Nicholson

Curtis, Anthony to Rebecca Williams   Nov. 11, 1812 (bond)
    Bondsman: Washington Curtis

Curtis, Benjamin to Betsey Dudley   March 9, 1825 (bond)
    Bondsman: Guilford Dudley

Curtis, Goodwin to Martha Ann Powers   Aug. 26, 1824 by Levin Edney, M.G.
    Bondsman: John B. Beech

Curtis, Goodwin to Julia White   May 22, 1845 by J.P. McKay, J.P.
    Bondsman: J. R. Hunter

Curtis, Moses to Patsey Staggs   Jan. 8, 1821 (bond)
    Bondsman: Thomas X Staggs

Curtis, William to Nancy Staggs   Oct. 11, 1815 (bond)
    Bondsman: John Staggs

Cutchan, John W. to Rhoda Denton Feb. 23, 1808 (bond)
    Bondsman: John McCutchan (groom's signature) and David Campbell

Cutchan, Thomas to Sarah F. Waller Aug. 15, 1820 by Wm. Anthony
    Bondsman: David House

Cuzach, James to Sally Tiffany Aug. 9, 1822 by J. Farrington
    Bondsman: James Cuzick and Wiley Estes

Cyrus, Bennett to Nancy Hamlet Oct. 25, 1831 by Wm. B. Carpenter
    Bondsman: Bennett Sires (signature) and Thomas M. Sconce

-D-

Dabney, Charles to Nancy Wall July 19, 1815 by Isham R. Trotter, J.P.
    Bondsman: William Dabney

Dabney, Charles A. to Mary Flournoy May 27, 1826 by John Alkinson, V.D.M.
    Bondsman: none given Date is of bond.

Dabney, John O. to Tabitha C. Morton May 27, 1841 by Martin Clark Elder,
    Bondsman: John D. Bond   (M.E. Church

Dabney, Robert C. to Narcissa R. Hunter Nov. 17, 1841 by Jas. C. Anderson, M.G.
    Bondsman: John D. Bond

Dabney, William to Eliza G. Hicks June 29, 1808 (bond)
    Bondsman: Robert Wait

Dabney, William W. to Suvicey B. Morton Jan. 26, 1848 by Wm. J. Barten, M.G.
    Bondsman: S. S. Mayfield

Dalton, John (X) to Catharine Wilson Dec. 15, 1827 by A.W. Morton, J.P.
    Bondsman: William Neal

Dalton, William to Elizabeth Owens Aug. 28, 1830 (bond)
    Bondsman: Hezekiah X Murphey

Dancy, Isaac to Mary Lamb Dec. 9, 1823 (bond)
    Bondsman: Archibald X Caudle

Daniel, George W. to Parthenia P. Edmondson March 14, 1846 by Wm. A. Whitsitt,
    Bondsman: David Sadler   (Bapt. Min. of United Effort Order

Daniel, Walters (X) to Anna Jones April 28, 1838 by Jacob Critz, J.P.
    Bondsman: Barnett Shaw

Daniel, Walter W. to Peggy Harlin June 14, 1827 by Tristram Patton
    Bondsman: David Mays

Daniels, Samuel M. to Jane J. Wade March 1, 1842 by Jas. King, M.G.
    Bondsman: James S. Wade

Dannah, Jacob to Sally Littleton Jan. 22, 1810 (bond)
    Bondsman: William Littleton

Daughrity, Joseph to Mary Dean Aug. 2, 1824 by H. Bailey, J.P.
    Bondsman: Havy Bailey

Davidson, Francis to Sally Leck (Leak?) May 18, 1808 (bond)
    Bondsman: George Teaveult

Davidson, George to Polly Addams Aug. 18, 1807 (bond)
    Bondsman: George Davidson Witness: John Holt

Davidson, George to Barsheba Tompkins Nov. 17, 1807 (bond)
    Bondsman: Daniel Davis

Davidson, George W. to Tabitha Ann Chesser June 16, 1841 by J.B. Boyd
    Bondsman: Jesse N. White

Davidson, John to Fanny Bradey May 6, 1807 by Tristram Patton, J.P.
    Bondsman: Stephen Childress (Childrep)

Davidson, John (X) to Nancy Potts Oct. 4, 1817 (bond)
    Bondsman: James Potts

Davidson, Joseph to Rebecca Irvin June 15, 1815 (bond)
    Bondsman: Barnabas X McVey

Davidson, Josiah to Charity Mitchell Feb. 1, 1816 by James Mison, J.P.
    Bondsman: Thomas Mitchell

Davidson, Samuel to Mary M. Haley May 10, 1838 by M.L. Andrews, M.G.
    Bondsman: William Harrison

Davidson, Thomas M. to Isabella Batey Oct. 9, 1836 (bond)
    Bondsman: Henry X Batey Witness: John W. Allen

Davidson, Thomas W. to Bethenia B. Blackburn Sept. 11, 1834 by Geo. J.
    Bondsman: Jason C. Wilson   (Poindexter, J.P.

Davie, Joseph to Annie Demos March 27, 1806 (bond)
    Bondsman: Hugh Ellison

Davis, Allen I to Sarah Landford Aug. 21, 1845 by Jn. Richardson, J.P.
    Bondsmen: Allen A. Davis (as signed) and Joseph A. Clayton

Davis, Amos to Betsey Wood May 4, 1809 by Nick Scales
    Bondsman: James Holbert

Davis, Benjamin to Livinia Sowells Nov. 8, 1840 by Thos. Prowell, J.P.
    Bondsman: Jame X Davis

Davis, Constant W. to Margaret Thompson Nov. 25, 1841 by M.L. Andrews, M.G.
    Bondsman: Charles H. Edmondson

Davis, Everett to Eliza R. Davis Oct. 4, 1832 (bond)
    Bondsman: Frederick Halfacre

Davis, Francis H. to Mary Ann Gray April 28, 1842 by Jesse Cox, M.G.
    Bondsman: Richard A. Graham

Davis, Frederick to Mary Cloud Feb. 21, 1849 by Rev. C.C. Mayhew
    Bondsman: George W. Morris

Davis, George to Polly Nolen Nov. 30, 1820 (bond)
    Bondsman: Turner Pinkston

Davis, Henry to Rebecca Hampton Feb. 11, 1805 (bond)
    Bondsman: Wilson Davis

Davis, Henry (X) to Elizabeth McIntire March 28, 1835 by Thos. Prowell, J.P.
    Bondsman: Hugh A. Fox

Davis, Henry W. to Hannah Irvin Feb. 3, 1823 (bond
    Bondsman: Nathaniel X Davis

Davis, Hilliard to Malinda Perry Oct. 16, 1832 by T.K. Speon, M.G. pastor
    Bondsman: John M. Dawson   (of Church of God at Berea

Davis, James to Bitsey Rupell (Russell?) Jan. 27, 1813 (bond)
    Bondsman: Rawley Dodson

Davis, James to Eliza Ann Hill March 23, 1814 (bond)
    Bondsman: William R. Hill Witness: William H. Stone

Davis, James (X) to Dicey Pigg Oct. 10, 1816 by Wm. Dussesgan?, J.P.
    Bondsman: James X Judge

Davis, James (X) to Elizabeth Smith June 20, 1842 by J.B. Boyd, J.P.
    Bondsman: Owen Prince

Davis, James (X) to Emeline Haley Oct. 12, 1847 by L.B. Johnson, J.P.
    Bondsman: Hardin X Toombs

Davis, James to Catharine A. Sneed Nov. 15, 1848 (bond)
    Bondsman: James Davis by George Hogan and C. P. Sneed

Davis, James A. to Lusetta S. Hay Oct. 23, 1846 by Thos. Prowell, J.P.
    Bondsman: Elijah M. Fox (groom also made mark)

Davis, James B. to Elizabeth Davis Dec. 30, 1847 by Thos. Prowell, J.P.
    Bondsman: James A. Riley

Davis, John to Sarah Gosage Feb. 10, 1808 (bond)
    Bondsman: Samuel Crawford

Davis, John to Priscilla Floyd Nov. 18, 1808 by Nick Scales
    Bondsman: James Holbert

Davis, John to Franky Chatman Nov. 24, 1812 (bond)
    Bondsman: Jarman Winsett

Davis, John D. to Mary Prowell March 27, 1836 by Thos. Prowell, J.P.
    Bondsman: James S. Davis

Davis, John J. (X) to Martha E. Dodd June 1, 1848 by John T. Cox, J.P.
    Bondsman: David A. Cowan

Davis, John L. to Jane Smith Jan. 4, 1811 (bond)
    Bondsman: Moses Steele

Davis, John S. to Mary Ann White Feb. 28, 1841 by Jno. Kelley, Min. of M.E.Cl
    Bondsman: M.L. Andrews

Davis, Jonathan P. to Elizabeth L. Alexander Jan. 1, 1826 by Andrew Craig
    Bondsman: Ebenezer Alexander

Davis, Nathan C. to Mary E. Wood Feb. 18, 1836 by Jesse Cox, M.G.
    Bondsman: none given

Davis, Nathaniel G. to Sarah E. A. Gleaves April 10, 1845 by Jno. Rushing, M.C
    Bondsman Samuel K. Rankins

Davis, Orlando to Martha McGee Aug. 12, 1840 by Thos. L. Douglass
    Bondsman: R. Alexander

Davis, Peter to Martha Young Dec. 24, 1828 by Geo. J. Poindexter, J.P.
    Bondsman: David Pinkston (groom "of Calloway County, Ky.")

Davis, Robert to Eliza H. Hudgins Mar. 20, 1833 by T.D. Porter
    Bondsman: Joseph Elliott

Davis, Seth F. to Susan Cloud Jan. 11, 1843 by R.A. Hill, J.P.
    Bondsman: P.W. (Philip) Cloud

Davis, Solomon to Jane Davis Nov. 1, 1809 (bond)
    Bondsman: Connaway Oldham

Davis, Stephen M. to Mary Jane Sanford Oct. 23, 1844 by Jesse Cox, M.G.
    Bondsman: Wm. T.J. Wood

Davis, Stokely A. to Ann Hartgroves March 29, 1821 by Levin Edney, M.G.
    Bondsman: John Armstrong

Davis, Stokely A. to Eveline Evans Sept. 5, 1836 (bond)
    Bondsman: John W. Allen

Davis, Thomas to Jane E. Westbrooks Dec. 22, 1847 by Jesse Cox, M.G.
    Bondsman: George W. Williams

Davis, Thomas H. to Avalin Miller April 1, 1841 by R.W. Robinson, J.P.
    Bondsman: Daniel M. Robinson

Davis, Thomas J. to Elvira Mullen Nov. 26, 1829 by Geo. Shannon, J.P.
    Bondsman: John Brown

Davis, William to Jane White Mar. 16, 1820 by Levin Edney, M.G. of Christ
    Bondsman: Wm. Johnson

Davis, William (X) to Lucy Walls Jan. 6, 1825 by Sam'l Merritt
    Bondsman: Samuel Merritt

Davis, William A. to Judith R. Owen Feb. 15, 1849 by Wm. A. Whitsitt, M.G.
    Bondsman: John H. Gowan of Davidson Co.

Davis, William H. to Mary H. Dotson Feb. 21, 1824 (bond)
    Bondsman: John W. Neelly

Davis, William S. to Rachel Barnes Jan. 14, 1847 by M.L. Andrews
    Bondsman: C. (Charles) F. Wall

Davis, Willis to Nancy Austin June 1, 1820 by F.D. Stone, J.P.
    Bondsman: John X Yates

Davis, Wilson to Sally Copeland Jan. 5, 1824 by G. Hunt
    Bondsman: Joshua Davis

Dawson, Ezekiel to Hannah McFadden July 19, 1808 (bond)
    Bondsman: Joseph Dawson

Dawson, James to Roseanna McFadden Aug. 3, 1815 (bond)
    Bondsman: Robert McFadden

Dawson, John to Helen Russell April 27, 1819 by Timothy Shaw, Jr., J.P.
    Bondsman: James Crowder

Dawson, John M. to Pheby Reynolds Aug. 19, 1825 (bond)
    Bondsman: John Dawson

Dawson, Martin P. to Jane Fields Sept. 30, 1835 (bond)
    Bondsman: James M. Watkins

Dawson, William B. to Nancy P. Hughes Jan. 15, 1835 by T.D. Porter
    Bondsman: John Hughes (groom signed "Dolson")

Dazey, Nathan A. to Eliza S. Adams Aug. 21, 1833 by T.D. Porter
    Bondsman: Kendall Dazey

Deal, Joseph to Elizabeth Cole May 3, 1806 (bond)
    Bondsman: Samuel Cole

Dean, Alexander to Parthenia Dean Jan. 8, 1829 by Robt. Henderson
    Bondsman: Wm. J. Yancy

Dean, Elijah H. to Jane B. McCarroll Nov. 1, 1832 by Tho. D. Porter
    Bondsman: Wm. H. Crouch

Dean, James to Catherine M. Redd March 16, 1834 by A.A. Wilson, J.P.
    Bondsman: Green B. X Dean (groom signed "Deen")

Dean, John to Eliza Andrews Feb. 16, 1825 by M.L. Andrews, J.P.
    Bondsman: Brockenbrough Andrews

Dean, William to Nancy A. Beard July 30, 1828 by M.L. Andrews, J.P.
    Bondsman: John Stephenson

Deane, Francis M. to Frances Gunter July 7, 1808 (bond)
    Bondsman: Francis Gunter (groom's initial may be U, M. Or W.)

Deason, Roland to Martha Henderson Oct. 18, 1828 by H.C. Horton, Minister
    Bondsman: H. C. Horton

Debnam, Thomas to Sarah McLemore March 27, 1818 (bond)
    Bondsman: Atkins McLemore

Dedman, William to Susan Camp April 29, 1840 by James M. Green, J.P.
    Bondsman: Thomas Glymp

Deens, Daniel to Nancy Williams June 16, 1816 by J.R. Trotter
    Bondsman: Henry Oliver

Degraffenreid, Matcalfe to Candice J. Pope May 26, 1830 by (Mih. failed to
    Bondsman: Hartwell H. Hobbs   (sign license)

Degraffenreid, Matcalfe to Lucy C. Gee Aug. 31, 1837 by Robert Davis, M.G.
    Bondsman: none given

Degraffenreid, Matthew F. to Margaret S. McLemore Nov. 11, 1841 by Thos. L.
    Bondsman: Beverly Reese   Douglass

Dement, Cader to Frances Hall March 15, 1824 (bond)
    Bondsman: John Landrum

De moss, Thomas to Mary Prowell Dec. 27, 1812 (bond)
    Bondsman: Fielden Shumate

Dempsey, Hugh to Nancy Allen Sept. 5, 1833 by M.L. Andrews, M.G.
    Bondsman: Alexander F. McKinney

Dempsey, Hugh to Catharine B. Bond Apr. 17, 1839 by M.L. Andrews, M.G.
    Bondsman: George Searight

Dempsey, William D. (X) to Nancy Brown Sept. 20, 1827 by G. Marshall, J.P.
    Bondsman: Elijah X Brown

Denson, William J. to Susan Wooldridge March 13, 1827 (bond)
    Bondsman: James C. Hill

Denton, Addison T. to Frances Ann Potter March 6, 1839 (bond)
    Bondsman: Richard G. Cowan

Denton, Arthur S. to Mary Jane Davis Dec. 3, 1835 by Jesse Cox, M.G.
    Bondsman: Abner Stacey

Denton, Jacob (X) to Polly Dobbs May 27, 1818 (bond)
    Bondsman: Burnette X Hardgroves

Denton, James W. to Sophia Shaw April 8, 1829 (bond)
    Bondsman: George W. Jones

Denton, Wilkins to Sarah Oden Jan. 1, 1840 by James Porter
    Bondsman: William H. Pointer

Denton, William to Charlotta Coleman Jan. 7, 1832 (bond)
    Bondsman: Jones R. Coleman

Derryberry, Albert G. to Milly J. Morgan Oct. 5, 1848 by Hiram Putman, M.G.
    Bondsman: James R. Sutton

Derryberry, David L. to Avelina Andrews   Dec. 15, 1831 by H.C. Horton, M.G.
    Bondsman: John Long

Derryberry, Jacob to Margaret Long   March 6, 1806 (bond)
    Bondsman: David Long   Test: Peter Long

Desaussure, Henry B. to Sally Jones Davie   Dec. 30, 1847 by W. Burns, M.G.
    Bondsman: William Burns

Devers, Amos to Polly Dellender   Jan. 12, 1813 (bond)
    Bondsman: Walter Owen

Devon, Marshall H. to Rebecca Vinible (Veneble)   Sept. 5, 1841 by W. R. Nunn
    Bondsman: Joseph Lovett

Dewbury (Dewberry), Henry to Martha Hadley   May 23, 1816 (bond)
    Bondsman: George Parham

Dial, Anthony (X) to Malvena Burch   Jan. 10, 1834 (bond)
    Bondsman: Wm. M. Wright and John McDaniel

Dial, Anthony Thomas (X) to Malinda Catherine Franklin   Feb. 5, 1834 (bond)
    Bondsman: Nathaniel L. Harrison and Elisha C. Williams

Dial, Eli to Eveline Craig   Feb. 10, 1828 by Joel Anderson, M.G.
    Bondsman: Andrew Montgomery

Dial, William to Jane C. Craig   Oct. 11, 1827 by Joel Anderson
    Bondsman: James Rice

Dickey, John to Nancy Page   Jan. 19, 1807 (bond)
    Bondsman: Samuel Braden

Dickinson, David W. to Sally B. Murfree   Oct. 17, 1841 by Philip Lindsey
    Bondsman: none given - license alone on file

Dickson, Thomas to Jane Moore   July 29, 1819 by G. Hunt, J.P.
    Bondsman: John Moore

Dickson, William to Nelly Gordon   Nov. 30, 1807 (bond)
    Bondsman: William Gordon

Dilliard, William to Jane Scruggs   Jan. 13, 1816 by John Nichols, J.P.
    Bondsman: Nicholas Dilliard

Dillon, John to Jane Graham   Sept. 15, 1839 by John Jones, M.G.
    Bondsman: none given

Dishon, Henry to Icy Roberts   Feb. 16, 1832 by John Morton
    Bondsman: Richard D. X Vaughn

Ditto, Henry A. to Lucy H. Walton   Oct. 17, 1844 by J. Richardson, J.P.
    Bondsman: W. L. Pate

Ditto, Hiram D. to Martha O. Cox   Oct. 13, 1846 by J. Richardson, J.P.
    Bondsman: Dooly Pate

Dobbins, John to Jane A. Cummins Aug. 11, 1825 (bond)
    Bondsman: Thos. J. Kirkpatrick

Dobson, Amos to Martha Ann Brooks April 28, 1831 by Robt. Davis, M.G.
    Bondsman: Spencer Dobson

Dobson, Hugh to Elizabeth Alexander Dec. 26, 1815 by Tristram Patton
    Bondsman: George Travis

Dobson, Mathew H. to Letitia Hughes Jan. 19, 1842 by Cowden McCord, J.P.
    Bondsman: M. N. Hughes

Dobson, Presley to Ann Harper Oct. 15, 1831 by John Alkinson, V.D.M.
    Bondsman: Presley X Dobson, Jr.

Dodd, Aaron to Lovey White May 16, 1825 (bond)
    Bondsman: Lewis J. Johnston

Dodd, Alexander to Catharine J. Davis Sept. 17, 1846 by S.S.A. Knott, J.P.
    Bondsman: David A. Cowan

Dodd, Samuel to Zerinah Johnson Nov. 7, 1815 (bond)
    Bondsman: Edward Swanson

Dodson, Beverly to Nancy Waller May 3, 1846 by Jas. King
    Bondsman: Bird Fitzgerald

Dodson, Bird to Judith Holland June 6, 1817 (bond)
    Bondsman: Presley Dodson

Dodson, Bird F. to Ann E. Burnett Jany. 15, 1849 by Jas. King
    Bondsman: William B. Patton

Dodson, Caleb to Mary Fitzgerald March 12, 1828 by Joel Anderson, M.G.
    Bondsman: Presley Dodson

Dodson, Ely to Adaline B. Kinnard Dec. 8, 1850 by Jesse Cox, M.G.
    Bondsman: Robert A. Toon

Dodson, Ruben to Nancy H. McConico Oct. 14, 1805 (bond)
    Bondsman: Thos. Walker

Dodson, Thomas to Jane Waddell Feb. 12, 1817 (bond)
    Bondsman: Hightower Dodson

Dodson, William D. to Mary A. Dudley Sept. 1, 1847 by M. B. Molloy, M.G.
    Bondsman: David T. Vestal

Dodson, William H. to Lucy Ann Boseley Dec. 12, 1850 (bond)
    Bondsman: John R. Dodson

Dogget, Chatten to Polly Wells Dec. 11, 1807 (bond)
    Bondsman: Wm. Hail

Donaldson, Buckley to Dida Mira Armstrong Feb. 2, 1811 (bond)
    Bondsman: Barnet Donaldson

Donelson, Barnett to Polly Andrews, Aug. 8, 1808 (bond)
    Bondsman: Samuel Andrews

Donelson, Robert to Peggy Feres Dec. 24, 1806 (bond)
    Bondsman: James Faris

Donnaly, Andrew to Jane Inman Jan. 22, 1812 (bond)
    Bondsman: John Davis

Donnell, Matthew O. to Eliza E. Edwards Feb. 13, 1818 (bond)
    Bondsman: Isaac Patton

Donywhite, Daniel to Elizabeth Perkins April 24, 1821 by Wm. Dunnegan, J.P.
    Bondsman: Thomas Kinsay

Dooley, Jacob to Susan Harris June 23, 1812 (bond)
    Bondsman: John McKinney

Dooley, Michael to Elizabeth Williams Dec. 19, 1810 (bond)
    Bondsman: James P. Rutledge

Doolin, Nathaniel to Susan Blackman Dec. 25, 1824 (bond)
    Bondsman: Alexander X Wood

Dortch, Willis R. to Elizabeth J. Stone Aug. 21, 1835 by James King, M.G.
    Bondsman: Asa Wattington

Dotson, Eli to Elizabeth Fitzgerald Aug. 31, 1820 by Henry Petty, M.G.
    Bondsman: James X Toon

Dotson, Hightower to Sally Dotson July 4, 1807 (bond)
    Bondsman: Roling Dotson

Dotson, James M. to Susan Hardeman Oct. 2, 1832 (bond)
    Bondsman: Washington Merritt

Dotson, Presley to Mary Boys Beach Sept. 16, 1823 by John Alkinson
    Bondsman: Obadiah Fitzgerald

Dotson, Samuel H. to Sally Chaney Aug. 28, 1828 by Wright Stanley, J.P.
    Bondsman: Sam'l Word

Dotson, Thomas to Nancy Ely Feb. 23, 1835 by H. B. North, M. G.
    Bondsman: Patrick Reese (groom signed "Dodson".

Dougherty, Samuel to Cincy Garrett Nov. 19, 1815 by G. Barney, J.P.
    Bondsman: William Penney

Douglass to Zilleam Parham July 7, 1821 (bond)
    Bondsman: William H. Short

Douglass, Dewitt C. to Martha A. Maury Jan. 2, 1850 by A.N. Cunningham, M.G.
    Bondsman: William H. Hill

Dowd, Andrew S. to Jemima L. Scales Oct. 21, 1850 by J.M. Macpherson
    Bondsman: Jesse G. Core

Dowd, John to Jean Powell Oct. 3, 1806 (bond)
    Bondsman: John Smith

Dowd, John R. to Mary Ann Duty Dec. 18, 1838 by W.D.F. Sawriee, M.G.
    Bondsman: James Hogan, Jr.

Dowdy, Allen to Martha Tucker Feb. 22, 1816 by Robt. McMillen
    Bondsman: William Dowdy

Dowdy, Allen to Betsey Sullivan Aug. 9, 1832 by Daniel White, M.G. "having
    Bondsman: Owen X Sullivan   care of 50 souls"

Dowdy, Charles to Martha Virginia Wells Oct. 28, 1848 by Jeremiah Stephens
    Bondsman: James Dowdy

Dowdy, Garner M. to Eliza Graham April 6, 1839 by Henry Walker, M.G.
    Bondsman: John Dowdy

Dowdy, John to Sally Tucker July 2, 1829 by Isaac Jones, M.G. in M.E. Church
    Bondsman: George M. Gillespie

Dowdy, Martin to Sophia Western Anderson Sept. 28, 1829 (as above)
    Bondsman: John Gordon

Dowdy, Micajah to Rebecca Tucker Nov. 20, 1810 (bond)
    Bondsman: Wm. Tucker

Dowdy, Micajah to Patsey Tally Dec. 19, 1822 by Edward Ragsdale, J.P.
    Bondsman: Anderson Hall

Dowdy, William to Elizabeth Edwards June 10, 1820 (license and bond)
    Bondsman: William X Tucker

Downing, William H. to Sarah Rucker March 1, 1826 (bond)
    Bondsman: none given

Doyle, Michael to Catharine Allen April 16, 1838 by T. Fanning, E.C.C.
    Bondsman: Turner Green

Drake, Boswell (X) to Henrietta Williams Nov. 5, 1829 by G.L. Nolen, J.P.
    Bondsman: George B. Mulherrn

Drake, David L. to Sarah H. Burnham Dec. 11, 1833
    Bondsman: John H. White

Drury, Richard C. to Martha L. McBride Feb. 1, 1813 (bond)
    Bondsman: William Neal Witness: H. Petway

Dryden, Nathaniel to Nancy Biggars Dec. 6, 1810 (bond)
    Bondsman: Joseph Biggars

Dudley, Christopher to Sarah E. Foster February 10, 1834 (bond)
    Bondsman: Thos. W. Blair

Due or Drury (both ways on bond), Perry to Mary Smith Nov. 5, 1807 (bond)
    Bondsman: Ezekiel Smith and Thomas Due

Duff, Ernis to Martha Wallace   March 3, 1826 by George Shannon, J.P.
    Bondsman: none given

Duff, Hugh to Caroline McCabe   June 18, 1827 by J. Farrington
    Bondsman: A. C. Carter

Duffel or Duff (illegible) to Lela Boven or Boren   (illegible) 1807
    Bondsman: Thos. Duff and James McCutchen

Duffel, William R. to Nancy Hungerford   May 8, 1811 (bond)
    Bondsman: Stephen Biles

Duffell, Allen to Susan McCarrell (McCanell?)   Dec. 25, 1821 by Wm. Anthony
    Bondsman: Allen T. Nolen

Duffle, Benjamin (X) to Eliza B allow   Jan. 11, 1844 by R.B.B. Cannon, J.P.
    Bondsman: George S. Gee

Duke, Burley J. to Mildred H. Young   Dec. 10, 1849 by M.L. Andrews, M.G.
    Bondsman: George Nichols

Duke, Green to Kerziah Timmons   Jan. 1, 1817 by Donnaldson Potter, M.G.
    Bondsman: John Hood   (groom made mark)

Duke, Henry C. to Nancy Pewit   Feb. 6, 1832 (bond)
    Bondsman: Frederick X Wright

Duke, William P. to Rebecca C. Kirk   March 9, 1820 by Henry P etty, M.G.
    Bondsman: Thos. Hardeman

Dunaway, Abraham (X) to Mary Broaden   Jan. 3, 1828 (bond)
    Bondsman: Z. H. German

Dunaway, Samuel to Elizabeth Childress   June 16, 1836 by Gilbert Marshall, JP.
    Bondsman: Josiah Neviels

Dunaway, Season (Leason?) H. to Rebecca Long   Nov. 22, 1832 by G. Marshall
    Bondsman: George Long

Duncan, James to Rebecca Tucker   Sept. 21, 1836 by William Lanier, J.P.
    Bondsman: Wellington Stinson

Duncan, Joseph to Peggy Davis   Nov. 12, 1812 (bond)
    Bondsman: James Sloan

Duncan, Wiley (X) to Sally Fisk   July 23, 1844 by James M. Green, J.P.
    Bondsman: Thomas X Griggs

Dunham, Daniel H. to Lewvania Adkins   Aug. 2, 1805 (bond)
    Bondsman: Joe D. Garrett

Dunham, William to Nancy Gunter   April 22, 1818 (bond)
    Bondsman: Alfred Edney

Dunkin, Amos to Christina Derryberry   Aug. 6, 1807 (bond)
    Bondsman: John Hicks

Dunlap, David to Fanny Read Feb. 4, 1820 (bond)
    Bondsman: Samuel Dunlap

Dunlap, Samuel to Nancy Riggs Dec. 23, 1818 (bond)
    Bondsman: Samuel Dunlap (same name as groom)

Dunlap, William (X) to Ellan Thomas Aug. 14, 1806 (bond)
    Bondsman: R. P. (X) Herrin

Dunn, Jacob to Priscilla Wright April 30, 1835 by C. McDaniel, J.P.
    Bondsman: John Hodgson

Dunn, John B. to Mary E. Frost Aug. 13, 1836 (bond)
    Bondsman: Mark A. Sneed

Dunn, Thomas D. to Louisiana Seay May 5, 1837 by Samuel Robinson, J.P.
    Bondsman: none given

Dunnavant, Leonard to Margaret Giddens Jan. 13, 1819 (bond)
    Bondsman: M. L. Bond

Dunnavant, Leonard to Sarah B. Reed (Rud?) Aug. 30, 1820
    Bondsman: H.R.W. Hill

Dupree, Samuel C. to Nancy Tisdale Oct. 1, 1823 by John Nichols
    Bondsman: Alfred McCown

Durden, Joshua to Eliza Oldham June 26, 1827 by John Pope, M.G.
    Bondsman: John Liscomb

Duty, Thomas to Polly Tarkington July 14, 1807 (bond)
    Bondsman: none given

Duty, William B. to Sarah Wilkins Feb. 4, 1832 (bond)
    Bondsman: Bolling C. North

Dwon?, Francis P. to Sabra Hazzlewood July 31, 1827 by Moses Span
    Bondsman: James W. Dwon

Dwyer, John S. to Matilda Jones Feb. 1, 1837 by N.P. Modrall?, M.G.
    Bondsman: none given

Dwyer, John S. to Elizabeth Webb Dec. 13, 1838 by J. Andrews, Baptist M.G.
    Bondsman: Benj. F. Ransom Witness: W. K. Ransom

Dyer, John M. to Elizabeth Bell Jan. 13, 1825 by N. Scales
    Bondsman: Douglas Ferguson

Dyer, Robert to Polley Sanford Sept. 1, 1816 by Nich's Scales
    Bondsman: John McPeake

Dyer, William to Jane Alston Aug. 3, 1837 by H.B. Hyde, J.P.
    Bondsman: none given

Dyer, William H. to Maacha? Field June 12, 1844 (bond)
    Bondsman: William Morton

-E-

Early, John W. to Lucy W. Moss   Aug. 2, 1830 (bond)
    Bondsman: Robert Hightower

Early, John W. to Catharine E. Hatcher   May 8, 1838 by M.L. Andrews, M.G.
    Bondsman: Richard Andrews

Early, Spotswood H. to Margaret S. Hatcher   Jan. 21, 1841 by M.L. Andrews
    Bondsman: Ethelbert H. Hatcher

Eastep, Samuel to Sarah Loyd   May 27, 1825 (bond)
    Bondsman: Absolem Weaver

Eatheridge, Jonathan to Caty Lewis   April 10, 1810 (bond)
    Bondsman: John L. Fielder

Eddington, Hugh H. to Sarah McCoy   July 25, 1836 by R.A. Hill, J.P.
    Bondsman: John W. Miller

Edgar, James to Selah Witherington   Jan. 6, 1816 (bond)
    Bondsman: Wm. Sparkman

Edgar, Samuel to Prudence Forehand   March 21, 1844 (bond)
    Bondsman: Jesse W. Fly

Edlis, Oswald to Polly Shelton   Feb. 11, 1812 (bond)
    Bondsman: Noah Shelton

Edmiston, Coveington (X) to Margaret Fleming   Dec. 22, 1816 by E. Hardeman
    Bondsman: John Holmes

Edmiston, Robert to Jane Gillispie   Jan. 8, 1818 (bond)
    Bondsman: Peter H. Martin   Test: Robert Davis

Edmiston, William to Priscilla Reid (Rud?)   March 10, 1818 (bond)
    Bondsman: German Lester

Edmonds, Thomas C. to Elizabeth Kennedy   Feb. 28, 1828 by Franklin McClaran,
    Bondsman: Joseph Kennedy   J.P.

Edmondson, Andrew J. to Sarah Jane Holland   Feb. 17, 1848 by Wm.A. Whitsitt
    Bondsman: John W. Allen

Edmondson, John to Mary Cummins   Sept. 18, 1827 by G. Hunt
    Bondsman: Robert T. Currin

Edmondson, John to Martha V. Owen   Dec. 24, 1850 by A.N. Cunningham, M.G.
    Bondsman: Robert F. Hill

Edmondson, John C. to Mary S. Coleman   March 3, 1835 by Joel Anderson, M.G.
    Bondsman: Samuel M. Edmondson

Edmondson, Samuel W. to Eliza Nolen   Dec. 21, 1832 (bond)
    Bondsman: Nevil A. Gee

Edmondson, Sidney P. to Lucy W. Hutson   Oct. 28, 1827 by Joel Anderson, J.P.
    Bondsman: Reuben Nance

Edmondson, Silas to Temperance C. Pomroy Sept. 1, 1839 by R.B.B. Cannon, J.P.
    Bondsman: Thomas I. Nolen

Edmondson, Silas to Sally A. Mullin Oct. 1, 1849 by B.R. Gant, M.G.
    Bondsman: William X Pomroy

Edmondson, William to Elixabeth Winsted Oct. 11, 1821 (bond)
    Bondsman: David Bell

Edmonson, William to Eveline Edmonson March 3, 1835 by Joel Anderson, M.G.
    Bondsman: John R. Gocey

Edney, Edmund to Nancy Davis Mar. 18, 1819 by Levin Edney, M.G.
    Bondsman: Wm. B. Edney

Edney, John D. to Sally Childress Dec. 25, 1823 by J.H.M. Thomas, J.P.
    Bondsman: Nicholas P. Perkins

Edney, Newton to Nelly Phipps Dec. 31, 1829 by Levin Edney, M.G.
    Bondsman: Edmund Edney

Edney, Samuel to Patsy Phipps March 11, 1818 (bond)
    Bondsman: David C. Waters

Edney, Winson to Nancy Potts Aug. 18, 1823 by S. Hunt
    Bondsman: John D. Edney

Edward, Edward E. to Lucy A. Bugg Sept. 6, 1846 by B.R. Gant, M.G.
    Bondsman: Jesse N. Oslin

Edwards, Franklin A. (X) to Nancy C. Lamb Jan. 14, 1850 by Jas. S. Owen, J.P.
    Bondsman: John A. X Edwards Wit.: N.W. Whitson & Wm. M. Lamb

Edwards, James to Hannah Dowdy Dec. 11, 1842 (bond)
    Bondsman: Jas. Edwards and Wm. Dowdy

Edwards, James A. to Susan Goodwin (bond)
    Bondsman: Samuel Peay

Edwards, John A. (X) to Elizabeth Hicks June 7, 1849 by Jas. S. Owen, J.P.
    Bondsman: James A. Neely

Edwards, Peter to Sally Humphreys Nov. 30, 1820 by G. Hunt
    Bondsman: D. J. Humphreys

Edwards, Samuel T. to Sally Matthews Aug. 11, 1821 (bond)
    Bondsman: Thomas Helm

Edwards, Silas to Mary Bagby Nov. 23, 1831 by S.S. Hawkins, J.P.
    Bondsman: John Mitchell

Edwards, William (X) to Rachael Curtis Oct. 12, 1821 (bond)
    Bondsman: Wm. N. X Edwards and Benj. X Curtis Test: Elisha L. Hall

Elam, Mathew to Mary W. Edmiston April 10, 1817 (bond)
    Bondsman: Caleb D. Pollard

Elam, Matthew to Nancy Jackson   May 7, 1817 (bond)
    Bondsman: Jeremiah X Pope Wit. Robert Davis

Elbeck, Henry to Elizabeth A. Carter   Aug. 28, 1838 by Robert Davis, M.G.
    Bondsman: William Johnson

Eliston, John to Ann Ridley   Nov. 7, 1816 by Garner McConnico, M.G.
    Bondsman: Thomas Hiter

Elkin, Robert to Permelia Francis   Sept. 21, 1830 by Robt. McCutchen, J.P.
    Bondsman: John Sawyer

Ellbeck, Henry to Sally Williamson   July 31, 1823 by Robt. Davis
    Bondsman: William P. Hays   (groom's sig. "Elmeck")

Ellington, George W. to Louisa Raney   Dec. 8, 1836 by Jacob Critz, J.P.
    Bondsman: none given

Elliott, Amos to Sally Porter   Feb. 19, 1822 by Henry Bailey, J.P.
    Bondsman: William X Hazlewood

Elliott, Charles L. to Marion Vernon   Nov. 11, 1840 by N.B. Owen, J.P.
    Bondsman: Samuel Vernon

Elliott, James to Mary Bobbitt   Feb. 27, 1831 by Nich's Scales, J.P.
    Bondsman: Hardaway Alston Wit. present: Preston Hay

Elliott, John to Mourning Drinkard   Jan. 25, 1816 (bond)
    Bondsman: Walter Elliott

Elliott, Seth to Martha E. Reams   Feb. 18, 1840 by M.L. Andrews, M.G.
    Bondsman: Thomas P. Anderson

Elliott, Thomas to Sally McKinny   Dec. 26, 1824 by N. Scales
    Bondsman: Jno. W. Cannon (groom's sig. "Elliot")

Elliott, William to Polley Elliott   Feb. 12, 1811 by Nick Scales
    Bondsman: John Elliott Wit: Wm. P. Harrison

Elliott, William A. to Polly Graves   Sept. 1, 1829 by Nathan L. Koonce, M.G.
    Bondsman: H. C. Whitworth

Ellis, George T. to Amanda M. Trimble   April 12, 1846 by Jas. King
    Bondsman: Clement J. Wood

Ellis, John J. to Sarah C. Irion   Sept. 26, 1817 (bond)
    Bondsman: David Mason

Ellis, Joseph W. to Sally Winslow   March 5, 1808 (bond)
    Bondsman: G. G. Washington   Test: A. Potter

Ellis, Thomas to Jane Allen   Feb. 8, 1815 (bond)
    Bondsman: Benjamin Parks

Elmon, Henry (X) to Parthenia Johnson   Nov. 9, 1825 by H. Bailey, J.P.
    Bondsman: Henry Wall

Elmore, William to Frances Groves (Graves?) Dec. 13, 1829 by Geo. J. Poin-
    Bondsman: William A. Elliott   (dexter, J.P.

Ely, John (X) to Elizabeth Lamb March 15, 1828 (bond)
    Bondsman: William Potter

Ensley, John M. to Christiana E. Burges Dec. 19, 1833 by M.L. Andrews, M.G.
    Bondsman: Wm. Williams (groom signed "Endsley")

Epperson, Littleberry to Patsey Fauer Sept. 27, 1810 (bond)
    Bondsman: George Gentry

Eppes, Freeman to Nancy Lavender July 20, 1826 (bond)
    Bondsman: none given

Epps, Francis B. to Mary McCord Aug. 23, 1832 by James B. Porter
    Bondsman: Alderson Maddin

Epps, Spencer (X) to Maria Lavender Sept. 9, 1828 (bond)
    Bondsman: John D. X Mays

Epps, Thomas E. (X) to Martha Ann Bates April 24, 1841 by Joseph Carle
    Bondsman: Joseph W. Baugh Letter attached: "State of Tennessee.
              Being called upon by Mr. Thomas Epps late of Virginia for
              a certified report relative to my knowledge of his gen-
              eology. I do certify that I am acquainted with him in his
              infancy. I was acquainted for many years with his father
              Edward Epps and his grandfather Thomas Epps and his great
              grandfather John Epps all of the county of Lewisburg and
              state of Virginia. They were reputed to be free white men
              of good reputable character owning lands and slaves.
              Sworn to and subscribed this 23rd day of April 1841.
              Robert Hayes Test: W.S. Webb, J.P." On outside letter:
              "Robert Hayes certificate of character for Thomas Epps.
              Examined by Messrs. Francis B. Fogg and Robert C. Foster,
              Esquire and pronounced by them sufficient evidence upon
              which marriage license might be issued. L.B. McConnico."

Erwin, Alexander R. to Louisa E. Boyd Nov. 27, 1837 (bond)
    Bondsman: Thomas W. Miles

Erwin, John E. to Elizabeth H. McFadden by Thos. D. Porter (bond dated
    Bondsman: Robert W. McFadden (Nov. 8, 1832, minister's return dated
                                  (Oct. 15, 1832. Latter date probably
                                  (should be Nov. 15, 1832.)

Escue, Robert to Elizabeth Stovall Feb. 4, 1814 (bond)
    Bondsman: Barth Stovall Wit.: Wm. H. Stone

Estes, David to Ellen Johnson July 24, 1842 by J.J. Bingham, J.P.
    Bondsman: Humphrey X Gardner

Estes, (Ester) to Polly Hicks May 14, 1807 (bond)
    Bondsman: Robert Ester and James P. Hicks

Estes, Samuel to Martha M. (U.) Gee Dec. 21, 1811 (bond
    Bondsman: James Hicks

Estes, Stephen (X) to Louisa Montgomery   Aug. 9, 1846 by John Nichols, J.P.
    Bondsman: George W. Shelton

Eubanks, Richard J. to Lucy A. Crowder   Nov. 15, 1837 by M.L. Andrews, M.G.
    Bondsman: Silas Edmonson

Evans, Benjamin to Elisabeth Reid   Feb. 7, 1822 by Joel Anderson
    Bondsman: Wm. Reed

Evans, Davis to Jane Townson   Sept. 30, 1812 (bond)
    Bondsman: Wm. H. Armistead

Evans, Duncan to Marilda A. Smith   April 4, 1844 by J.B. Boyd, J.P.
    Bondsman: Samuel S. Chrisman

Evans, Enos S. to Priscilla Shelton   June 20, 1826 by J. Farrington, J.P.
    Bondsman: none given

Evans, Etheldred to Nancy Poarch (Poasch?) June 2, 1812 (bond)
    Bondsman: Donaldson Potter

Evans, Isham to Susan Cates   Aug. 21, 1813 (bond)
    Bondsman: Isham Evins? and Shelby Corzine

Evans, James D. to Mary Ann Wood   May 7, 1828 by Thos. D. Porter, M.G.
    Bondsman: Stephen Wood

Evans, Jese to Ann McConnico   Oct. 14, 1809 (bond)
    Bondsman: Harvey Puckett

Evans, John to Wealthy Forehand   Oct. 7, 1830 by James Ivy, J.P.
    Bondsman: Wm. B. Bray

Evans, John to Amanda Shell   Aug. 7, 1838 by Robert Davis, M.G.
    Bondsman: John W. Miller

Evans, John (X) to Eliza Warren   Aug. 29, 1838 by Wm. Edmondson, J.P.
    Bondsman: Silas Edmonson

Evans, John J. to Nancy D. Mullen   June 12, 1823 by George Shannon, J.P.
    Bondsman: John A. Holland

Evans, Lawrence to Nancy Bennett   April 2, 1819 (bond)
    Bondsman: Peter Smith

Evans, Robert to Sally Lark Potter   Jan. 11, 1825 (bond)
    Bondsman: Robt. A. Reed

Evans, William to Elisabeth Cowan   March 18, 1815 by S. Hills, Jr.
    Bondsman: David Johnston

Everly, George to Polly Dobbins   Nov. 13, 1819 (bond)
    Bondsman: John Brown

Everly, Jacob to Louisa Word   Aug. 17, 1830 by Robert Davis, M.G.
    Bondsman: Thos. Montgomery

Evins, William to Mourning McPherson Feb. 26, 1829 by John Alkinson, V.D.M.
    Bondsman: John Forehand

Ewin, Henry C. to Betsey Hill Jan. 12, 1815 (bond)
    Bondsman: William H. Hill

Ewing, Felix to Rachel S.L.C.M. McCrory Sept. 2, 1824 by Wm. Hume, V.D.M.
    Bondsman: M.H.R.H. Smith

Ewing, Jesse H. to Margaret A. Johnston Jan. 7, 1841 by W.B. Carpenter
    Bondsman: Robert H. Campbell

Ezell, Balaam to Keziah Tarkington July 18, 1805 by Tristram Patton
    Bondsman: Jesse Tarkington

Ezell, Fedrick to Matilda Cloyd 24th, 1824 (no month given)
    Bondsman: Herbert Owen

Ezell, Fielder (Fielden) to Elizabeth Dodd July 9, 1820 by Henry Petty, M.G.
    Bondsman: Samuel Dodd

Ezell, Frederick to Polly Dodd Jan. 4, 1812 (bond)
    Bondsman: Swanson Johnston

Ezell, Littleberry to Martha H. Smith Dec. 29, 1836 by James King
    Bondsman: none given

Ezell, Samuel to Mary D. Barnes Sept. 17, 1844 by John Z. Wrenn, J.P.
    Bondsman: Henry X Hawks

Ezell, William to Frances Madden Nov. 25, 1841 by Jas. King, M.G.
    Bondsman: Thomas A. Graham

Ezell, William C. to Elizabeth A. Smith Dec. 8, 1841 by Carmack Stephens
    Bondsman: William A. Jones

-F-

Fagan, Thomas H. to America Bennet Feb. 12, 1849 by John King
    Bondsman: Van sweeden Gillespie

Faircloth, Cordial (X) to Sally Reynolds Oct. 31, 1816 by Garner McConnico
    Bondsman: M.C. DeGraffenreid

Ferguson, James T. to Elizabeth Shannon Dec. 7, 1818 (bond)
    Bondsman: Charles Mason

Faris, Jonathan J. to Bethenia E. Bond Nov. 12, 1840 by J.C. Anderson, M.G.
    Bondsman: John O. Crump

Fariss, John B. to Leah Donelson Nov. 15, 1837 by M.L. Andrews, M.G.
    Bondsman: none given

Fariss, William to Ann H. Russell Dec. 7, 1837 by N.P. Modrall, M.G.
    Bondsman: none given

Farmer, Hiram (X) to Lucinda L. Shelton   July 30, 1843 by M.L. Andrews, M.G.
    Bondsman: Jadock X Johnson

Farmer, John to Elizabeth B. Gibson   Sept. 21, 1844 by Pettus Shelburne, J.P.
    Bondsman: Simon Venable

Farmer, Lemuel to Merinda McGan   Dec. 28, 1841 by M.L. Andrews, M.G.
    Bondsman: Henderson McMahan

Farmer, Lemuel to Mary M. Hardeman   July 2, 1845 (bond)
    Bondsman: Frank Hardeman

Farmer, Moses E. to Wilmoth Boyd   June 12, 1828 by John Alkinson, V.D.M.
    Bondsman: Nich's P. Stone

Farmer, Moses to Jane Williams   Aug. 30, 1831 by James W. Rea, M.G.
    Bondsman: Johnson D. Williams

Farmer, Napoleon B. to Martha A.E. Harvey   Jan. 5, 1842 by B.B. Toon, J.P.
    Bondsman: Holcomb P. Harvey

Farmer, Samuel to Rachel McMahon   Feb. 13, 1822 (bond)
    Bondsman: James Patton

Farnsworth, Samuel H. to Jane Cowsert   April 29, 1826 (bond)
    Bondsman: none given

Farrar, Abraham to Rebecca Moore   Nov. 18, 1812 (bond)
    Bondsman: William Moore

Farrow, Elisha to Lydia Ann Chrisman   Dec. 14, 1830 by John Wall, J.P.
    Bondsman: Thomas Chrisman

Faster, (Foster?) Robert C., Jr. to Louisa L. Sanders   Oct. 28, 1819 (bond)
    Bondsman: E.B. Robertson

Faught, Joseph W. to America P. Warren   Aug. 8, 1839 by R.W. Robinson, J.P.
    Bondsman: Charles W. X Woods

Faught, Samuel to Nancy Dean   May 6, 1810 (bond)
    Bondsman: Joseph Inman

Faulkenbury, John A. to Eliza J. Orman   Jan. 12, 1832 (bond)
    Bondsman: Richard L. Andrews

Fay, Andrew to Sarah Dwyers   April 24, 1823 (bond)
    Bondsman: Jeremiah Dwyers

Fedrick, John to Susan Jones   Feb. 16, 1824 (bond)
    Bondsman: David Jones

Feltes, James W. to Polly Ann Sea   Jan. 29, 1829 by Lent Brown
    Bondsman: Eli A. X Sea

Felts, Frederick J. to Mary F. Weathers   May 19, 1847 by Peter Owen, M.P.
    Bondsman: Richard Felts

Ferguson, Deongald to Nancy Dyer Sept. 2, 1820 by Wm. Anthony, J.P.
    Bondsman: Joseph A.C. Kindrick

Ferguson, Doctor F. to Mary A. Campbell Nov. 16, 1841 by J. Bernett, J.P.
    Bondsman: Arthur S. Aikin

Ferguson, George W. to Elizabeth A. Hunter Dec. 13, 1848 by Jas. King
    Bondsman: Alexander Black

Ferguson, James to Tabitha Dyers Dec. 13, 1823 (bond)
    Bondsman: John M. Dyers

Ferguson, Jerome to Elizabeth Jones Nov. 18, 1841 by James King, M.G.
    Bondsman: Arthur S. Aikin

Ferguson, John to Margaret A. Gillispie Nov. 10, 1831 by Wm. Allison, J.P.
    Bondsman: Philip V. X Doss

Ferguson, John R. to Susan Ann Gray Dec. 17, 1842 by Jesse Cox, M.G.
    Bondsman: Daniel F. Collins

Ferguson, Joseph to Nancy Ferguson Jan. 28, 1847 by Reuben White, J.P.
    Bondsman: Thomas Chrisman

Ferguson, Marshall J. to Elizabeth Lunn Jan. 9, 1848 (Min.'s name omitted)
    Bondsman: John Baugh

Ferguson, William S. to Dorcas Aikin Nov. 1, 1834 by S.S. McEwen? (illegible)
    Bondsman: John N. Cates

Ferrel, Josiah to Catharine Inman Jan. 28, 1818 (bond)
    Bondsman: William Kenney Letter attached: "William Kenney go to
              the county clark in Franklin for licence to marry Josiah
              Ferrel and Catherine Inman and go my Security for the same
              and you will oblige Yours Josiah Ferrel"

Field, Absolem to Lucy Hester Dec. 26, 1824 by Thos. S. King, J.P.
    Bondsman: J. Field

Field, George W. (X) to Sarah Jane Tindall Sept. 11, 1848 by Jas.S.Owen,J.P.
    Bondsman: George W. Barnes

Field, Jackson (X) to Jemima Barnes Mar. 16, 1824 (bond)
    Bondsman: Sylvester Jones

Field, Jesse to Rebecca Curtis Nov. 25, 1845 by Jas. King
    Bondsman: Stephen B. Field

Field, John to Polly Gossett April 7, 1828 (bond)
    Bondsman: Andrew Field

Field, John J. to Catharine Curtis July 16, 1839 by Jas. B. Potter
    Bondsman: Moses B. Caskey

Fielder, John L. to Mary Campbell Feb. 13, 1821 by John Witherspoon
    Bondsman: Benjamin White

Fielder, John S. to Sally Hamlet Nov. 9, 1818 (bond)
    Bondsman: R. H. Mason

Fielding, Thomas W. to Elizabeth Hunter Jan. 23, 1818 (bond)
    Bondsman: none given Witness: N.P. Hardeman

Fields, Henry (X) to Elizabeth Clark Jan. 19, 1842 by N.R. Owen, J.P.
    Bondsman: Ryleigh D. Murray

Fields, Jeremiah to Mary Odum March 13, 1837 (bond)
    Bondsman: none given. No marriage date or by whom performed.

Fields, John H. B. to Mildred W. Scales Aug. 22, 1850 by J.M. Macpherson
    Bondsman: Joseph W. Scales

Fields, Leonard (X) to Kesiah Hamblet Sept. 13, 1827 by Thos. S. King, J.P.
    Bondsman: Thomas Peay

Fields, Lewis to Margaret Hunter March 11, 1823 by Tristram Patton, J.P.
    Bondsman: Nitherland Tate

Fields, Peter P. to Mary E. Bell March 5, 1845 by W.A. Whitsitt
    Bondsman: Young G. Cannon

Fields, Samuel (X) to Julia Johnson Dec. 6, 1849 by Wm. Walgreen, J.P.
    Bondsman: John Massey

Fields, William to Mary Loyd July 26, 1837 by J.W. Rea, M.G.
    Bondsman: none given

Figures, Thomas N. to Bethenia Hardeman Sept. 23, 1843 (bond)
    Bondsman: Turner S. Foster

Fisar, John to Elizabeth Kerfman Sept. 26, 1822 by C. McDaniel, J.P.
    Bondsman: William Wolfe

Fisher, Frederick to Rebecca S. McCurdy Dec. 23, 1834 by John McCurdy, M.G.
    Bondsman: Benjamin Appleby

Fisher, Frederick to Elizabeth C. Horton Dec. 18, 1845 by M.L. Andrews, M.G.
    Bondsman: William Y. Bennett

Fisher, Frederick to Lucy R. Andrews Dec. 25, 1849 by M.L. Andrews
    Bondsman: Wm. Y. Bennett

Fisher, John to Martha Still April 13, 1847 (bond)
    Bondsman: Richard Alexander

Fisk, John to Peggy Duffel July 19, 1813 (bond)
    Bondsman: John Duffel

Fisk, Joseph K. (X) to Mary H. Layne Nov. 12, 1845 by L.P. Johnson, J.P.
    Bondsman: Benjamin W. Lane

Fisk, Robert (X) to Henrietta Mariah Curry June 3, 1834 by John Morton
    Bondsman: Elijah S.S. Dean

Fisk, Samuel to Ellenor Vernon   July 6, 1833 (bond)
    Bondsman: Simon T. Green

Fisk, Samuel B. to Sarah B. Rivers   June 22, 1847 by Wm. Carter, J.P.
    Bondsman: Thos. J. Miller

Fisk, William (X) to Mary Neelly   Dec. 31, 1841 by N.K. Owen, J.P.
    Bondsman: Dossey B. Thomas

Fitts, John W.H. to Minerva R. Cooper   Dec. 16, 1845 by Peter Owen
    Bondsman: Russell P. Cooper

Fitts, Marcus to Mary Tignor   Dec. 9, 1829 (bond)
    Bondsman: Henry Riddle (groom made mark)

Fits, Felix G. (X) to Mary Hood   Nov. 28, 1839 by Geo. B. Boyd, J.P.
    Bondsman: James X Hood

Fitzgarrell, James to Fanny Hanks   Aug. 7, 1807 (bond)
    Bondsman: Sam H. Dotson

Fitzgerald, John, Jr. to Frances Mays   Sept. 3, 1843 by Jas. King
    Bondsman: Ely Dodson

Fitzgerald, Obediah to Martha Mays   Nov. 19, 1827 (bond)
    Bondsman: Bird Fitzgerald

Fitzpatrick, John to Lucy Freeman   July 15, 1812 (bond)
    Bondsman: none given   Witness: James Pratt

Fitzpatrick, Morgan to Fanny Evans   Dec. 30, 1806 (bond)
    Bondsman: John Allen

Flack, James to Jane H. Neelly   Nov. 24, 1836 by H.B. North, M.G.
    Bondsman: Brice M. Hughes

Fleety, William to Francis Burford   Sept. 7, 1819 (bond)
    Bondsman: Richard H. Rudder (groom of "Richard Rudder' place")

Fleming, David R. to Emily M.F. Andrews   June 29, 1848 by M.L. Andrews, M.G.
    Bondsman: William D. Andrews

Fleming, James to Lethe Jordan   Aug. 18, 1825 by H.B. Hyde, J.P.
    Bondsman: Zacheriah X Smith

Fleming, James M. to Nancy Nolen   Dec. 23, 1824 by Geo. Shannon, J.P.
    Bondsman: Bennett Phillips

Fleming, John T. to Harriett N. Reilly   Nov. 25, 1845 by H.B. North, M.G.
    Bondsman: Frederick A. Thompson

Fleming, Josiah to Jane B. Sharp   Dec. 4, 1828 by Thos. D. Porter
    Bondsman: Samuel M. Pannill

Fleming, Samuel to Jane Thompson   July 29, 1819 by D. Brown
    Bondsman: Absolem Thompson (Letter attached: "This is to certify
              that I have given Leave that Samuel Fleming may reseive
              License at your office to marry my Daughter Jane
              John Thompson July 24, 1819")

Fleming, William to Mickey Thompson   July 15, 1815 (bond)
    Bondsman: John Thompson

Fletcher, James to Isabella M. Cherry   June 12, 1839 (bond)
    Bondsman: James X Cherry and William N. X Cherry

Fletcher, Willie J. to Mary Ann Jordan   April 4, 1839 (bond)
    Bondsman: James B. Jordan

Flippin, Jesse S. to Mary Southall   Aug. 3, 1826 by John Alkinson, V.D.M.
    Bondsman: none given

Flippin, Phillip H. of Maury Co. to Rebecca Harper of Wm'son Co. Sept.6,1832
    Bondsmen: Philip H. Flippin by Jesse S. Flippin, Robert C. Foster by
              Jesse S. Flippin. Letter attached: "Mr. Thos. Hardeman:
              Sir please to issue to my brother Jesse S. Flippin marriage
              license to marry myself and Mrs. Rebecca Harper and by so
              doing you will oblige Philip H. Flippin Sept. 4, 1832"

Floid, Joseph (X) to Sally Gilbert   Jan. 11, 1819 (bond)
    Bondsman: James Glover Witness: Thomas Miller, Jr.

Floyd, Drury to Ann Rowlett   June 30, 1846 by A. Matthews, M.G.
    Bondsman: James M. Gault

Floyd, James to Catharine K. Webb   Dec. 12, 1843 by John Landrum, Baptist M.
    Bondsman: Wm. A. Webb

Floyd, John to Betsey Logan   May 10, 1806 (bond)
    Bondsman: David Logan

Floyd, John to Mary Smith   April 13, 1809 (bond)
    Bondsman: John F. Childress

Floyd, John H. to Sarah Johnson   Dec. 17, 1829 by Robert Pate, J.P.
    Bondsman: Elijah Adams

Floyd, John H. to Anna Manire   Aug. 12, 1846 by John King, M.G.
    Bondsman: John E. Rainey

Floyd, Wm. to Sally Morfet   Feb. 11, 1811 (license and bond)
    Bondsman: Benjamin Brown

Floyd, William to Julia G. Edmondson   Jan. 16, 1840 by Berry F. Weakley,M.G.
    Bondsman: William E. McNail

Floyd, William to Martha Johnson   Aug. 7, 1849 by M.C. Jordan, J.P.
    Bondsman: Joseph McPeak

Fly, Caleb to Elizabeth Holland   Jan. 23, 1834 by Geo Shannon, J.P.
    Bondsman: Harry Tindall

Fly, David (X) to Patsey Younger   Nov. 19, 1818 (bond)
    Bondsman: Thos. Younger

Fly, Elisha to Elizabeth Cutchen   Nov. 30, 1816 by Thos. Boaz, Minister
    Bondsman: William Shelton

Fly, George to Winny Ann Eliza Lacy   Aug. 16, 1832 by George Shannon, J.P.
    Bondsman: Jeremiah Hill

Fly, John (X) to Frances Belcher   May 2, 1844 (bond)
    Bondsman: Samuel I.C. X Coleman

Fly, Sterling B. to Emeline Barnes   Nov. 16, 1842 by T.W. Haynes, M.G.
    Bondsman: Jessie Morris

Foley, Stephen to Polly Bonds   Oct. 22, 1835 by M. Johnston, J.P.
    Bondsman: David Burnham

Folwell, Joseph to Catherine Ford   Dec. 31, 1833 by Jno. W. Miller, J.P.
    Bondsman: Wm. D. Taylor   Wit. present: J.A.M.E. Stewart

Folwell, Joseph to Ellendor Ford   Nov. 27, 1845 (bond)
    Bondsman: M.L. Andrews

Ford, Abram to Polly Howard   Sept. 5, 1827 (bond)
    Bondsman: Samuel Crouse (groom made mark)

Ford, William (X) to Isabella Hill   April 14, 1843 (bond)
    Bondsman: Bennett Blackburn

Forehand, Newton to Mary Ann Hutton   Dec. 14, 1828 by Wm. Roach
    Bondsman: John Forehand

Forehand, Samuel to Sally Mcpherson   Jan. 8, 1825 by Levin Edney, M.G.
    Bondsman: John Forehand

Forehand, Thomas to Elizabeth Grimes   Sept. 11, 1809 (bond)
    Bondsman: James Jackson

Forehand, Vincent to Betsey Marlin   Sept. 28, 1820 (bond)
    Bondsman: Daniel Gray

Forehand, William C. to Mary Hobbs   March 13, 1850 by W.J. Tucker, J.P.
    Bondsman: William X McPherson

Foster, Andrew J. to Amanda McNabb   Aug. 28, 1845 by M.L. Andrews, M.G.
    Bondsman: Tillman Pench (illegible)

Foster, Bennett T. to Louisa Barman   July 19, 1843 by S.S. Nunn, J.P.
    Bondsman: John B. Porter

Foster, James G. (X) to Hannah Stratram?   March 29, 1824 by G. Hunt
    Bondsman: Wm. Lovel

Foster, Maloy J. to Margaret A. Pewitt   April 25, 1844 by Chesley Williams, J.P.
    Bondsman: Samuel Davis

Foster, William T. to Ruth Thomas   Nov. 26, 1836 (bond)
    Bondsman: John B. Beech (Bush?)

Foulkes, John W. to Jean Wood   Dec. 26, 1805 (bond)
    Bondsman: Elisha White

Fowler, Edward to Martha Venable Feb. 22, 1808 by N. Scales
    Bondsman: John Gardner

Fowler, James to Nancy Fisher Oct. 27, 1840 by James M. Green, J.P.
    Bondsman: George D. Bell

Fowler, John to Patcy Foster May 13, 1817 (bond)
    Bondsman: Drury Warren

Fowler, Thomas to Rebecca Key Aug. 3, 1820 (bond)
    Bondsman: John Brimm

Fowler, Thomas to Mary F. Fisher April 29, 1847 by Wm. A. Whitsitt, Bap.Min.
    Bondsman: James Wilkins

Fowlkes, Thompson to Prepellar (Pressellar?) Hyde Nov. 15, 1806 by N. Scales
    Bondsman: Thompson Wood

Fox, Elijah M. to Nancy C. Wakefield Oct. 27, 1847 by Thos. Prowell, J.P.
    Bondsman: John R. McIntosh

Fox, Hugh A. to Margaret Wakefield Feb. 21, 1837 by James Fox, J.P.
    Bondsman: none given

Fox, James to Susan Fox Jan. 17, 1837 by Thos. Prowell, J.P.
    Bondsman: none given

Fox, Milus to Mary Wakefield Jan. 30, 1834 by James Fox, J.P.
    Bondsman: Joseph Wakefield

Fox, Thomas to Delilah Jane Walker Oct. 31, 1839 by S.W. Newsom, J.P. (illeg)
    Bondsman: Washington Wollard

Francis, Moses B. to Sarah Dickson March 1, 1811 (bond)
    Bondsman: Jacob Harder

Frankham, Edmund (X) to Lydia Loftin Oct. 14, 1835 (bond)
    Bondsman: Smith Bridges

Frantham, Floyd (X) to Betsey Gunter Aug. 24, 1822 (bond)
    Bondsman: Henry X Holliday

Frantham, James to Peggy Peach Nov. 22, 1821 (bond)
    Bondsman: Jno. K. Campbell (groom made mark)

Frantham, Jesee (X) to Sally Holliday Dec. 17, 1818 (bond)
    Bondsman: Martin X Frantham

Frantham, Marten (X) to Charlotte Gardiner July 1, 1816 by Wm. Dyer, J.P.
    Bondsman: Martin Franthum

Frantham, Martin to Rachel Holliday Jan. 4, 1812 (bond)
    Bondsman: Cornelius Crenshaw

Frantham, William (X) to Rebecca Pinkston March 7, 1821 by Berry Nolen, J.P.
    Bondsman: J. I. Thomas

Frantham, William D. to Amy C. Floyd   Dec. 30, 1845 (bond)
   Bondsman: Alexander Dodd

Frazer, Henry S. to Elizabeth M. Murfree   Nov. 1, 1848 by A.N.Cunningham,M.G.
   Bondsman: John W. Burton

Frazier, Augustus D. to Lavinia Leigh   March 2, 1834 (bond)
   Bondsman: Charles W. Crouch

Freeman, Byram R. to Elizabeth M. McCurdy   Oct. 10, 1850 by C.B. Faris,G.M.
   Bondsman: Jas. P. Rankin

Freeman, Sanders to Patsey Brown   Sept. 26, 1812 (bond)
   Bondsman: Sterling Brown

Frierson, George to Mava A. Moore   Dec. 21, 1808 (bond)
   Bondsman: D. Squier

Frost, James C. to Ann L. (or S.) Pope   Aug. 15, 1839 by H.B. North, M.G.
   Bondsman: Sutherland S. Mayfield

Frost, Sterling B. to Martha E. Pollard   Dec. 22, 1847 by M.W. Gray, M.G. of
   Bondsman: Wm. T. Carmack   (M.E. Church South

Fry, James (X) to Polly Walker   Sept. 13, 1815 (bond)
   Bondsman: Joshua Roberts

Fry, Joseph H. to Amanda C. Giddens   April 4, 1830 by Thos. L. Douglass
   Bondsman: Felix Ewing

Fuel?, James to Mrs. Sidney Smith   April 8, 1823 by Joel Anderson
   Bondsman: Joel Anderson

Fugett, William to Eley Deviling (Devlin?)   Nov. 29, 1815 (bond)
   Bondsman: Elias Brassell

Fulghum, Theophilus to Polly Williams   Jan. 2, 1810 (bond)
   Bondsman: Stephen Biles

Fulkes, Gabriel to Jency Hyde   May 23, 1806 (bond)
   Bondsman: Thomas Wood

Fuller, John to Nancy Johnston   Dec. 17, 1814 (bond)
   Bondsman: James S. Wilson

Fulton, Joseph B. to Mary A. Reynolds   July 7, 1842 (bond)
   Bondsman: Jas. Williams, Jr.

-G-

Gadsey, John E. to Sarah Hamilton   May 12, 1831 by Thos. D. Porter
   Bondsman: Washington Shelton

Gallaway, Enoch to Anna Taylor   July 19, 1810 (bond)
   Bondsman: Joab Patterson

Gambill, George W. C. to Mary Jane Joice   Sept. 16, 1845 (bond)
    Bondsman: Thos. A. Bostick

Gambill, Milton to Tempey Howell   June 13, 1810 (bond)
    Bondsman: Samuel Harper

Gamble, Bradley to Elizabeth Baucom   July 28, 1819 by Thos. Wilson
    Bondsman: Joseph Kendrick

Gamble, George W. to Minerva Nunn   Dec. 22, 1836 by N.P. Modrall
    Bondsman: James X Gambill (groom signed "Gambill")

Gamble, William C. to Eliza Tarkington   April 24, 1824 by G. Hunt
    Bondsman: Thos. Potter

Gamblin, James W. to Lucy Ann Bond   Dec. 19, 1833 by M. Johnston, J.P.
    Bondsman: John H. White

Gamblin, John W. to Margaret Ann Cartwright   Jan. 28, 1850 by James M. Reed, J.P.
    Bondsman: Ira E. Burnham

Gambrill, John to Lena McLain   July 10, 1828 by Jabez Owen
    Bondsman: Ira X Burnham

Gannoway, Walker to Louisa Lester   Sept. 5, 1814 by John Adkerson
    Bondsman: none given Witness: N.P. Hardeman

Gant, Benjamin R. to Angelina Bugg   Aug. 13, 1833 by H.C. Horton, M.G.
    Bondsman: Benjamin B. Lanier

Gant, Howard S. (X) to Isabell Price   Aug. 19, 1841 by J. Hatcher, J.P.
    Bondsman: Robert Biggers

Gant, Joel to Sarah Phillips   May 27, 1816 (bond)
    Bondsman: Jesse Weatherly

Gant, John M. to Temperance Simmons   Aug. 14, 1828 by L. Brown, M.G.
    Bondsman: John H. Gant

Gant, Joseph M.C. to Elizabeth Bugg   Jan. 15, 1840 by H.C. Horton, M.G.
    Bondsman: Harwood S. X Gant

Gant, William G. to Elizabeth C. Hendrix   Sept. 21, 1836 by S.B. Robinson, J.P.
    Bondsman: Francis H. Jackson

Gardiner, John to Jenny Venable   Feb. 23, 1808 by N. Scales
    Bondsman: Thos. Venable

Gardiner, Thos. to Jean Page   Nov. 4, 1806 (bond)
    Bondsman: John Gardiner

Gardiner, Walter (X) to Mary Gardiner   Jan. 5, 1832 by S.S. Newman, J.P.
    Bondsman: Joseph P. Johnson

Gardner, Daniel S. to Elizabeth Thompson   Feb. 27 1838 by Jos. Burnet, J.P.
    Bondsman: Humphrey X Gardner

Gardner, Griffin W. to Sarah M. Poyner   April 12, 1838 by J.P. McKay, J.P.
    Bondsman: Thomas X Chambers

Gardner, Humphrey (X) to Martha Gardner   July 19, 1840 by S.S.R.A. Knott, JP
    Bondsman: Hugh X Thompson

Gardner, Jackson (X) to Dicey Dollar   Sept. 23, 1840 (bond)
    Bondsman: Samuel Skelley

Gardner, James to Abba Davis   March 22, 1849 (bond)
    Bondsman: Samuel X Gardner

Gardner, Noah (X) to Harriet Corsby   Nov. 21, 1820 (bond)
    Bondsman: Thomas Gardner

Gardner, Samuel (X) to Nancy Thompson   Jan. 30, 1845 by S.S.A.P. Knott, J.P.
    Bondsman: Hugh X D. Thompson

Gardner, Thomas, Jr. to Sarah Johnston   March 4, 1822 by Wm. Dunnegan, J.P.
    Bondsman: Wiley Estes

Garner, Britain to Patsy Gilbert   Jan. 17, 1807 (bond)
    Bondsmen: John Gilbert and Sampson Flake

Garner, Jesse to Clarissa Rutherford   Jan. 4, 1831 by T.D. Porter, M.G.
    Bondsman: Benjamin Palmore

Garner, John to Sally Cochran   June 20, 1807 (bond)
    Bondsman: William Cochran

Garner, Philip (X) to Susan White   July 1, 1824 by N. Scales
    Bondsman: James Ozburn

Garner, Thomas to Nancy Gooch   Feb. 7, 1820 (bond)
    Bondsman: John C. Gooch

Garner, William to Martha White   Dec. 10, 1844 (bond)
    Bondsman: John W. X White

Garner, William N. (X) to Mary E. Wilson   Sept. 15, 1842 by J.B. Boyd, J.P.
    Bondsman: Robert X Ramsey

Garnett, James H. to Mary Jane McDaniel   Oct. 3, 1847 by M.L. Andrews, M.G.
    Bondsman: William McDaniel

Garrett, Caleb to Elizabeth Hamilton   Dec. 24, 1816 by J. Farrington
    Bondsman: Edward Bevil

Garrett, Caleb to Elizabeth Hambleton   Sept. 16, 1830 by Jas. Rea, M.G.
    Bondsman: Jeremiah Field

Garrett, Coleman (Coalman) W. to Scina Rounsavall   Nov. 20, 1823 by G.Marshall
    Bondsman: Wm. A. Temple

Garrett, Fenton to Oliva E. Crosley   Aug. 31, 1837 by S. Green, J.P.
    Bondsman: none given

Garrett, George W. to Harriett Anderson Feb. 10, 1817 (bond)
    Bondsman: Brane H. Anderson

Garrett, James to Jane Spence Sept. 21, 1842 by John Crick, J.P.
    Bondsman: Stephen Jordan

Garrett, John (X) to Edy Hardcastle Aug. 10, 1818 (bond)
    Bondsman: Samuel Daugherty

Garrett, Matthew to Matilda White June 20, 1844 by J.A. Cunningham, J.P.
    Bondsman: Henry S. Hendrix

Garrett, Richard C. to Elizabeth F. Wood April 5, 1843 by John Richardsson,
    Bondsman: James Collier   J.P.

Garrett, Thomas B. to Levicy Evans June 24, 1820 (bond)
    Bondsman: J. H. Maury

Garrett, Wesley to Ann Thurman April 22, 1848 (bond)
    Bondsman: Jeremiah Thurman

Gary, James to Susan Williamson April 10, 1817 (bond)
    Bondsman: H.R. Hill

Gary, Thomas W. to Delia Ann Andrews June 2, 1842 by M.L. Andrews, M.G.
    Bondsman: James H. Gary

Gaston, George to Eliza L. Bird Aug. 8, 1844 by J.A. Cunningham, J.P.
    Bondsman: Wiley B. White

Gates, James to Patsey Rusel Sept. 25, 1815 (bond)
    Bondsman: Benjamin X Rusel (groom also made mark)

Gates, Joseph to Elizabeth Ostean Nov. 21, 1816 by N. Scales
    Bondsman: Reeves Jordan (groom made mark)

Gatlin, Alfred to Martha H. Ham Feb. 22, 1830 by E.R. Parish, J.P.
    Bondsman: Jos. J. Yarbrough

Gatlin, Benjamin F. (X) to Anna Crenshaw Feb. 18, 1845 by J.F. McMahan, J.P.
    Bondsman: Lewis Midgett

Gatlin, Hardy to Rhoda Knight July 7, 1841 by Wm. Moor, J.P.
    Bondsman: Thomas W. Little

Gatlin, James to Sarah Pinkleton Dec. 29, 1845 (bond)
    Bondsman: William H. McMahan

Gatlin, Lazarus to Elenor Lyttle April 16, 1816 by S. Hunt, J.P.
    Bondsman: J. B. Thompson

Gatlin, Thomas L. to Jane Marling Jan. 13, 1848 (bond)
    Bondsman: John M. X Grimes

Gautt, Hugh M. to Martha Floyd Oct. 21, 1829 by Horatio Burns, M.G. in M.E.
    Bondsman: John H. Floyd   Church

Gault, Isiah C. to Mary Raney Nov. 30, 1834 by Joseph Ralston, J.P.
    Bondsman: Samuel Bochnes?

Gault, James M. to Mary Jane Boelmus Oct. 25, 1831 by Thos. D. Porter
    Bondsman: Wm. Crouch

Gault, James M. to Matilda F. McPherson Jan. 16, 1844 by S.G. Burney
    Bondsman: John W. Miller

Gault, John M. to Martha Ann Taylor Aug. 27, 1830 (bond)
    Bondsman: Nathaniel H. Thomas

Gault, Renwick A. to Elizabeth N. Floyd Feb. 13, 1833 (bond)
    Bondsman: James M. Gault

Gaut, Alfred S. to Pamelia P. Bugg Nov. 14, 1837 by William Lanier, J.P.
    Bondsman: none given

Gee, Benjamin O. to Virginia H. Tanner Sept. 10, 1828 by M.L. Andrews, J.P.
    Bondsman: Henry Gee

Gee, George S. to Sarah I. Rash Dec. 8, 1836 by Levi Crosley, J.P.
    Bondsman: none given

Gee, John H. to Julia A. Tanner Dec. 5, 1832 by M.L. Andrews, J.P.
    Bondsman: Benjamin O. Gee

Gee, Robert F. to Adaline D. Irion Sept. 1, 1830 (bond)
    Bondsman: Robert S. Thomas

Gee, Willie to Adaline McKnabb Dec. 22, 1835 (bond)
    Bondsman: John W. Witherspoon

Gentry, George to Patsey Carson July 2, 1813 (bond)
    Bondsman: John M. Walker

Gentry, Joseph S. to Mary E. Rucker Jan. 15, 1850 by W. Burns, M.G.
    Bondsman: Wm. H. Crouch

Gentry, Meredith P. to Caledonia Brown Nov. 19, 1846 by A.N. Cunningham, M.G.
    Bondsman: L. B. McConnico

Gentry, Nicholas to Sally Browder Feb. 19, 1805 (bond)
    Bondsman: Jove Boyd

Gentry, Nicholas to Polly Nunn Oct. 26, 1818 (bond)
    Bondsman: Sam Shelburne

Gentry, Reuben A. to Ruth T. Rogers Oct. 21, 1834 by Jas.H.Otey, Bishop of
    Bondsman: Hartwell H. Hobbs   Diocese of Tenn.

Gentry, Samuel to Mary A. Bailey July 24, 1834 by Michael Finney, J.P.
    Bondsman: Darrington Garrett

Gentry, Theopulus L. to Rebecca B. Sappington Mar. 24, 1825 by J. Anderson
    Bondsman: Reuben A. Gentry

Gentry, Theophilas S. to Mary Dabney   Jan. 22, 1839 by Jas. King, M.G.
    Bondsman: H. H. Hobbs

Gentry, Theophilus L. or S. to Mary S. Pugh   Aug. 2, 1848 by Jas. King, M.G.
    Bondsman: Edward B. Pugh

German, Dan to Fanny Puckett   Jan. 7, 1807 (bond)
    Bondsman: Joseph Germain (groom's name spelled "Germain" once.)

German, Daniel to Elizabeth Rounsevall   Jan. 26, 1828 (bond)
    Bondsman: Joshua W. McCown

German, Joseph to Jean McCandless   Nov. 20, 1806 (bond)
    Bondsman: John McCandless

German, Zacheus to Nancy Cooper   Feb. 22, 1817 by S. Hunt, Jr.
    Bondsman: Daniel German

German, Zacheus H. to Emeline McEwen   Dec. 13, 1820 (1828?) (bond)
    Bondsman: M. M. McConnico

Gholson, John to Sally G. Theweatt   June 6, 1809 (bond)
    Bondsman: John Sample

Gibson, John to Jenny Wilson   March 22, 1809 (bond)
    Bondsman: Mark Wilson

Gibson, John W. to Martha H. Lester   Dec. 31, 1840 by Pettus Shelburne, J.P.
    Bondsman: Wm. J. Smithson

Gibson, Patrick to Parmelia N. Smithson   Jan. 7, 1847 by Pettus Shelburne, JP
    Bondsman: Charles W. Smithson

Gibson, Winfrey L. to Cinthia Norris   Aug. 30, 1827 by Daniel White, M.G.
    Bondsman: George X Potts

Giddens, James to Priscilla Buford   April 2, 1806 (bond)
    Bondsman: James Buford (Note attached written by bride's father, Jas. Buford, dated Mar. 29, 1806 granting permission to issue license.

Giddens, James M. to Caroline A. Thomason   Sept. 19, 1837 by H.B.North, M.G.
    Bondsman: none given

Gilbert, Benjamin to Catharine Robertson   Oct. 24, 1808 (bond)
    Bondsman: Benj. Gilbert

Gilbert, Joshua (X) to Martha Montgomery   June 22, 1845 (bond)
    Bondsman: John X Burnett

Gilbert, William B. to Frances Adams   June 23, 1833 by S.S. Harkness, J.P.
    Bondsman: Riley X Sunn?

Giles, Cyrus to Susan Potts   Aug. 12, 1824 by Wm. Dunnegan, J.P.
    Bondsman: John Potts

Giles, Edward J. to Milly Johnston   Dec. 20, 1832 by Wm. Rucker, J.P.
    Bondsman: Charles S. McCall

Giles, James H. to Sarah Dobson   July 31, 1823 (bond)
    Bondsman: John Hassell

Giles, John to Martha Blackman   Dec. 24, 1843 by M.L. Andrews, M.G.
    Bondsman: Garrett P. Wells

Giles, Josiah E. to Mary Gibson   July 21, 1818 (bond)
    Bondsman: James Gibson

Giles, Mortimer W. to Sarah B. Loftin   Oct. 3, 1850 by Jeremiah Stephens, M.G.
    Bondsman: Christopher Giles

Giles, Nicholas P. to Frances Jane Giles   Dec. 21, 1848 by Jere. Stephens, M.G
    Bondsman: Christopher Giles

Giles, Paschal to Tabitha C. Orwin?   Nov. 29, 1836 by (name not given)
    Bondsman: none given

Giles, Richard (X) to Sarah Jane Johnson   Nov. 11, 1839 (bond
    Bondsman: William Giles

Giles, Robertson to Susan A. Evans   Aug. 7, 1843 (bond)
    Bondsman: John Giles

Giles, Robertson to Frances A. Smith   Dec. 2, 1850 (bond)
    Bondsman: Edward J. Giles

Giles, Thomas to Prudence Ranea   Jan. 16, 1833 by M.L. Andrews, M.G.
    Bondsman: Clabourn Johnson

Giles, Thomas to Sarah Ann Horton   Nov. 3, 1847 (bond)
    Bondsman: John H. Allen

Giles, William to Mary Young   Dec. 13, 1834 by Andrew Craig, M.G.
    Bondsman: Clement Smith

Giles, William E. to Sarah Ann Young   Dec. 15, 1840 (bond)
    Bondsman: Charles X Smithson

Gill, Daniel to Catherine Thweatt   Dec. 6, 1815 by J.R. Trotter, Jr.
    Bondsman: Harwood Thweatt   Note found: Permission given by William
        Thweatt and Francis Thweatt for Catharine to marry.

Gillaspie, Thomas to Lucy Tully (Gully?)   Aug. 26, 1828 by M.L. Andrews, J.P.
    Bondsman: Samuel Henderson

Gillespie, David A. to Anna Bigger   Feb. 3, 1831 by M.L. Andrews, M.G.
    Bondsman: Ezekiel Wall

Gillespie, George to Nancy Owen Roberts   June 16, 1830 by Rev. James H. Shield
    Bondsman: A.B. Ewing (groom signed "Gillaspie")

Gillespie, George to Eliza Goodwin Cowles Feb. 13, 1839 by H.B. North, M.G.
    Bondsman: Andrew Park

Gillespie, George to Ann McClellan Nov. 21, 1843 by Robert C. Garrison, M.G.
    Bondsman: Sutherland S. Mayfield "married before competent number of witnesses in Presbyterian Ch."

Gillespie, George M. to Frances L. Morton Jan. 12 (2?), 1832 by John Wilson
    Bondsman: Alexander B. Morton

Gillespie, John S. to Tabitha Gray Dec. 23, 1834 by M.L. Andrews, M.G.
    Bondsman: John M. Gillespie

Gillespie, Robert to Marietta Gleeves Aug. 8, 1833 by Michael Finney, J.P.
    Bondsman: Thos. S. Berry

Gillespie, Thomas T. to Jane Walker July 20, 1812 (bond)
    Bondsman: Hance H. Walker

Gillespie, Van sweeden to Margaret Ann White Aug. 18, 1850 by M.C. Jordan, J.P.
    Bondsman: John T. Wilson

Gillispie, William to Betsey Haile Oct. 20, 1818 (bond)
    Bondsman: William Swann

Gilliam, Benjamin F. to Eliza Jane Isriel April 2, 1846 by John P. McKay, J.P.
    Bondsman: Wm. Thompson

Gilliam, Thomas E. to Celia Hardgraves Feb. 5, 1819 by Levin Edney, M.G.
    Bondsman: Wm. McCollum

Gilliam, William A. to Martha D. Smithson Dec. 5, 1822 by Joel Anderson
    Bondsman: Thos. Reynolds

Gilliam, William A. to Elvira H. H. Smith May 2, 1847 by Philip Ball, M.G.
    Bondsman: Wm. P. Campbell

Gilpin, John (X) to Pamelia Shaw Dec. 19, 1829 (bond)
    Bondsman: John Shaw

Gilpin, John to Mary Shaw Oct. 20, 1841 by J. Burnett, J.P.
    Bondsman: Benjamin A. Clardy

Gipson, Emanuel to Martha Ann Norris Feb. 27, 1834 (bond)
    Bondsman: Winfrey Gibson

Givin, James to Nancy Carson Oct. 27, 1825 (bond)
    Bondsman: Moses B. Spann

Givings, Ephraim to Fanney Jordan Nov. 6, 1811 (bond)
    Bondsman: Benjamin Jordan

Givens, Martin (X) to Elizabeth McNeil Feb. 20, 1850 by J. Hendricks, J.P.
    Bondsman: James F. McNeil

Givens, William to Racheal Inman Nov. 23, 1843 by R. White, J.P.
    Bondsman: Trimm S. Foster

Givens, William to Judy Brown   June 10, 1846 by R. White, J.P.
    Bondsman: John B. McEwen

Givens, George W. to Dicenda Inman   Dec. 24, 1841 by R. White, J.P.
    Bondsman: Wiley W. Pewit

Givens, William to Mary Inman   August 5, 1835 (bond)
    Bondsman: Malachi Pewitt

Gladden, Joseph (X) to Betsey Rhodes   April 2, 1827 (bond)
    Bondsman: Eldridge Cland?

Gladden, William W. to Rebecca Hutcherson   June 21, 1827 by David White
    Bondsman: William X Burnham

Glascock, George to Elisabeth Graham   May 1, 1806 (bond)
    Bondsman: Martin Madden

Glascock, Richard to Elizabeth Bullock   March 11, 1828 by H. Bailey, J.P.
    Bondsman: Eli Lunn

Glass, Hector to Sarah C. Nolen   Mar. 10, 1831 by Andrew Craig, M.G.
    Bondsman: Thos. J. White

Glass, Hector to Hardemia Nolen   July 4, 1833 by H.B. North, M.G.
    Bondsman: Hardemia (Hardeman?) Nolen

Glass, Lemuel to Caty Zachry   Aug. 3, 1818 (bond)
    Bondsman: George Sleeker

Glass, Samuel F. to Sarah Melone   Sept. 7, 1815 (bond)
    Bondsman: Benjamin D. Rutherford

Glass, Samuel F., Jr. to Agnes W. Hunter   Sept. 21, 1842 by Jas.C.Anderson
    Bondsman: Jas. R. Bridges

Glass, Willie B. to Jane A. Dobbins   April 21, 1836 by James W. Rea, M.G.
    Bondsman: none given

Gleaves, Benjamin to Jane Crockett   Jan. 20, 1848 by A.N. Cunningham, M.G.
    Bondsman: Andrew Crockett, Jr.

Gleaves, William to Louisa P. Morgan   April 7, 1846 by Hiram Putman
    Bondsman: N. G. Davis

Glem, Samuel M. to Lavinia P. Powell   Feb. 6, 1845 by L.C. Bryan
    Bondsman: Archibald Glem (Glenn?)

Glenn, Abram to Susan Raney   Jan. 12, 1831 by J. Gault, J.P.
    Bondsman: James Glenn

Glenn, Daniel to Lucy Rowlett   Jan. 31, 1825 (bond)
    Bondsman: Jason Winsett

Glenn, David to Nancy Raney   Jan. 2, 1826 (bond)
    Bondsman: none given

Glenn, Simon to Sally McEwen   April 27, 1819 (bond)
    Bondsman: John L. McEwen

Glenn, William (X) to Zilpah Magness   June 16, 1831 by Thos. L. Porter
    Bondsman: John Glenn

Glimp, George to Martha Passons?   Feb. 1, 1838 by L. Crosley, J.P.
    Bondsman: Jesse Glimp

Glimp, James B. (X) to Amanda Wynne   June 7, 1849 by E.P. Scales, J.P.
    Bondsman: James A. House

Glimp, Jesse to Mary Ann Wheeler   May 9, 1837 by Levi Crosley, J.P.
    Bondsman: none given

Glimp, John A. to Frances J. Wheeler   April 9, 1847 by L.B. Johnson, J.P.
    Bondsman: William C. Wilkins

Glimp, Thomas to Elizabeth McLemore   Jan. 14, 1829 by Jas. Williams, M.G.
    Bondsman: Littlebury Griggs

Glymph, Thomas to Louisiana J. Green   Nov. 4, 1841 by N.K. Owen, J.P.
    Bondsman: Williamson A. Wheeler (groom signed "Glimp")

Glimph, William to Fanny Taylor   April 19, 1827 by Thos. King, J.P.
    Bondsman: Richard W. Robeson (Groom signed "Glimph")

Glover, Jones to Betsey Laatey, Loatey, Lastly or Looty   May 16, 1816 by
    Bondsman: John X Asqua (groom made mark)   E. Hardeman

Glum?, James to Sarah A.E. Carter   May 28, 1840 (no J.P. or min. mentioned)
    Bondsman: William F. Carter

Glum?, James H. to Ruth A. Christopher   April 26, 1849 by G. Marshall, J.P.
    Bondsman: William F. Carter

Goad, John (X) to Drucinda Dawson   Sept. 18, 1823 by Geo. Tilman, J.P.
    Bondsman: John M. Dawson

Gocey, Moses C. to Mary Nevils   July 30, 1846 by Green S. Simmons, Min. M.E.
    Bondsman: Wm. C. West   Church

Godwin, George W. to Mary T. McCollum   Nov. 18, 1835 by Andrew McCrady
    Bondsman: Wyatt Coleman

Godwin, James S. to Mary Ann Shelton   April 23, 1837 by J. Burnett, J.P.
    Bondsman: none given

Godwin, Kinchen (X) to Susan Beasley   Dec. 14, 1843 by J. Burnett, J.P.
    Bondsman: Reddick X Godwin

Godwin, Reddick to Mesina Rustin   Feb. 17, 1829 (bond)
    Bondsman: Lawrence X Smith

Godwin, Seth to Nancy Lester   March 2, 1820 (bond)
    Bondsman: Jay Vestal

Goff, Ira C. to Nancy S. or L. Swanson   Nov. 19, 1840 by H. B. North, M.G.
    Bondsman: J.O.H.A. Charter

Goff, Isaac to Rebecca Densan   Oct. 25, 1819 (bond)
    Bondsman: James C. Hill

Goff, John to Ibby McEwen   Oct. 24, 1808 (bond)
    Bondsman: Thomas Goff

Goff, William, Jr. to Nancy Moore   Oct. 14, 1829 (bond)
    Bondsman: Andrew Halfacre

Goforth, Beaty to Violet K. M. West   Oct. 19, 1830 (bond)
    Bondsman: Isaac X West

Gooch, David R. to Tabitha Mayo   Jan. 3, 1818 (bond)
    Bondsman: James Kidd

Goodman, Archabal to Delaney Davis   March 11, 1806 (bond)
    Bondsman: Henry Davis and William Gunley

Goodman, James to Peggy Goodman   Oct. 21, 1819 by Edward Ragsdale, J.P.
    Bondsman: Jas. Brown

Goodrich, John to Milly Short   Sept. 1, 1831 by John Alkinson, V.D.M.
    Bondsman: Elijah A. Loyd

Goodrum, Thomas H. to Polly S. Dickson   April 2, 1840 by John S. Davis, M.G.
    Bondsman: James X McNabb

Goodwin, George W. to Mary B. Buchanan   Jan. 7, 1838 (min. name omitted)
    Bondsman: Green B. Goodwin

Goodwin, James H. to Mildredge Ann White   May 23, 1849 by Lycurgus McCall, J.P.
    Bondsman: Washington Hartly   (groom made mark)

Goodwin, Thomas C. to Sarah A. Hatcher   Oct. 14, 1847 by Lycurgus McCall, J.P.
    Bondsman: Alexander Hatcher

Gordon, David to Susan M. Caperton   Aug. 24, 1824 (bond)
    Bondsman: Samuel Caperton

Gordon, Francis to Betsey Caperton   Sept. 18, 1817 (bond)
    Bondsman: John Caperton

Gordon, James to Nancy Carlin   Aug. 19, 1827 (bond)
    Bondsman: James Caperton

Gordon, James (X) to Eliza Mullen   Oct. 14, 1836 by J.A. Holland, J.P.
    Bondsman: Hugh Kelly

Gordon, John to Calista Gibson   June 23, 1828 by Thos. L. Douglass
    Bondsman: Thomas Helm

Gordon, Kinchen (X) to Margaret Barnes   May 20, 1841 by J. Burnett, J.P.
    Bondsman: Allen S. Sparkman

Gordon, William to Rachel Barnes Aug. 16, 1823 (bond)
    Bondsman: James Barnes (groom also made mark)

Gordon, William R. to Lockey Meadows Feb. 3, 1824 by J. Farrington
    Bondsman: Davis Lamb

Goswick, George to Elizabeth Powers Oct. 9, 1828 by Lemuel Manire, J.P.
    Bondsman: Elias Barnett

Gowan, James to Anne Price Feb. 19, 1808 (bond)
    Bondsman: Samuel Eskridge

Gracy, John to Polly Shoares Feb. 17, 1818 (bond)
    Bondsman: Newel Gracy

Gracy, John to Lockey Gordon May 19, 1838 (bond)
    Bondsman: Jasper N. Meadow

Gracy, John D. to Polly McBride Oct. 28, 1819 (bond)
    Bondsman: George Davis

Gracy, Newel to Peggy Shores Nov. 20, 1807 (bond)
    Bondsman: Robert McCracken

Gradon, James to Nancy Edwards Sept. 10, 1807 (bond)
    Bondsman: Charles Edwards

Graham, Adonijah to Mary Ann Noland Dec. 31, 1844 by John Wrenn, J.P.
    Bondsman: M.L. Andrews

Graham, Charles to Harriet E. McDaniel Nov. 20, 1834 by J.H. Harris, J.P.
    Bondsman: Branden Fields

Graham, George W. to Lucinda Wright Dec. 24, 1839 by Robert Davis, M.G.
    Bondsman: Richard Hayes

Graham, James to Sidney Gatlin (Galton?) Aug. 2, 1823 (bond)
    Bondsman: Thomas Matthews (groom signed "Grehem")

Graham, James to Nancy Jane Walker Oct. 24, 1842 by Jeremiah Stephens, M.G.
    Bondsman: Spence Waddey

Graham, John H. to Lucinda E. McGavock May 20, 1847 by M.L. Andrews, M.G.
    Bondsman: John W. Richardson

Graham, Jonathan R. (X) to Arminta Giles April 6, 1845 by J. Stephens
    Bondsman: Spence Waddy

Graham, Samuel to Jane Thompson May 5, 1833 by Andrew McCrady, J.P.
    Bondsman: John H. Bullock

Graham, Samuel (X) to Martha Giles Dec. 14, 1848 by Jeremiah Stephens, M.G.
    Bondsman: H. W. Steagall

Graham, Thomas A. to Sarah E. Core March 25, 1847 (bond)
    Bondsman: Preston S. Childress

Graham, William A. to Lucinda E. Graham Sept. 24, 1848 by Wm. M. Wright, J.P.
    Bondsman: Nashville Wright

Gray, Alexander W. to Mariah M. Thompson Nov. 12, 1840 by Jarvis W. Rea
    Bondsman: Alden C. Beech

Gray, Archibald (X) to Nancy Kirby Nov. 3, 1817 (bond)
    Bondsman: Malachi Kirby

Gray, Charles H. to Sarah E. Hughes Feb. 27, 1836 by James W. Rea, M.G.
    Bondsman: none given

Gray, Daniel to Nancy Pewett Nov. 13, 1810 (bond)
    Bondsman: Deliverence Gray

Gray, Elijah to Anna Brooks Oct. 8, 1823 by Geo. Shannon, J.P.
    Bondsman: Matthew X Brooks

Gray, Harry to Parmelia Turner Mar. 19, 1835 by Gilbert Marshall, J.P.
    Bondsman: W.D. Ferguson (groom signed "Henry")

Gray, Harvey (X) to Malinda Wood Jan. 14, 1831 by Jas. P. Brown, J.P.
    Bondsman: Joseph X Pewitt

Gray, Henry (X) to Delia Nolen Jan. 31, 1822 (bond)
    Bondsman: James Shannon

Gray, Henry (X) to Sarah Owen Dec. 6, 1827 by G. Hunt
    Bondsman: Howell Woodruff

Gray, Henry P. to Sarah Jane Southall Dec. 4, 1844 by M.L. Andrews, M.G.
    Bondsman: William D. Andrews

Gray, James to Elisabeth Adams July 14, 1808 (bond)
    Bondsman: Woodson Hailey

Gray, James to Lucy Sledge Nov. 9, 1820 by Wm. Petty, M.G.
    Bondsman: Henry X Sledge

Gray, James to Mary Ann McDaniel Feb. 18, 1836 by Joel Anderson
    Bondsman: none given

Gray, James A. to Martha A. McCrady Jan. 29, 1837 by John P. McKay
    Bondsman: none given

Gray, James W. to Lucinda H. Owen Nov. 26, 1833 by Rev. Jas. King
    Bondsman: Henry J. Walker

Gray, John, Jr. to Susan Blackman Nov. 16, 1820 by P. Russell
    Bondsman: Stephen West

Gray, John D. to Cecilia C. McCrady May 18, 1837 by Robert Davis, M.G.
    Bondsman: none given

Gray, Joseph L. to Polly Crowder May 11, 1825 (bond)
    Bondsman: James Demoss

Gray, Price to Tilpha Blackman   Dec. 24, 1810   (bond)
    Bondsman: Robert Gray

Gray, Robert to Patsey M. Holland   Jan. 3, 1822 by Joel Anderson
    Bondsman: Rodham Jones

Gray, Sandford F. to Elizabeth B. Ormes   Dec. 30, 1824 by G. Hunt
    Bondsman: Alexander M. Gray

Gray, Thomas W. to Sally Stone   July 25, 1824 by G. Hill, E.M. E.C.
    Bondsman: John Stacy

Gray, William (X) to Nancy Mays   Oct. 25, 1815   (bond)
    Bondsman: Jese X Turner

Gray, William to Susan P. Brooks   Jan. 28, 1837   (bond)
    Bondsman: none given

Gray, William to Mary W. Freeman   July 15, 1847 by W. Burns, M.G.
    Bondsman: William A. Jarratt

Gray, William F. to Sophia Stockett   Oct. 8, 1848 by Jas. Marshall, M.G.
    Bondsman: Francis H. Davis

Green, Berry to Elizabeth Hamlett   Jan. 27, 1830 by James Williams
    Bondsman: Lemuel Birch

Green, Isham S. to Parmelia Fisher   Mar. 19, 1840 by Jas. M. Green
    Bondsman: William Dedman

Green, James C. to Elizabeth Ann White   June 18, 1840 by R. White, J.P.
    Bondsman: Joseph Hendrix

Green, Jonathan (X) to Penelope Jones   Sept. 12, 1842   (bond)
    Bondsman: Benjamin X Jones

Green, Lewis to Mary Hodge   July 30, 1835 by C. McDaniel, J.P.
    Bondsman: George A.S. Mayfield

Green, Lewis to Priscilla G. Tate   May 30, 1837 by Levi Crosley, J.P.
    Bondsman: none given

Green, Robert (X) to Judy Sadler   Dec. 8, 1842   (bond)
    Bondsman: John Haley

Green, Shearwood to Mary Ozburn Johnston   May 21, 1829 by Thos. Wilson
    Bondsman: Berry Johnson

Green, Simon T. to Jane Elizabeth Waller   Nov. 12, 1835 by W.B. Carpenter
    Bondsman: James Waller

Green, Thomas C. to Martha L. Denson   Jan. 5, 1828 by John Alkinson, V.D.M.
    Bondsman: Henry Christmas

Green, Willis K. to Sarah A. Holloway   Jan. 12, 1848 by Wm. A. Whitsitt, M.G.
    Bondsman: Samuel C. Fly

Greer, Abraham to Peggy Kinney   Aug. 13, 1825 (bond)
    Bondsman: Thos. Craige

Greer, James W. to Michael E. Brown   July 26, 1826 (bond) by Levin Edney, M.G.
    Bondsman: none given

Greer, Richard (X) to Henrietta Brown   Oct. 1, 1839 (bond)
    Bondsman: Wiley Adams

Greer, Vincent to Patsey Garrett   Nov. 30, 1809 (bond)
    Bondsman: James Hargraves (groom signed "Vinson")

Greer, William (X) to Emeline Patton   Aug. 30, 1841 (bond)
    Bondsman: Genry Greer

Gregory, Charles H. to Elizabeth C. Robertson   May 3, 1842 by H. C. Horton
    Bondsman: James P. Sharpe

Gregory, James to Elizabeth Gentry   Dec. 24, 1828 by D.S. Jude
    Bondsman: Thos. Cheatham

Gregory, Tully to Rosanna Anderson   Feb. 10, 1820 by James Shelburne, J.P.
    Bondsman: John Layne

Gregory, William T. to Martha A.P.T. Robertson   May 11, 1843 by H.C.Horton,MG
    Bondsman: J.H. (James) Gregory

Griffin, James E. to Eliza Williams   Aug. 22, 1826 by J. Witherspoon
    Bondsman: none given

Griffith, Samuel to Mary Smith   Nov. 17, 1807 (bond)
    Bondsman: Geo. Davidson and Daniel Davis

Griffith, Thomas to Elizabeth Taylor   Jan. 16, 1810 (bond)
    Bondsman: Frederick Taylor

Grigg, Lewis M. to Sarah M. Yeargin   Oct. 12, 1831 by Thos. D. Porter
    Bondsman: Bartlett Yeargin

Griggs, Henry (X) to Hannah Polk   April 15, 1824 by Geo. Shannon, J.P.
    Bondsman: Atkins McLemore

Griggs, Rhodum (X) to Sally Griggs   Mar. 21, 1821 by O.T. Watkins, J.P.
    Bondsman: Richard X Griggs

Griggs, Richard (X) to Edy Walker   May 15, 1821 by O.T.Watkins, J.P.
    Bondsman: William Walker (X)

Griggs, Thomas to Martha McKinley   Jan. 1, 1846 by L.P. Johnson, J.P.
    Bondsman: Thomas Burch

Griggs, Thomas S. to Clarissa Pearce   Oct. 9, 1822 by G. Barnes, J.P.
    Bondsman: Atkins McLemore

Griggs, Willie to Louise Glymple?   Feb. 11, 1830 by Abner M.Dowell
    Bondsman: John X Griggs

Griggs, Willie to Elizabeth Glymp June 18, 1840 by James M. Green
    Bondsman: Green B. Green (signed "G.B.")

Grigsby, Benjamin to Mary E. Nicholson Feb. 1, 1846 by James Porter, M.G.
    Bondsman: John Jamison

Grigsby, William to Celina F. Hatcher June 14, 1849 by H.B. North, M.G.
    Bondsman: none given (License issued in Maury County)

Grimes, James (X) to Elizabeth Little April 16, 1816 by S. Hunt, J.P.
    Bondsman: J.B. Thompson

Grimes, William to Sally Little April 15, 1813 (bond)
    Bondsman: Wm. P. Harrison

Grooms, Bright to Catherine Windows Aug. 14, 1813 (bond)
    Bondsman: James Brown

Grubbs, Thomas to Polly Hiter Dec. 11, 1811 (bond)
    Bondsman: Thos. Hiter

Guin, Benjamin to Catherine Beard July 29, 1818 (bond)
    Bondsman: Moses X Beard

Guin, Literal to Elizabeth Modlin Jan. 6, 1842 by Thos. S. Nolen, J.P.
    Bondsman: Christopher X Guin

Guinn, Christopher (X) to Martha R. Roberson Feb. 26, 1835 by Geo. Shannon
    Bondsman: Wm. J. Buford

Gully (Tully), Needy to Lucy Henderson Aug. 22, 1816 by John W. Kirkpatrick
    Bondsman: Charles Byron

Gunter, Claibourne J. to Nancy Ann Allen Dec. 6, 1823 by John Atkinson
    Bondsman: William Atkinson

Gunter, Felix G. to Martha Ann Duffer May 2, 1839 by Robt. Davis, M.G.
    Bondsman: Miles White

Gunter, Felix G. to Ann Hampton April 16, 1848
    Bondsman: Will Ewing (date of mar. omitted. On outside license:
                "no property found Will Ewing")

Gunter, Francis to Frankey May Aug. 6, 1807 (bond)
    Bondsman: Jas. B. Tuttle

Gunter, Hezekiah (X) to Polly Kelly Dec. 19, 1818 (bond)
    Bondsman: Thomas Thompson

Gurley, Benjamin to Nancy York Aug. 1, 1811 (bond)
    Bondsman: Walter Hill

Gurley, Lewis to Dorcas Oliver June 16, 1816 by A. Mebane, J.P.
    Bondsmen: Lewis Gurley by Jonathan Coor and Wm. Coor

Gurley, William to Abby Deans Jan. 6, 1806 (bond)
    Bondsman: William Davis and Henry Sharp

Gurney, Samuel to Rebecca J. Thomas   Mar. 30, 1844 by Pettus Shelburne, J.P.
    Bondsman: John H. Thomas

Gutherie, David H. to Sally V. Carter   May 11, 1818 (bond)
    Bondsman: H.R.W. Hill

Gutherie, Edwin A. (X) to Lucy Bomar   June 14, 1831 by H.C. Horton, M.G.
    Bondsman: Pleasant Hawkins

Guthrie, John N. to Elizabeth J. Woolf   Feb. 18, 1834 (bond)
    Bondsman: Luke Jinkins

Guthrie, Robert to Matilda H. Maury   Jan. 18, 1816 (bond)
    Bondsman: Richard Maury

Guthrie, William to Sally Meadow   July 15, 1820 (bond)
    Bondsman: Sparkman Holland (groom signed "Guthry")

Guy, James to Sarah Housden   April 18, 1841 by R.B.B. Cannon, J.P.
    Bondsman: Asa X Harper

Guy, James J. to Elvira Perkins   Aug. 29, 1838 by M.L. Andrews, M.G.
    Bondsman: R.W.H. Bostick

Gwin, Jesse (X) to Sally Kennedy   Aug. 18, 1825 by R. McCutchen, J.P.
    Bondsman: John X Garrett

Gwinn, James to Nancy Carson   Oct. 31, 1824 by M.T. Spann, J.P.
    Bondsman: none given

-H-

Haden, Mathew R. to Catherine Jane Davis   Mar. 26, 1834 by Abner McDowell
    Bondsman: Robert B. Owen

Haddick, John G. to Elizabeth Taylor   Dec. 23, 1830 by John Morton
    Bondsman: Frederick May

Haddick, Thomas R. to Nancy Tailor   Sept. 3, 1833 by John Morton
    Bondsman: Isaac Johnson

Haddox, John to Susan M. Reilly   July 30, 1846 by R.C. Garrison, V.D.M.N.S.P.
    Bondsman: Wm. K. Bond

Hadley, Denny P. to Elizabeth Smith   Jan. 23, 1821 by Geo. Blackburn, D.M.
    Bondsman: John L. Hadly

Hadley, William to Mary Smith Hightower   Aug. 17, 1820 by Wm. Hulme, V.D.M.
    Bondsman: Hugh F. Bell

Hafford, John to Lucy Price   Dec. 27, 1825 (bond)
    Bondsman: Solomon P. Catt

Haggard, Edmund to Betsey Andrews   Feb. 12, 1809 by N. Scales
    Bondsman: Jas. Bradley

Haggard, Samuel to Elisabeth Peterson Mar. 26, 1806 (bond)
    Bondsman: George Oldham

Hagins, Bernard to Harriott Armstrong Dec. 25, 1811 (bond)
    Bondsmen: Wm. Sanders and James Armstrong

Hail, Michich (X) to Rachel Ray Oct. 22, 1849 by John King, M.G.
    Bondsman: John I. Mankin

Hail, Robert E. to Mary E. Gault Feb. 27, 1850 by John King, M.G.
    Bondsman: M. X Hail

Hail, Samuel to Polly Elam March 6, 1814 (bond)
    Bondsman: Robert Cannon

Haile, Isaac G. to Sarah Rozzell April 5, 1829 by A.W. Morton, J.P.
    Bondsman: Alfred Chrisman

Haile, Samuel to Rebecca Berry Feb. 4, 1819 by Nich's Scales
    Bondsman: Robert Murray

Hailey, James to Elizabeth Moore Nov. 18, 1815 (bond)
    Bondsman: William J. Boyd (groom signed "Haley")

Hailey, Walter C. to Bethenia Reynolds Aug. 30, 1817 (bond)
    Bondsman: Thos. Reynolds

Hailey, Woodson to Polly Neil March 29, 1809 (bond)
    Bondsman: Thos. M. Poteet

Haladay, Henry (X) to Elizabeth Trantham Feb. 23, 1815 (bond)
    Bondsman: Simon X Batman

Halbert, James to Elizabeth Smith Aug. 3, 1810 (bond)
    Bondsman: Oliver Williams

Halbrooks, John to Mecca F. Moore Nov. 3, 1831 by Wm. Rucker, J.P.
    Bondsman: Isiah X A. Moore

Hale, Jobe (X) to Keziah or Heziah Ragsdale May 17, 1815 (bond)
    Bondsman: Lankester X Ragsdale

Haley, Benjamin W. to Martha Jane McCord Feb. 13, 1842 by Cowden McCord, JP
    Bondsman: Newton McCord

Haley, Carroll B. (X) to Catharine Lamb Nov. 13, 1834 (bond)
    Bondsman: S. B. Robinson

Haley, James to Claressa Taylor Feb. 7, 1829 by Thos. Potts, M.G.
    Bondsman: Jacob Crick

Haley, John to Betsey Kennedy Dec. 6, 1825 by Levin Edney, M.G.
    Bondsman: John Kennedy and James Davis

Haley, John to Frances Hamlett Nov. 8, 1843 (bond)
    Bondsman: David Sires

Haley, Marquis S. to Jane E. Huggins Nov. 7, 1844 by John Beard, M.G.
    Bondsman: James Rogers

Haley, Thomas (X) to Hannah Venable Dec. 11, 1827 by Nich's Scales
    Bondsman: William X Palmore

Haley, William W. to Wincy W. Lavender Aug. 30, 1820 (bond)
    Bondsman: Wm. Wallis (groom signed "Hailey")

Haley, Wyatt to Sarah Jordan Jan. 19, 1848 by N. D. Jordan, J.P.
    Bondsman: Robert C. Pewitt

Halfacre, Andrew to Mary W. Barnes Aug. 21, 1834 by Robert Davis, M.G.
    Bondsman: Abner M. Wallace

Halfacre, David to Judith Vaughan Nov. 23, 1836 by George Long, J.P.
    Bondsman: Josiah Nevills

Halfacre, Henry to Priscilla B. McBride Feb. 1, 1834 by Matt Marshall
    Bondsman: none given

Halfacre, Jacob to Elizabeth Crisman Aug. 8, 1822 by Thos. Nelson
    Bondsman: Isaac Chrisman

Halfacre, Jacob (X) to Elizabeth Rucks Feb. 21, 1833 by Andrew Craig, M.G.
    Bondsman: Andrew Craig

Hall, Abram to Jane Martin Oct 27, 1850 by J.A. McCaul, J.P.
    Bondsman: none given

Hall, John to J. N. Warmoth Sept. 19, 1849 by W. M. Nunn, J.P.
    Bondsman: Wm. Neal

Hall, John H. to Martha S. Sherwood Aug. 23, 1848 by John King, M.G.
    Bondsman: George X W. Russell

Haly, John H. (X) to Saluda B. Redman March 28, 1843 by A.K. Nunn, J.P.
    Bondsman: Young Redman (groom signed "John A. X Haly")

Haley, William N. to Mary C. Crowder Jan. 13, 1842 by M.L. Andrews, M.G.
    Bondsman: Benjamin W. Haly

Haly, Wyat A. to Mary C. Riggs Nov. 29, 1846 by W.M. Nunn, J.P.
    Bondsman: Wm. B. Morton

Ham, Asa to Zane M. Rogers Aug. 29, 1833 by Robt. Davis, M.G.
    Bondsman: Alfred McGan

Ham, Davis to Susannah Clark Dec. 16, 1816 (bond)
    Bondsman: Orange X Ham

Ham, Elijah to Nancy D. Alford May 11, 1836 by John McCurdy, M.G.
    Bondsman: none given

Ham, Francis M. to Parmelia A. Frith Jan. 1, 1845 by G.W. Armstrong, J.P.
    Bondsman: John C. McDowell

Ham, James G. to Mary Ivy Feb. 6, 1840 by Wm. R. Hooten, M.G.
    Bondsman: John H. Allen

H am, Jesse (X) to Jane Beech June 11, 1834 (bond)
    Bondsman: Daniel Sinclair

Ham, John S. (X) to Rebecca Moss April 23, 1840 by Wm. R. Hooten, M.G.
    Bondsman: Alexander Allison

Ham, Orange to Sally Atkinson May 15, 1817 (bond)
    Bondsman: William Short

Ham, Solomon (X) to Elizabeth Saucer? July 6, 1832 by Daniel Baugh, J.P.
    Bondsman: Bolling C. North

Hama, John H. to Salina P. Kirkpatrick Sept. 8, 1825 by Robt. W. Galloway, AB
    Bondsman: none given

Hambleton, William to Nancy Berry March 6, 1814 (bond)
    Bondsman: John Torter (Porter?)

Hamblett, Richard (X) to Martha Coble July 10, 1831 by Wm. B. Carpenter
    Bondsman: Samuel Burke?

Hamer, Daniel to Charlotte Roberts Jan. 30, 1823 by Thos. Nelson
    Bondsman: Harris Hamer

Hamer, Frederick D. to Charlotte N. Hamer Aug. 6, 1843 by Peter Owen, M.G.
    Bondsman: Robert C. Mayfield

Hamer, Harry to Polly Brown Sept. 5, 1814 (bond)
    Bondsman: William Hamer

Hamer, John to Susanah Roberts Sept. 25, 1813 (bond)
    Bondsman: Sterling Brown and James Hamer

Hamer, John H. to Ann Brown Nov. 1, 1827 by T. Nelson, J.P.
    Bondsman: Daniel Hamer

Hamer, Leander S. to Mady D. Allen July 12, 1838 by Peter Owen
    Bondsman: John M. Winstead

Hamer, Leander S. to Mary Halfacre Nov. 11, 1842 by T.W. Haynes, M.G.
    Bondsman: George King

Hamer, Reese P. to Nancy C. Vernon Nov. 7, 1839 by N.B. Owen, J.P.
    Bondsman: S. Vernon, Jr. (groom signed "Reez")

Hamer, William to Maranda Roberts Dec. 8, 1827 by Thomas Nelson
    Bondsman: Daniel Hamer

Hamilton, Andrew to Elizabeth Rhoads July 19, 1806 (bond)
    Bondsman: Allen Corbert

Hamilton, James to Anna Houston Swisher Dec. 22, 1811 (bond)
    Bondsman: John Porter (Uncertain which was bride's last name)

Hamilton, James N. to Caroline Boyd Feb. 1, 1839 (bond)
    Bondsman: Wm. B. Stanfield

Hamilton, James W. to Nancy R. Betty Nov. 19, 1844 by A.N. Cunningham, M.G.
    Bondsman: James W. Gray

Hamilton, John J. to Elizabeth H. Blackburn April 15, 1816 (bond)
    Bondsman: William S. Hamilton

Hamilton, John W. to Elizabeth Goff Nov. 30, 1826 by Joel Anderson
    Bondsman: none given

Hamilton, Josiah M. to Malvira Ezell June 19, 1849 by John M.M. Murray, J.P.
    Bondsman: William E. Rash

Hamilton, Samuel to Martisha Stanfield March 30, 1820 by G. Barnes, J.P.
    Bondsman: Goodloe Stanfield

Hamilton, William S. to Sarah Johnston Aug. 22, 1826 (bond)
    Bondsman: none given

Hamlet, James S. to Catharine Hamlet Sept. 15, 1825 by Thomas Nelson
    Bondsman: John L. Fielder

Hamlet, James S. to Jane Waller July 16, 1850 by John Hay, J.P.
    Bondsman: Lazarus Sires

Hamlet, Thomas (X) to Sarah Wisenor April 7, 1832 by Wm. B. Carpenter
    Bondsman: Robert Wisenor

Hamlett, Richard (X) to Mary Waller May 24, 1841 by N.R. Owen
    Bondsman: W. Y. Ozburn

Hamlett, Thomas (X) to Elizabeth Knight Sept. 19, 1849 by Wm.A. Whitsitt
    Bondsman: Wm. H.S. Hill

Hamlin, James H. to Mary A.E. Brown April 27, 1847 by M.L. Andrews, M.G.
    Bondsman: W. La F. McConnico

Hammer, Samuel A. to Blanche P. Old May 6, 1824 by Robert David, M.G.
    Bondsman: B. R. DeGraffenried

Hammond, David to Tilpha Strickland Nov. 1, 1809 (bond)
    Bondsman: Sam'l Cox

Hammons, James to Amanda Shaw Nov. 10, 1836 by J. Burnett, J.P.
    Bondsman: Albert W. Blackburn

Hammons, William to Mary Ingram Dec. 30, 1834 (bond)
    Bondsman: Samuel Eastep (Eastess?) (groom signed "Hammon")

Hamoch, Daniel B. (X) to Nancy Houston July 24, 1832 (bond)
    Bondsman: William A. Jordan (groom's name may be Hancock)

Hampton, Andrew S. to Jane Tarpley April 10, 1820 by Jas. Boyd, J.P.
    Bondsman: George Fisher

Hampton, Andrew S. to Milly Christly Nov. 5, 1834 (bond)
    Bondsman: Absolom Thompson

Hampton, David A. to Mary E. F. Mitchell Jan. 17, 1849 by Wm. A. Whitsitt, MG
    Bondsman: John H. Carmichael

Hampton, Henry to Elizabeth Stanfield Feb. 14, 1838 by Wm. Edmondson, J.P.
    Bondsman: Richard D. X Vaughan

Hampton, Jeremiah to Ann Eliza Fields July 22, 1847 by Wm. A. Whitsitt,
    Bondsman: Robert F. Hill   (Baptist Minister

Hampton, John C. to Ann Drannan March 24, 1834 by Jno. Nichols
    Bondsman: Samuel L. Graham

Hampton, Joseph H. to Nancy Kidd Oct. 13, 1842 by Rev. T.W. Haynes
    Bondsman: Thomas P. Carsey

Hampton, Preston to Sally Beavers Sept. 1, 1807 (bond)
    Bondsman: John Davis

Hampton, Smith (X) to Hulda S. McCall March 26, 1840 by J. Wall, J.P.
    Bondsman: John W. Goodwin

Hampton, Willis to Nancy Hicks Jan. 3, 1826 by Joel Anderson, J.P.
    Bondsman: none given

Hancock, Daniel B. (See Hamoch, Daniel B.

Hancock, Richard C. to Elizabeth Guy Dec. 20, 1821 by W.M. Hogan
    Bondsman: Richard C. Hancock by his attorney Rich. Hauck and
        Stephen W. Hancock and Thos. J. Hardeman

Hancock, Thomas W. to Jane W. Guy Sept. 18, 1828 by David C. Kinnard, J.P.
    Bondsman: Thos. H. Caperton

Hancock, William M. to Harriet E. Reynolds Feb. 15, 1837 by James W. Carson
    Bondsman: none given

Handy, Thomas H. to Maria Henderson Sept. 16, 1834 by Jas. H. Otey, Bishop
    Bondsman: Robert C. Foster   (Diocese of Tenn.

Hanks, Gayden to Mary Dorrel Dec. 28, 1819 by Jno. Alkinson, M.D.
    Bondsman: Robert Stringfellow

Hannah, Jacob to Sally Littleton Jan. 22, 1810 (bond)
    Bondsman: Wm. Littleton

Hanner, John W. to Elizabeth R. Park May 27, 1834 by Thos. L. Douglass
    Bondsman: Loving H. Woldridge

Hardeman, Bailey to Rebecca A.F. Wilson June 20, 1820 by Geo. Blackburn, M.G.
    Bondsman: Thos. Hardeman and Jn. P. McCutchan

Hardeman, Constant to Mary Little Dec. 12, 1824 by G. McConnico
    Bondsman: Thos. Hardeman

115.

Hardeman, Thomas to Bethunia H. Perkins   Aug. 26, 1830 by Jas. H. Otey,
    Bondsman: John Marshall   (Rector St.Paul's Episcopal Church

Hardeman, Thomas to Lucretia Nash Hardeman   Sept. 15, 1835 by Nathan Watson
    Bondsman: Constance Sneed   (Munroe, ass't min. St. Paul's

Hardeman, Thomas, Jr. to Ann Green Perkins   Dec. 27, 1820 by G. McConnico,MG
    Bondsman: Aaron V. Brown

Harden, Jeremiah to Sally McCutchen   July 26, 1814 (bond)
    Bondsman: Jeremiah Harden and Jere Harden

Harderson, Thos. to Polly Wilson   Oct. 30, 1813 (bond)
    Bondsman: James Howe

Hardin, John to Mary Tilman   Jan. 19, 1818 (bond)
    Bondsman: James Nowlen

Hardin, John to Susanna Appleton   Dec. 29, 1815 (bond)
    Bondsman: John Hardin

Hardin, Presley W. to Mary Williams   Sept. 24, 1839 by Rev. Joel Anderson
    Bondsman: J. Williams (Josepheus)

Harding, George to Eliza Stuart   April 16, 1844 by W.B. Carpenter
    Bondsman: Ennis Murray

Harris H. Harding to Susan McMullin   May 22, 1816 by J. Farrington, J.P.
    Bondsman: James McCombs   (groom signed "Horace Harding")

Harding, John to Cynthia M. Motherel   Sept. 22, 1845 (bond)
    Bondsman: James S. Demoss

Harding, Thos. to Lucy Nolen   Aug. 7, 1807 (bond)
    Bondsman: Lewis Mansker

Harding, William to Elizabeth McGavock   Jan. 2, 1840 by A.H. Dashielle
    Bondsman: Joseph Vaulx?

Hardison, Joshua to Narcissa J. Blackburn   Feb. 10, 1841 (bond)
    Bondsman: Robert A. Glum (Glenn?)

Hardison, William to Polly Hardison   Dec. 29, 1812 (bond)
    Bondsman: Bryant Wells

Hargis, James K. to Lavinia W. Read   July 27, 1824 (bond)
    Bondsman: Andrew Reed

Hargraves, Henderson to Mary Ann Butts   April 9, 1850 by Jas. S. Owen, J.P.
    Bondsman: Wm. H. Hamilton

Hargrove, Bennet to Clarissa Skellington   March 9, 1826 by M.L. Andrews, M.G.
    Bondsman: none given

Hargrove, Bennet A. (X) to Mary Ann Williams   Aug. 20, 1846 by L. McCall, JP
    Bondsman: D.S. X Williams

Hargrove, James A. (X) to Ellen Jane Brown Sept. 11, 1843 by William W. Bond
    Bondsman: Spencer W. Skinner

Hargrove, John to Nancy Chapman March 16, 1834 by J. Wall, J.P.
    Bondsman: Robert X White

Hargrove, Joseph to Martha Hartley March 27, 1822 by Edward Ragsdale, J.P.
    Bondsman: Edward Ragsdale

Hargrove, Joseph to Frances Williams Feb. 5, 1846 by Lycurgus McCall, M.G.
    Bondsman: Daniel X Williams

Hargrove, Newton (X) to Milly Emeline McCall July 27, 1847 (bond)
    Bondsman: Evans X Hargrove

Hartgrove, Samuel (X) to Polly M. McCall Nov. 5, 1824 (bond)
    Bondsman: Charles X McCall

Hargrove, William to Martha Chriswell Oct. 26, 1837 by J. Wall, J.P.
    Bondsman: none given

Harkreader, John to Judith Oldham Dec. 30, 1833 (bond)
    Bondsman: Davis Hargraves

Harkreader, Samuel to Nancy M. Hardgraves Jan. 10, 1833 by Jas. W. Rea, M.G.
    Bondsman: James H. Harkreader (bride's name sp. "Hargraves" on lic.

Harpending, Hiram A. to Parthenia Stone Dec. 11, 1842 by R. White, J.P.
    Bondsman: John T. Cook

Harper, Asa (X) to Rebecca Burge Nov. 8, 1843 by R.B.B. Cannon, J.P.
    Bondsman: Carter Stanfield

Harper, Berryman to Elizabeth Carpenter Dec. 26, 1821 by Robert Davis, M.G.
    Bondsman: James C. Hill

Harper, John to Lovey Freeman May 31, 1808 (bond)
    Bondsman: Lewis Watkins

Harper, Richard R. to Sarah Merritt Oct. 12, 1831 by Joel Anderson, M.G.
    Bondsman: Robert S. Thomas

Harper, Sterling to Viney Scott Oct. 22, 1833 (bond)
    Bondsman: William H. Wills (Wells?)

Harper, Thomas T. to Rebecca Southall July 14, 1824 (bond)
    Bondsman: John Mayfield

Harrell, James to Sally Small Dec. 25, 1807 (bond)
    Bondsman: John Kidwell

Harrelson, Ezekiel to Eve Cirkles Sept. 8, 1807 (bond)
    Bondsman: John Armstrong

Harris, Carey A. to Martha F. Maury Jan. 14, 1829 by Jas. H. Otey
    Bondsman: John Marshall

117.

Harris, Edward to Caroline F. Wood   June 25, 1817 (bond)
    Bondsman: John Shadick

Harris, James to Susannah Christopher   Feb. 27, 1816 by Geo. Tillman, M.D.
    Bondsman: Newton Walls   (groom's name may be "Jonas")

Harris, Thomas (X) to Ellen Adams   Dec. 24, 1841 by Tho. Prowell, J.P.
    Bondsman: Wiley E. Beasley

Harris, Sampson (X) to Rebecca Sampson   Sept. 11, 1839 (bond)
    Bondsman: Smith S. Sampson

Harris, Samuel to Mary M. Harris   March 31, 1822 by W.R. Nunn, J.P.
    Bondsman: Richard Tanner

Harrison, Allen to Hannah Herron   Oct. 7, 1819 by D. Brown, V.D.M.
    Bondsman: David C. Kinnard

Harrison, Allen to Lucy H. Tanner   Jan. 22, 1829 by M.L. Andrews, J.P.
    Bondsman: Edmund Tappan

Harrison, James to Elizabeth York   Dec. 27, 1820 (bond)
    Bondsman: Jas. X York

Harrison, John P. to Malvira D. Greer   Jan. 31, 1850 by Green J. Simmons,
    Bondsman: Thomas L. McCrory   Min of Methodist Protestant Ch.

Harrison, Nathaniel to Fanny Haily   Dec. 11, 1815 (bond)
    Bondsman: William Harrison

Harrison, Nathaniel to Christianna T. Knight   Nov. 10, 1830 by E.R. Parish, J.P.
    Bondsman: Henry X Jones

Harrison, William to Ann P. Smith   June 29, 1823 by G. Hulme, J.P.
    Bondsman: Henry M. Huton?

Harrison, William to Martha Terrell   Oct. 3, 1839 by H.B. North, M.G.
    Bondsman: Isham Lamb

Harrison, William to Mary M. Webb   Oct. 3, 1844 by M.L. Andrews, M.G.
    Bondsman: Lemuel B. McConnico

Harrison, William B. to Elizabeth Island   Dec. 8, 1832 by Elijah R. Parrish,
    Bondsman: none given   (license alone)   Esq.

Harrison, William P. to Caroline Crosby   Jan. 13, 1846 by B.D. Neal, M.G.
    Bondsman: Nicholas P. Hardeman

Harrison, William to Edith Holt   March 15, 1810 (bond)
    Bondsman: Nicholas P. Hardeman

Hart, George (X) to Mary Hampton   Feb. 20, 1849 by John Nichols, J.P.
    Bondsman: John X Bennett

Hartley, Labern (X) to Nancy Cason   Nov. 21, 1816 by Wm. R. Nunn, J.P.
    Bondsman: John X D. Pope

Hartly, Laben to Harriet C. McCall   Oct. 21, 1847 by Lycurgus McCall, J.P.
    Bondsman: J. C. Bigger   (groom signed "Laban Hartly")

Harvey, Benjamin B. to Lucinda Warren   Oct. 11, 1838 by R.W. Robinson, J.P.
    Bondsman: Thomas McGuire

Harvey, Hillary J. to Elizabeth P. Williams   Dec. 23, 1847 by M.L. Andrews
    Bondsman: George P. Brimm   (groom signed: "Hilry J. Harvy")

Harvey, Holcomb B. to Mary C. Wilson   Mar. 2, 1843 by Thos. H. Roberts, J.P.
    Bondsman: G. B. (George) Brimm

Harvill, John to Nancy Powell   Oct. 9, 1809 (bond)
    Bondsman: John Powell

Harwell, Feathuston to Eliza Owen (bond) (date omitted)
    Bondsman: Peter J. Walker

Hasel, William J. (X) to Zylpha Tarkington   July 12, 1820 by Henry Petty, M.G.
    Bondsman: James X Blackman

Haselwood, Thomas (X) to Rebecca Rusel   Sept. 15, 1815 by N. Scales
    Bondsman: Jeremiah X Rusel

Hasley, David to Patsey Crenshaw   April 4, 1811 (bond)
    Bondsman: Corneluus Crenshaw

Hasley, Samuel to Elizabeth Edwards   Sept. 29, 1846 (bond)
    Bondsman: Benjamin Martin   (groom's name may be "Halsey")

Hassell (Hasel), Elisha M. to Nancy Hawkins   Oct. 18, 1809 (bond)
    Bondsman: James Hicks

Hassell, Elisha M. to Mary Ann Shaw   May 5, 1837 by Jacob Critz, J.P.
    Bondsman: none given

Hassell, James (X) to Elizabeth Shaw   April 8, 1829 (bond)
    Bondsman: Bannister W. Shaw

Hassell, John to Sally Stoddart   Feb. 15, 1806 (bond)
    Bondsman: Midijah Collins

Hassell, John W. to Charlotte Orms   Jan. 22, 1834 by C.E. McEwen, J.P.
    Bondsman: Henry Gray, Jr.

Hassel, Zebulon to Unity Shields   Mar. 4, 1832 by M. Davitt, M.G.
    Bondsman: Zebulon Shields and John B. Beech

Hastings, Henry to Sally Hudlow   Dec. 29, 1815 by Tristram Patton
    Bondsman: Alexander Mebane

Hastings, Stephen to Catherine Hudlow   Dec. 6, 1815 (bond)
    Bondsman: John Harshaw (Kershaw?)

Hatcher, Alexander to Naoma White   July 29, 1850 by Thos. P. Wells, M.G.
    Bondsman: John T. Wilson

Hatcher, Bernard M. to Susannah F. Wood   May 23, 1850 by Jesse Cox, M.G.
    Bondsman: J. J. Toon

Hatcher, Octavius C. to Caledonia B. Pillow   Aug. 23, 1843 by W. Burns
    Bondsman: Wm. A. Jarrat

Hatchett, John to Nancy Freeman   March 1, 1821 by Nich's Scales
    Bondsman: Robert C. Foster, Jr.

Hawk, Henry (X) to Bethenia Ezell   May 7, 1839 (bond)
    Bondsman: James Hogan, Jr.

Hawkins, Amasa (X) to Polly Horton   Oct. 11, 1817 (bond)
    Bondsman: J. M. Durford

Hawks, Henry to Ann Eliza Barnes   Jan. 8, 1846 by M.L. Andrews, M.G.
    Bondsman: J.H.W. Allen

Hawks, Jeremiah to Amanda Johnson   May 21, 1836 (bond)
    Bondsman: William S. Bennett

Hay, Benjamin to Sally Thompkins   Aug. 16, 1808 (bond)
    Bondsman: Jones Glover

Hay, John to Betsey Bullock   Jan. 17, 1811 (bond)
    Bondsman: Wm. May

Hay, John to Frances A. Johnson   Dec. 2, 1828 by Francis A. Owen, P.G.
    Bondsman: Ewing D. Thompson

Hay, John to Mary O. Green   April 30, 1848 by Wm. A. Whitsitt, Minister
    Bondsman: Franklin A. Burke

Hay, James S. to Elizabeth Holland   Oct. 4, 1827 by John Holland, V.D.M.
    Bondsman: William Mosley

Hay, James S. to Mary Ann Ivey   Nov. 8, 1849 (bond)
    B ondsman: Dooly Pate

Hay, James T. to Rebecca Wakefield (bond)
    Bondsman: Hugh A. Fox

Hay, Pettus S. to Cena Underwood   Jan. 20, 1842 by Jeremiah Stephens, M.G.
    Bondsman: Christopher W. Kinnard

Hay, Pleasant to Louisa E. Doolin   Feb. 21, 1844 by Thomas J. Miller, J.P.
    Bondsman: Joseph R. Hunter

Hay, Richard to Martha Radford   July 29, 1816 (bond)
    Bondsman: Henry Walker

Hay, Richard (X) to Susan Walker   Nov. 1, 1832 by James King
    Bondsman: James Shelburne

Hayes, James (X) to Nancy Jarrott   Sept. 27, 1838 by Matthew Marable, J.P.
    Bondsman: Everett X Haynes

Hayes, Lewis to Anna Long   Oct. 1, 1811 by Nick Scales
    Bondsman: Richard M. Hyde

Hayes, Reuben P. to Eliza W. Gunter   Jan. 17, 1829 (1828?) by T.L. Douglass
    Bondsman: John W. Miller

Hayes, Wm. to Margaret Johnson   April 29, 1809 (bond)
    Bondsman: Jacob Gray

Haynes, Abram to Sarah Haynes   Nov. 15, 1832 by Nich's Scales
    Bondsman: William Span

Haynes, Franklin B. to Nancy Jane Atkerson   Feb. 14, 1843 by M.L. Andrews
    Bondsman: James B. Bridges

Haynes, George to Mildred Newman   Sept. 15, 1815 (bond)
    Bondsman: Green Seat

Haynes, Hugh to Temperess Gray   Dec. 27, 1812 (bond)
    Bondsman: Wm. Purkston

Haynes, James to Asanath or Acenath Wilson   Nov. 12, 1810 (bond)
    Bondsman: Thomas Wilson

Haynes, James to Marcha Fields   Jan. 18, 1842 by M.L. Andrews, M.G.
    Bondsman: N. S. Haynes (groom signed "Haines")

Haynes, James M. to Tilitha A. Beasley   Jan. 12, 1841 (bond)
    Bondsman: John I. Beasley

Haynes, James S. to Rizpah Wilson   Sept. 7, 1830 by J. Wall, J.P.
    Bondsman: Cyrus Haynes

Haynes, John to Anna Terrill   Feb. 13, 1812 (bond)
    Bondsman: Pleasant Watkins

Haynes, John (X) to Virginia Kennedy   Jan. 29, 1835 by J. Ralston, J.P.
    Bondsman: W. A. Haynes

Haynes, John L. or S. to Nancy Vanatta   Jan. 11, 1816 (bond)
    Bondsman: John Saminas? (illegible)

Haynes, John M. to Elizabeth Royster   Mar. 5, 1840 by J. Richardson, J.P.
    Bondsman: John Haley (groom's name may be "Hayms")

Haynes, Joseph T. (X) to Sally Boatright   Sept. 15, 1830 by J. Gault, J.P.
    Bondsman: William Morress

Haynes, Natus H. to Elizabeth H. Andrews   Oct. 14, 1841 by Robert L. Andrews
    Bondsman: James W. Hampton

Haynes, Patrick to Mary Peebles   July 14, 1823 (bond)
    Bondsman: Morris S. Bond

Haynes, Thomas to Susan Peebles   April 15, 1812 (bond)
    Bondsman: Silas Stephens

Haynes, Thomas H. to Susan J. Stephenson   April 21, 1849 by A.N. Cunningham
    Bondsman: D. R. Crutcher

Haynes, Thomas K. to Eliza M. Hill   Feb. 23, 1842 (bond)
    Bondsman: Thomas H. Haynes and Wm. J. Hill

Haynes, William R. to Virginia S. Andrews   Dec. 18, 1845 by M.L. Andrews, MG
    Bondsman: William D. Andrews

Haynes, William T. to Lucinda Stokes   Nov. 17, 1824 (bond)
    Bondsman: John S. Haynes

Hays, Henry W. (X) to Henrietta Freeman   Sept. 30, 1833 by Robt. Pate, J.P.
    Bondsman: Wm. J. X Hays

Hays, James C. to Portia E. Thomas   Nov. 30, 1841 by Jonathan Rothrock, J.P.
    Bondsman: John T. Miller

Hays, John A. to Eliza Southall   Oct. 26, 1837 by H. B. North, M.G.
    Bondsman: none given

Hays, Michael (X) to Rebecca Gates   Nov. 11, 1838 by H. B. Hyde, J.P.
    Bondsman: William N. Jones

Hays, Oliver B. to Sally C. Hightower   Feb. 3, 1812 (bond)
    Bondsman: Joseph Phillips

Hays, Reuben P. to Louisa Thomas   June 18, 1840 by Philip P. Neely, M.G.
    Bondsman: John W. Miller

Hays, William to Mary Wilson   Dec. 24, 1828 by Balaam Ezell
    Bondsman: John X Burns

Hays, William P. to Polly W. Davis   Nov. 12, 1818 (bond)
    Bondsman: H. R. W. Hill

Hays, William to Portia C. Hays   June 6, 1849 by M.L. Andrews, M.G.
    Bondsman: Ferdinand S. Woldridge

Hazlewood, Fleming (X) to Nancy Fuqua   Feb. 3, 1825 by H. Bailey, J.P.
    Bondsman: Abraham X Hill

Hazlewood, James (X) to Gilly (Tilly?) Featherston   Jan. 20, 1836 by A.A.
    Bondsman: Moses Lillard   (Wilson, J.P.

Hazlewood, John J. to Mary E. T. Whaley   Nov. 15, 1843 by W. Burns, M.G.
    Bondsman: Meredith P. Gentry

Hazlewood, Thomas (X) to Cynthia Mangum   March 13, 1828 by David C. Kinnard
    Bondsman: Fleming X Hazlewood

Hazlewood, Thomas (X) to Sarah Sutton   Dec. 31, 1834 by A.A. Wilson, J.P.
    Bondsman: James X Hazlewood

Hazelwood, William to Rebecca Simpson   July 29, 1820 by Thos. Wilson
    Bondsman: George Fisher

Heaten, James to Sally Dobson   Dec. 10, 1805 by Tristram Patton
    Bondsman: none given (badly torn)

Heath, Lewis to Elizabeth Ray   Sept. 6, 1817 (bond)
    Bondsman: Benajah X Carlton

Heathcock, Lemuel G. to Narcissa Jane Young   Jan. 24, 1847 by H. Thomson, JP
    Bondsman: George W X Young (groom signed "Haithcock")

Helm, Benjamin C. to Pamelia M. Andrews   May 21, 1833 (bond)
    Bondsman: Claborne Johnson

Helm, Fieldin to Nancy Holland   Feb. 8, 1813 (bond)
    Bondsman: Frederick Holland

Helm, Henderson to Mary Eliza Beale   Nov. 15, 1848 by H.B. North, M.G.
    Bondsman: S. M. Crump

Helm, James to Susannah Hubbard   Feb. 13, 1837 by M.L. Andrews, M.G.
    Bondsman: none given

Helm, Thomas to Elizabeth Carl   Feb. 17, 1825 by Robert Davis, M.G.
    Bondsman: John Thompson

Helm, William M. to Mary E. Bond   Oct. 5, 1837 by Robert Hardin, M.G.
    Bondsman: none given

Hembree, Joseph to Elizabeth Robinson   Mar. 10, 1840 by Robert Davis, M.G.
    Bondsman: John A. Bohems (groom's name "Henly" in one place)

Hemphill, George to Anna M. Calhoon   Mar. 23, 1824 (bond)
    Bondsman: Bennett Phillips

Hemphill, Sam'l to Nancy Alsup   Feb. 21, 1808 (bond)
    Bondsman: David P. Anderson

Henderson, James G. to Theodicia G. Scales   Mar. 10, 1831 by Thos.D. Porter
    Bondsman: Samuel Clark

Henderson, James G. to Emily Pugh   Nov. 8, 1843 (bond)
    Bondsman: James H. Scales

Henderson, James G. to Emily R. Pugh   Nov. 9, 1844 by Robert L. Andrews
    Bondsman: none given (may be same as above)

Henderson, Ramsey to Eliza A. Ott   Aug. 18, 1831 by Robert Henderson
    Bondsman: Alfred Henderson

Henderson, Richard to Jane Baldridge   March 2, 1806 (bond)
    Bondsman: John Baldridge

Henderson, Robert to Peggy Shipman   June 30, 1807 (bond)
    Bondsman: Jas. Shannon

Henderson, Robt. to Nancy Wooten   June 3, 1809 (bond)
    Bondsman: Wm. McCalpin

Henderson, Robert to Ann Elizar Henderson   July 14, 1816 by Geo. Blackburn
    Bondsman: Wm. Smith

Henderson, Samuel to Rachel Jane Hughes   Mar. 14, 1844 by M.L. Andrews, M.G.
    Bondsman: William Harrison

Henderson, William S. to Mary R. Scales   Dec. 10, 1840 by M.L. Andrews, M.G.
    Bondsman: Samuel Henderson

Hendley, John J. to Susan Reeves   Jan. 9, 1838 by H. McNish, J.P.
    Bondsman: Frederick Bibb   (groom made mark)

Hendrick, Allen to Polly Jackson   April 25, 1815   (bond)
    Bondsman: Thomas Jackson

Hendricks, Solomon (X) to Nancy Hutchinson   Aug. 3, 1823 by Lewis Loyd, J.P.
    Bondsman: John Crouse

Hendrix, Andrew (X) to Ann Rebecca Causby   Sept. 9, 1829 by Arthur Sherrod,
    Bondsman: Noah X Gardner   (A.P.M.E.C.)

Hendrix, Francis I (X) to Caroline Paschall   Sept. 17, 1841 by E.W. Hendrix,
    Bondsman: Charles McBride, Jr.   M.G.

Hendrix, Joseph to Lucinda Green   July 15, 1840   (bond)
    Bondsman: James C. Green

Hendrix, Thomas L. to Elizabeth Prince   Sept. 20, 1838 by Sam B. Robinson, JP
    Bondsman: Wm. K. Ransom

Henley, James to Jane Nolen   Dec. 23, 1841 by B.B. Toon, J.P.
    Bondsman: John H. Carmichael

Henley, Thomas D. to Rebecca N. (M?) Campbell   Jan. 8, 1835 by Robt. Lapsley
    Bondsman: John Charsball?

Henrickson, Archelaus M.D. to Mary A.E. Patterson   June 16, 1847 by Thos. H.
    Bondsman: Azariah L. Kimbrough   (Roberts, J.P.)

Henry, Theophilus to Abegail Graham   Oct. 6, 1825 by H.C. Horton, M.G.
    Bondsman: John Rupard (Russard?)

Henry, William to Ascenatte S. Owen   Oct. 10, 1847 by R.M. McDaniel, J.P.
    Bondsman: Edwin T. Cloud

Herbert, John B. to Temperance Hunt   Dec. 18, 1832 by Jabez Owen, J.P.
    Bondsman: Herbert Owen

Herbert, Richard N. to Sarah Ann Stevens   May 6, 1834 by Gilbert Marshall, JP
    Bondsman: William Sudberry

Herbert, Robert N. to Elizabeth L. Cummins   Nov. 4, 1831 by G. Hunt
    Bondsman: John M. Currin

Herron, George to Rebecca Patton   Aug. 1, 1822 by D. Brown, D.V.M.
    Bondsman: Thos. Helm

Herron, Henry to Sintha Harris Dec. 8, 1818 (bond)
    Bondsman: John D. Garrett

Herron, James H. to Maria B. Bond July 9, 1827 (bond)
    Bondsman: Moses Steele

Herron (Huron?), John to Nancy A. Warren Dec. 20, 1832 by M.L. Andrews, MG
    Bondsman: Andrew G. Porter

Herron, Samuel F. to Susannah G.E. Parrish Sept. 25, 1834 by Jas.B. Porter
    Bondsman: James Herron

Herron, Thomas to Ruth E. Moss Dec. 17, 1848 by R.W. Moss, J.P.
    Bondsman: O. C. Dillahunty (groom signed "Herrin")

Herron, William W. to Catharine B. McCutchen Aug. 11, 1841 by R.A. Lapsley
    Bondsman: Robert C. Dysart

Hershaw, John (see Kershaw) to Polly Hudlow Dec. 24, 1811 (bond)
    Bondsman: William Rawlstone

Hickman, Elliott to India Ann Dudley Sept. 11, 1810 (bond)
    Bondsman: Arch Potter

Hicks, Arthur to Polly Fisher April 4, 1815 (license and bond)
    Bondsman: Jahu Baker

Hicks, Benjamin A. to Nancy Holloway Dec. 16, 1828 by Geo. Shannon, J.P.
    Bondsman: John X Poyner

Hicks, George W. to Permelia McNeil July 30, 1846 by J.J. Bingham, J.P.
    Bondsman: Young X McNeil (groom made mark)

Hicks, James (X) to Susan Carlile Sept. 2, 1815 (bond)
    Bondsman: Philip Haley

Hicks, James to Nancy D. Vaughan June 2, 1840 by Gilbert Marshall, J.P.
    Bondsman: Stephen W. X Hicks

Hicks, Matthew (X) to Mary Lewis Sept. 26, 1833 by Gilbert Marshall, J.P.
    Bondsman: Burnel Warren Wit. present: W.H. Bailey

Hicks, Reuben (X) to Rebecca Simons Brooks May (Mar.?) 18, 1824 by John
    Bondsman: Alfred McCown   (Nichols, JP

Hicks, Richard (X) to Sarah E. Inman Nov. 28, 1849 by John S.Williams, M.G.
    Bondsman: Laben Pewitt "at Residence of William Kirby"

Hicks, Stephen to Catharine O. Poynor June 13, 1828 by Geo. Shannon, J.P.
    Bondsman: John X Poynor

Hicks, Stephen W. (X) to Mary Griggs June 6, 1839 by Jesse Cox, M.G.
    Bondsman: Thomas S. Russell

Hicks, William to Mary Ann Green July 9, 1828 by P. Green
    Bondsman: O. T. Watkins

Hicks, William C. to Susan A. Sampkin Aug. 28, 1839 by Stephen Nolen, J.P.
    Bondsman: Edmond Lewis

Higginbottom, Caleb to Frances Smith Dec. 15, 1807 (bond)
    Bondsman: James Shields

Hightower, Richard R. to Ann E. Foster April 29, 1840 by P.P. Neely, M.P.
    Bondsman: Sam N. Stephens

Hilburn, Richard (X) to Elizabeth Campbell Dec. 26, 1818 (bond)
    Bondsman: John Campbell

Hill, Abraham to Frankey Roar Nov. 28, 1812 (bond)
    Bondsman: Richard Smith

Hill, Benjamin to Polly Barnes Feb. 13, 1823 by G. Hunt
    Bondsman: Geo. W. Alford

Hill, Constillo S. to Susan Woodruff Jan. 16, 1830 by John Alkinson, V.D.M.
    Bondsman: Wilson X Woodruff

Hill, Green to Martha Ann Kirkpatrick July 24, 1834 by Andrew Craig, M.G.
    Bondsman: Daniel Williams

Hill, Henry R.W. to Margaret E. McAlister Aug. 8, 1827 by Thos. L. Douglass
    Bondsman: Joshua W. McCown

Hill, Hezekiah to Ann Humphreys June 28, 1821 by G. Hunt
    Bondsman: Jeremiah Hill

Hill, Hugh to Polly Demoss Jan. 23, 1809 (bond)
    Bondsman: Isaac Greer

Hill, Jacob to Jane Lemon Nov. 28, 1819 by Henry Petty, M.G.
    Bondsman: Henry L. Crutcher

Hill, James to Delilah Gore Jan. 27, 1812 (bond)
    Bondsman: Matthew McGaugh

Hill, James B. to Narcissa Hughes May 19, 1831 by Jas. W. Rea, M.G.
    Bondsman: James T. Morris

Hill, James C. to Mary Dudley Sept. 16, 1830 by Thos. L. Douglass
    Bondsman: John T. Smith

Hill, James F. to Elizabeth W. Layne Oct. 18, 1832 by Thos. D. Porter, M.G.
    Bondsman: Jno. W.M. Hill

Hill, Jeremiah to Matilda Fly Dec. 26, 1838 by P.B.B. Cannon, J.P.
    Bondsman: Peter B. Ladd

Hill, John to Rebecca Wade April 22, 1809 (bond)
    Bondsman: Obadiah Wade

Hill, John D. to Annis L. Hodges Aug. 14, 1834 by S. Brown, M.G.
    Bondsman: James Mankins

Hill, John G. to Jemima Cook Feb. 11, 1827 by Tristram Patton, J.P.
    Bondsman: Presley Dotson, Jr.

Hill, John H. to Susan A. Cose? July 17, 1839 by James W. Rea, M.G.
    Bondsman: Barnett R. Hughes

Hill, John H. to Susan E. Hughes Feb. 2, 1842 by James W. Rea, M.G.
    Bondsman: James Cox

Hill, John W. H. to Mary S. Clark June 7, 1836 by H.G. North, M.G.
    Bondsman: John S. Clark

Hill, John W.M. to Emily S. Hamilton Nov. 5, 1829 by Thos. D. Porter, M.G.
    Bondsman: Littleberry Pate

Hill, Jonathan to Elizabeth Holt Feb. 2, 1819 by G. Barnes, J.P.
    Bondsman: Jonathan Hill by Wm. Holt and William N. Holt

Hill, Joseph L. F. to Nancy Jackson Oct. 8, 1833 by the Rev. James W. Rea
    Bondsman: James Smith

Hill, Joshua C. to Lemiza Lanier May 27, 1816 (bond)
    Bondsman: Henry Hill

Hill, Richard J. to Meda Jordan Oct. 20, 1827 (bond)
    Bondsman: Samuel Peay

Hill, Robert to Eliza C. Perkins Jan. 23, 1823 by Geo. Blackburn, V.D.M.
    Bondsman: John B. Craighead

Hill, Spencer to Betsey Ezbern Feb. 9, 1807 (bond)
    Bondsman: Jeremiah Fly

Hill, Thomas I. to Elizabeth Culbertson Oct. 27, 1842 by Thomas H. Roberts
    Bondsman: John D. Wood

Hill, Thomas J. to Frances Wood Jan. 22, 1829 by Thos. D. Porter
    Bondsman: Peyton M. Bass

Hill, Thomas W. to Virginia W. Pryor Mar. 3, 1842 by E.W. Hendrix, M.G.
    Bondsman: Prier fears (sp. as written)

Hill, William to Nancy Hendricks July 8, 1811 (license and bond)
    Bondsman: Matthew McGaugh

Hilliard, Philemon to Emily Manning July 8, 1829 by Wm. Moor, J.P.
    Bondsman: Martin S. Little

Hilton, William W. to Sarah Newsom Jan. 24, 1849 by John Nichols, J.P.
    Bondsman: William A. Hogan

Hines, Owen to Polly Phillips Feb. 27, 1812 (bond)
    Bondsman: Grover Sharp

Hiter, Thomas to Sally S. McCrory Jany. 29, 1811 (bond)
    Bondsman: Charles McAlister

Hobbs, Fredrick to Sarah Garrett Feb. 4, 1822 (bond)
    Bondsman: Wilkins Whitfield

Hobbs, Hartwell H. to Harriet E. Berson May 26, 1835 by Robert Davis, M.G.
    Bondsman: John M. Currin

Hobbs, John to Judah Robertson Dec. 21, 1809 (bond)
    Bondsman: Thomas Goff

Hobbs, John (X) to Marthena Ann Haskin Dec. 23, 1830 by Wm. Rucker, J.P.
    Bondsman: William X G. Adams

Hobbs, Solomon (X) to Patsey Robertson July 20, 1815 (bond)
    Bondsman: George Everly

Hodge, Andrew to Louisa C. Orms Sept. or Oct. 18, 1834 by Robt. Davis, M.G.
    Bondsman: Calvin J. Fields

Hodge, Francis to Bridget Malone May 28, 1812 (bond)
    Bondsman: Thomas Malone

Hodge, Francis S. (X) to Mary Polk Dec. 18, 1834 by T.D. Porter
    Bondsman: Charles Smithson and C.E. Williams

Hodge, James to Nancy B. Atkinson Oct. 30, 1832 (bond)
    Bondsman: Dossey Atkinson

Hodge, John to Jane Carothers July 14, 1818 (bond)
    Bondsman: Joseph Stockett

Hodge, Philip to Margaret Sammons April 29, 1819 by Horatio Burns
    Bondsman: Woodson Walker

Hodge, William R. to Frances S. Atkinson Sept. 2, 1834 by Jas. King
    Bondsman: Solomon Berson

Hodges, Albert P. to Mary Jane Hill (bond)
    Bondsman: Christopher A. Hill

Hodges, Edward (X) to Nancy Sills Aug. 5, 1824 (bond)
    Bondsman: John Smith

Hodges, George to Betsey Mandley Dec. 8, 1806 (bond)
    Bondsman: Thompson Wood

Hodges, James (X) to Maria Vannatta April 24, 1824 (bond)
    Bondsman: Watson X Salmons

Hodges, William to Polly Beavens Sept. 22, 1806 (bond)
    Bondsman: William Wilson

Hogan, David to Fanny Toon April 3, 1826 by John Alkinson, V.D.M.
    Bondsman: none given (mar. date not given)

Hogan, Jacob F. or R. to Harriett D. Talliaferro Oct. 13, 1835 by L.P.Green,
    Bondsman: John B. Edmondson   M.G.

Hogan, John to Nancy Rigar Nov. 23, 1807 (bond)
    Bondsman: Drury Alsup

Hogan, Powell E. to Nancy M. Wall Aug. 21, 1846 (bond)
    Bondsman: John G. Reynolds

Hogans, William (X) to Lany? Taylor Dec. 7, 1816 (bond)
    Bondsman: Benijah X Cotton or Catton

Hogg, Calvin to Leah Wilson Nov. 20, 1845 by Fred J.F. Wilson
    Bondsman: Wm. A. Baucom

Hogg, Joshua to Elizabeth Stacks Dec. 29, 1822 by E. Ragsdale, J.P.
    Bondsman: John W. X McMillen

Holden, Grandison to Elizabeth F. Neal Dec. 28, 1847 (bond)
    Bondsman: C. W. Holden

Holiday, John (X) to Sally Truett Sept. 2, 1829 (bond)
    Bondsman: Henry X Truett

Hollady, Peter to Lettisia Hartgrave Feb. 7, 1812 (bond)
    Bondsman: Alexander Sampson

Holladay, Thomas to Margaret Butticks April 11, 1812 (bond)
    Bondsman: William Scott

Holland, Benjamin F. to Parmelia A. Powers Dec. 21, 1843 by J.J. Bingham, JP
    Bondsman: John J. Ham

Holland, Felix C. to Sarah Jane Atkinson Feb. 23, 1843 by Joseph Carle, M.G.
    Bondsman: Andrew J. Toon

Holland, George B. to Lucy Henry Bond Mar. 24, 1827 by John Alkinson, V.D.M.
    Bondsman: Wm. Bonds

Holland, Gustavus to Mary P. Brown July 31, 1845 by Gilbert Marshall, J.P.
    Bondsman: Stephen Nolen

Holland, John A. to Sarah Gray July 31, 1823 by George Shannon, J.P.
    Bondsman: Robert M.C.W. Shannon

Holland, Kemp S. to Elizabeth M. Maury July 12, 1823 by T.L. Douglass
    Bondsman: Richard Maury

Holland, Thomas H. to Elizabeth Scott June 23, 1839 by Jno.P. McKay, J.P.
    Bondsman: Benjamin F. Holland

Holland, Spearman to Nancy Hicks June 15, 1821 (bond)
    Bondsman: H.R.W. Hill

Holland, William S. to Mary Edmondson April 7, 1847 by M.L. Andrews, M.G.
    Bondsman: George W. Barnes

Holliday, John (X) to Sally Frantham Jan. 26, 1824 (bond)
    Bondsman: Henry X Holliday

Hollier, Christopher A. to Mary Wing   Oct. 6, 1838 (bond)
    Bondsman: Thomas Parkes

Holliman (Holleman), Jacob to Peggy Keylar, Heylar or Keglar   Aug. 24, 1808
    Bondsman: Joseph Sumners or Summers   (bond) (illegible)

Hollis, Thomas to Patsey McPherson   July 22, 1819 by Timothy Shaw
    Bondsman: Willis X Chamberlin

Holloway, James D. to Martha Gray   Jan. 8, 1850 by Green J. Simmons, Meth.Min.
    Bondsman: Thomas Waldron

Holloway, Joseph P. to Lucretia Lewis   Aug. 7, 1839 by Stephen Nolen, J.P.
    Bondsman: Elisha C. Williams

Holloway, William (X) to Lucinda Sampkins   Aug. 22, 1833 by Geo. Shannon, J.P.
    Bondsman: Thomas Carmichael

Holmes, John to Polly Woods   Dec. 14, 1807 (bond)
    Bondsman: John Denny

Holmes, John to Betsy Price   Dec. (no day) 1817 (bond)
    Bondsman: Isham Matthews

Holmes (Holmer), Luke M. to Lucy Sanford   Dec. 10, 1813 (bond)
    Bondsman: John Matthews

Holstead, Benjamin to Elizabeth Webb   May 17, 1838 (mar. date and by whom
    Bondsman: John Sanderson   omitted)

Holstead, Joseph (X) to Amanda Sharp   July 4, 1838 by Sam B. Robison, J.P.
    Bondsman: Joseph Sharber

Holt, Harden P. to Faney Andrews   Feby. 19, 1816 (bond)
    Bondsman: Thos. H. Perkins

Holt, Jacob to Susanna Crenshaw   Sept. 6, 1809 (bond)
    Bondsman: Thomas Crenshaw

Holt, John R. (X) to Jane Jarrett   June 23, 1841 by Cowden McCord, J.P.
    Bondsman: Edmund D. Hays

Holt, Louis to Emily Cummins   Oct. 27, 1834 by James W. Rea, M.G.
    Bondsman: Parker Bateman   (groom signed "Lewis")

Holt, Nicholas P. to Talitha (Tabitha?) E. Hughes   July 24, 1833 by J. King,
    Bondsman: Andrew Halfacre   M.G.

Holt, William to Polly White   Dec. 18, 1834 by John Ragsdale, J.P.
    Bondsman: S. Cainy X Johnson

Holt, William N. to Martha Ridley   Jan. 17, 1821 by G. Barnes, J.P.
    Bondsman: Elisha L. Hall

Holt, William R. to Nancy Jane Clark   Aug. 3, 1848 by W.F.A. Shaw, J.P.
    Bondsman: Lewis X S. Johnson

Holton, Andrew to Letsey Winsett   Sept. 25, 1828 by Horatio Burns, D.M.E.E.
    Bondsman: Silas Winsett

Hommel, Isaac (X) to Hannah Smith   Aug. 20, 1835 (bond)
    Bondsman: Samuel Eastep (Eastess?)

Hood, Bryant to Peggy Hunter   April 30, 1827 (bond)
    Bondsman: John A. Wilkins (groom signed "Briant")

Hood, James (X) to Mary A.E. Williams   Dec. 16, 1838 by Daniel Baugh, J.P.
    Bondsman: John G. Graham

Hood, John to Polly Best   Feb. 5, 1815 (bond and license)
    Bondsman: Jonathan Best

Hood, Leonard (X) to Eliza Ann Thompson   Oct. 31, 1844 by H.B. North, M.G.
    Bondsman: John T. Fleming

Hood, Peter to Elizabeth Ezzell   July 1, 1816 by Allen Hill, J.P.
    Bondsman: Isaac Tignor

Hood, Thomas to Rosetta Isom   Aug. 29, 1821 (bond)
    Bondsman: John X McKay

Hood, William (X) to Mary Potts   June 16, 1834 (bond and license)
    Bondsman: Thomas Peebles

Hooks, David to Clarissa Craig   July 8, 1828 by David C. Kinnard, J.P.
    Bondsman: B. M. Nicholson

Hooks, John W. to Elizabeth Inman   Nov. 19, 1837 by Reuben White, J.P.
    Bondsman: none given

Hopkins, George to Elizabeth Creek   Nov. 29, 1832 by R. Ransom, J.P.
    Bondsman: Newton C. Creek

Hopkins, Gray J. to Margaret Roland   Oct. 12, 1840 (bond)
    Bondsman: Wm. F. Abernathy

Hopkins, John to Margaret Fox   Jan. 12, 1818 (bond)
    Bondsman: Hugh Fox

Hopkins, William D. to Cynthia Copeland   Aug. 23, 1825 by G.H.
    Bondsman: Alfred Edmiston ("20 mi past 7 o'clock time of ceremony")

Hopper, Hance H. to Nancy Littleton   Sept. 9, 1835 by Jas. W. Rea, M.G.
    Bondsman: none given (license only)

Horseford, Spencer to Isabella Boyd Beaty   Feb. 22, 1842 by J.B. Boyd, J.P.
    Bondsman: James Beaty

Horsford, John (X) to Fanny Boon   Feb. 28, 1836 (bond)
    Bondsman: Thomas Powell

Horsford, Matthew (X) to Polly Ford   Oct. 28, 1835 (bond)
    Bondsman: George Allen

Hosford, James (X) to Lucy Atkinson   Feb. 21, 1830 by J. Wall, J.P.
    Bondsman: Silas Chrisman

Hosford, John to Sarah Helton   June 22, 1837 by L. Powell, M.G.
    Bondsman: none given

Horton, Allison to Sarah Anderson   Feb. 19, 1849 by Wm.W. Bond, Esqr.
    Bondsman: Thomas Russell   (groom signed "A. W.")

Horton, Clabun M. to Malvira E. Harrison   April 8, 1847 by M.L. Andrews
    Bondsman: W. D. Andrews

Horton, Everett to Jane Horton   Dec. 13, 1830 by H. C. Horton, M.G.
    Bondsman: Isaac Vanzant

Horton, Minoah to Catherine Bugg   Oct. 10, 1836 by H.C. Horton, M.G.
    Bondsman: Wm. C. Woods

Horton, McKendre (X) to Elizabeth Wilie   Aug. 20, 1832   (bond)
    Bondsman: Reuben T. Craig

Hough, William L. to Susan Griggs   Dec. 30, 1850 by John Cox, J.P.
    Bondsman: John B. McEwen

Housden, Benjamin (X) to Hannah Luke (Leeke?)   July 16, 1839 by R.B.B. Cannon
    Bondsman: Samuel H. Barnes   J.P.

House, Andrew L. to Martha Caroline Shaw   July 15, 1847 by H.B. North, M.G.
    Bondsman: John N. House

House, Benjamin B. to Elizabeth J. House   Jan. 20, 1834   (bond)
    Bondsman: John H. Neelley

House, David to Sally Adams   Oct. 30, 1815   (bond)
    Bondsman: Jacob X House

House, George A. to Mary Ann Raney   Jan. 13, 1842 by H. B. Hyde, J.P.
    Bondsman: James A. House

House, Isaac H. to Elizabeth A. Vaughan   Dec. 22, 1846 by John Lam?, M.G.
    Bondsman: Stephen M. Glenn or Glem

House, James to Fanny Neelly   Feb. 3, 1810   (bond)
    Bondsman: B. Neelly

House, James to Mary Walton   Oct. 27, 1823   (bond)
    Bondsman: John Tignor

House, James A. to Drucilla Barnwell   Dec. 27, 1830   (bond)
    Bondsman: David House

House, John to Polly M. Dabney   Dec. 20, 1813   (bond)
    Bondsman: Joseph Crockett

House, John to Peggy Walker   April 5, 1818   (bond)
    Bondsman: Jacob X Ham

House, John (X) to Sally Gillan (Gillian) Mar. 19, 1821 by Wm. Anthony, J.P.
    Bondsman: John Adams

House, John F. to Cynthia Swisher Dec. 7, 1827 (bond)
    Bondsman: William Brown

House, John N. to Nancy Jane Neely Nov. 23, 1845 by Jesse Cox, M.G.
    Bondsman: John W. Neely

House, Joseph G. to Elizabeth Fish March 25, 1837 by John Morton
    Bondsman: none given

House, Samuel S. H. to Sarah Jane Parks Sept. 25, 1845 by R.G. Irvin, M.G.
    Bondsman: William E. Green

House, Thomas (X) to Elizabeth Ragsdale Dec. 24, 1838 by John Ragsdale
    Bondsman: William Ragsdale

House, Thomas (X) to Nancy Ragsdale Feb. 4, 1847 by S. Sparkman, J.P.
    Bondsman: Jesse Ragsdale

Housen, James to Elizabeth Crocker Jan. 12, 1837 by J.A. Holland, J.P.
    Bondsman: none given

Houston, Edward to Sarah McAdoo July 15, 1818 (bond)
    Bondsman: Jones Houston

Houston, John B. to Charlotte M. Kinnard June 18, 1826 by Joel Anderson
    Bondsman: none given

Houston, Joseph (X) to Mary Jane Goodwin Oct. 28, 1847 by W.M. Nunn, J.P.
    Bondsman: James X H. Goodwin

Houzedin?, Benjamin to Susan Guy May 19, 1836 by Wm. Edmondson, J.P.
    Bondsman: none given

Howall, William (X) to Sarah Jane Forehand Sept. 15, 1840 by Wm.R. Horton, M.G.
    Bondsman: William H. Short

Howard, Benjamin A. to Laetitia A. Caperton Jan.15, 1845 by M.B.Molloy,G.M.
    Bondsman: Robert Ragsdale

Howard, John to Fanny Pinkston Aug. 11, 1807 (bond)
    Bondsman: Hugh Pinkston

Howard, Robert (X) to Sally Crouse Jan. 4, 1825 by Samuel White "preacher of the Gospel"
    Bondsman: John Crouse

Howel, David to Cintha Hunt Jan. 15, 1806 (bond)
    Bondsman: Jacob Gray

Howel, Henry to Nancy Smith Aug. 3, 1837 by B.F. Bingham, J.P.
    Bondsman: none given

Howel, William H.H. to Catharine Humble Aug. 25, 1842 by Geo. W. Mayberry, J.P.
    Bondsman: William Howel

Howington (Herrington?), James W. to Mary Ann McNeal   Jan. 1, 1840 (bond)
    Bondsman: Boyd M. Nicholson

Hubbard, James T. to Mary Jane Spencer   May 17, 1849 by W.B. Carpenter
    Bondsman: Isaac S. Webb

Hubbard, Ransom L. to Susan Kellow   Jan. 7, 1838 by Levi Crosley, J.P.
    Bondsman: Griffin G. Zachary

Huddleston, James to Isabella McKenley   Jan. 29, 1807 (bond)
    Bondsman: David Huddleston

Hudgans, King D. to Sarah Witherington   March 23, 1825 (bond)
    Bondsman: James X Peach

Hudgens, James A. to Nancy Vaughan   Dec. 15, 1831 by T.D. Porter
    Bondsman: Sam Peay

Hudgens, John J. to Mary Ann Coleman   Feb. 28, 1833 by Thos. D. Porter, M.G.
    Bondsman: Robert Davis

Hudson, Miles R. to Mary Jane Shaw   Feb. 4, 1847 by M.L. Andrews, M.G.
    Bondsman: W. H. Spratt

Hudson, Thomas to Rebekah Hulme   July 22, 1815 (bond)
    Bondsman: William Hungerford

Huff, William to Ann Pace   July 31, 1842 by I. Bennett, J.P.
    Bondsman: Isaac X Page

Huggins, Nathaniel (X) to Mary Graham   March 12, 1817 (bond)
    Bondsman: George Glasscock

Hughan, Alexander to Lucinda Gray   Dec. 25, 1846 by James M. Reed, J.P.
    Bondsman: William Henry

Hughes, Archilaus P. to Mary E. Webb   Nov. 29, 1824 (bond)
    Bondsman: James Brown

Hughes, Archilaus to Sarah Dunneber   Oct. 18, 1846 by N.R. Jordan, J.P.
    Bondsman: Constantine Jordan

Hughes, Barnet R. to Elizabeth P. Cose   Aug. 25, 1841 by James W. Rea, M.G.
    Bondsman: Wm. Cummins

Hughes, Benjamin (X) to Frances Moppin?   June 23, 1827 by Geo. J. Poindexter, J.P.
    Bondsman: James Mogan

Hughes, Brice M. to Susan E. Fleming   Sept. 26, 1839 by M.L. Andrews, M.G.
    Bondsman: J. W. Baugh (Joseph)

Hughes, James to Elizabeth Robins   Dec. 4, 1827 by Ware Henley, J.P.
    Bondsman: Ephraim X Gordan

Hughes, James (X) to Martha Whitby   Dec. 15, 1841 (bond)
    Bondsman: Robert Layne

Hughes, James, Jr. to Rosanna Holland   July 12, 1824 (bond)
    Bondsman: Fountain B. Carter

Hughes, James E. (X) to Tabitha M. Allen   Dec. 18, 1839 by Jas. W. Rea, M.G.
    Bondsman: Barnett R. Hughes

Hughes, John A. to Susan Williams   Aug. 13, 1841 by Cowden McCord, J.P.
    Bondsman: James S. Ogilvie

Hughes, John A. to Mary E. Bond   March 28, 1844 by John Nichols, J.P.
    Bondsman: Joseph B.S. Wyatt

Hughes, John B. to Louisa McMahan   July 31, 1846 by Thomas Reed
    Bondsman: W. Lafayette X Hughes and W. L. Hughes

Hughes, John F. to Jane B. Baldridge   Nov. 13, 1832 by D.C. McLeod, A.M.G.
    Bondsman: Jesse Thomas

Hughes, John M. to Sarah J. Warren   Feb. 22, 1849 by G.W. Pollard, J.P.
    Bondsman: John C. Neelly (groom made mark)

Hughes, Levi to Jincy Gibson   Sept. 19, 1807 (bond)
    Bondsman: Hardy L. Fennell

Hughes, Nicholas to Amanda Cummins   Aug. 27, 1827 by John Alkinson, V.D.M.
    Bondsman: Richard L. Maury

Hughes, Pryor R. to Martha A. Boyd   July 2, 1825 (bond)
    Bondsman: Wilkins Oldham (groom may be Pryor B.)

Hughes, Pryor R. to Kizzy Williams Williams   Sept. 20, 1837 by Joseph Carle
    Bondsman: none given

Hughes, Reece J. to Elizabeth Bryant   July 5, 1850 by Wm. Wright, J.P.
    Bondsman: Green W. Locke

Hughes, Richard to Manerva Duty   Nov. 26, 1835 by Robert Davis, M.G.
    Bondsman: William E. Hughes

Hughes, Robert M. to Elizabeth R. Brown   Aug. 6, 1850 (bond)
    Bondsman: Littleberry R. Brown

Hughes, Samuel C. to Nancy W. Anderson   Aug. 18, 1831 by Andrew Craig, M.G.
    Bondsman: William Martin

Hughes, Thomas to Lucy M. Bond   Dec. 21, 1830 by Robt. Davis, M.G.
    Bondsman: Nich's P. Stone

Hughes, William E. to Eliza C. Wilkins   Jan. 31, 1837 by Joseph Carle
    Bondsman: none given

Hughes, Wm. E. to Virginia M. Stone   Nov. 6, 1839 by James C. Anderson ,
    Bondsman: Wm. White   (teacher of Christian Relig

Hughes, William M. to Martha P. Dobson   Feb. 19, 1829 by Thos. D. Porter
    Bondsman: William Martin

Hughes, William T. to Mary Jane Henning Aug. 19, 1846 by M.L. Andrews, M.G.
    Bondsman: Wm. G. Ozburn

Hughs, Pryor R. to Martha A. Boyd July 2, 1826 by John Alkinson, V.D.M.
    Bondsman: none given

Hulan, George to Peggy Sharp April 16, 1813 (bond)
    Bondsman: Leon Hunt

Hulme, George W. to Elizabeth Whittenton June 11, 1823 (bond)
    Bondsman: Ephraim Best

Hulme, George W. to Serena Porter Jan. 29, 1829 by Wm. Moor, J.P.
    Bondsman: Benjamin P. Dillin

Hulme, Thomas to Susan Childress July 22, 1812 (bond)
    Bondsman: Jonathan Currin

Hulme, William to Elizabeth Childress Jan. 18, 1811 (bond)
    Bondsman: Thomas Hiter

Hulme, William B. to Mary Leigh Feb. 26, 1833 by Levin Edney, M.G.
    Bondsman: John B. Hulme

Humphreys, Charles L. to Elisabeth North Dec. 13, 1820 by D. Brown, V.D.M.
    Bondsman: John L. McEwen

Humphreys, David W. to Frances H. Baugh Sept. 26, 1848 by M.L. Andrews, M.G.
    Bondsman: Wm. B. Patton

Humphreys, Michael to Patsey Wells May 23, 1811 (bond)
    Bondsman: Charles Kavanaugh

Hunly, Humphrey (illeg.) to Polly Outtry (illeg.) April 6, 1820 (bond)
    Bondsman: Joel Garner (groom made mark)

Hunt, Andrew W. to Susan Ann Nichols Jan. 17, 1837 by M. Marshall
    Bondsman: none given

Hunt, Edward to Margaret M. Hazlett May 30, 1833 by Thos. L. Douglass
    Bondsman: Mansfield House

Hunt, George to Terrissa P. Cooper May 9, 1818
    Bondsman: Benjamin Guinn

Hunt, Green W. to Fanny G. Watkins Dec. 29, 1830 (bond)
    Bondsman: Hiram Edmondston

Hunt, Jonathan S. to Frances M. Turner Sept. 30, 1822 (bond)
    Bondsman: J. N. Charter

Hunt, Robert A. to Sally Chriswell Oct. 13, 1834 by Wm. Carson J.P.
    Bondsman: Jenkins Scantland

Hunt, Squier to Sydney Cooper March 17, 1818 (bond)
    Bondsman: Arthur Ayres

Hunter, Henry to Jane Bennets   Oct. 9, 1821 (bond)
    Bondsman: James Wilkins

Hunter, James to Sally Young   July 12, 1806 (bond)
    Bondsman: George Strambler?

Hunter, James H. to Margaret Burnett Oct. 1, 1827 (bond)
    Bondsman: John A. Wilkins

Hunter, James M. to Elizabeth F. Norris Sept. 15, 1847 by Jas. Marshall, MG
    Bondsman: John R. Marshall

Hunter, Joseph R. to Priscilla W. Cloud Nov. 22, 1842 by James C. Anderson,
    Bondsman: Thos. N. Figures   M.G.

Hunter, Perkins to Mary Dodson Dec. 27, 1827 by Joel Anderson A J.P.
    Bondsman: Bird Fitzgerald and N. T. Edwards

Hunter, William H. to Sarah M. Moss Nov. 3, 1835 (bond)
    Bondsman: Alexander M. Wortham

Hurt, Elijah to Martha Ragsdale Oct. 27, 1827 by Wm. Craig
    Bondsman: Jameson M. Ragsdale

Hurt, Elijah R. to Dosha Field Dec. 6, 1830 (bond)
    Bondsman: Drury H. Field

Hurt, William (X) to Louisa Long Feb. 29, 1844 by G. H. Leigh, J.P.
    Bondsman: J. B. McPherson (James)

Husbands, Miles to Sophia W. Nicholson Jan. 30, 1833 (bond)
    Bondsman: David Moss

Hutcherson, George W. to Margaret A. Redman Dec. 19, 1844 by J.R. Pearcy, JP
    Bondsman: B. D. Redman

Hutcherson, John W. (X) to Mary White Dec. 29, 1836 (bond)
    Bondsman: Joseph X Sampley

Hutcherson, Lewis J. (X) to Cynthia White Aug. 5, 1838 by (omitted)
    Bondsman: Ira E. X Burnham

Hutcheson, Spencer to Peggy Alexander July 26, 1813 (bond)
    Bondsman: Thomas Alexander

Hutchinson, John D. to Parallee Pewitt Dec. 30, 1837 by Reuben White, J.P.
    Bondsman: none given

Hutchison, Charles (X) to Elizabeth Mont (Wont?) Nov. 17, 1824 by Lewis Loyd,
    Bondsman: John Crouse   JP

Hutchison, Thomas (X) to Nancy Givens Dec. 29, 1829 by M.L. Andrews, M.G.
    Bondsman: G. W. Givens (Geo. W.)

Hutson, Cuthbert B. to Susan Bryant Jan. 20, 1818 (bond)
    Bondsman: Wilson Bryant and "Cutbirth" B. Hutson

Hutson, Richard to Mary Gatlin Aug. 7, 1842 by J.F. McMahan, J.P.
    Bondsman: James B. Campbell

Hutton, Alexander to Elizabeth Montgomery Feb. 12, 1834 by Wm. Moor, J.P.
    Bondsman: John M. Hutton

Hutton, Henry to Nancy Williamson Jan. 15, 1817 (bond)
    Bondsman: David Manning

Hutton, James to Winafred Weathers April 12, 1821 by Henry Petty, M.G.
    Bondsman: Joseph S. Hamilton

Hutton, John M. to Sally Doyle Jan. 6, 1820 by G. Hunt
    Bondsman: J. E. Williamson

Hutton, John M. to Polly Priest March 10, 1825 by Robert Davis, M.G.
    Bondsman: John W. Miller

Hutton, Patrick to Eley Germain March 22, 1806 (bond)
    Bondsman: Dan'l Germain

Hyde, Hartwell B. to Elizabeth P. Alston May 17, 1822 (bond)
    Bondsman: John S. Russwurm?

Hyde, Joseph John to Elizabeth Ann Jordan Jan. 28, 1847 by Jesse Cox, M.G.
    Bondsman: J. (Joseph) W. Scales

-I-

Ingram, George to Elizabeth Thompson Sept. 12, 1835 (bond)
    Bondsman: Samuel S. Patton

Ingram, Hezekiah to Elizabeth Scott April 29, 1830 by Geo. Shannon, J.P.
    Bondsman: Jocob X Scott

Ingram, Thomas to Susannah Gee Dec. 22, 1806 (bond)
    Bondsman: James Hicks

Inman, Benjamin to Jane Alexander Jan. 11, 1825 (bond)
    Bondsman: Thomas Hulme

Inman, Benjamin to Ann Givens Aug. 10, 1843 (bond)
    Bondsman: Malachi X Scott

Inman, Benjamin M.C to Eliza Kelly Jan. 4, 1845 by R. White, J.P.
    Bondsman: John X Inman

Inman, Ezekiel to Cary Perkins April 4, 1811 (bond)
    Bondsman: Thomas Alexander

Inman, Ezekiel to Lillie Edgar Feb. 24, 1816 (bond)
    Bondsman: Lazarus Inman

Inman, Ezekiel to Eliza Branch Aug. 5, 1824 by Wm. Dunnegan, J.P.
    Bondsman: F. Dunnegan

Inman, Granville G. (X) to Barbara Pewitt   July 28, 1842 by R. White, J.P.
    Bondsman: Wiley W. Pewitt

Inman, James A. to Emeline Edmondson   July 7, 1846 by Wm. A. Whitsitt, Bap-
    Bondsman: Rufus Hampton   (tist Min. of the Effort Order

Inman, John (X) to Sarah Kearby   Sept. 2 , 1816 by Wm. Dunessan?, J.P.
    Bondsman: Hamilton Montgomery

Inman, John (X) to Parmelia Alexander   Jan. 6, 1820 by Wm. Dunnegan, J.P.
    Bondsman: John X Bradley

Inman, Lewis D. to Nancy M. Goff   Aug. 1, 1833 (bond)
    Bondsman: Elijah Gray

Inman, Samuel to Hannah Little   July 10, 1813 (bond)
    Bondsman: William Grimes

Inman, Samuel to Mary Wilkinson   May 24, 1831 by C. McDaniel, J.P.
    Bondsman: Lewis Inman

Inman, Wesley S. to Sarah Ann Cotton   Nov. 4, 1850 by M.L. Andrews, M.G.
    Bondsman: W. B. White

Inman, William (X) to Rachel Kirbey   March 6, 1828 by Daniel White
    Bondsman: Joseph X Pewitt

Inman, William B. to Jane Bird   Nov. 5, 1837 by Reuben White, J.P.
    Bondsman: none given

Inscore, William to Jane Hasting   Dec. 29, 1831 by Tristram Patton, J.P.
    Bondsman: Thos. R. Shaw

Irion, Philip J. to Sarah A. Carsey   Sept. 6, 1832 by T.D. Porter
    Bondsman: Elijah H. Dean

Irland, Daniel to Peggy Cochran   Sept. 15, 1812 (bond)
    Bondsman: John Cochran

Irvin, Andrew to Elizabeth Evans   July 27, 1826 by M.L. Andrews, M.G.
    Bondsman: none given

Irvin, Christopher to Elizabeth Irvin   Nov. 9, 1841 by John Wall, J.P.
    Bondsman: James X Irvin

Irvin, Jackson C. to Amelia Ann Reams   June 25, 1849 by (not given)
    Bondsman: Isaac S. Page

Irwin, Robert to Susannah Hairgrave   Feb. 1, 1817 (bond)
    Bondsman: Nicholas Gentry

Irwin, Robert to Hannah Davidson   March 22, 1817 (bond)
    Bondsman: Joseph Davidson

Isbell (Ishell?), James to Edy Riggins   July 14, 1826 by W.B. Carpenter
    Bondsman: none given

Ivie, Benjamin W. to Eliza Ivie   Oct. 29, 1825 (bond)
    Bondsman: William Atkinson

Ivie, James B. to Sarah Reynolds   Mar. 2, 1841 by J. B. Boyd, J.P.
    Bondsman: J. B. Fulton

Ivie, Reuben I. to Elizabeth C. Owen   Sept. 27, 1848 (bond)
    Bondsman: William N. Smith

Ivy, John W. (X) to Martha Ann Tally   Nov. 13, 1846 by F. Ivy, J.P.
    Bondsman: James Talley

-J-

Jackson, Andrew W. to Rebecca M. Webb   Dec. 22, 1842 by E.W. Hendrix, M.G.
    Bondsman: Isaac X Hendrix

Jackson, David to Polly Wilbanks   Oct. 7, 1830 by John Rushing, M.G.
    Bondsman: Littleton Clark

Jackson, Durant H. to Amanda E. Reams   Mar. 1, 1849 by James Marshall, M.G.
    Bondsman: Charles W. Crowder

Jackson, Durant K. to Nancy Temple   Nov. 7, 1821 (bond)
    Bondsman: Clairborne Runsarall?

Jackson, Francis (X) to Martha Davenport   Dec. 27, 1832 by Tristram Patton, JP
    Bondsman: William M. House

Jackson, Francis to Sally Revel   June 16, 1835 by John Landrum
    Bondsman: Francis Jackson by R. Jackson and Richard Jackson
        "Whereas I the said Francis Jackson having a desire to
        obtain license to be married to Salley Revel of your
        county and it being inconvenient for me to travel to your
        office; therefore pray you ... to issue and deliver said
        license to bearer hereof after said bearer enters himself
        security that there is no lawful cause to obstruct the
        marriage. Under my hand this 11th day June, 1835 Fran J."

Jackson, Francis M. to Barbara Allen   Oct. 9, 1838 by M.L. Andrews, M.G.
    Bondsman: James Allen

Jackson, Henry to Nancy Chrisman   Dec. 24, 1822 by Thomas Nelson
    Bondsman: Jacob Halfacre

Jackson, Henry B. to Polly Clay   Sept. 21, 1821 (bond)
    Bondsman: Elisha North

Jackson, James (X) to Martha J. Tomlinson   Sept. 10, 1844
    Bondsman: Robert H. Williams

Jackson, James to Mary A. Brown   June 21, 1846 by John King, M.G.
    Bondsman: Hugh Sherwood

Jackson, John to Elizabeth Elam Dec. 22, 1818 (bond)
    Bondsman: Matthew Elam

Jackson, John to Susan Manska (Mansker) Aug. 25, 1838 by Gilbert Marshall, JP
    Bondsman: Larkin Burch

Jackson, John (X) to Elizabeth Kingston Jan. 5, 1847 by Jonas Sutton
    Bondsman: Wilson X Calhoon

Jackson, John A. to Frances M. Anderson Oct. 31, 1841 by Thomas L. Douglass
    Bondsman: Jonathan Rothrock

Jackson, Josiah to Sally Lewis Sept. 21, 1822 (bond)
    Bondsman: Cornelius Vaughn (groom signed "Joseas")

Jackson, Raleigh M. to Canzady? Putman Oct. 5, 1848 by John Landrum, Bap.Min.
    Bondsman: William M. Lamb

Jackson, Richard G. to Elizabeth Scales Aug. 16 or 17, 1843 by R.G. Irvine
    Bondsman: Mark L. Andrews

Jackson, Robert to Nancy Jackson June 25, 1818 (bond)
    Bondsman: Thos. Jackson

Jackson, Robert to Barbary G. Sharp May 14, 1850 by (omitted)
    Bondsman: none given (This is Maury County license)

Jackson, Robert H. to Susan Dalton June 4, 1822 (bond)
    Bondsman: D. P. Perkins

Jackson, Samuel to Betsey Welch May 30, 1826 (bond date) by R. McCutchen, JP
    Bondsman: none given

Jackson, Thomas to Ruth Hendricks Aug. 10, 1813 (bond)
    Bondsman: John Dillon

Jackson, Thompson F. to Frances T. Atkinson Dec. 10, 1833 by John Alkinson,
    Bondsman: Armine T. Reese V.D.M.

Jackson, Westley to Mary C. Evans July 16, 1834 by Levin Edney, M.G.
    Bondsman: Charles Cartright (groom signed "Wesley")

Jackson, Wesley to Mary Jane Davis Mar. 30, 1839 (bond)
    Bondsman: Turner Smith

Jackson, William to Catherine Brooks Jan. 6, 1820 (bond)
    Bondsman: Pleasant Todd

Jackson, William to Agnes Witt Jan. 8, 1826 (bond)
    Bondsman: none given

Jackson, William (X) to Mary Ann Nancy Jenkins June 29, 1835 by J. Allison,
    Bondsman: Charles A. Merrill J.P.

Jackson, William to Elizabeth Nelson Jan. 23, 1839 by Jno. R. Pearcy, J.P.
    Bondsman: John R. Pearcy

Jackson, William to Martha E. Hawkins Nov. 1, 1848 by G.W. Rolland, J.P.
    Bondsman: John A. Griggs

Jaggers, Thomas J. to Frances A. Bateman Jan. 7, 1835 by C.E. McEwen, J.P.
    Bondsman: Parker Bateman

James, George H. to Catharine Bradley July 24, 1811 (bond)
    Bondsman: Archibald Potter

James, Thomas A. to Elizabeth A. Bailey Aug. 30, 1831 by Cary James, D.M.E.C.
    Bondsman: Thomas S. Williamson

Jamison, Henry D. to Sarah W. Thomas July 23, 1835 by Jesse Cox, M.G.
    Bondsman: H.D. Jamison by Christopher Beasley and R.P. Currin
    ".. I wish you to send marriage license by my friend Mr. Beasley.
    .. Please sign bond for me if Mr. Beasley will not answer for security wish you would procure Mr. Maury(?) or some other security.. The young ladies name is Sarah W. Thomas and send me the bond .. I will sign it with my security and return it by Mr. Cox who will be the preacher when he returns the license. I understand that you are a little particular in those matters therefore I have suggested these two propositions, presuming either will be legal. I would not put you to this trouble but am not in good health and wish to avoid riding in the sun. Resp'lly H.D. Jamison July 23, 1835 N.B. I mentioned Mr. Maney? he being a friend of mine. Also mention P.N.Smith R.P. Currin & John Liscomb if Mr. Maney is not in town. H.D.Jamison"

Jamison, John to Montgomery Wells Jan. 29, 1846 by James B. Porter, M.G.
    Bondsman: Benjamin Grigsby

Jamison, John B. to Sarah Angelia Pinkston Nov. 12, 1840 by R.W. Robinson, JP
    Bondsman: David J. Patterson

Jamison, Marshal to Rebecca Ridley Jan. 30, 1818 (bond)
    Bondsman: Beverley Ridley

Jamison, Samuel (X) to Sarah Carson Feb. 10, 1825 by M.T. Span, J.P.
    Bondsman: William Manning

Jamison, Wiley (X) to Elizabeth Hardeson March 10, 1827 (bond)
    Bondsman: Samuel X Jamison

Jefferson, Stillman A. to Frances A. Con? Feb. 20, 1850 by H.B. North, M.G.
    Bondsman: Bolling C. North

Jenkins, Duke to Louisa Still Jan. 14, 1836 by H.B. North, M.G.
    Bondsman: Nathan Newsom

Jenkins, Henry (X) to Cynthia B. Sconce Nov. 22, 1827 by Thos. King, J.P.
    Bondsman: Leonard Vernon

Jenkins, Jeremiah to Sally Glymph Oct. 9, 1832 (bond)
    Bondsman: Paul Jones

Jenkins, Walter L. to Agnes P. Stone Nov. 13, 1816 by D. Brown, Dr. of Ministry
    Bondsman: Peter Pryor

Jernigan, Riley to Nancy Oliver   Aug. 1, 1829 by Wm. Craig
    Bondsman: William Oliver

Jeter, William W. to Elizabeth Jeter   May 10, 1832 by Robert Davis, M.G.
    Bondsman: Wm. M. Wright

Job, Aaron to Masdrey Bradley   June 29, 1812 (bond)
    Bondsman: Samuel Carson

Job, Anthony (X) to Lorinda Franklin   Aug. 23, 1834 (bond)
    Bondsman: Thos. Williams

Johns, John to Evelind Hopkins   Jan. 16, 1831 by John Little
    Bondsman: Samuel Cox

Johnson, Allen W. to Narcissa Edmondson   May 11, 1848 by Wm. M. Nunn, J.P.
    Bondsman: John T. X Erskine

Johnson, Anderson to Caroline Nolen   Dec. 19, 1825 (bond)
    Bondsman: Robert Grimmer (Trimmer?)

Johnson, Andrew to Judith Word   Dec. 1, 1836 by Robert Davis, M.G.
    Bondsman: none given

Johnson, Benjamin A. to Martha J. Robison   Nov. 28, 1850 by E.B. Matthews, MG
    Bondsman: G. P. Brien

Johnson, Charles to Mary J. White   Jan. 28, 1836 by W. Pearson, M.G.
    Bondsman: David Campbell

Johnson, Claibourne to Sarah Ann Horton   April 20, 1836 by H.C. Horton, M.G.
    Bondsman: none given

Johnson, Elcamy (X) to Sarah Ragsdale   Dec. 10, 1825 (bond)
    Bondsman: William Holt

Johnson, Freeman to Sarah McGuire   Jan. 1, 1835 by Wm. Rucker, J.P.
    Bondsman: Eli M. Corzine

Johnson, George T. to Martha A. Hall   Dec. 29, 1844 by Jno. P. McKay, J.P.
    Bondsman: Natus J. Haynes

Johnson, Henry to Narcissa Wilson   Dec. 17, 1844 by H.C. Horton, G.M.
    Bondsman: Wiley M. X Horton

Johnson, Isaac to Secy Williams   Dec. 6, 1834 (bond)
    Bondsman: Thomas Haddick

Johnson, James to Narcissa Merritt   Oct. 24, 1834 by Jas. King
    Bondsman: David Campbell

Johnson, James (X) to Rachel Johnson   May 24, 1844 by M.L. Andrews, M.G.
    Bondsman: Joac X Pace

Johnson, James C. to Louisa Cochran   Feb. 8, 1850 (bond)
    Bondsman: Joel S. King

Johnson, James H. to Frances Nolen   April 11, 1820 by Wm. Anthony, J.P.
    Bondsman: Wiley Jones

Johnson, James M. to Susan O. W. Yeargin   Nov. 29, 1844 by C.B. Feriss, G.M.
    Bondsman: Joseph W. Sharber

Johnson, Jeffry (X) to Eliza Peach   Feb. 28, 1850 by Jno. T. Cox, J.P.
    Bondsman: James Brooks

Johnson, Jesse to Dolly Smithson   Oct. 8, 1828 (bond)
    Bondsman: Joseph A. Brimm

Johnson, Jesse (X) to Milley Ann Johnson   Aug. 28, 1846 by S.S.P.A. Knott, JP
    Bondsman: John X Johnson

Johnson, John to Nancy Reynolds   Oct. 7, 1813 (bond)
    Bondsman: Thomay Reynolds

Johnson, John to Caroline M. Barham   Jan. 17, 1843 by M.L. Andrews, M.G.
    Bondsman: John E. Gadsey

Johnson, John to Wincey Merritt   Oct. 29, 1846 (bond)
    Bondsman: James Merritt

Johnson, Joseph to Martha Vestal   Aug. 10, 1830 by Jonathan Rothrock, J.P.
    Bondsman: Nathan Gilbert

Johnson, Josiah to Michy B. Jefferson   May 1, 1819 by Nich's Scales
    Bondsman: W. B. Hyde

Johnson, Josiah to Ferreby Hyde   Sept. 31, 1825 by Andrew Craig, M.G.
    Bondsman: H. B. Hyde

Johnson, Joshua to Minerva Jordan   Jan. 1, 1835 by T.D. Porter
    Bondsman: Freeman W. Jordan

Johnson, Lemuel (X) to Rhodda Merritt   Nov. 20, 1845 by G.S. White, M.G.
    Bondsman: John X Johnson

Johnson, Littleton to Jane Berryman   June 19, 1815 (bond)
    Bondsman: David Mason

Johnson, Meredy (X) to Rachael Pace   Nov. 21, 1825 by Andrew McCrady, J.P.
    Bondsman: Richard Jones

Johnson, Stephen to Patsey Jordan   Dec. 15, 1806 (bond)
    Bondsman: Thompson Wood

Johnson, Thomas to Nancy E. Pate   Dec. 15, 1846 by J. H. Wilson
    Bondsman: Jesse T. Pate

Johnson, Thomas P. to Lucy F. Taliafero   May 17, 1836 by W. Dearson, M.G.
    Bondsman: none given

Johnson, Watty P. (X) to Eleanor Gardner   Feb. 20, 1838 by W.H. Meadow, J.P.
    Bondsman: Vardy McAlpin

Johnson, William to Sarah E. King May 4, 1837 by A.T. Scruggs Min. of M.E.Ch.
    Bondsman: none given

Johnson, William B. to Adelia C. Nolen Feb. 5, 1835 by H.B. North, M.G.
    Bondsman: Richard W. Robinson

Johnson, Willis R. (X) to Jane Pinkerton Feb. 17, 1841 by John P. McKay, J.P.
    Bondsman: Peter X Sweeney

Johnson, Wilson to Naomy Graham Dec. 22, 1839 by J. Rothrock, J.P.
    Bondsman: Wilson X Graham and Thos. J. Cook

Johnson, Zadock to Lucy Ann Pate Oct. 15, 1845 (bond)
    Bondsman: Jesse T. Pate

Johnston, Andrew (X) to Sally Hicks May 29, 1821 by George Blackburn, M.G.
    Bondsman: Jeremiah Fields

Johnston, Andrew, Jr. to Amanda C. Moore Dec. 24, 1844 by M.L. Andrews, M.G.
    Bondsman: Thomas White

Johnston, Benjamin to Susan Brogdon July 5, 1823 by Thomas Nelson
    Bondsman: Stephen Frazer

Johnston, David to Harrett Barfield Dec. 3, 1823 by Joel Anderson
    Bondsman: Lewis Barfield

Johnston, David to Jane Merritt Oct. 22, 1827 by Joel Anderson
    Bondsman: Henry J. Merritt

Johnston, Edmund to Nancy Johnston Dec. 18, 1807 (bond)
    Bondsman: Josiah Johnston

Johnston, Eldred to Nancy Elmore Oct. 20, 1830 by Geo. J. Poindexter, J.P.
    Bondsman: Sylvanus W. Smith

Johnston, Gregory to Rachael M. Corzine Jan. 13, 1831 by Wm. Rucker, J.P.
    Bondsman: Eli M. Corzine

Johnston, James to Gracy Gault June 5, 1805 (bond)
    Bondsman: Ephraim Brown

Johnston, Jas. D. to Susan Waddill July 22, 1808 (bond)
    Bondsman: John White

Johnston, Joel (X) to Sally White Jan. 9, 1815 (bond)
    Bondsman: Wiley Johnson (groom gave name "Johnson" on bond)

Johnston, John to Mary Terrell Jan. 27, 1831 by Thos. L. Douglass, M.G.
    Bondsman: John E. Gadsey

Johnston, John (X) to Mahala Ragsdale May 26, 1833 by Andrew McCrady, J.P.
    Bondsman: Felix Lunn (groom's name "Johnson" on bond)

Johnston, John W. to Narcisa Hayne May 21, 1815 by N. Scales
    Bondsman: Wm. McKnight

Johnston, Jordan to Polly Dowdy Oct. 24, 1822 by Edward Ragsdale, J.P.
    Bondsman: Gibson Dowdy

Johnston, Lewis to Nancy Wilkins Jan. 29, 1829 (bond)
    Bondsman: Wm. D. Taylor

Johnston, Littleberry to Ann Nolen Sept. 18, 1827 by Thos. King, J.P.
    Bondsman: Richard W. Robinson

Johnston, Robert to Susan Merritt July 29, 1829 by Joel Anderson, M.G.
    Bondsman: W.S.S. Harris

Johnston, Wiley to Mary Smith Aug. 5, 1816 (bond)
    Bondsman: Edward X Holt

Johnston, William to Louisa Crockett Jan. 26, 1821 by Geo. Blackburn, Min.
    Bondsman: James C. Hill

Johnston, William (X) to Polly Holt April 2, 1821 (bond)
    Bondsman: William Clarke

Johnston, William to Mary Dickson Feb. 25, 1838 by H. McNish, J.P.
    Bondsman: none given (sp. "Johnson" on outside of bond. Also,
        date March 29, 1837 is on bond)

Johnston, William W. to Sarah K. Alston July 21, 1831 by H.B. Hyde, J.P.
    Bondsman: Green W. Hunt (groom signed "Johnson")

Johnston, Willis (X) to Polly Nall Sept. 15, 1821 (bond)
    Bondsman: William Nall

Joice, Ree to Sally Allen Mar. 8, 1821 by G. Barnes, J.P.
    Bondsman: James Peay

Jones, Abner to Sally Smith May 23, 1833 by Joseph Carle
    Bondsman: John Graham

Jones, Amza to Eliza Haywood Marable Feb. 1, 1815 by Levin Edney, M.G.
    Bondsmen: E.H. Marable, Benjamin White, Wiley Royal

Jones, Amza (X) to Fanny Ham July 23, 1835 by Wm. Roach, J.P.
    Bondsman: Kelly Mc Rhodes

Jones, Barnett to Mary Marlin Dec. 1, 1831 by S.S. Newman, J.P.
    Bondsman: John Cowan

Jones, Benjamin to Nancy Allen Dec. 20, 1814 (bond)
    Bondsman: Andrew S. Andrews

Jones, Benjamin to Elizabeth E. Adams Aug. 13, 1835 by Nelson P. Modrall, MG
    Bondsman: William Spann

Jones, Charles O. to Frances Meacham Sept. 13, 1843 by J.J. Bingham, J.P.
    Bondsman: Elisha Meacheam (sp. as signed)

Jones, Daniel H. to Sarah Hampton Jan. 21, 1830 by E. R. Parish, J.P.
    Bondsman: Isaac Secrest

Jones, David to Matilda Wilson Feb. 16, 1824 (bond)
    Bondsman: John Fedrick

Jones, Decatur P. to Elizabeth Ann Powell Oct. 14, 1846 by Jas. King
    Bondsman: George Lavender

Jones, Dempsey to Julia Davis Sept. 26, 1829 by Wm. Armstrong, J.P.
    Bondsman: Alex. Y. Simmons

Jones, Enoch H. to Rebecca F. Hunt Sept. 17, 1839 by R.B.B. Cannon, J.P.
    Bondsman: Enoch Hunt

Jones, Holland M. to Eliza N. Harrison Feb. 26, 1835 by Joel Anderson
    Bondsman: James Anderson

Jones, Holland M. to Sarah Edwards Aug. 15, 1841 by M.L. Andrews, M.G.
    Bondsman: William Jones

Jones, James to Augusta Ann Scruggs Jan. 10, 1829 by Thos. L. Douglass
    Bondsman: John H. Scruggs

Jones, James (X) to Elizabeth Sharp Dec. 24, 1840 by John Landrum
    Bondsman: Chesley J. Coursey

Jones, James G. to Elizabeth Sharp Sept. 15, 1812 (bond)
    Bondsman: Jas. M. Gray

Jones, James G. to Manerva Jordan Nov. 15, 1831 by H. B. Hyde, J.P.
    Bondsman: Hartwell B. Hyde

Jones, James H. to Rhoda L. Marlin Aug. 4, 1842 by J.J. Bingham, J.P.
    Bondsman: Joseph Beasley (groom made mark)

Jones, James M. to Marthusa Shumate June 3, 1841 by Monroe Short, J.P.
    Bondsman: William M. Shumate

Jones, Joel W. to Elizabeth Temple Feb. 1, 1816 by Levin L. Edney, M.G.
    Bondsman: William Jones

Jones, John to Polly Hutcherson Feb. 1, 1814 (bond)
    Bondsman: J. B. Avery

Jones, John (X) to Mary Tucker Dec. 18, 1836 by J.A. Holland, J.P.
    Bondsman: James X Harper

Jones, John (X) to Milly Ann Harrison Dec. 22, 1842 by Joseph Carle, M.G.
    Bondsman: William W. Wall

Jones, John W. to Mary Ann Gray Dec. 9, 1846 by Jas. M. Green, J.P.
    Bondsman: John A. Burke

Jones, Joseph (X) to Betsey Taylor Aug. 1, 1831 by Levin Edney (no date)
    Bondsman: Isaac X Jones

Jones, Judson to Keziah Waters Oct. 12, 1812 (bond)
    Bondsman: General Lee Dolen

147.

Jones, Lewis to Susan McAffee   Aug. 21, 1811   (bond)
   Bondsman: Abraham Truit

Jones, Lewis T. (X) to Matilda Lock   July 16, 1845 by J.J. Bingham, J.P.
   Bondsman: Elisha Meacheam

Jones, McLauren H. to Ann Elizabeth Haly   July 15, 1847 by W.N. Nunn, J.P.
   Bondsman: J. S. Gentry

Jones, Maury to Mary Hulme   March 15, 1832 by Levin Edney, M.Gospel Christ
   Bondsman: John W. Hulme

Jones, Mordecai (X) to Susan Harper   Dec. 26, 1833 by Ware Henley, J.P.
   Bondsman: John X Owen

Jones, Peter (X) to Peggy Nolen   Aug. 1, 1844 by R.B.B. Cannon, J.P.
   Bondsman: John H. Winstead

Jones, Presley to Dorothy Garrett   Feb. 26, 1826 by M.T. Span, J.P.
   Bondsman: none given

Jones, Richard B. to Elizabeth Andrews   Oct. 15, 1818   (bond)
   Bondsman: Robert G. Jones

Jones, Richard C. to Brittania Johnson   Dec. 4, 1832 by Felin Helm, J.P.
   Bondsman: John B. Beasley

Jones, Robert A. G. to Polly Green   Sept. 25, 1842 by James A. Cunningham, JP
   Bondsman: Benjamin X Jones

Jones, Samuel (X) to Eliza Brogdam (illeg.)   June 18, 1827 by T. Nelson
   Bondsman: William X Linton

Jones, Sylvester to Anna Frazier   Feb. 1, 1825 by Thos. King, J.P.
   Bondsman: Thomas P. Carsey

Jones, Taylor to Martha Vowell   April 28, 1848 by John F. Cox, J.P.
   Bondsman: John W. Miller

Jones, Thomas to Julia Jones   Nov. 26, 1808   (bond)
   Bondsman: Benjamin White

Jones, Thomas to Polly Bass   Feb. 28, 1809   (bond)
   Bondsman: John Bass

Jones, Thomas to Margarite Allen   Dec. 26, 1818   (bond)
   Bondsman: Benjamin X Jones

Jones, Thomas to Mary Criswell   Aug. 15, 1828 by J. Wall, J.P.
   Bondsman: J. B. Ragsdale

Jones, Thomas to Susan Riddle   July 26, 1833 by John N. Nolen, J.P.
   Bondsman: Albert Poteete

Jones, Thomas to Elizabeth Hartley   Feb. 27, 1839 by Henry Walker, M.G.
   Bondsman: Andrew Hartley

Jones, Thomas M. to Marietta Perkins Dec. 25, 1838 by H.J. Leacock, Rector
   Bondsman: Neill S. Brown   (St.Paul Ep. Church

Jones, Washington (X) to Hester Perry McLaughlin Mar. 6, 1849 by J.Hendricks,
   Bondsman: Matthew Garrett   J.P.

Jones, Wiley (X) to Nancy Guy Dec. 29, 1839 by R.B.B. Cannon, J.P.
   Bondsman: Asa X Harper

Jones, Wiley to Nancy Nolen Aug. 1, 1820 by Wm. Anthony
   Bondsman: William Nolen Junior

Jones, Wiley to Rebecca Berry Sept. 7, 1843 by James King
   Bondsman: Washington Shelton (groom signed "Willer")

Jones, William to Patsey Adkins May 28, 1806 (bond)
   Bondsman: John J. Winston

Jones, William to Julia Ann Cromer Dec. 23, 1828 by Franklin McClaran, J.P.
   Bondsman: Hugh M. Gault

Jones, William to Ferriby Johnson April 5, 1837 by W.H. Meadow, J.P.
   Bondsman: none given

Jones, William to Ann E. Edwards Dec. 22, 1842 by M.L. Andrews, M.G.
   Bondsman: John R. Hatcher

Jones, William G. to Lucinda Williamson May 12, 1836 by Lewis Magee, J.P.
   Bondsman: none given

Jones, William N. to Sarah F. Jordan Nov. 1, 1843 by John Richardson, J.P.
   Bondsman: James M. Jones

Jones, Willis to Celia A. Strickland Aug. 31, 1829 (bond)
   Bondsman: W. B. Sweeney

Jones, Willis G. or T. to Margaret G. House Sept. 3, 1835 by Matt Marshall,
   Bondsman: Amasa Webb   J.P.

Jordain, Clement to Martha Matthews Dec. 20, 1821 by W.R. Nunn, J.P.
   Bondsman: Christopher McConnico

Jordan, Benjamin to Sally Wood April 6, 1812 (bond)
   Bondsman: Benjamin Jordan

Jordan, Benjamin (X) to Sarah P. Adams Aug. 4, 1846 by Jn. Richardson, J.P.
   Bondsman: G. M. Pate

Jordan, Freeman W. to Martha Ann Carothurs June 8, 1837 by Jesse Cox, M.G.
   Bondsman: none given

Jordan, Garner M. to Rebecca G. Burton Dec. 20, 1824 (bond)
   Bondsman: Thomas J. Goff

Jordan, George to Sally Puckett Dec. 12, 1815 (bond)
   Bondsman: Jared McConnico

Jordan, James to Franky Spencer Sept. 7, 1813 (bond)
   Bondsman: James Read

Jordan, John to Lucinda Turner Jan. 27, 1827 (bond)
   Bondsman: John Page

Jordan, John to Grizzle Taylor Dec. 22, 1831 by L. Manire, J.P.
   Bondsman: John M. Gault (Bride's name Grizelda?)

Jordan, John A. to Emily A. Fletcher June 5, 1845 by Jesse Cox, M.G.
   Bondsman: Johnson Wood

Jordan, Johnson to Rachael Hill Dec. 28, 1808 by Nick Scales, J.P.
   Bondsman: Martin Symms Test: David Mason and A. Potter

Jordan, Johnson to Nancy Beasley March 26, 1822 by Horatio Burns
   Bondsman: John Jordan

Jordan, Johnson, Jr. to Martha Williams April 25, 1843 by J. Dyer, J.P.
   Bondsman: James Williams, Jr.

Jordan, Minus (Minos) C. to Elizabeth Jordan July 20, 1842 by Jesse Cox, MG
   Bondsman: Rufus E. Philips

Jordan, Newton to Mary G. Jordan Oct. 27, 1824 (bond)
   Bondsman: Harrison Jordan

Jordan, Robert D. to Nancy D. Martin Sept. 30, 1836 by N. Patterson Modrall,
   Bondsman: Thos. E. Jordan   M.G.

Jordan, Stephen A. to Mary Carothers Sept. 8, 1846 by Jesse Cox, M.G.
   Bondsman: R. B. Carothers

Jordan, Thomas to Nancy Peay Sept. 5, 1849 by B.R. Gant, M.G.
   Bondsman: Sam'l Peay

Jordan, William to Medy Boyd Aug. 28, 1810 by N. Scales
   Bondsman: Johnson Jordan

Jordan, William to Ann B. Sappington Dec. 8, 1830 by Joel Anderson, M.G.
   Bondsman: Alexander Hughes

Jordan, William to Mary H. Bell Jan. 2, 1833 by T.D. Porter
   Bondsman: Albert G. Hill

Jordan, William to Elizabeth E. Boyd Dec. 12, 1833 by T.D. Porter
   Bondsman: Thomas Edmondson

Jordan, William to Sarah J. Wood Dec. 31, 1840 by Jesse Cox, M.G.
   Bondsman: Newton Jordan

Jordan, William H. to Elizabeth Pettus Feb. 14, 1850 by Jesse Cox, M.G.
   Bondsman: Johnson Wood

Jordan, Williamson to Sarah E. Davis Sept. 5, 1844 by A.W. Meacham, M.G.
   Bondsman: Blount Jordan

Jummerson, James A. to Eleanor Quinn Dec. 29, 1817 (bond)
    Bondsman: Jesse Barnes (groom made mark. Jammeson?)

-K-

Kaiglar, David to Nancy Miles Sept. 8, 1816 by Nich's Scales
    Bondsman: John Pillow

Karr, James C. to Julia A. Haynes July 11, 1832 by Jas. B. Porter
    Bondsman: John Moore

Kasby (Illeg.), William to Dinah Kennad? June 17, 1807 (bond)
    Bondsman: Benjamin Prichard

Kavenaugh, Williams to Margaret McKenny July 25, 1816 by A. Mebane, J.P.
    Bondsman: Thos. E. Dudley (groom's name "William" on bond)

Keeling, Edward A. to Ann Slater Jan. 15, 1815 (bond)
    Bondsman: John Anderson

Keen, Thomas G. to Eleanor H. Jones Sept. 26, 1839 by H.I. Leacock, Rector
    Bondsman: Samuel N. Stephens   (L.P.E. Church in Franklin

Keffer, James to Caroline E. Breast Sept. 27, 1822 by Thos. L. Douglass
    Bondsman: James Park

Keiglar, William to Elizabeth Beasley April 15, 1812 (bond)
    Bondsman: Wm. Martin

Kelley, Enoch B. to Jane Floyd Mar. 7, 1850 by John King, M.G.
    Bondsman: Wm. A. McCord

Kelley, William to Ruth Alexander Dec. 29, 1813 (bond)
    Bondsman: Thomas Alexander

Kellor, Samuel to Arman P. Neely Feb. 27, 1846 by Charles N. Poyner
    Bondsman: Samuel Kelloe and William Yeargin

Kellor, Thomas B. and Eliza Lampkins Jan. 15, 1837 by J.A. Holland, J.P.
    Bondsman: none given

Kellow, Arthur (X) to Frances H. Neelly Dec. 8, 1836 by J. Holland
    Bondsman: William J. Moody

Kellow, Thomas H. to Sarah Ann Vaughan Nov. 30, 1837 by Wm. Edmondson, J.P.
    Bondsman: none given

Kelly, Agricola M.W. to Peny E. White Dec. 22, 1850 by M.L. Andrews, M.G.
    Bondsman: James S. Roberts

Kelly, Allen P. to Milly Turbiville Sept. 14, 1819 by Thos. Wilson
    Bondsman: Lewis H. Perry

Kelly, Asbury M. to Sarah B. Womack Oct. 20, 1831 by James King, M.G.
    Bondsman: James S. Swisher

Kelly, Elijah (X) to Adeline White Dec. 28, 1833 (bond)
    Bondsman: Henry W. X Harpending

Kelly, Hugh to Juliet Berson Jan. 26, 1837 by M. Marshall
    Bondsman: none given

Kelly, Thomas to Betsy Hicks Oct. 13, 1808 (bond)
    Bondsman: Nathaniel Armstrong

Kelton, William R. to Martha Cummins Jan. 1, 1840 by W.H. Baldridge
    Bondsman: John P. Bond

Kemper, James to Sarah D. Mullen Feb. 11, 1829 by Jabez Owen, J.P.
    Bondsman: Benjamin D. Smith

Kendrick, Starling (X) to Sally Singletery Nov. 28, 1815 (bond)
    Bondsman: John X Kendrick

Kennedy, Evender to Mary Goff Aug. 15, 1816 by Geo. Blackburn, M.G.
    Bondsman: James McCombs

Kennedy, James to Elizabeth P. Bennett Sept. 1, 1831 by Robt. Hardin, M.G.
    Bondsman: Andrew Herron

Kennedy, James (X) to Lavinia Long Jan. 5, 1833 by Robt. McCutchen, J.P.
    Bondsman: Henry X Trewitt

Kennedy, Price to Sally K. Demsey May 24, 1826 (bond)
    Bondsman: none given

Kennedy, Robert to Annis Ferrill (Ferill) June 10, 1816 by Robt. McMillin, JP
    Bondsman: Dempsey Sayers

Kenney, William C. to Elizabeth Oldham Sept. 4, 1838 by R.W.H. Baldridge
    Bondsman: Henry Wilson

Kenny, John to Jane G. Douglass Dec. 10, 1833 by D.C. McLeod, M.G.
    Bondsman: Jesse Thomas (groom signed "Kinny")

Kerr, Egbert B. to Nancy A. Cowsert Feb. 16, 1845 by Rev. Milton B. Molloy
    Bondsman: Calvin C. Chapman

Kerr, John to Ann Moncrief Nov. 7, 1850 by E.P. Scales, J.P.
    Bondsman: Samuel Lewis

Kershaw (see Hershaw)
Ketchum, James (see Catchum, James)

Key, George (X) to Puina Tignor March 30, 1821 (bond)
    Bondsman: Thos. Hardeman

Kidd, George W. to Elizabeth C. Still Dec. 24, 1841 by J.W. Green, J.P.
    Bondsman: George P. King

Kidd, James to Frances Gooch Jan. 3, 1818 (bond)
    Bondsman: David R. Gooch

Kidd, Thomas to Catharine D. Clark   Jan. 12, 1842 by L.B. Johnson, J.P.
    Bondsman:. Wm. E. Morton

Kidd, William to Zelpha Kimbrough   Dec. 23, 1809 (bond)
    Bondsman: Elisha Kimbrough

Kilcrease, Davis to Mahala Mandley   Nov. 9, 1817 (bond)
    Bondsman: Chapman Manly

Killough, Allen to Ann Peeler (illeg.)   July 31, 1808 (bond)
    Bondsman: Frederick Peeler

Kilpatrick, Samuel W. to Margaret W. Campbell   May 9, 1832 by Jabez Owen, JP
    Bondsman: James L. Smith

Kimbro, Rolly P.S. to Sinai V. Crutcher   Oct. 15, 1844 by M.L. Andrews, M.G.
    Bondsman: Richard H. Ogilvie

Kimbroe, Elisha L. to Martha Taylor   Aug. 16, 1821 (bond)
    Bondsman: James X Kidd

King, Anthony (X) to Jane Campbell   Nov. 6, 1849 by M.L. Andrews, M.G.
    Bondsman: John Hafner

King, Benjamin T. to Susan J. Matthews   Oct. 29, 1835 by T.D. Porter
    Bondsman: James M. Green

King, George to Lucinda Gooch   Feb. 13, 1832 (bond date) by Jno. G. Hay, D.C.
    Bondsman: Audley S. Hamilton

King, James to Elizabeth Dabney   Dec. 11, 1830 (bond)
    Bondsman: Lemuel B. McConnico

King, James B. to Nancy McGee   Sept. 25, 1845 by J.A. Cunningham, J.P.
    Bondsman: Henry S. Hendricks

King, James P. to Mary Ann Jordan   Dec. 24, 1840 by A.J. Nunn, J.P.
    Bondsman: David D. Russell

King, John to Lucy Ann Alston   Jan. 2, 1834 by T.D. Porter, M.G.
    Bondsman: Bolen C. Barnes

King, John to Sarah Taylor   July 31, 1834 by G. Hunt
    Bondsman: Thomas Carmichael

King, Michael to Jane McFawl   Nov. 14, 1820 (bond)
    Bondsman: John Quigley

King, Oswin H. to William Carroll   Dec. 3, 1829 by G. Hunt
    Bondsman: W. H. Womack   (bride and groom may have names reversed)

King, Richard to Nancy Daley   Oct. 2, 1827 by H.C. Horton, M.G.
    Bondsman: H. C. Horton

King, Robert to Elizabeth Wood   Aug. 22, 1832 by Daniel White, M.G.
    Bondsman: William Moray

King, Thomas B. to Eliza Thomas   Feb. 1, 1842 by Jesse Cox, M.G.
    Bondsman: John A. Oden

King, Thomas B. to Louiza Thornbrough Dec. 22, 1849 (bond)
    Bondsman: James H. Jones (groom made mark)

King, Thomas B. (X) to Eliza E. Thornbrough Sept. 3, 1850 by M.C. Jordan, JP
    Bondsman: Benjamin F. Martin

King, Thomas L. to Delia C. Nolen Aug. 7, 1817 (bond)
    Bondsman: Stephen Nolen (groom's initial may be "S")

King, Thompson H. (X) to Allebury Stanfield Aug. 7, 1838 by R.B.B. Cannon, JP
    Bondsman: John King

King, William (X) to Rebecca Marim? Dec. 16, 1834 by G. Hunt, J.P.
    Bondsman: W. C. Hunt

King, William to Rebecca W. Buchanan Oct. 3, 1850 by C.B. Faris, G.M.
    Bondsman: none given

King, William B. to Eliza Jane Manire Sept. 30, 1841 by William Davis, Min.
    Bondsman: Daniel D. Russell

King, William B. to Jane F. Lytle Jan. 27, 1842 by A.L.P. Green, M.G.
    Bondsman: Wm. B. King by Wm. Johnson and Wm. Johnson

King, William S. to Sarah Edwards May 31, 1838 by R.B.B. Cannon, J.P.
    Bondsman: Jacob Morton

King, William S. to Rebecca W. Rash Sept. 16, 1849 by B.R. Gant, M.G.
    Bondsman: Hezekiah Hill

Kington, John C. to Martha Shelton Dec. 27, 1836 by James King, M.G.
    Bondsman: none given

Kinnard, Christopher W. to Elizabeth H. Watkins Dec. 14, 1843 by Jesse Cox,
    Bondsman: Patrick G. Giles   M.G.

Kinnard, Christopher W. to Martha V. Watkins May 24, 1849 by Jesse Cox, M.G.
    Bondsman: Thos. E. Hall

Kinnard, Claibourne H. to Elizabeth A. Fleming Feb. 20, 1834 by James King
    Bondsman: John I. Watson

Kinnard, David C. to Hannah Miller Jan. 3, 1821 (bond)
    Bondsman: Robert Parrish

Kinnard, David C. to Sarah T. Olgilvie Nov. 27, 1822 by Henry Bailey, J.P.
    Bondsman: Robert Parrish

Kinnard, George C. to Mary A. Jordan Oct. 18, 1846 by W. Burns, M.G.
    Bondsman: Joseph S. Gentry

Kinnard, James P. to Nancy Ogilvie Dec. 15, 1827 by Joel Anderson
    Bondsman: Boyd M. Nicholson

Kinnard, Michael to Adeline McConnico   April 5, 1821 by Joel Anderson
    Bondsman: R. B. Marshall

Kinnard, Richard O. to Elizabeth B. Fleming   Mar. 13, 1848 by Robert C. Gar-
    Bondsman: Claibourne Kinnard   (rison, V.D.M.N.S.P.

Kinsey, Benjamin to Catharine Sherrin   Dec. 11, 1830 by Daniel White, Min.
    Bondsman: Thos. R. Shaw

Kinsey, William B. to Arrena Bates   Nov. 4, 1841 by (name omitted)
    Bondsman: Franklin B. X Haynes

Kirby, William J. to Peana White   Mar. 29, 1838 by J.J. Bingham
    Bondsman: Wiley B. White

Kirk, Jessee L. to Polly Wilkins   July 31, 1813 (bond)
    Bondsman: William Bond

Kirk, John to Ann Pruet   March 12, 1807 (bond)
    Bondsman: Theo. Brenthley

Kirk, William A. A. to Ann R. Clark   Aug. 14, 1821 (bond)
    Bondsman: William P. Hays

Kirkes, William to Mary Sampson   April 3, 1839 by J. Wall, J.P.
    Bondsman: Smith X Sampson

Kirkpatrick, John to Catharine Anderson   Aug. 8, 1823 by Andrew Craig, M.G.
    Bondsman: Alex Russell

Kirkpatrick, John O. to Julia F. Atkinson   Aug. 12, 1846 by J.C. Anderson, MG
    Bondsman: R. P. Moss

Kirkpatrick, Samuel to Jane Dobbins   Oct. 9, 1815 (bond)
    Bondsman: Thos. Craig

Kirkpatrick, Thomas E. to Nancy L. Willie (Wylie?)   June 5, 1828 by M.L.And-
    Bondsman: John C. Wylie   rews, M.G.

Kirkpatrick, Thomas J. to Anna Dobbins   Mar. 20, 1826 by John Alkinson,V.D.M.
    Bondsman: none given (date is bond date)

Kirkpatrick, William J. to Mary Herron   Oct. 2, 1833 (bond)
    Bondsman: A.T. Reese

Kirsey, Drury to Agnes Thompson   Jan. 6, 1831 by Thos. Prowell, J.P.
    Bondsman: William Younger

Knight, James (X) to Sally Sawyers   Dec. 8, 1841 (bond)
    Bondsman: Shadrack Cayce

Knott, Ivison to Jane E. Owen   Oct. 9, 1843 by L.B. Johnson
    Bondsman: John Knott

Knott, James R. to Mary L. Bracey   Dec. 21, 1848 by W.M. Nunn, J.P.
    Bondsman: John C. Helm

Knott, William M. to Martha P. Smithson   Jan. 6, 1841 by Pettus Shelburne, JP
    Bondsman: John C. Johnston   (date discrepancy on bond and license,-
                                        marriage may have taken place in 1840

Koonce, Wright to Mary Loyd   Mar. 1, 1822 by Leven Edney, M.G.
    Bondsman: James C. Koach   (groom signed "Right")

Korman, James to Martha E. McLaughlin   Sept. 1, 1846 by Richard P. Miles,
    Bondsman: Alexander Rosboroughs   Bishop of Nashville

-L-

Lacey (Locey), Lorenza (X) D. to Ruthy Hartly   Sept. 1, 1850 by M.H. Dobson,
    Bondsman: John Lister   JP

Lackey, Andrew K. to Nancy D. Bond   Nov. 22, 1850 by J.C. Anderson, M.G.
    Bondsman: Robt. W. Bond

Lacy, Hopkins to Martha Allen   Feb. 14, 1828 by H. Bailey, J.P.
    Bondsman: William W. Johnson

Ladd, Constantine D. (X) to Sarah Hicks   Sept. 12, 1835 by Geo. Shannon, J.P.
    Bondsman: William J. Moody

Ladd, Peter B. to Matilda Fly   July 2, 1837 by R.W. Robinson, J.P.
    Bondsman: none given

Ladd, Thornton G. to Mary Jane Smithson   Aug. 4, 1841 by Pettus Shelburne, JP
    Bondsman: William P. Ladd

Laden, Thomas to Margaret Pearce (Pearse?)   Oct. 2, 1823 by Robt. Davis, M.G.
    Bondsman: Spencer R. Wyatt   (groom signed "Layden")

Lagron, William to Mary Halfacre   Oct. 24, 1814   (bond)
    Bondsman: Jacob Halfacre

Lamb, Abram (X) to Elizabeth Prince   Feb. 1, 1848   (bond)
    Bondsman: John P. Stevens

Lamb, David to Esther Landram   Oct. 7, 1813   (bond)
    Bondsman: James Hill

Lamb, David (X) to Susan Lamb   July 8, 1824 by Wm. Pollard
    Bondsman: William Hill

Lamb, Drury M. to Ruth McCullum   Dec. 6, 1837 by R.W. Morris, E.U? P. Church
    Bondsman: none given

Lamb, Enoch (X) to Rebecca Milton   Aug. 8, 1840 by John Lanksin?, B.M.
    Bondsman: James X Jones

Lamb, Isham to Martha B. House   March 27, 1845 by H.B. North, M.G.
    Bondsman: James L. Armstrong

Lamb, Jonathan to Elizabeth Hale   Sept. 4, 1830   (bond)
    Bondsman: David Jackson

Lamb, Martin to Francis Hill Oct. 31, 1816 by Meriman Landrum
    Bondsman: William X Hill

Lamb, Merriman to Elizabeth Pope Oct. 27, 1837 by Jno. Landrum
    Bondsman: none given

Lamb, Thomas to Parry (Purry?) Putnam May 6, 1821 (bond)
    Bondsman: Thomas Wright

Lamb, William to Hannah Putman July 31, 1829 by L. Manire, J.P:
    Bondsman: Jesse H. Carson

Lamb, William (X) to Nancy Crick Sept. 4, 1838 by Sam B. Robinson, J.P.
    Bondsman: William Lewis

Lamb, William (X) to Elizabeth Crick March 5, 1841 by John Landrum, J.P.
    Bondsman: John Lamb

Lamb, William to Mary Knot Mar. 29, 1844 by Chesley Williams, J.P.
    Bondsman: Mark L. Crick

Lamb, William D. to Nancy C. Webster Jan. 28, 1841 by N.R. Owen, J.P.
    Bondsman: Jacob G. Page

Lambert, Abner to Ibby Scott April 27, 1825 by Jas. Scott, M.G.
    Bondsman: William Amis

Lampkin, William to Ann Eliza Adams May 30, 1844 by (name omitted)
    Bondsman: Benjamin X Malone

Lampkins, James H. to Susan Price May 11, 1845 by M.L. Andrews, M.G.
    Bondsman: John B. McEwen

Lancaster, David to Nancy Radford Feb. 21, 1807 (bond)
    Bondsman: Peter Swanson

Landrum, John to Delpha Hall Dec. 24, 1822 by Jonathan Norman
    Bondsman: Joshua Landrum and John Webb

Landrum, William to Winney Pope Oct. 27, 1827 by Sam B. Robinson, J.P.
    Bondsman: none given

Lane, Benjamin to Rebecca Walker Nov. 7, 1825 by Tristram Patton
    Bondsman: John M. Lane

Lane, James to Rebecca McPherson Sept. 25, 1849 by John P. McKay, J.P.
    Bondsman: Woodward X Hart

Lane, Martin to Margaret D. McEwen Sept. 5, 1817 (bond)
    Bondsman: Christopher E. McEwen

Lane, Reuben to Sarah Long May 22, 1823 by Hartwell B. Hyde, J.P.
    Bondsman: Nath'l X Cannon (groom signed "Layne")

Lang, Edward to Jane Kenney Dec. 14, 1828 by J. Farrington, J.P.
    Bondsman: James P. Dillin

Lang, George W. to Rebekah Priest Dec. 15, 1819 by T. Farrington, J.P.
    Bondsmen: J.C. Hill and Wm. Johnson

Langley, Levi (X) to Arcadia Horton Feb. 2, 1819 by John Thurston
    Bondsman: Thomas Hilliard

Langley, William to Rebecca J. Ingram Jan. 16, 1850 by John C. Wiley, J.P.
    Bondsman: George W. Allen

Lanier, Benjamin B. to Mary Donelson Oct. 30, 1838 by M.L. Andrews, M.G.
    Bondsman: Thomas Helm

Lanier, Benjamin S. to Mary A. Boone March 29, 1845 (bond)
    Bondsman: William W. Peace

Lanier, William to Martha C. Tanner Dec. 11, 1830 by M.L. Andrews, M.G.
    Bondsman: Alanson Oslin

Laslin, William to Sarah Shaderick Oct. 6, 1817 (bond)
    Bondsman: Edward Harris

Lathem, James to Sally Gray Dec. 24, 1812 (bond)
    Bondsman: John McGee

Laughlin (Loughlin?), James to Elizabeth Roy (Ray?) Dec. 22, 1810 (bond)
    Bondsman: Benjamin Parks

Laughlin, Lynden to Caroline Nall Sept. 19, 1835 (bond)
    Bondsman: Isaac Anderson

Lavendar, William (X) to Abigail Blake Apr. 22, 1819 by Tristram Patton, JP
    Bondsman: Jeremiah Terry

Lavender, Anthony to Parraller Sprott Jan. 26, 1837 by M.L. Andrews, M.G.
    Bondsman: none given

Lavender, Nelson Jr. (X) to Pamelia White Mar. 1, 1832 by Wm. Rucker, J.P.
    Bondsman: George M. X White

Lavender, Nicholas (X) to Nancy Sloan March 2, 1822 (bond)
    Bondsman: Richius X Lavender

Lawhorn, Charles (X) to Peggy McIntosh Dec. 18, 1822 by Jas. Reid, J.P.
    Bondsman: Henry Martin

Lawhorn, John to Catharine Ruder Jan. 27, 1831 by Robt. Davis, M.G.
    Bondsman: John H. Bullock

Lawrence, Edward to Mary J. Marling March 18, 1848 (bond)
    Bondsman: John W. Chandler

Lawrence, John C. to Jane B. Jones Dec. 16, 1845 by M.L. Andrews, M.G.
    Bondsman: Pleasant W. Brown

Laws, Theldred to Nancy Poarch Jan. 2, 1812 (bond)
    Bondsman: none given

Laymasters, John (X) to Mary Ann McPherson Jany. 15, 1825 (bond)
    Bondsman: Henry X Truit

Layne, Benjamin W. to Dilly Fisk Sept. 12, 1847 by Thos. J. Miller, J.P.
    Bondsman: Geo. A. J. Mayfield (groom signed "Lane")

Layne, Henry to Nancy Hogwood (Haywood?) July 24, 1828 by Lent Brown, M.G.
    Bondsman: Allen X Salmons

Layne, John to Frances Hughes Feb. 23, 1820 by Eleazar Hardeman, J.P.
    Bondsman: William Layne

Layne, John B. to Lucy H. Hogan Jan. 7, 1846 by W. Burns
    Bondsman: George W. Layne

Layne, Robert to Nancy Hickman Feb. 1, 1819 by Nich's Scales
    Bondsman: Wm. K. Layne

Layne, Robert to Susan Anne Glenn Sept. 4, 1845 by Wm. F. Carter, J.P.
    Bondsman: John B. Layne

Layne, William T. to Elizabeth M. Walton July 25, 1839 by Jesse Cox, M.G.
    Bondsman: none given

Lazenby, John (X) to Sarah E. Morris Mar. 24, 1845 (bond)
    Bondsman: Thomas L. McCrory

Leath, Michael M. to Martha B. Clark Oct. 30, 1836 by Wm. B. Carpenter
    Bondsman: Stephen L. Vaught

Leathers, David L to Catherine Philips Mar. 2, 1837 by Lent Brown
    Bondsman: none given

Leaysbeck, Thomas to Leannah Andrews March 27, 1805 (bond)
    Bondsman: Lazarus Andrews

Ledbetter, William to Eliza Adaline Wellborn Apr. 24, 1828 by German Baker
    Bondsman: H. D. Neilson (groom of Rutherford Co.)

Lee, Benjamin to Patsey Barlett (Bartleff or Bartlett) May 3, 1814 (bond)
    Bondsman: Henry Hadger

Lee, Hubbard J. to Polly Guthrie Sept. 3, 1817 (bond)
    Bondsman: Roderick Temple (groom signed "Herbert")

Lee, John (X) to Polly Ann Scott Feb. 21, 1849 by Thos. J. Nolen, J.P.
    Bondsman: William X Pumroy

Lee, William to Mary Love Jan. 9, 1809 (bond)
    Bondsman: Joel Hobbs

Lee, William S. to Mary Field Sept. 9, 1835 by James Johnson, J.P.
    Bondsman: J. Thomas Parrish and James McAlister

Leek, Samuel P. to Anna Barnes April 1, 1818 (bond)
    Bondsman: Ansylum Barnes

Leflore, Greenwood to Priscilla Donly June 9, 1834 by S.B. McConnico, J.P.
    Bondsman: Edward Breathitt

Leftwich, Jesse to Mary R. Lewis Dec. 24, 1850 by A. N. Cunningham, M.G.
    Bondsman: Thomas S. Porter

Legate, Charles S. to Sally Gray Feb. 20, 1805 (bond)
    Bondsman: John Secrest

Legate, James to Fanny Wilson Nov. 22, 1817 (bond)
    Bondsman: James Wilson

Lester, Charles S. to Parmelia F. Marable Oct. 23, 1839 by H. B. Hyde, J.P.
    Bondsman: Joseph H. Ladd

Lester, German to Catharine Reed (Rud?) Feb. 10, 1818 (bond)
    Bondsman: Wm. Edmiston

Lester, James to Mary D. McConnico Dec. 21, 1820 by John Alkinson, Minister
    Bondsman: James C. Hill

Lester, James W. to Elizabeth Tucker Feb. 14, 1832 (bond)
    Bondsman: John McHally

Lester, Robert H. to Martha M. Allen Dec. 23, 1848 (bond)
    Bondsman: Braxton J. Wall

Lester, Samuel (X) to Priscilla Meadows Feb. 24, 1839 by J.P. Bingham
    Bondsman: Edwin J. H. Reese

Lester, Silas S. to Frances J. Wood (bond)
    Bondsman: Johnson X Wood

Lester, Whitehead to Rebecca Thweatt June 3, 1827 by Ware Henley, J.P.
    Bondsman: Samuel Blake

Lester, William P. to Rebecca Pinkston Dec. 11, 1832 by M. L. Andrews, M.G.
    Bondsman: William Andrews

Lester, William P. to Nancy H. Watson Oct. 28, 1847 by W. Burns, M.G.
    Bondsman: David Pinkston, Jr.

Lewallen, Aron to Sarah Young Jan. 14, 1819 by G. Hunt, J.P.
    Bondsman: John Sherin

Lewis, Benjamin (X) to Betsey Roberts Nov. 11, 1823 (bond)
    Bondsman: Benjamin Roberts

Lewis, Elam to Elizabeth Wood Jan. 12, 1832 by T. D. Porter
    Bondsman: Joshua M. Kelly

Lewis, Elam to Mary E. Glenn Nov. 28, 1843 by H. B. Hyde, J.P.
    Bondsman: Johnson Wood

Lewis, Gravitt T. or L. to Polly Fuqua (bond)
    Bondsman: Doctor F. Fuqua

Lewis, Richard to Ann Roberts Sept. 30, 1835 by T.D. Porter
    Bondsman: Robert Grummer?

Lewis, Richard C. (X) to Elizabeth Palmon (Palmore?) Oct. 20, 1841 (bond)
    Bondsman: Benjamin F. Lewis

Liggett, John to Mary H. Wade Oct. 18, 1841 by J. B. Boyd, J.P.
    Bondsman: William M. Smith

Liggett, Wade H. to Jane Secrest Jan. 29, 1829 by Joel Anderson, M.G.
    Bondsman: John Secrest

Lightfoot, Tapley M. (X) to Elizabeth Aldridge Nov. 20, 1843 by S.S.R.A.
    Bondsman: Smith Sampson (groom aged 85, bride aged 18) Knott, JP

Lillard, Moses to Eliza Ann Featherstone Feb. 11, 1829 by D.C. Kinnard, J.P.
    Bondsman: Samuel Neal

Lillard, Thomas J. to Nancy Irvin Mar. 24, 1831 by Wm. Allison, J.P.
    Bondsman: Abram F. Lillard

Linam, John W. to Sarah A. Potts Aug. 29, 1850 by W.B. Carpenter
    Bondsman: William Cartwright

Lindsay, Elemore to Margaret A. Wilson July 16, 1837 by J.B.W. (illeg.) J.P.
    Bondsman: none given

Lindsey, John (X) to Milley Coore Feb. 17, 1819 (bond)
    Bondsman: William Coore

Lindsey, William to Mary Wilson Oct. 22, 1810 (bond)
    Bondsman: Robert Kennedy

Linton, Samuel to Nancy Burnham Sept. 2, 1817 (bond)
    Bondsman: Frederick Ivy

Lister (Lester?), Henry to Sarah Ann Sample Nov. 12, 1845 (bond)
    Bondsman: John Lister

Lite, Charles T. to Mary E. Wood Nov. 28, 1848 by H. B. North, M.G.
    Bondsman: R. E. Thompson

Little, Alfred S. to Martha Pope Dec. 30, 1834 by E.G. Porter
    Bondsman: Sanford H. Little

Little, Charles (X) to Saphronia Butter June 8, 1843 by Jas. F. McMahan, J.P.
    Bondsman: Simeon Venable

Little, David G. to Mary Webb July 12, 1835 by J. Landrum
    Bondsman: Alfred L. Little

Little, George (X) to Elizabeth Anderson Dec. 14, 1815 by W.R. Nunn
    Bondsman: John Clinton

Little, Isaac N. (X) to Elizabeth White Oct. 31, 1833 by Wm. Moor, J.P.
    Bondsman: Wm. W. Robb

Little, James (X) to Nancy Locke   July 2, 1843 by J.F. McMahan, J.P.
    Bondsman: Thomas X Gatlin

Little, James H. to Mary Stanley   Nov. 1, 1836 by J.S. Bartlett, J.P.
    Bondsman: Nelson Grimes

Little, John M. (X) to Mary Knight   Dec. 31, 1834 by Robert Davis, M.G.
    Bondsman: Gassaway Peach

Little, Joseph to Missouri Pope   Feb. 2, 1829 (bond)
    Bondsman: David Jackson

Little, Martin S. to Mary Dobson   Sept. 13, 1829 by Wright Stanley, J.P.
    Bondsman: Wm. W. Robb

Little, Sanford H. (D?) to Adaline Birdwell   May 7, 1834 by James M. Carson,
    Bondsman: James C. Taylor   JP

Little, Stephen to Ellender Bailey   June 30, 1808 (bond)
    Bondsman: Wm. Bailey

Little, Thomas W. to Mary Ann King   Nov. 21, 1846 (bond)
    Bondsman: T. S. Gatlin

Littleton, Joseph S. to Susan McDaniel   Nov. 30, 1837 by Robert Davis, M.G.
    Bondsman: none given

Littleton, Reuben to Hannah Willett   Dec. 21, 1815 (bond)
    Bondsman: David W. Gee

Littleton, William (X) to McCandles Ridge   Mar. 5, 1817 (bond)
    Bondsman: Nathan'l X Huggins

Littleton, William (X) to Polly Whitby   Aug. 22, 1832 by Wm. Moor, J.P.
    Bondsman: John H. Bulloch

Littleton, William (X) to Martha Larimore   April 8, 1838 by Wm. Moor, J.P.
    Bondsman: Henry X Truett

Littleton, William (X) to Rebecca Murphy   Jan. 11, 1842 by Joseph Carle
    Bondsman: Thos. Kidd

Litton, Elihu (X) to Mary A. Davis   Feb. 6, 1849 by W.F.A. Shaw, J.P.
    Bondsman: Eliphas R. Davis

Litton, Henry (X) to Nancy Davis   Mar. 14, 1840 by Thos. Prowell, J.P.
    Bondsman: Eliphas R. Davis

Litton, James M. to Sarah Jane Davis   Dec. 30, 1847 by Thos. Prowell, J.P.
    Bondsman: William X Davis

Litton, Thomas to Anna Davis   Mar. 16, 1836 by Thos. Prowell, J.P.
    Bondsman: Henry William X Davis

Livesey, Carter to Betsey Wright   Oct. 13, 1810 (bond)
    Bondsman: Jacob Simmons

Lock, Walter to Sally Bell March 19, 1805 (bond)
    Bondsman: Abe May

Lock, William to Patsey Carothers Oct. 10, 1805 (bond)
    Bondsman: Alexander Smith

Locke, Green W. to Sarah Ann Jones Dec. 26, 1844 by J.J. Bingham, J.P.
    Bondsman: William W. Brookes

Locke, Knacy H. to Susan R. Andrews Oct. 24, 1843 by M.L. Andrews, M.G.
    Bondsman: none given (license only)

Locke, Richard Stith to Elizabeth Andrews Dec. 21, 1805 (bond)
    Bondsman: Kinacy Andrews

Locke, Thomas (X) to Martha M. Blackburn Aug. 22, 1844 by S.S.P.A. Knott, JP
    Bondsman: Rice J. Hughes

Locke, William to Rhoda Boyd Jones July 3, 1850 by John P. McKay, J.P.
    Bondsman: Jesse D. Brown

Lockett, Joel (X) to Paraller Bonds Feb. 10, 1843 by W.B. Carpenter
    Bondsman: John P. McKay

Lockett, Uriah to Harriott Gray July 11, 1816 by Berry Vaden
    Bondsman: John Gray

Lockridge, Cannon H. to Elizabeth H. Durdon Jan. 9, 1847 by M.B. Molloy, MG
    Bondsman: Elbert J. Nichols

Lockridge, Robert P. to Virginia King Sept. 2, 1844 (bond)
    Bondsman: Thomas S. Crawford

Lockridge, William to Rebecca Herron Feb. 29, 1824 by D. Brown, V.D.M.
    Bondsman: Thomas M. Lockridge

Lockridge, William J. to Margaret E. Horton (bond)
    Bondsman: James W. Crawford

Loftin, Harbert C. to Mary Ann Barker Sept. 30, 1836 by James King
    Bondsman: Addison H. Walker

Loftin, Herbert C. to Martha Jane Barker Dec. 16, 1847 by H.B. North, M.G.
    Bondsman: Wm. B. Patton

Loftin, John (X) to Nancy Thomas Jan. 11, 1825 by R. McCutchen, J.P.
    Bondsman: Lewis Hardgrove

Loftin, Joseph J.B. to Lucinda R. Raney Nov. 1, 1843 by H.B. Hyde, J.P.
    Bondsman: Nathan A. Boyd

Logan, Coatsworth P. to Susan R. Horton Dec. 27, 1846 by Robert L. Andrews
    Bondsman: L. C. Beale (Livingston Beale)

Long, George to Mary R. Primm Jan. 18, 1844 by R.G. Irvine, M.G.
    Bondsman: James N. Neelly

Long, George W. to Elizabeth Cocey March 14, 1822 by Thos. L. Douglass
    Bondsman: James R. Davis

Long, Henry (X) to Elizabeth Turner Dec. 27, 1833
    Bondsman: Freeman Johnston (no mar. date or by whom performed)

Long, Isaac to Susannah Tooms March 16, 1809 (bond)
    Bondsman: Benjamin Tarkington

Long, James to Jane F. Hughs Dec. 26, 1825 by Joel Anderson
    Bondsman: Wm. Allison

Long, James to Caroline M. Early May 31, 1838 by H.H. North, M.G.
    Bondsman: Thomas X Chambers

Long, John to Elizabeth Little June 5, 1825 by H. B. Hyde, J.P.
    Bondsman: Edward Anderson

Long, Josiah to Letitia Cromer Sept. 14, 1848 by W.F. Erwin, M.G.
    Bondsman: John W. Parks

Long, Nicholas to Judith R. Dudley May 23, 1822 by John N. Blackburn, M.G.
    Bondsman: Ferdinand Stith

Long, Richard T. to Sinia Gentry Jan. 25, 1821 by W. R. Nunn
    Bondsman: David Humphreys

Long, William (X) to Emeline Burnett Apr. 13, 1844 by Stokley A. Davis, J.P.
    Bondsman: James X Canada

Long, William C. to Polly P. Tinsley April 30, 1812 (bond)
    Bondsman: James W. Gray

Long, William L. to Polly P. Findley April 30, 1812 (bond)
    Bondsman: Sam Crockett (note similarity with above)

Love, John to Agnes Hays May 25, 1805 (bond)
    Bondsman: Wm. Hays

Love, John G. to Rebecca Axem July 18, 1811 (bond)
    Bondsman: Joseph Love

Love, Joseph to Frances Douglass Feb. 15, 1848 by Rufus Ledbetter
    Bondsman: John Marshall

Love, Samuel to Nancy Axum March 4, 1812 (bond)
    Bondsman: David B. Love

Lovell, Markham to Polly Polk April 15, 1836 (bond)
    Bondsman: Beverly Ridley

Lovell, Thomas to Nancy Gentry Aug. 19, 1815 (bond)
    Bondsman: Thos. Gentry

Lovell, William to Peggy Stephenson Jan. 7, 1812 (bond)
    Bondsman: Samuel Patton

Lovell, William D. to Leah P. P. Scales May 20, 1821 by Peyton Smith, M.G.
    Bondsman: Thos. Hardeman, Jr.

Lovet, Moses (X) to Margaret Featherston Oct. 7, 1834 by A.A. Wilson, J.P.
    Bondsman: Jesse N. White

Lovett, Joseph to Martha Devore Dec. 19, 1831 by J. Norman, J.P.
    Bondsman: Jesse N. White

Lovett, David to Fanny Saunders Sept. 22, 1806 (bond)
    Bondsman: Elijah Saunders and Luke Pryor

Low, Gabriel R. to Vinia (Viney) H. Yarbrough March 21, 1839 by Mark L. Andrews, MG
    Bondsman: Blount Jordan

Low, James to Eleanor Alexander April 18, 1822 by Jonathan Norman
    Bondsman: Garrett X Simmons

Low, James to Martha Wills April 14, 1836 by Nelson P. Modrall, M.G.
    Bondsman: Joseph R. Sutton

Loyd, Lewis to Parmelia Talley Dec. 13, 1811 (bond)
    Bondsman: Philip Loyd

Ludbury, William D. to Sally Criddle July 3, 1820 (bond)
    Bondsman: William Johnson

Luna, Jackson to Nancy Andrews Aug. 2, 1832 by M.L. Andrews, M.G.
    Bondsman: James Brooks (groom made mark)

Lunn, Alfred to Nancy Bullock Oct. 31, 1827 by H. Bailey, J.P.
    Bondsman: Amos Dobson

Lunn, Eli to Eliza Glascock Feb. 20, 1828 by John Witherspoon
    Bondsman: Alfred Lunn

Lunn, Felix G. to Ruth Radford Feb. 22, 1841 (bond)
    Bondsman: James Walker

Lunn, John to Eleanor Graham June 24, 1819 by Henry Petty, M.G.
    Bondsman: W.W. Hill

Lunn, William to Ester Graham Jan. 9, 1826 (bond)
    Bondsman: none given

Lutey, James (X) to Rebecca Anderson April 9, 1822 by Eleazar Hardeman
    Bondsman: Edward Anderson

Luther, John (X) to Laura Anderson August 27, 1838 (bond)
    Bondsman: David X Brown

Luty, David to Margaret Woodson Feb. 2, 1819 by Eleazar Hardeman
    Bondsman: John Layne

Lyon, Charles P. to Mary Ann Jones Dec. 18, 1833 (bond)
    Bondsman: John Evans, Jr.

Lyon, Stephen H. to Matilda Crockett   Jan. 25, 1830 by T.D. Porter
    Bondsman: Peter Perkins

Lytle, Archibald to Elizabeth C. Cole   June 27, 1822 by Geo. Blackburn,V.D.M.
    Bondsman: H. R. W. Hill

Lytle, John C. to Sarah E. Graham   Aug. 29, 1837 by A.T. Scruggs, M.G.
    Bondsman: none given

Lytle, William F. to Mary T. Logan   June 10, 1835 by William Eagleton, V.D.M.
    Bondsman: Jas. J. Guy

****

    This is such a large task it is necessary for two type-writers to be busy, and of course errors will creep in, for it is very difficult to read the old faded script on many of the bonds and licenses, and equally hard to keep typing errors from creeping in, but we are trying to have it as nearly correct as possible for you.

****

The following marriages have been found after the pages on which they should have appeared were printed, hence they are added here and will appear in the index.

Adams, Elijah to Lucy Ann Elliott   Mar. 22, 1834 by
    J. Richardson, JP.   William Ditto, Bondsman

Cox, Samuel to Elizabeth Hopkins   Feb. 27, 1827
    Bondsman: Joshua W. McCown (Bond alone filed)

Watkins, David (X) to Rhoda Galysan   Nov. 1, 1827 by
    Wright Stanley, JP.   Josiah (X) Galyean, Bondsman

Wiles, Joel B. to Rebecca Bryan   Feb. 26, 1829 by
    C. McDaniel, JP   Thomas K. Cotton, Bondsman

Wilkerson, Johnson B. to Sarah Ann E. Beach   May 6, 1841 by
    M. L. Andrews, M.G.   Thomas C. Carsey, Bondsman

Wilkerson, Joshua F. (X) to Letitia Johnson   June 2, 1847 by
    John Nichols, JP.   Harvey (X) Cartright, Bondsman

Wilkes, Daniel to Jane Montgomery   Nov. 6, 1827 by
    Thos. L. Douglass   Francis (X) Rice, Bondsman

Wilkes, Joshua T. to Sarah F. Pewitt   Dec. 23, 1849 by
    W. Burns, Minister   Allen G. Nevills, Bondsman

"M"

Mayberry, John (X) to Mary Younger Jan 25, 1817 bond
    Bd: Thos. Younger   Test: Ennis Murrey

Mayberry, John C.(X) to Minerva Eliza Ann Thompson Aug.26,
    1830 by Thos. Prowell JP BD: Peter Thompson

Mabrey, Ezekiel to Frances Chambers Mar 4, 1834 by Jas.
    Carothers JP BD: Frederick Mabry

Mabry, Job to Nancy Thweatt 24 Dec 1818 (bond)
    Bds: Henry Kinzer Wit: Thos. Hardeman Jr.

Mabry, Philip (X) to Mary Ann J. Wren Nov. 19, 1833
    Bd: Thorton Westbrook By Tilbert Marshall JP

Macham, Nathan to Ellen Akin Dec 21, 1837 W.H.Meadow JP

Maclin, Henry to Mary Ann Farmer Dec 19, 1838 John McCurdy
    BD: James Hogan Jr. Signed Henry W. Maclin.

Maclin, Isaac E. to Eliza P. Farmer Dec 22, 1836 by
    John McCurdy, MG BD: John M. Currin

Maclin, William T. to Ann M. M. Brooks Dec. 13, 1837

Madden, Alderson to Mahala Bugg July 29, 1835 BD: J.B.Porter

Maddocks, George to Elizabeth Potts Feb. 22, 1816
    Bd: James Potts (X) - signed George (X) Maddocks

Madison, Presley (X) to Polly Mairs June 20, 1824 by J.
    Farrington Bd: James Gary

MaGee, Elijah (X) to Polly Shepherd Dec 22, 1827 bond
    Bd: Lewis Magee Wit: Will Hardeman

Magness, Josiah to Parlee (?) Williams Dec 6, 1827 by
    John Witherspoon Bd: Josiah Magness -Wm.D. Hutton

Magness, Zacheriah (X) to Frances Ragsdale Jan 3, 1828
    By M. L. Andrews JP BD: Martin Little

Mairs, Isaac to Hannah Blackshore May 3, 1806 Bd:Geo.Gramler

Mairs, Josiah to Druscilla Christmas Feb. 9,1805 BD:Geo.Patton

Maiton, William (Wm.) to Sally Hutson Sept 18, 1828 by
    Hartwell B. Hyde JP BD: Obediah G. Stegall

Mallard, Joseph W. to Sarah Ransom Sept 27,1831 by
    J. Norman JP BD: Lemuel Ransom

Mallory, John to Sally Crockett   Apr 18, 1812
    Bds: Andrew Crockett   Wit. Wm. P. Harrison

Mallory, John Jr. to Catharine B. Caldwell   Sept 17, 1846
    By Robert A. Lapsley   Bd: John B. Crockett

Mallory, Thomas G. to Margaret S. McLemore   Sept. 14, 1824 b
    Bd: Sion Hunt

Mallory, William H. to Theodosia Graves   June 3, 1846 by
    L. C. Bryan, MG   Bd: H. C. Lockett

Malone, Jordan to Letitia C. Andrews   Feb. 1, 1838 by
    M. L. Andrews MG   Bd: Benjamin C. Helm

Malone, William to Martha Ann Ray   Jan 14, 1826 (Bond)

Malugin, Thomas (signed Mallagin) to Joanna Wilkins   Mar 19,
    1824 W. Smith, JP BD: R. Charten & Elisha L. Hall

Mangham, Plummer A. to Elizabeth Jackson   June 30, 1844 by
    Monroe Short, JP   BD Thos. A. Graham

Mangrum, Allen to Winnefred Pope   Apr 19, 1835 BD:Sam.Allen

Mangrum, James (aged 70) to Nancy Hughes (aged 60) Mar. 6,
    1841 by J. W. Robinson   Bd: John A. (X) Barnes

Mangrum, James M. (X) to Sarah A. Elliott   Dec. 30, 1841, bond
    Bd: H. Henry Mangrum (X)

Mangrum, Plumer to Susan Walton   Dec. 29, 1827, bond
    Bd: Samuel Houston

Mangrum, Silas (X) to Mary E. Whitby   Dec. 23, 1847 by
    Wm. G. Carter, J. P.   Bd: Lewis Whitby (X)

Mangrum, William (X) to Catharine Halfacre   Dec. 27, 1849 by
    Gilbert Marshall, J. P.   Bd: Jacob Halfacre Jr.

Manier, Lemuel to Susannah Jackson   Sept. 25, 1814
    Bd: Cooper Bennett   Clk & Wit: N. P. Hardeman

Manier, George W. (X) to Harriette Wisenor   Dec. 3, 1828 by
    Jabez Owen J.P.   Bd: William Holmes

Manire, John A. to Frances J. Lee   July 14, 1847 bond   Bd:
    John L. Webb

Manire, John W. to Mary Hendrix   Jan. 8, 1846 by E. W. Hendrix, M. G.   Bd: John T. Webb

Manire, Stephen to Mary M. Patterson March 11, 1846 by
    John King, M. G.   Bd: John H. Floyd

Mankin, John (X) to Agnes Owen May 8, 1832 by Wm. Little,
    J.P. Bd: George R. Mulherrin

Mankins, William to Martha Dunn Apr. 28, 1834 by John
    Richardson, J.P.   Bd: Abner Salmons (X)

Manly, Edward to Eunice Bateman Apr. 26, 1846 by W. B. Carpenter Bd: Henry B. Reams

Maney, Lewis M. to R Adeline Cannon Dec. 3, 1846 by E. D.
    Elliott, M. G.   Bd: Lewis M. Maney by L. B. McConnico
    Wm. H. Maney. Letter attached to Bond quoted:
    "I hereby empower and authorise the Clerk of the County Court or his deputy to sign my name to all or any bond or bonds required by the Laws of Tennessee to be by me executed for the obtainment of license to any minister of the Gospel, Judge or Justice of the Peace in and for the State of Tennessee or to any other person qualified by law to solemnise the rites of matrimony between me and R. Adeline Cannon of Williamson County. Given under my hand and seal this 20th day of November 1846. Seal   Lewis M. Maney

Mann, David B. to Sarah Riely (?) June 23, 1828 Married at
    7:30 in the evening by G. Hunt   Bd: Miles White

Manning, Mark to Nancy Sharber Sept. 6, 1832 by Lemuel
    Manire, J. P.   Bd: Rezin Lazenby

Manning, Smith to Frances Lazenberry Jan. 18, 1832 Bond
    Bd: Richard Berry

Manning, William (X) to Betsey Wade Jan. 29, 1820 by
    H. Adams, J. P.   Bd: John Manning

Manning, William to Nancy Bass Dec. 14, 1820 by Tristram
    Patton, J.P.   Bd: Thomas T. Harper

Manning, William to Nancy Bass Dec. 5, 1820 by Robert Davis,
    E.M.C. (must be same as above)

Mansker, George W. (X) to Susannah Lowry May 10, 1834 Bd:
    John W. Miller

Mansker, Lewis W. to Betsey Simpkins Sept. 31, 1811 by Nick
    Scales, J. P. Bd: George Mansker

Mansker, Wm. to Luvicy Briley Sept. 7, 1808 (Bond) Bd:
    George Parsons, Jno. Garner

Marbury, Leonard W. to Mary Kidd Feb. 4, 1823 Bd: James Kidd

Marine, Thomas I. (X) to Ann Ray Oct. 15, 1836 by G. W. Hunt
    Bd: Wm. G. Moody

Marlin, Edward to Sally Smith Aug. 1, 1815 (Bond) Bd:
    John Hilliard

Marlin, George to Amy Morris March 1, 1810 Bd: Francis Gunter

Marlin, Henry to Nancy Doyle Apr. 14, 1821 by Levin Edney,
    Min. Gospel of Christ Bd: Thomas Cooper

Marlin, James to Jenny Ross Dec. 24, 1807 Bd: Francis Gunter

Marlin, James to Betsey Pinkerton Feb. 21, 1812 Bd: Wm. Alden

Marlin, Robert (X) to Susannah Jones Sept. 19, 1832 Bd:
    William Baxter

Marling, James to Elizabeth S. Peay Sept. 8, 1836 by J.
    Burnett, J. P. Bd: Reuben White

Marling, Samuel C. to Sarah Allen May 29, 1848 by W. Lafay-
    ette McConnico, D. C. Bd: George H. Wheeler

Marr, William M. to Nancy G. Perkins Dec. 17, 1807 Bd:
    Peter Hardeman

Marshall, Gilbert to Louisa W. Nash Feb. 15, 1832 by Andrew
    Craig, M. G. Bd: James Marshall

Marshall, Humphrey Jr. to Frances E. McAlister Jan. 23, 1833
    Solemnized on the evening of Jan. 23, 1833 by Jas. H.
    Otey, Min. Prot. Ep. Ch. Bd. John Marshall

Marshall, James to Nancy S. Simmons Dec. 16, 1828 by Andrew
    Craig, M.G. Bd: Frederick Halfacre

Marshall, John to Margaret P. Campbell May 16, 1833, Thursday
    evening, by Jas. H. Otey, Rector St. Paul's Ep. Ch.
    Franklin. Bd: Joseph I. Pugh

Marshall, John to Frances Crockett Nov. 20, 1845 (Bond)
    Bd: Will S. Campbell

Marshall, Robert A. to Sarah Jane Brown June 3, 1847 (Bond)
    Bd: R. P. Moss (Robert)

Marshall, Thomas W. to Mary Ann Pinkard May 17, 1843 by M. L.
    Andrews, M. G. Bd: John Clemm

Marshall, William A. to Eliza McEwen Sept. 8, 1836 by Matt
    Marshall. Bd: Robert A. Marshall

Marshall, William S. to Mary R. Mitchell Feb. 26, 1829 by
    D. C. Kennard, J. P. Bd: Isaac N. Mayfield

Marshall, William S. to Mary Gillespie Aug. 26, 1841 by
    J. R. Cearcy, J. P. Bd: Christppher M. Brooks

Marshall, William W. (X) to Sally Holloway Jan. 3, 1826 by
    Geo. Shannon, J. P. Bd: M. L. Warren

Martin, Alexander to Elizabeth Cain Nov. 4, 1819 by J. Farrington   Bd: Jacob Critz

Martin, Benjamin F. to Jane D. Alston July 13, 1840 (Bond)
    Bd: James W. Peebles

Martin, Daniel G. (X) to Elizabeth Ann Crick Jan. 17, 1848
    by Lycurgus McCall, J.P. Bd: James Martin

Martin, George to Tabitha Deshazo May 7, 1825 Bd: Jas.
    Deshazo

Martin, Iverson B. to Sarah Ann Roberts Nov. 1, 1847 (Bond)
    Bd: John H. Garrett

Martin, James I. (X) to Dicey Jane Ragsdale June 20, 1839 by
    E. P. White Bd: Redmond J. Edwards

Martin, James T. to Hannah Jane Criswell Mar. 3, 1836 by
    L. McCall, J. P. Bd: Wm. L. White

Martin, Jefferson to Esther Stewart Jan. 8, 1829 by Robt.
    Henderson Bd.: Thos. Stuart (as signed)

Martin, John D. to Osee Tiffang July 1, 1821 by P. Russell
    Bd: Wiley Estes

Martin, John W. to Margaret J. Childress Dec. 24, 1839 by
    Robert A. Lapsley

Martindale, Miles (X) to Nancy Hill Jan. 7, 1815 Bd:
    William Tunney (X)

Martin, Samuel N. to Polly Allison Dec. 27, 1815 Bd: Harry Hill

Martin, Samuel F. to Caledonia Tindale Aug. 8, 1850 by John
    L. Hill, M. G. Bd: Joel Champion

Martin, Thomas to Elizabeth J. Scruggs Mar. 30, 1812 Bd:
    Anderson Berryman

Martin, Thomas E. to Mary C. Wray Oct. 15, 1844 by Chesley
    Williams Bd: James T. Byler

Martin, Tignal to Franky Welch Aug. 1, 1814 Bd: Geo. Gentry

Martin, Tignell (X) to Emily Tanksley July 18, 1821 by Edward Ragsdale, J. P. Bd: Henry Martin

Martin, William (X) to Frances A. Belcher Sept. 25, 1850 by John F. Cox, J.P. Bd: McDonald Rodgers (X)

Martin, William C. to Eliza H. Davis Aug. 7, 1839 by C. T. Owen Bd: William Floyd

Martin, Zadock to Minerva T. Nalls Dec. 28, 1850 by J. Hendricks, J.P. Bd: Thomas G. N. McCord (X)

Mason, Allen J. to Lucy Ann Still Feb. 16, 1847 by N. L. Norvill Bd: John H. Carmichael

Mason (signed Mayson), Elijah to Hannah Johnston Dec. 17, 1828 by C. McDaniel, J.P. Bd: David Watkins (X)

Mason, Henry P. to Mary D. Stevens Sept. 29, 1833 by Wilford H. Rains, J.P. Bd: Andrew Halfacre

Mason, Isaak to Sarah Hale Sept. 26, 1817 Bd: Thos. Prithett

Mason, Jacob to Patsey Curry (?) July 12, 1805 Bd: Isaac Mason

Mason, Joseph to Edith McClure June 29, 1812 Bd: Isaac Mason

Matthews, Berryman S. to Angeline Allen Dec. 8, 1846 by John C. Wiley, J.P. Bd: Mark L. Andrews

Matthews, Edward W. to Mary M. Alston (?) Aug. 2, 1824 (Must be an error; see below).

Matthews, Edward W. to Mary R. Ralston Aug. 6, 1824 Bd: Thos. Hardeman

Matthews, Isaac to Susan Parker Jan. 10, 1821 Bd: Ree Joyce

Matthews, Isham S. to Elizabeth J. Parks Aug. 16, 1849 by M. W. Gray, M. G. Bd: Thomas Boyd

Matthews, James S. to Mary M. Chiles Apr. 20, 1824 Bd: Jacob Morton

Matthews, James T. to Nancy A. J. Revis Dec. 8, 1850 by J. M. Macpherson Bd: Wm. H. Hamilton

Matthews, Richard M. (X) to Emeline Ragan Dec. 24, 1848 by Ely Dodson, J. P. Bd: Henry C. Smithson

Matthews, Samuel to Martha L. Ralston   June 17, 1830 by H. L. Norvell, M. G.   Bd: Williamson Smith

Matthews, Thomas to Susan S. Gatlin   Nov. 4, 1824 Bd:Geo. Andrews

Matthews, Thomas F. to Louisa V. Reams   Sept. 27, 1849   Bd: John D. Roper

Matthews, William to Catharine Morris   Oct. 15, 1826 by Jas. Scott, M. G.

Matthews, William I. (X) to Mary Ann Gates July 20, 1836 by T. D. Porter   Bd: Fielding Seavers

Matthews, William L. to Betsy Shumate   Dec. 9, 1817   Bd: William J. Shumate

Maugham, Joseph (X) to Mary White   Dec. 21, 1836 Bd:Thos.R. Sears

Maugham, William H.(X) to Charity Walker   June 17, 1840 by R. W. Robinson   Bd: Benjamin W. Layne

Maupin, Jesse G. to Elizabeth Taylor   Jan. 6, 1826

Maury, James H. to Lucinda Smith   May 29, 1822 Bd: N.P. Perkins

Maury, Richard L. to Margaret A. Bond Jan. 8, 1828 by John M. Holland   Bd: Sunford White

Maury, Zebulon M. P. to Virginia L. Ashlin   Feb. 27, 1845 by M. L. Andrews, M. G.   Bd: James P. Harvey

Mavine (Marine),George W (X) to Sarah Bazwell Oct 25, 1832 by Jabez Owen JP - BD: John P. (X) Cunningham

Maxcy, Stephen (X) to Nancy Stephenson   June 16, 1820   Bd: William Maxey   Wit: Thos. Hardeman

Maxwell, Albert M. to Sarah C. Winsitt   Jan 23, 1843 bond   Bd: William (X) Gesit

Maxwell, James B. to Nancy Palmer   Jan 29, 1846 Bd.Bird.Palmer

Maxwell, Jesse and Elizabeth Carson May 4, 1826 by M.T.Span JP

Maxwell, Jesse to Myra Rucker Mar. 4, 1847   Bd: Jesee H. Philips

May, David to Mary Ann Gardiner   June 26, 1833 by. S. S. Harkness JP   Bd: Andrew D. Blackburn

May, Frederick to Sicily Williams   Oct. 22   Bd: R.L. Saunders

May, Frederick to Eunice Cochran   Dec. 22, 1840 Bd: Nathan W. Cochran

May, John A. (X) to Mary Jane Warren   Oct. 26, 1849   by G. W. Rolland J.P. Bd: Oscar Reams

Mayberry, Amoricus C. to Elizabeth M. Dodson   Feb. 25, 1847   Bd: Ferdinand B. Russell (Bond only)

Mayberry, David to Susan L. Joice   May 13, 1847 by Nathan Lyon, Minst. Bd: James Hughes

Mayberry, George W. to Lucy Orton   Dec. 4, 1827 Bd: Page Bond

Mayberry, Henry G. to Adelicia Swanson   May 4, 1843 by Henry B. North, M.G. Bd: J. A. (John) Wilkins

Mayberry, Henry G. W. to Sophronia Hunter   Jan. 11, 1849 by M. L. Andrews, M.G. Bd: John H. Morton

Mayfield, Ambrose to Nancy Brooks   Dec. 24, 1822 by George Tilman, J.P. Bd: Cyres Montgomery

Mayfield, Elijah to Amelia Gillaspie Dec. 15, 1816 Bd: Sam'l Brooks

Mayfield, Elias to Jenny Fleming Sept. 7, 1811 Bd: James Boyd

Mayfield, Isaac Newton to Louisa Spencer Feb. 8, 1832 by Wm. Allison, J.P. Bd: Wm. C. Nunn

Mayfield, James to Sally Nunn   Feb. 1, 1808   Bd: Geo. Gentry

Mayfield, James to Polly Gooch Mar. 24, 1831 Bd: Henry Wyme

Mayfield, John to Nancy Carle Oct. 11, 1821   Bd: Thos. T. Harper

Mayfield, Robert C. to Eliza A. Dickson   Nov. 7, 1844 by W. B. Carpenter Bd: Donald Cameron

Mayfield, Sutherland to Sally Parks Feb. 2, 1813 Bd: Reuben Parks Wit: Wm. P. Harrison

Maryfeld (or Merryfield) Thomas to Mirah Leahorn Aug. 23, 1806 Bd: Jonas Hunter Wit: R. P. Currin

Mayfield, Thomas S. to Lucy Ann Reams Nov. 18, 1834 Bd: Thos. W. Sconce

Mayfield, Thomas S. to Martha Still   Mar. 12, 1840 by W. B. Carpenter   Bd: Mastin Clay

Mayhew, Carroll C. to Pauline C. Comer   Nov. 13, 1848   Bd: William J. Walker   (Bond alone)

Mays, Gardner to Polly Lemons   May 23, 1827   Bd:Reuben Mays

Mays, Geo. G. to Savenia Davis   Aug. 12, 1833   Bd:Newsom Barham

Mays, Reuben to Rebecca Dancy   Jan. 21, 1828   Bd: Chas. Lemon

Meacheam, Elisha to Elizabeth Jones   Aug. 31, 1843 by J. J. Bingham, J.P.   Bd: Charles O. Jones

Meacham, Green to Elizabeth Bingham   May 30, 1850 by Jas. King   Bd: James Meacham

Meecham (signed Meacheam) James to Rosanna Cowen   Mar. 11, 1830 by Joseph Carl   Bd: Jonathan Carl

Meacham, Matthew to Mary Ann Cowan   Dec. 14, 1837

Meadon, Joseph R. to Rebecca Parham   July 30, 1835 by Rev. Jas. W. Rea, M.G.   Bd: Wm. H. Meadon, Jones R. Coleman

Meador, Wm. to Priscy Allen   Aug. 3, 1829   Bd: James Meachem

Meadow, Anderson (signed Andrew (X)) to Mary Williams   Apr. 30, 1821   Bd: Joseph Meadow

Meadows, Anderson (signed A.(X)) to Elizabeth Orr   Oct. 8, 1822   Bd: John Gracy

Meadows, James W. to Eliza W. Alexander   Jan. 6, 1827 by Geo. Shannon, J.P.   Bd: Ennis H. Duffee

Meadow, Jasper N. (signed Meador) to Mary Ann Foster   Apr. 7, 1836 by James W. Rea, M.G.   Bd: Joshua Young

Meadows, Samuel (X) to Mary F. Sadler, Sept. 27, 1843 by J. J. Bingham, J.P.   Bd: Francis W. Byers

Meadows, Spearman to Sarah Gunter   Mar. 28, 1822 by F.D.D.J. Stone, J.P.   Bd: F. B. Carter

Meadow, Wm. to Margaret Williams   Feb. 6, 1819   Bd:Jos. Meadow

Meadows, Wm. D. to Elizabeth A. Harris   Nov. 22, 1837 by Joseph Carle

Meairs(Mars) John to Nancy Germain   Oct. 30, 1807   Bd:Jos.Meairs

Mearcham, Wm. to Sally Hood   Aug. 16,1824   Bd: A. Clark

Mebane, Allen to Hannah Norwood Sept. 18,1839   Bd:Wm.W. Peace

Mebane, Geo. to Katharine Buford (no date) Bd:John Hodge

Mebane, Wm. to Micky Burton   Mar. 13,1823 by Joel Anderson,
    J.P.   Bd: Nathaniel H. Mebane

Medle (Wedle) George to Polly Primm July 24, 1819   Bd: Green
    H. Primm

Meek, John to Rachel Blackburn July 11, 1816 Bd:Lucas Kennedy

Metling, Ansel(X) to Tiersey Briant Feb. 7, 1824 Bd: John (X)
    Underwood   Wit: Elisha L. Hall

Melton, Balam (X) to Sarah Melton   Jan. 23,1838 Bd:Jas.(X)
    Melton

Meredith, Benjamin C. to Margaret Broadmore   Feb.16, 1842 by
    M. L. Andrews, M.G.   Bd: Americus B. Beech

Meredith, Francis D. to Frances Brodnax Feb. 7, 1840 by Jacob
    Critz   Bd: James M. Critz

Merrill, Charles A. to Louisiana Everly Oct. 9, 1838 by T.
    Fanning, M. G.   Bd: Wm. H. Crouch

Merritt, Bennett B. to Martha Johnston Mar. 27, 1834 by C. M.
    McDaniel, J.P.   Bd: James Johnson

Merritt, Benjamin to Elizabeth Barnett Jan. 16, 1813 Bd:
    Edward H. McNail

Merritt, James (X) to Sarah A. Crosen Sept. 22, 1847 Bd:
    Robert G. . Logsdon   (Bond alone filed)

Merritt, John A. to Ann Burton Aug. 19, 1830 Bd: Thos.A. Battle

Merritt, Washington to Louesa E. Owen July 24, 1838 Bd: Henry
    J. Walker

Mias, John to Judah Downey Jan. 16,1820   Bd.:Henry (X) Pate

Middleditch, Cyrus to Martha Hungarford June 13, 1815 Bd:
    Cutherth B. Hudson

Midget, Lancaster (X) to Harriett Ormes Oct. 21,1828 Bd:
    James P. Dillin

Midyett, Lewis to Mary W. Gee Dec. 19,1843 Bd:Lemuel Farmer

Milegen (or Meligan) Thomas to Sarah Dungan Sept. 18,1827 by Nichs. Scales Bd: Thomas Mason

Miles, John B. (Mills) to Mary J. Edmondson Dec.8, 1831 by Thos. D. Porter, M.G. Bd: Sam'l R. Sallee

Miles, Thomas to Peggy Smith Nov. 25, 1808 Bd: Jno. Wright

Miller, Charles F. To Elizabeth Wilburn June 21,1844 by A. P. Cunningham, M.G. Bd: Turner S. Foster

Miller, Henry to Polly Mansco Feb. 12, 1812 Bd:Wm. Mansco

Miller, Isaac to Nancy McMean May 9,1807 Bd: Wm. Miller

Miller, John T. to Sarah Haynes Nov.16,1841 Bd:Jas. Hogan Jr.

Miller, John W. to Christiana B. Miller July 17,1828 Bd: Thomas Woolridge

Milsted, Zealous to Elizabeth Blair Apr. 5,1806 Bd:Frederick Raidgen Wit: Peter Hardeman

Milton (X) James to Ann Lamb July 8,1840 Bd:William Lamb

Milton, John to Sarah Crick Jan.2, 1844 Bd:James P. Smith

Milton, Nathaniel(X) to Susannah Pewitt Dec.23,1828 Bd: Joseph (X) Pewitt

Milton, Tilford (X) to Winneford Milton June 24, 1846 by Hiram Putman Bd: Newton (X) Milton

Mincy, Richard R. to Louiza E. Red July 25, 1847 by Lycurgus McCall, J.P. Bd: Henry Johnson

Minnis, Wm. to Elizabeth Shook Oct. 14,1815 Bd: John Hilliard

Mitchell, David A. to Eliza Lindsey Dec. 10,1829 by Jabenz Owen, J.P. Bd: Samuel H. Ogilvie

Mitchell, David A. to Sarah J. Davis Apr. 3, 1848 by Wm. A. Whitsitt, Min. Bd: James H. Still

Mitchell, Hambling H. to Zerilda T. Graves July 14,1839 by Pettus Shelburne, J.P. Bd: Nathaniel Cranshaw

Mitchell, Robert W. to Margaret W. Wilson Dec. 20, 1827 by D. C. Kinnard, J.P. Bd: Zaucheus Wilson

Mitchell, Vachel to Naomy Armstrong Apr. 9, 1821 by Levin Edney, M.G. Bd: Right Koonce

Mize, Andrew (X) to Sarah Brandon June 7, 1834 Bd:Jesse N.White

Modin, Reuben to Nancy Deavenport Jan. 26,1826 by R. McCutchen

Modlin, Berry(X) to Mary Pomroy Sept. 24,1836 Bd:Reuben Overman

Modlin, James to Elizabeth Pomeroy Nov.4,1830 Bd:**Alfred** Moore

Modlin, Nathan to Polly Star Jan. 31,1826 by R. McCutchen,J.P.

Modlin, Samuel(X) to Lucy Harrison Mar.2,1845 Bd: John G. Ormes

Moffeit, Orson D.(signed Orran Moffet) to Elizabeth Wilkins June 25, 1823 Bd:Joseph Bennett Witn:Wilson McCown

Mondrelewski, Felix to Mary Thomas Edward Apr. 30,1846 by R. White, J.P. Bd: Benjamin (X) Morton

Montague, Albert to Mary Haynes Mar. 17,1830 Bd:Jos. H. Fry

Montague, Albert G. to Ann C. Smith May 31,1847 Bd:Jno.T.Miller

Montgomery, Alexander to Margaret Craig Jan. 16,1807 by Tristram Patton Bd: James Craig Test: A. Potter

Montgomery, Benjamin to Mary E. Ivy Jan.9,1839 Bd:Sam'l Thompson

Montgomery, Cyrus to Susan Walker Mar.5,1839 Bd:Isaac Folenbee

Montgomery, Eli to Martha Atkins Mar.11,1829 Bd: Dempsey Ragsdale (X)

Montgomery, Eli to Sally Pitts Aug. 9, 1832 Bd: Dempsey (X) Ragsdale

Montgomery, Eli to Gilly Hazelwood Dec. 12, 1842 Bd: Dempsey (X) Ragsdale

Montgomery, John to Joannah Demos Nov. 9,1815 Bd:Lewis Demos

Montgomery, John to Dicey Ragsdale Sept. 28, 1845 Bd: John (X) Taylor

Montgomery, John D. to Martha Clark (Bond) Mar.19, 1839 Bd: Benjamin Montgomery (signed B. Mentgumery)

Montgomery, Porter to Rhoda Ragsdale Oct. 28,1824 Bd: Jas. Edwards

Montgomery, Robert to Betsey Wilson Feb. 3, 1828 Bd:Jas. H. Logan

Montgomery, Thomas to Nancy McCabe Oct. 24, 1822 by Geo. Blackburn, VDM Bd: E. T. Clouston

Montgomery, Wm. to Malinda Craig Feb. 26,1820 Bd:Andrew Montgomery

Montgomery, Wm. to Sarah Brownlee Mar. 5,1831 Bd: Henry Wyme

Montgomery, William (X) to Betsey Ferguson Dec. 21,1833 by Tristram Patton, J.P. Bd: Calvin Shaw

Montgomery, Wm. to Margaret Fprehand Apr. 10,1839 Bd: Shadrack Cayce

Moody, John to Anne Johnston Dec. 10, 1807 Bd: Richard Orton

Moody, Wm. to Eliza Elizabeth Hill Jan.16,1828 Bd: Wm. Young

Moody, Wm. T. to Eliza Roy Mar. 14,1837 by J.A. Holland,J.P.

Moon, Green H. to Selina P. Butt Dec. 6,1838 Bd:Jas.E.Thompson

Moon, Isiah to Hester Ann Gant June 29,1842 Bd:E.D. Rushing

Moon, James to Mary Hiter Feb. 18,1845 Bd: George E. Trimble

Moon, Thomas to Peggy Hampton June 26,1806 Bd:John Fitzpatrick, James Hampton Test: John Hawkins

Moor, Isaiah A. (X) to Mary W. Atkinson July 5,1833 Bd: Albert G. Hill

Moor, Wm. to Lucy Cooper Dec. 20, 1819 Bd: Jno. G. Williamson

Moore, Abraham to Nancy Merritt Dec. 8,1824 Bd:Thos. J. Goff

Moore, Benjamin (X) to Edy Harris July 9,1818 Bd: Joshua Farrington

Moore, Carey H. to Mary Ashlin Feb. 1,1821 Bd: David A. Moore

Moore, David A. to Francis Ashlin Sept. 30,1822 Bd:Abram White

Moore, Elijah to Mildred Ruffin July 11, 1817 Bd:Joshua Cutchin

Moore, James to Ann Cahoon July 2,1807 Bd:George Cahoon

Moore, James to Margaret Cahoon Jan. 22, 1808 Bd:Geo. Cahoon

Moore, James to Nancy Hulme June 21,1819 Bd:Luther Brown

Moore, James A. to Jane W. Jordan Nov.16,1837 by Jesse Cox,MG

Moore, John to Nancy Rogers Feb. 3, 1806 Witn:N.P. Hardeman

Moore, John to Susan Craig Jan. 15, 1820 Bd:John C. Gillaspie

Moore, Joseph A. to Nancy D. Hawks(Bond Feb.10,1846 Bd: Samuel Ezell

Moore, Lewis to Charity Rosebum July 30,1824 Bd:Uzariah (X) Anderson

Moore, Macon (X) to Adeline Orman Mar. 14, 1844 Bd: John A. Wilkins

Moore, Richard G. to Mary Huggins Mar. 18, 1846 by Jno. Z. Wren, J.P. Bd: Allen W. Mangrum

Moore, Thos. to Mary T. Perkins Sept. 16,1823 Bd:Will Hardeman

Moore, Thos. J. to Elizabeth Campbell May 19,1836 by Jas. H. Otey Bp. of Prot. Ep. Church Bd:John W. Campbell

Moppin, Geo. W. to Mary Corzine Jan. 7,1847 by Wm. Y. Carter J.P. Bd: Middleton F. Warren

Moppin, James M. (X) to Milly Warren July 17, 1845 by C. M. Peyton, J.P. Bd: John (X) Warren

Moppen, Jesse (signed Maupin) to Sarah Newcorn Dec. 28, 1840 Bd: John B. Jamison

Moppin, John (X) to Elizabeth Bazdell Dec. 18,1834 by W. B. Capenter Bd: William (X) Warren

Moran, Charles to Lavinia Brown Dec. 24, 1816 Bd: Robert Martin

Moran, Thomas B.(X) to Susan Ann Ham June 30,1844 Bd:John M. Porter

Morgan, Edmund to Rachel Calvert Jan. 31, 1809 Bd:Sam'l Brown

Morgan, Harwood to Sarah W. Gremmer July 8,1830 by Peyton Smith Bd: Lemuel B. McConnico

Morgan, James (X) to Elizabeth Hughes Nov. 30,1821 by E. Hardeman Bd: John (X) Rosenbum

Morgan, James G. to Sarah Whitby Dec. 21,1848 Bd:S.S. Matthews

Morgan, Samuel S. to Martha Carson Apr.17,1839 Bd: Blount Jordan Witn: Chesley Williams

Morgan,Wm. (X) to Eliza Hogwood Oct.20,1831 Bd: Daniel Yates

Morgan, Wm. X to Martha Thornborough Nov. 13, 1839 by J. W. Crick, J.P. Bd: Samuel S. Morgan

Morgan, Wm. (X) to Nancy Hutson Oct. 10, 1842 Bd: Owen Briant

Morris, Allen to Milly Watkins Feb. 19, 1812 Bd: Pleasant Watkins

Morris, Archibald to Jane Christopher July 24, 1825 by Jas. Reid, J.P. Bd: Morton Wade

Morris, Benjamin W. to Martha J. Horton Nov. 11, 1835 by M. L. Andrews, M.G. Bd: Elliott R. Waddey

Morris, C.B. to Margaret L. Bond May 6, 1848 Bd: Jas. Waddey (Bond alone filed)

Morris, Geo. W. to Susan Cland June 20, 1838 Bd: Turner Smith

Morris, Jacob T. (X) to Ann L. Campbell Nov., 23, 1831 by Jas. W. Rea, M.G. Bd: Charles P. Lyon

Morris, James L. to Rhoda Williamson Feb. 12, 1823 Bd: H. L. Crutcher

Morris, James M. to Lydia Phagan Jan. 4, 1813 Bd: David Riggs

Morris, Jesse to Ann Eliza Morris Mar. 17, 1847 Bd: James H. Still

Morris, Joseph to Betsey Anderson Jan. 22, 1811 Bd: Sam'l McCall

Morris, Joseph (X) to Chloe Kennedy Nov. 27, 1821 by H. Adams, J.P. Bd: Woodruff (X) Clay

Morris, Joseph (X) to Mary Abigail Simmons Oct. 11, 1842 by Isaiah Dyer. Bd: Isaiah Dyer

Morris, Morgan (X) to Elizabeth Park Jan. 1, 1823 by M. L. Andrews, J.P. Bd: Edmund (X) Morris

Morris, Nathan E. to Elizabeth Davis July 5, 1847 by J. C. Anderson, M. G. Bd: Thos. N. Figures

Morris, William to Jane Frantham Dec. 7, 1824 Bd: Morris Frantham

Morris, Wm. (X) to Annis Kinsey Sept. 28, 1830 Bd: Daniel (X) Sullivan

Morrison, Robert D. to Nancy E. Morgan Aug. 2, 1841 by A.H. Nunn, J.P. Bd: Thos. L. Rives

Morrison, Robert W. to Elizabeth Montgomery Oct. 21, 1833 by J. Wall, J.P. Bd: Douglas Jones

Morrison, Zenus C. to Elizabeth Maxwell June 13, 1841 by A. H. Nunn, J.P. Bd: Addison H. Nunn

Morse, Parsons W. to Elizabeth Nichols May 9, 1832 by Joel Anderson, M. G. Bd: James Brown

Morse, Wm. H. to Sarah E. Giddens Dec. 28, 1833 Bd: John W. Early.

Morton, Abner to Penizer Lanier Apr. 1, 1813 Bd: Wm. Morton

Morton, Abraham B. to Leticia Cannon Dec. 23, 1812 Bd: Don F. Bostick

Morton, Jacob to Elizabeth D. Burge Dec. 16, 1811 Bd: Abner Morton

Morton, Jacob H. to Susan P. Mayberry Sept. 17, 1846 by James C. Anderson, M.G. (License only filed)

Morton, Jesse B. to Sarah A. Wood Feb. 21, 1843 by H. B. Hyde, J. P. Bd: Wilfred C. Coleman

Morton, John Sr. to Cynthia M. Broomfield Nov. 26, 1846 by S. S. P. Knott, J.P. Bd: Alex Craig

Morton, John W. to Sarah B. Goodwin June 14, 1838 by T. Fanning, M. G. Bd: Wm. R. McDougall

Morton, Samuel to Polly Pillows July 26, 1832 Bd: Peter J. Walker

Morton, Samuel to Sicily Gooch Apr. 20, 1837 by T. D. Porter

Morton, Samuel G. to Sarah E. Lillard (Bond) Apr. 24, 1844 Bd: Blount Jordan

Morton, Samuel S. to Ann P. Dabney May 26, 1841 Bd: John O. Crump

Morton, Samuel to Jane (Patsey) Kidd Jan. 14, 1817 by Thos. Boaz Bd: Stephen Morton

Morton, Solomon H. to Sarah H. Green Sept. 22, 1825 by Thos. S. King, J.P. Bd: Jacob Morton

Morton, Wm. to Susan Gremmer Apr. 1, 1813 Bd: Abner Morton

Morton, Wm. B. to Virginia C. Waddey Nov. 30, 1843 by W. Burns, M. G. Bd: Johnson Jordan

Morton, Wm. B. to Margaret A. Patton Mar. 20, 1849 Bd: Jos. R. Hunter

Mosely,(X) George W. to Elizabeth Waters July 19, 1841 by Gilbert Marshall Bd: James B. Young

Mosely, Jesse to Arispha Red Feb. 15, 1844 Bd. James Robison

Moseley, Peter E. to Catharine M. Starnes Oct. 27, 1846 by Martin Clark, Elder in M.E. C. Bd. Everett Owen

Moseley, Lycurgus H to Mary A. Starnes Nov. 28, 1838 by A.L. S. Green, MG. Bd. Bennett B. Wilkinson

Moseley, William to Hannah Redford May 1, 1823 by Joel Anderson Bd: Athelston Ransom

Moseley, Jesse to Barbara Hay Feb. 21, 1822 Bds: Everett Haynes and William Mosley

Moses, Abraham to Patsey Winstead Oct 25, 1819 BD. Fred. Ezell

Moss, Abner W. to Mary Jane Barham Sept. 7, 1842 by James C. Anderson, M.G. Bd: Harrison H. Merritt

Moss, Abram M. to Rebecca Ivy Mar. 24, 1834 Bd. Andrew Webb

Moss, David T. to Mary W. Gideon Dec. 23, 1834 Bd. Dabney Collier

Moss, John T. to Louesa A. Giddens Jan 12, 1839 Bd. Patrick Reese

Moss, William to Martha C. Farmer Dec. 22, 1836 by J. McCurdy

Motherall, James to Margaret U. Edmiston April 10, 1817 by S. Hunt BD: J. H. Lockett Test: Robert Davis

Moulton, Thomas S. to Amanda F. Merritt July 26, 1843 by Jessee Cox, MG, Bd. Lancelot Johnston

Mullen, Job (X) to Sally Childrep Apr 23, 1825 Bd. Jesse Mullen

Mullen, Joseph W. to Jane Wright July 13, 1807 Bd. Dennis (X) Wright Attest: Peter Hardeman

Mullen, Henry to Polly Cochran Aug 9, 1814 Wit: N.P. Hardeman

Mullin, Abner (X) to Mary Stanfield Dec 22, 1834 by George Shannon Bd: William Griggs

Mullin,(X) George to Betsey Childrup* June 3, 1824 by Gilbert Marshall JP. Bd. Beriah K. Thompson

Mullin, George to Polly Brown May 17, 1836 by J. A. Holland JP
(* There seem to be Childrups, Childreps, and Childress's in the records.)

Mullin, Josiah (X) to Frances Edmondson Nov. 10, 1841 by
    N. R. Owen JP   Bd. John B. Barnes

Murphy, John (X) to Eliza Stokes June 7,1839 Bd. John(X) Fitz
    Witness present: L. B. McConnico

Murphy, John (X) to Charlotte Newsom Dec.8,1841 Bd. Ingram Peebles

Murphy, (X) William to Nancy Elam Apr.19, 1819 Bd. Joseph(X) Murphy

Murray, Ennis to Anna Buchanan Dec. 19,1818 by John Pillow Agt.
    Bd. John Pillow Wit: Thos Hardeman Jr.

Murrey, Ennis to Sarah Early Dec. 9, 1846 Bd. M. L. Andrews MG.

Murray, Francis to Jane Rutherford Dec.18,1810 Bd. Matthew
    Johnston Wit: Wm. P. Harrison

Murray, Henry to Matilda Denny Apr 25,1823 Bd. John W. Dyer

Murrey, John B. to Adeline E. Wilson Oct.10,1844 Bd. Ennis Murrey

Murray, Joseph H. to Margaret Sloan   July 15, 1850 by B. R. Gant
    M.G. Bd. Candor M. Sanford

Murray, Robert to Margaret Rutherford May 28,1812 Bd.Jason Hopkins

Murray (or Maury as signed) Thomas (X) to Olive Louder Nov.1,
    1820 by Franc Jackson JP Bd. John Smith Test: E.Hall

Murray, Thomas P. to Catharine Wilson Nov. 7, 1843 by M. L.
    Andrews, MG   Bd: Samuel M. Caldwell

Murrey, William C. to Catharine E. Early Nov 30, 1847 by
    H. B. North, MG

Myers, Isaac (signed Mayers) to Gennett Daniel Mar 22, 1839
    by Robert Davis, M.G.   Bd: Jackson Smith

Myrick, David N. to Mary Swanson Aug.27,1825 Bd.Williard W.
    Kellyrick

                "Mc"
McAlister, Charles to Elizabeth Wright Apr. 2, 1811
    Bd. John Sample Wit: Wm. P. Harrison

McAlister, Charles to Martha Cator Feb. 17, 1837 by Wm. Moor JP

McAlister, Charles P. to Priscilla A. Hodge June 27, 1837

McAlpin,William to Mary H. Adams Mar. 24, 1842 by Jas C. Owen
    J.P. Bd: Robert A. Reed

"Mc"

McAlpin, Vardy (X) to Elizabeth Gardner Jan. 18, 1838 by
    W. H. Meadow, JP   Bd: McAlpin (X) Johnson

McBride, Hugh to Susanna Patterson Aug 11, 1813 Bd. Wm. Pinkston

McBride, James to Peggy Duncan Nov. 7, 1822 Bd. Matthew Pinkston

McCabe, Hugh to Sarah Squire Aug. 2, 1819 Bd. Charles McCabe

McCabe, James L. to Susan B. Miller July 28, 1824 Bd Dan. Shearwood

McCabe, William to Mary Shell Sept. 9, 1846 Bd. George White

McCaddam, Irvin to Darcass McClain Mar. 18, 1809 Bd: Absolom
    Whitesides

McCall, Charles to Cynthia Johnson Oct. 6, 1827 Bd: Thos. Johnson

McCall, John A. (signed McCaul) to Elizabeth Boon May 22, 1839
    by J. Wall J.P.   Bd: C. P. Logan

McCall, Lycurgus to Emeline M. Hartly Jan. 26, 1837

McCall, Rufus A. to Adeline J. Andrews Mar. 26, 1846 by Acton
    Young, M. G.   Bd: C. P. Logan

McCall, Smith G. to Cynthia Skillington Nov. 4, 1831 by M. L.
    Andrews, M. G.   Bd: John A. Skillington

McCall, Thomas to Fanny Rutledge Sept. 16, 1824 Bd: Jacob Cahoon

McCall, Willie (X) to Anna Christy (Christa) Feb. 13, 1820 by
    Edward Ragsdale Bd: William Glover

McCallister, Joseph to Elizabeth Moore Jan. 3, 1808 Bd: Mitchell
    Robinson

McCallum or McCollum, Cloud to Betsey Taylor Apr. 14, 1808 Bd:
    John Moore

McCalpin, Daniel to Elizabeth Muchum(?) Mar. 27, 1827 Bd: Silas
    Edwards Witness present: J. W. McCown

McCalpin, John to Priscilla Gibson Apr. 13, 1815 Bd: Wm. McCalpin

McCalpin, Wm. to Patsey Wooten (or Wooton) July 17, 1307 Bd:
    John Honderson

McCandlass, John (X) to Mary E. Morris July 30, 1846 by John
    Monady, M. G. Bd: Joseph Sprott

McCandlass, John (X) to Phebe Ann Walker Nov. 17, 1847 Bd: Silas
    Edmondson

McCandless, William (X) to Esther Roller Oct. 18, 1841 by R. B. B. Cannon, J.P. Bd: John B. Potter

McCandless, Wm. to Sally Golly Aug. 29, 1809 Bd: Stephen Biles

McCanles, James (X) to Nancy Pumroy Aug. 19,1823 Bd:Wilson Davis

McCannon, David to Deborah Denton Aug.25,1808 Bd: Moses Johnston

McCarley, Ezekiel to Margaret Langston Apr. 14,1808 by Tristram Patton Bd: Dornton Patton

McCarrell, Abner to Narcessa Orton Dec.9,1819 Bd:Jas. Rutherford

McCarroll, Israel to Rachael Giddens no date except 1830 Bd: Wm. H. Crouch

McCaslen, Harman to Teresa Andrews Aug. 13,1816 Bd:John McCaslen

McCaslin, Webster(X) to Nancy Hicks Apr.5,1817 Bd:John X McKinsey

McCasline(?) John to Ruth Andrews Feb. 24,1816 Bd:Jas. Shelly

McClain, Allen to Amy Bateman Oct. 18,1806 Bd:Enoch Bateman

McClaran, Alexander P. to Martha M. House Aug.30,1831 by Thos. L. Porter Bd: Daniel C. McClaran

McClaran, Alexander P. to Mary Scales Feb. 25,1841 by M. L. Andrews, M.G. Bd: Charles A. House

McClaran, Franklin to Mouren (Morney ?) Bellenfent Mar. 20, 1815 Bd: Garland M. McClaran

McClaran, John to Lucy Potts June 26,1816 Bd:Stringer Potts

McClaren, Felix G. to Nancy C. Marable Oct. 23,1838 by Sam. B. Robinson,J.P. Bd: John Marable

McClary, Daniel (X) to Susannah Rutledge Oct. 1,1816 by Wm. Logan, J.P. (License and bond filed)

McCleary, James A. to Elizabeth A. Moore Aug. 5,1809 Bd: James Ewing Witn: Wm. P. Harrison

McCleland, Wm. B. to Mary B. Anthony Nov. 24,1819 Bd:Jas.H. Johnston

McClellan, Uriah (X) to Rebecca Sullivan Aug.20,1833 Bd:Wm. (X) Raburn Witn:W. H. Bailey, Thos. W. Talbot

McClellan,Wilson to Elizabeth Dean Oct.19,1820 Bd:JohnW.Osburn

McClellan, Wilson to Sarah Thompson Oct. 8,1828 Bd:B. B. Lanier

McClish, James to Batsey Blythe Mar. 6,1814 Bd: Joseph Spratt

McClish, John to Eleanor Blythe Jan. 7,1819 Bd:Joseph Blythe

McClure, Henry to Manerva Peay May 12,1833 Bd: John King

McClure, Huston to Amy Ogilvie July 20,1814 Bd:Richard Ogilvie

McClure, James to Mary Tapley Feb. 16,1825 Bd: Benajah Gray

McCollum, John to Fanny McCollum Oct. 19,1828 Bd: Henry Wall

McConel, Walter to Polly Barker June 29,1807 Bd:Zachereah Parker

McConnico, Christopher W. to Susan C. Drake Nov. 25, 1822 by Joel Anderson Bd: B. S. Tappan

McConnico, Garner Y. to Catharine Kinnard Oct. 25,1827 by Joel Anderson. Bd: Jno. S. Buchanan

McConnico, Jared H. to Henritta Kinnard Mar. 5,1816 Bd:Joel Stevens

McConnico, Lemuel B. to Lucinda M. Grennier Jan. 13,1824 Bd: Morris L. Bond

McConnico, Lemuel B. to Frances W. Cloud Nov.6,1839 by Robert A. Hill, J.P. Bd: John O. H. P. Charter

McConnico, Washington Lafayette to Caroline F. Cloud Jan. 5,1845 by W. Henderson, J.P. Bd: Wm. Anderson

McCord, Aaron C. to Elemina M. Caskey Sept. 16,1843 Bd:Jos.Sprott

McCord, Abner to Mary Rudder June 14,1820 Bd: Richard H. Rudder

McCord, Allen N. to Jane Jordan Dec. 26,1833 Bd:Albert Gallatin Hill

McCord, Allen N. to Mary Jane Ogilvie July 18,1850 Bd:Newton McCord

McCord, James to Rebekkah Curtis Jan.14,1814 Bd: Joshua Curtis

McCord, James to Sarah Tomlinson Feb.22,1843 Bd:Benj.C.Stephenson

McCord, Newton to Sarah Ann Knott Nov.3,1842 Bd: Ben W. Haley

McCorkle, Alexander to Jane Cooper July 4,1811 Bd:Jas. Andrews

McCorkle, John to Jane M. Blackburn Apr. 17,1827 Bd:Bluford (X) Blackburn

McCormack, James to Susannah Gault July ? 1805 Bd:Ephraim Brown

McCorwell, Peter W. to Purity Campbell Feb. 24,1848 Bd:JohnBaugh Bond alone filed

McCown, Alexander to Nancy Tomblin Oct. 25,1810 Bd:Jno.Rachfordd

McCoy, Daniel to Polly Eddington Feb.26,1815 Bd: James Brown

McCoy, Elijah C. (X) to Sarah S. Daniels Dec. 31,1840 by Jas. D. King Bd: Samuel M. Daniels

McCrabb, Joseph F. to Lydia R. Simon Nov.9,1830 Bd:Robt. Simon

McCracken, Robert to Tenny Priest Apr. 6,1809 Bd:Joel T. Rivers

McCracken, Samuel to Margaret McGuire Dec. 26,1807 Bd:Ephraim McCracken

McCrory, Franklin A. to Eliza Jane Hobbs Oct. 13,1844 by G. W. Armstrong Bd: J. M. Whitfield

McCrory, Hugh to Martha C. Whitworth Nov. 20, 1843 Bd:Joseph W. Sharber

McCrory, James to Rebecca Porter July 16, 1845 Bd:Jas.X Wiggins

McCrory, Legate(signed McKory) to Sally Johnston June 15,1822 Bd: Noble Stockett

McCuistion, Benjamin to Sally Jordan Apr. 17, 1807 Bd: John McCuistion

McCuiston, John to Peggy Ingram May 12,1806 Bd: George Wrenn

McCullough, James to Catharine McFadden Dec. 16,1830 by Peyton Smith Bd: Calvin Clark

McCurdy, Allen to Elizabeth Herrin Feb. 9,1828 Bd:Jas.B. Herren

McCurdy, David to Rebecca Andrews July 26,1820 Bd:Geo. Andrews

McCurdy, John to Elisabeth Andrews Apr.23,1821 Bd:Tappley B. Andrews

McCurdy, Wm. to Elizabeth Cheatham Dec.28,1814 Bd:Thos.Cheatham

McCutchan, Jas. to Eleanor T. Edminston Jan.9,1823 by Geo. Blackburn,V.D.M. Bd: Andrew Crockett

McCutchan, John to Rhoda Denton Feb. 23,1808 Bd:David Campbell

McCutchan, John to Margaret W. Edmondson Jan.27,1825 by Wm. Hume V.D.M. Bd: John Edmondson

McCutchen, Robert to Martha G. Edmiston Jan. 6,1817 Bd:David Bell

McCutchen, Samuel to Betsey Lizenbury Sept.16,1830 Bd:Wm. Spencer

McCutchen, Wm. to Matilda Collins May 6,1816 Bd:Hodijah Collins

McCutchen, Wm. H. to Mary R. Edmiston Sept.30,1830 Bd:John Marshall

McDade, Charles to Sarah Francis Dec. 25,1819 Bd:Rath N. Forbes

McDaniel, Alexander to Sally Jackson Oct. 5,1820 Bd:Abner Boyd

McDaniel, John to Nancy Peebles or Peoples July 17,1817 Bd: W. W. Hill

McDaniel, Robert to Betsey Young Feb. 19,1807 Bd:Thos. Kennedy

McDaniel, Wm. U. to Sally Garrett Jan. 15,1811 Bd: Samuel Ware

McDonald, Francis to Sally Stanley Aug. 15,1810 Bd:Geo. Hodge

McDougall, Wm. R. to Rebecca S. Hamilton June 14,1838 by T. Fanning, M. G. Bd: John W. Morton

McDowel, Matthew to Maranda Windrow Dec. 24,1835 Bd: Wayne W. Murphy of Rutherford

McDowell, Harvey to Catherine Sawyers June 3,1824 Bd: Robert Dannedy, Wm. X Sawyers, James H. McDowell

McDowell, John C. (X) to Mary Cartright Dec. 29,1839 by Jno. P. McKay Bd: Thos. S. Wyatt

McDowell, Joseph C. to Patsey Slicker Aug. 5,1827 Bd:John Reed

McDowell, Joseph P.(X) to Malinda Jane West Sept.2,1843 by R. M. McDaniel, J.P. Bd: David L. Drake

McDowell, Joseph P. to Jane Orms Jan.15,1849 Bd:G. W. Hughes

McElhuny (signed McElhennyey), Joseph to Patsey Kiles Dec. 20, 1815 Bd: Barbanbas C. Kiles

McEwen, Cyrus to Susan Kinnard Feb. 2,1825 Bd:Thomas Goff

McEwen, Cyrus to Eliza Ann Bell Nov.6,1833 Bd: C. E. McEwen

McEwen, John B. to Cynthia Z. Graham Oct. 13,1842 Bd:Thos. N. Figures

McEwen, John L. to Tabitha Barfield Apr. 14,1820 Bd:Jas. McEwen

McFadden, Nathan Hays to Eliza Lucinda McFadden Feb. 22,1834 Bd: Ralph S. McFadden

McFadden, Reuban to Amy Hartgrave Sept. 23,1823 Bd:Sam'l Barclift

McFadden, Wm. to Lucy Armstrong Aug. 23,1832 Bd:Thos. H. Osburn

McFall, John to Aley Dobbins May,1806 Bd: James Wilkins

McFarland, Wm. to Caroline Barnes Sept.6,1836 Bd:Thos.B. Kellow

McFerrin, Anderson P. to Minerva Porter Apr. 27, 1842 by A. L. P. Green, M. G. Bd: James Park, Anderson P. McFerrin by James Park. Copy of letter attached to bond: "Nashville, April 21, 1842. Bro. Park: Will you be so kind as to apply at the Clerk's office for a marriage License? The names are Anderson P. McFerrin and Miss Minerva Porter. My brother and Miss Porter are of your county. By complying with the above you will confer a favor on my brother and save him a ride to your town. I will identify you in way of endorsement. It is no runaway affair. Send to my office by return mail. Yours respectfully, J. B. McFerrin."

McFerrin, Wm. M. to Manerva Oldham June 23,1835 Bd:Hardin P. Bostick

McGan, Alfred to Emily M. Edney Dec. 19,1833 Bd:John A. Hudson

McGan, Eli to Polly Estes Nov. 22,1817 Bd:Jabe Mayberry

McGaughy, James (X) to Nancy Mcord sometime 1817 Bd:Joshua White

McGaughey, Thos. B. to Virginia T. Griggs Dec. 18,1849 by A. N. Cunningham, M. G. Bd: Alford McGaughey

McGavock, Oscar Hugh to America N. Bryan May 22, 1845 (Bond only) Bd: John Smith

McGee, Chiles to Nancy McConnico Apr. 10,1817 Bd:James Brown

McGee, Elijah - see Magee

McGee(signed Megee), John to Ritty White Aug. 20,1822 by Lewis Loyd, J.P. Bd: Lewis (X) Sheppard

McGee, Lewis to Rhoda Beard Jan. 1,1822 Bd: Thomas Kinsey

McGee, Wm. to Elizabeth H. Old Apr.7,1819 Bd:M.F. DeGraffenreid

McGee, Wm.(X) to Jinny King Feb. 26,1846 Bd:Henry Hendricks

McGee, Wm. E. (X) to Elizabeth Fitz Mar. 8,1843 Bd:John M.Stevens

McGehee, George Washington to Cynthia Ann Campbell Apr.6,1826
    Nathan Ewing, Clerk of Davidson County Court

McGilvory, Wm. (X) to Polly Craig Dec. 5,1816 Bd:M. L. Bond

McGinnis, Robert to Nancy Robertson Mar. 5,1845 Bd:Davis X Danada

McGrew, Geo. W. to Nancy Ann Southall Dec. 4,1844 by M. L. Andrews, M. G. Bd: Robert Wilkinson

McGuire, James to Rachel Cannada McCutchan Nov. 22,1810 Bd:
    John Brim

McGuire, Patrick to Patsey Kavanaugh Dec. 31, 1812 Bd:Sam'l Craig

McGuire, Thos. to Martha J. Young Oct. 11,1840 Bd:Alphonzp Andrews

McIntire, John to Nancy Wall Nov. 18,1841 Bd:Henry W.(X) Davis

McIntosh, Colin(signed Collon) to Jane Fox Oct. 17,1839 by Thos.
    Prowell, J. P. Bd: A. M. (Andrew) Adair

McIntosh, John R. to Cynthia Fox Aug. 20,1848 Bd:Wm. L.Sparkman

McJordan, Garner to Mary Petway Oct.20,1839 Bd:Zilman F. Walker

McKane, Wm. to Elizabeth Cullom Dec. 31,1822 Bd: Wm. Nolen Jr.

McKay, John L. to Elizabeth N. Polk Nov. 21,1843 by J. H. Campbell Bd: Cameron H. Lockridge

McKay, John P. to Margaret Scott Sept. 21, 1824 Bd: Wm. Scott

McKay, Melton R. to Jane Miller Jan.6,1831 Bd: Charles M. Scott

McKay, Wm. A. to Margaret McEwen Mar. 9,1836 by James W.Rea,M.G.

McKennie, John (X) to Harriett Anderson May 16,1822 by Nichs.
    Scales Bd: Jno. W. Osborn

McKenzie, Wm. to Mary Garrett Aug.23,1837 by J.W. Rea, M. G.

McKibbin, Jas. to Mary Field Feb.16,1846 Bd: Hugh Dempsey

McKinney, Alexander F. to Grizzell Lane Apr. 19, 1837 by S. G. Burney, M. G.

McKinney, Randolph (X) to Parthenia Dungan Sept. 26, 1825 Bd: Nathan Dungan

McKnight, James to Nancy McClellan Oct. 10, 1807 Bd: Sam McKnight

McKnight, James to Mary Price Sept. 17, 1820 Bd: M. Bostick

McKnight, Samuel B. to Arrabella Hunter May 17, 1806 (Bond) Bd: Richard Henderson

McKnight, Samuel B. to Jane R. Shannon July 10, 1812 Bd: John McKnight

McKnight, Wm. to Nancy Harper May 6, 1817 Bd: Charles Depriest

McKory, Legate - see McCrory

McLain, Ephraim H. to Elizabeth S. Ogilvie Aug. 23, 1832 Bd: Richard Weldon

McLane, Henry M. to Nancy B. Lane July 27, 1836 Bd: Cephas Adams

McLemon, Young to Frances Elizabeth McLemon Sept. 1, 1847 by L. B. Johnson, J.P. Bd: Adkins McLemon

McLemore, Abraham (X) to Dicey Jones Dec. 28, 1827 Bd: Lewis Green

McLemore, Abram (X) to Pamelia Camp Nov. 21, 1839 Bd: Isham Greer

McLemore, Atkins to Sabrina Maury June 14, 1834 Bd: Simon Green

McLemore, Atkins J. to Bethenia Dabney Sept. 7, 1821 Bd: J. N. Charten

McLemore, Burrell to Nancy Williamson Feb. 7, 1814 (Bond) Bd: Nich- P. Hardeman

McLemore, Giles to Elizabeth B. Debnam Nov. 15, 1823 (Bond) Bd: Edward J. McLemore

McLemore, Robert to Leah P. Perkins Dec. 14, 1805 Bd: Y. A. Gray

McLemore, Robert to Peggy S. Dabney June 8, 1812 Bd: Hardin Perkins

McLemore, Robt. W. to Harriet S. Figures Sept. 17, 1840 by A. H. Dashiell. Bd: Zebulon W. P. Maury

McLemore, Sugars to Bethenia Ann McLemore Jan. 9, 1823 by John R. Blackburn, M.G. Bd: James C. Hill

McLemore, Sugars to Elizabeth P. Bond Mar. 8,1836 by Jos. Carle

McLeod, Dickson C. to Martha Thomas Nov. 30,1830 Bd:Ellbeck,Henry

McMahon, Ansley to Susan Little Nov. 8,1820 Bd:John Edmiston

McMahon, Joseph F. to Jane L. Goff Feb. 2,1832 Bd:Jas. C. Carr

McMahon, Wm. to Rachel J. Perkins Aug. 6,1817 Bd: T. Saunders

McMahan, Wm. H. to Mary Jane Vaughan Jan. 31,1849 Bd:Ira Peach

McManns, Wm. to Nancy McCaslin Feb. 2, 1826 by John Atkinson,VMD

McManus, Jonathan C. to Susanna McCaslin Oct. 31,1825 Bd: John McCaslin

McMeans, David N. to Mary Jane Caskey Sept. 19,1849 Bd:J.N. Neely

McMeans, John to Nancy McKifee 1805 Bd: Ephraim Brown

McMillan, James N. to Elizabeth C. McCall Jan. 2,1848 by Lycurgus McCall, J.P. Bd: J. S. Whitehead

McMillen, Alexander to Letty N. Bowman Feb. 2,1820 Bd: Charles L. Humphreys

McMimms(signed McMeens) David N. to Sarah F. Stevenson June 19, 1845 Bd: R. J. Baugh

McMullin, Thos. to Margaret Patterson Dec. 4,1811 Bd:Wm. Pinkston

McMurray, Silas to Susan F. Rash Dec. 14, 1847 by Wm. A. Whitsitt, M. G. Bd: J. William C. Rash

McMurray, Wm. to Mary T. Kimbrough Oct. 9,1838 Bd:Wm.A. Vernon

McMurry, Samuel to Dicy Morton Oct. 14,1815 Bd: Jacob Morton

McMurry, Wm. to Polly Morton June 11, 1810 Bd:Elisha Morton

McNabb, James (X) to Elizabeth Burch Apr. 2,1840 by Philip P. Neely, M.P. Bd: Thomas H. Goodrum

McNeal(McNail), Edward to Ann Edmiston Aug. 17, 1815 Bd: John Buchanan

McNeal, Neal to Polly Yates July 27, 1825 Bd:Pearson X Taylor

McNeil, Henry to Caroline E. Homble May 5, 1842 Bd:JohnG.Brown

McPeak, Matthew to Polly Powell Oct.20,1824 Bd:Wm. D. Hutton

McPhail, Angus to Nancy Sharp Dec. 15, 1812 Bd: Wm. Neal

McPhail, Angus to Sally Glass Dec. 30, 1828 Bd: Wm. Johnson

McPhail, Angus to Sarah Carter Oct. 28, 1844 Bd:E.G. Christian

McPhail, Daniel to Sarah Whitfield Oct. 11, 1831 Bd:John Wheaton

McPherson, George (X) to Parthenia Turner Aug. 21, 1828 by Wm. Moor, J. P. Bd: Thompson (X) Riggins

McPherson, Green (X) to Emeline Forehand Dec. 29, 1846 by J. C. Anderson, M. G. Bd: Edwin T. Cloud

McPherson, James to Hannah Cartright Sept. 19, 1823 Bd:Jas. Haley

McPherson Jas. B. to Ann Marlin Jan. 20, 1824 Bd: John Coles

McPherson, John to Ruth Casey Feb. 24, 1823 Bd:Irey X Casey

McPherson, John M. to Martha S. King Sept. 18, 1845 Bd:Wm. Crouch

McPherson, Joseph (X) to Nancy Forehand Nov.15,1843 by S. A. David, J. P. Bd: James B. McPherson

McPherson, Rhesa R. to Abigail S. Jones Aug. 31, 1843 by Joseph Carle, M. G. Bd: Wm. H. Trimble

McPherson, Vardy (X) to Emily Heath Dec. 21, 1843 Bd:Seth T.Davis

McPherson, Wm. (X) to Elizabeth Pritchett Jan. 13, 1847 Bd: George (X) Forehand

McRady, James L. to Virginia Cash June 17, 1844 Bd:Geo. Long

McThompson, John to Emeline Bosley Dec. 31, 1839 by R. B. B. Cannon, J. P. Bd: Wm. Edmondson

Nail, Nicholas to Sally Williams June 16,1813 Bd: Julian Nail

Nall, Andrew I. (X) to Nancy Loflin Feb. 8, 1840 Bd:Fred. Ivy

Nall, James C. to Naomy Underhill Feb. 20,1842 Bd:John Nall

Nall, John to Rachel Campbell Aug. 14,1818 Bd:Thos. (X) Kelly

Nance, Bird to Sally Mack June 25,1808(Bond) Bd: Richard Orton

Nance, Henry to Sarah Nelson Dec. 29,1825 Bd:Geo. W. Sanford

Nance, Jas. H. to Ann M. Brown Dec. 19,1833 Bd:Stanhope H. Braly

Nance, Joseph to Ellenor Black Mar. 20, 1815 Bd: Joseph Crenshaw

Nance, Josiah C. to Bethunia H. Snaed Bd: William McGee

Nance, Reuben to Frances Armstrong (in one place Ingram) Bd:
John Matthews, Thos. Matthews

Nance, William to Polly Bowlin July 1, 1819 Bd: John W. Osborn

Nash, Demsey to Lucy Garrett Sept. 17, 1805 Bd: Wm. Hume

Neal, Armistead R. (X) to Sarah G. Haley Dec. 15, 1831 Bd:
David Caldwell Witn: Jno. G. Hay

Neal, Benjamin D. to Mary S. Tulloss Aug. 4, 1840 Bd: Jas.M. Payne

Neal, Charles to Jane Donaldson Feb. 25,1830 Bd:John Neel (bride-
groom's name signed Charles Neil)

Neal, James to Mary Rhodes Oct. 7, 1828 Bd. William Clemmons
Wit: Nich^S. Scales -Sig. James Neel

Neal, James J. to Emily F. Hays Jan 25, 1838 Bd. Rich.M.Hayes

Neal, John C. to Ann Cahoon Sept. 29,1832 Bd. John Patton

Neal, John H. to Martha J. Mason Aug. 30, 1837 by John Kelley MG

Neal, Perry M. to Sarah Ann Crockett Oct. 25, 1842 Bd. J.R. Hunter

Neal, William to Elizabeth Trimble Dec. 15,1812 Bd. Angus McPhail
Wit: Wm. P. Harrison

Neal, William to Martha Wynne Mar. 17, 1824 Bd: Henry Wynne
Wit: Elisha L. Hall. By W. R. Nunn, JP.

Neal, William P. to Mary A. (Gor J.) Parham Aug. 9, 1831

Neal, William S. to Margaret Robinson Sept 8, 1836 by William
Lanier JP. Bd? Joseph Robinson

Neelly, Charles L. to Sarah Wells (Weels) Dec. 20, 1819 by
Tristrum Patton Bd. John Neelly Jr

Neelly, George L. to Rhoda Ann E. House Nov.1, 1843 Bd. J.A.Neelly

Neelly, George W. to Rhoda L. Priest June 18, 1829 Bd. Abram Priest

Neelly, Isaac to Sarah Burk Sept. 19, 1841 by N. R. Owen, JP
Groom sig. Neely - Bd. William K) Fish

Neelly, Isaac G. to Elizabeth J. Crutcher July 13, 1842
Bd. Isaac G. Gentry (?) Jas. Hogan Jr.

Neelly, James A. to Mary J. Long   Oct 2, 1845 by R. G. Irvine,
         MG. Bd. Sam'l S. House

Neelly (Neely) James A. to Sarah E. Edwards   Jan 4, 1849 by
         Jas. S. Owen Bd. Nathan C. Burke

Neelly, John C. to Elizabeth Warren   July 4, 1816 by David
         Shannon, JP. Bd. Burret (X) Warren

Neely, John H. to Susan H. Woldridge   June 18, 1833 by G.
         Marshall JP. Bd. Bird Fitzgerald

Neely, John W. to Jane J. House   Nov. 26, 1845 by H. Bridges,
         J.P. Bd. John N. House

Neely (Neelly), Philip P. to Henrietta P. Keffer   Oct 20, 1840
         by Wm. Randle, MG. Bd. James Young

Neelly, Samuel to Sally Neelly   Jan. 12, 1806   Bd. Elliot Hickman

Neely, Thomas to Elizabeth Neely   Dec. 15, 1834   Bd. Creed W. Ellington

Neelly, William to Elizabeth Priest   June 9, 1827   Bd. John W. Miller

Neelly, William to Lucinda C. House   Aug. 11, 1842   Bd. John H. Neelly

Neelly, William L. to Elizabeth Blackwell   Mar. 1, 1832 by
         Thos. L. Douglass Bd: Joseph S. Waller

Neil, James H. to Elizabeth Brown   Apr 8, 1830   Bd. Lem. H. Ogilvie

Neilson, Charles B. to Catherine Patterson   Nov. 23, 1807
         Bd. Arch Potter

Nelson, George to Delila Brown   Dec. 21, 1816   Bd: John Brown

Nelson, Joseph H. to Elizabeth Dalton (on Bond) dated Dec. 18
Nelson, Joseph H. to Elizabeth Scales (on license) dated
         Dec. 26, 1832 by Thos. D. Porter. Bd. Madison H.
         Dalton (probably her kinsman so Dalton prob. right.)

Nesbet, William B. to Rebecca H. Aikin   Jan. 15, 1829   James Akin

Nesbitt, John D. to Martha M. Allen   Dec. 21, 1843   Bd. John Akin

Nevils, Isaac J. to Ann Boyd   Dec. 2, 1830   Bd. Josiah Nevils

Nevils, Josiah to Sarah B. Beach   June 21, 1821   Rich. B. Beach Bd.

Nevins, William to Belinda Nolen   Feb. 15, 1832   Wm. Caldwell Bd.

Newby, Ozwell to Martha Green   May 20, 1832   John W. F. Boxley Bd

Newcomb, (X) Nelson to Sarah R. Pope   Jan. 2, 1838   Preston S. Childrep

Newcomb, William to Louisa Nicholson Dec.11,1841 John S. Park Bd

Newman, John to Sabry Lowder Mar.3, 1812 Richard W. Hyde, Bd.
　　　　Wit: William P. Harrison

Newsom, Godfrey S., to Sarah W. Nolen Jan. 19, 1837

Newsom, Micajah J. to Mary C. Causey Oct.29,1846 Richard Fitts b

Newsom, Thomas H. to Barbara J. Martin Jan.8,1850 J.B.McEwen Bd.

Newton, Ebenezer (X) to Mahala Clark Oct.26,1830 B. S. S. Weekman,
　　　　JP. Hamilton W. Davis,Bd.

Newton, Ebenezer B. (X) to Elizabeth Lightfoot May 19,1850
　　　　by W. F. A. Shaw, JP. W. B. White, Bd.

Nichol, James (signed Nichel) to Sarah C. McPhail Dec.4,1849
　　　　by J.W. Rogers,Presbyter of Franklin Episcopal
　　　　Church. Bd. JohnL. McEwen

Nichols, Andrew T. to Susan T. Temple Nov. 8, 1842 John W. Wall

Nichols, Asa to Priscilla O. Duty July 8,1835 Robt. Davis,Bd.

Nichols, Geo.(X) to Lucy Jane Young Dec.20,1838 Wm. Nichols,Bd.

Nichols, Harrison to Mary Moon Sept.5,1838 Stuart Patterson,Bd.

Nichols, Jeremiah B. to Sarah Young Aug.8,1828 Wm. Hays, Bd.

Nichols, John to Elizabeth McCown Oct.29,1814 (bond) Alexander
　　　　McCown, Bd.

Nichols, Wm. to Martha S. Hamilton Dec.20,1848 Jno. B. Gray,Bd.

Nicholson, Cordy to Polly Caperton Dec.22,1813 Bd:Jno.Nicholson

Nicholson, David W. to Salina Potter May 25,1830 Radford Sat-
　　　　terfield, Bd.

Nicholson, Malachi H. to Elizabeth M. Jamison Jan. 5,1837

Nickens, Joseph(X) to Mary Red Oct.5,1839 Bd:Marcus(X)Nickens

Nickens,Thomas(X) to Nancy Bass Sept.22,1847 Marcus(X)Nickens Bd.

Nickens, Wm.(X) to Chloe D. Matthews Sept.3,1842 Bd:Bernard S.
　　　　Matthews

Nobles, John to Betsey Ragsdale Apr.23,1819 Abel(X) Ragsdale,Bd.

Nobles, Nathaniel to Nina(could be Nima)Jackson Feb. 13,1825
　　　　Elijah Gibson, Bd. by Wm. Dunnegan, J.P.

Nolen, Allen T. to Francis A. Davis July31, 1822 T.A. Thomson,Bd.

Nolen, Felix G. to Margaret A. Dial Nov.24,1830 by G. L. Nolen, J.P. Bd: Wm. G. Merritt

Nolen, General L. to Polly Turner Apr.25,1810 Bd:Stephen Nolen

Nolen, Green to Frances M. Morton Sept.29,1832"by the subscriber Peter S. Gayle" Bd: Richard W. Robinson

Nolen, John to Mary Newsom Jan.22,1834 Bd: Wm. M. Turner

Nolen, Joseph to Tempe Young Jan. 18, 1817 Bd:Thomas P. Cassey

Nolen, Joseph to Peggy Brown Dec.23, 1817 Bd:William Brown Test: Robert Davis

Nolen, Micatah to Nancy White Feb.19,1807 Bd:Chas. Campbell, Jas. McCutchan

Nolen, Stephen to Michal Nolen July 23,1816 Bd:Elijah Davis

Nolen (Nowlin)Stephen to Martha Tilman Dec.8,1817 Bd:Silas Tilman

Nolen,Wm. M. to Sarah Ann Crump Nov.25,1840 Bd:John Ballenfant

Nolen,Wm. M. W. to Martha J. Webb Nov.28,1839 Jas. Hogan Jr.,Bd:

Nolin, Thomas to Sally Thomas July 23,1808 Bd:Mark Thomas

Norris, Wm. to Cynthia Campbell Mar.19,1826

North, James to Narcissa Edwards Feb.22,1825 Bd:John Baugh

North, John to Mary Davis Aug. 6,1831 Bd:Jno. E. Denson

North, Wm. to to Mary F. Buford Dec.30,1833 Bd:Boling C. North

North, Wm. T. to Mary Zerilda A. Helm Sept. 21,1839 James L. Armstrong, Bd. (Bond alone)

Norton, Wm. to Eliza Wilson Jan. 10,1810 Bd:John Easton, Chas. McAlister Wit: Wm. P. Harrison

Notgrass, Thomas to Mary Armstrong Oct.16,1832 Bd:David Baugh

Nawlin, James to Elizabeth Tilman Oct.15,1815 Silas Tilman,Bd.

Nowlin, Wade to Frances Tilman Mar.4,1824 H. L. Atkinson, Bd.

Nunn, Joel to Elizabeth G. Williams Jan.12,1822 Bd:Robert Stone

Nunn, Robert S. to Mary Jane Allison Nov.5,1850 Bd:Young W.Redmon

Nunn, Thomas to Julia Fryette Sept.26,1816 Erastus Collins, bd.

Nunn, William M. to Jane M. Jones Sept.10,1841 A. L. Capelman,Bd.

Nye, Shaderick to Martha J. Hall Aug.8,1820 Aaron V. Brown,Bd.

Oakes,Isaac(X) to Lotty Ham Aug.21,1822 John Witherspoon,Bd.

Oakley, Jesse A.(X)(signed James A.) to Nancy Roach Oct.25,1838
    Bd: Caleb Fly

Oakly (or Oakley) Jesse to Patience Perkins Jan13,1822 Noah
        Gardner, Bd. Witn: D. Hardeman

Oakley, Robert to Emily Stephens Aug. 12,1830 Wm. W. Coleman,Bd.

O'Brant, David(X) to Jane Newsom Feb.3,1839 Willis O'Brant,Bd.

O'Bryant, Willis(X) to Polly Ann Melton Nov.8,1838 Balaam Melton (X), Bd. Witn: Sam B. Robinson

Oden, Hezekiah to Vituria A. Reams Sept. 22,1847 John F. House,Bd.

Oden,Thos. H. to Rebecca H. Reams Oct. 11,1847(on separate piece
        of tablet paper among bonds)

Oden, Wm. to Martha A. E. Davis Nov.29,1842 Bd:Charles M. Scott

Odil, David M. to Sarah Jane Stanley Jan.15,1841 Cameron H.
        Lockridge, Bd. By A. L. T. Green, M. G.

Odil, James M. to Margaret E. Giddens Sept.7,1837

Odil, John to Polly Kerr June 25,1808 Thos. G. Caldwell, Bd.

Odle (signed Odil) Anderson to Fanny McCarrel April 1,1817 Bd:
        Leonard Dunavant West: Robert Davis

Ogilvie, Alfred S. to Mira M. Riggs May 4,1836 byN.P.Modrall,M.G.

Ogilvie, Jackson W. to Mary Jane Davidson Oct.27,1833 Johnson
        D. Williams, Bd.

Ogilvie, James S. to Rachel M. Webb Feb.28,1844 Richard H. Ogilvie, Bd.   By M. L. Andrews, M. G.

Ogilvie, John R. to Bethenia P. Sneed July 18,1847 by John Rains
        M. G.   Bd: James F. Simmonds

Ogilvie, Kimbrough T. to Elizabeth P. Wilson Jan.28,1829 Bd:
        Lemuel H. Ogilvie

Ogilvie, Lemuel H. to Martha Moses Mar.27,1823 Frederick Ezell,Bd

Ogilvie, Wm. to Elizabeth N. Dummuber Dec. 21,1838 Jas.Hogan Jr.

Old, John E. to Jackey E. Jones June 22, 1816 Robt.B. Harney,Bd.

Old, Thomas H. to Susan W. Crunk Aug.5,1828 Bd:Mordica C. H. Puryear

Oldham, Lee to Susanna Doherty Feb.4,1813 Washington Doherty,Bd.

Oldham, Washington to Polly Doherty Jan.19,1813 Benjamin Reader

Oliver, Alexander to Norry Roddery Dec.15,1823 Wm. Dowers, Bd.

Oliver, Harbert N. to Elizabeth Ballow Sept.12,1833 J.F.F. Hill

Oliver, Jesse to Flora Ann Love Oct.30,1833 Richard Haley Jr.,Bd.

Oliver, John to Celia Bridges Nov.3,1816 Henry Oliver, Bd.

Oliver, Levi to Anna Collins Dec.23,1805 Bd:John Hassell, Elisha Hassell   Witn: John Hardeman

Oliver, Robert to Rebecca Fitzpatrick Feb. 19,1814 Samuel Fitzpatrick, Bd. Witn: N. P. Hardeman, Wm. H. Stone

Oliver, Wm. to Mary Ann Ferrel Nov.27,1820 Jackson Tinsley,Bd. Witn: John G. Hay

Ollephant, James to Sally Henderson June 9,1807 Bd: Wm. Dunlap, Reason B. Bishop Wit: N. P. Hardeman

Olmsted, Charles G. to Elizabeth McAlister Sept. 4,1823 Bd: H. R. W. Hill.Witn: Joshua W. McCown

Oneall (Or Omall) Elisha F. to Rebecca Lindsey Feb. 19, 1835 Bd: L. M. Frost

O Neal, Wm. P. to Elizabeth Oden Feb.24,1830 Theodrick Carter,Bd.

Oram, Wm. to Eliza Padgett Sept. 14,1836 Bd: George W. Graham (bridgeroom signed as William H. Orum)

Orman, Adam to Patsey Reams Dec. 17,1816 Bd:Geo. Mebane

Orman, James to Harriet Epps Apr.15,1847 W. M. Pope, Bd.

Orman, Wm. D. to Addeline Dodd Oct.25,1843 Bd:Wm. Burns

Orman, Wm. D. to Jane Turner Nov.22, 1846 James W. Roach, Bd.

Orman, Wm. L. to Mary A.R. North Nov.7,1838 Jas. L. Armstrong,Bd.

Ormes, John D. to Cassy Buttrey Oct.10,1828 Howell S. Woodruff

Orr, Ebenezer W. to Nancy S. Dobbins Nov.15,1824 Wm. M. Orr, Bd.

Orr, Hugh R. to Elizabeth Sudbury June 10,1841.Wm. M. Wright, Bd.

Orr, Hugh Read to Sarah Patton Dec. 9,1811 Bd:John R. Orr, John J. Henry

Orr, Robert to Polly Ann Cummins Mar.22,1824 Bd:John Dobbins Witn: Elisha L. Hall

Orton, David to Jane Humphreys Mar.6,1806 Bd: James Donaldson

Orton, Johnson to Sarah Ann Lacy Nov.28,1833 Sam'l B.Orton,Bd.

Ortoh, Ray S. to Mary M. Nicholson Mar.26,1850 Thos.B.Bond, Bd. Witn:John G. Hay

Orton, Richard to Lucy Bond Jan.24,1810 Bd: Wm. Hulme

Orton, Samuel B. to Harriett Humphreys Sept.26,1822 F. B. Carter

Orton, Wm. B. to Harriett S. Guthrie Jan.18,1838 Andrew J.Floyd

Osburne, Noble to Hannah Garner Dec.19,1811 Joseph Sumners,Bd.

Oslin, Alexander to Keziah Wood Jan. 12,1832 Bradley K.Gambill

Oslin, Wm. S. to Nancy Lanier Mar.27,1823 M. Lang Bond, Bd.

Osteen, David to Elizabeth Smith Apr.6,1809 Bd:Weak Smith

Osteen, John to Elizabeth Mizell Aug.15,1812 Bd:Levi Mizell

Otterburry, Michael to Sarah Pearce May 27,1822 S.D. Pearce,Bd.

Overall, Jackson M. to Miry P. Jordan Sept.7,1842 Bd: James B. Jordan. Witn: Edward L. Jordan, Stephen Jordan

Overman, Reuben to Melinda McKay Apr. 3, 1837 by C.M. McDaniel,JP

Overton,X Edwin W. to Sarah Jane Harvey Oct.24,1839 Bd:John W. Harvey

Overton, Jese to Tilpha Tarkington July 10,1810 Richard Swanson

Owen, Addison G. to Tabitha C. Johnson Nov.3,1848 John H. Carmichael, Bd. By M. L. Andrews, M. G.

Owen, Benjamin G. to Mary A. Reeves Sept.18,1833 Thos.L.Rives,Bd.

Owen, David R. to Christiana T. Hughes Jan.10,1833 John H.Rives

Owen, Everett to Anna Gray Nov. 11,1824 Nathan Owen, Bd.

Owen, Franklin L. to Elizabeth C. Maury Sept.13,1827 Wm. K. McAlister, Bd. Witn:J. W. McCown

Owen, Frederick to Nancy Nelson Jan.24,1818 Herbert Owen,Bd.

Owen, Glenn to Betsey Hardeman Feb.22,1809 Bd:Robt. Musgrove

Owen, Greenberry R. to Mary A. Rives Oct.26,1833 Wm.L. Tate, Bd. By Levin Edney,M.G. (one entry says Grumley R. Owen)

Owen, Herbert to Martha A. R. Thompson Jan.1,1835 Bd:Wm. T. Roberts, James P. Stevens. Letter attached:"Mr. Thomas Hardiman, You Will please issue for me to Mr. Roberts a marriage licens and oblige yours with Respect Herbit Owen"

Owen, Ira H. to Eliza Ann Owen Jan.30,1834 Curtis Stevens,Bd.

Owen, Isaac(X) to Diana Forgersan Mar.21,1816 David Black,Bd.

Owen, James(X) to Martha Vault July 11,1824 Daniel(X)Ireland,Bd.

Owen, James B. to Mrs. Mary McCutchen Mar.7,1844 Geo.A.J.Mayfield, Bd.

Owen, James T. to Margaret E. McCormick Oct.30,1839 James D. Trimble (or Tremble) Bd.

Owen, Jesse M. to Sarah Atkinson Dec. 11,1828 Bd:Allen N.McCord

Owen, John to Sarah P. Owen Feb. 6,1828 Bd: Philip Owen

Owen, John G. to Ann D. Brooks Jan.10,1837

Owen, Joseph to Sally M. Street June 12,1826

Owen, Joshua to Polly Hall Mar. 4,1805 Bd:Richardson Williamson Witn: Robert Sample

Owen, Nathan to Jincy Hightower Aug.11,1807 Jaser Owen, Bd. Witn:J. Hicks

Owen, Nathaniel R. to Susan H. Johnston Sept.1,1821 Bd: Henry McClure

Owen, Peter to Matilda T. Brooks Jan.2,1842 Cowden McCord,Bd.

Owen, Reuben R. to Nancy Floyd Mar.15,1843 Noah R. Morrow, Bd.

Owen, Richard A. to Mary Temple Feb.2,1837 by J.W. Rea, M.G.

Owen, Robert to Martha Blackwell Feb.11,1839 Bd:Hugh Thomson(Bond)

Owen, Robert C. to Eliza Whitfield Oct.25,1825 Bd:Sandy Owen

Owen, Robert W. to Lucinda F. Wells Dec.25,1850 by Jeremiah Stephens, MG Bd:John H. (X)Ragsdale

Owen, Samuel(X) to Martha Quinn Oct.5,1823 John(X) Owen, Bd.

Owen, Sterling to Jane Goodrum Dec.24,1835 Nathaniel R. Owen,Bd.

Owen, Sterling W. to Sarah C. Nicholson Jan.24,1833 John Owen,Bd.

Owen, Thomas(X) to Martha McDaniel June 26,1834 Chas.(X)Burke,Bd.

Owen, Wm. to Mary F. Johnson Dec.2,1850 Bd: William H. Owen

Owen, William E. to Ann A. Campbell Apr.24,1817 Robt.Curry,Bd.

Owen, William E. to Catherine P. James Feb.2,1826

Owen, William F. to Elizabeth C. McCormick June 6,1838 Bd: Franklin Ferguson

Owens, Walter to Jenny Hamilton Dillender Feb.27,1810

Owens, Wm. to Elizabeth Brown Sept. 8, 1814 Nathaniel Peay,Bd.

Ozburn, Richie to Nancy Crockett Jan.2,1840 Bd:Samuel Waters

Ozburn, Robert to Caroline Shelton Nov. 19,1840 James Owen,Bd.

Ozburn, Wm. G. to Mary G. Scales Mar.3,1847 Bd:Simon Venable

Ozment, John H.(X) to Elizabeth Owen Aug.17,1850 Thos.W.Collins

Pacand (or Pacaud), Ferdinand to Mary Mumford Oct.29,1839 Bd: Thos. L. Robinson

Pace, Joac (X) to Jane Dotson Aug.16,1843 Jas. Hogan Jr., Bd.

Pace, Thomas (X) to Nancy M. Logsdon Mar.18,1845 Jas.(X)Johnson

Padgett, Henry G. to Mary W. Andrews Nov.30,1821 H.L.Crutcher,Bd.

Padgett, Wm. to Eliza Dunlap Feb.25,1829 Bd:Robt. Crutcher

Page, David D. to Charity Evans Mar.25,1817 Bd:Laurence G.Evans

Page, David E. to Hannah Bush Parsons Nov.10,1810 Dixon Vaughn

Page, Jacob to Mary Jane Harrison Jan.26,1843 Bd:John H. Thomas

Page, James N. to Susan Stockett Dec. 23,1846 Bd:Wm. N.Motherall

Page, John to Margaret Ann Wilson May 11,1830 Bd:Miles H. Owen

Page, Milton Harvey to Malvina S. Wilson June 24,1833 Bd:Thomas M. Sconce

Page, Wm. to Ginny McFadden Jan. 3,1814 Bd:Charles Gum

Palmer, Bird to Anna Carson Feb. 16,1826

Palmer, Willie to Eliza Mitchell Dec.28,1843 Bd:Gilman Wadley Bond alone.

Palmon, James to Nancy Alston Oct. 19,1840 Bd:Jas.Palmon(cousin)

Palmon, Thomas to Mary R. Carter Sept.22,1841 Sam'lT.Crockett,Bd.

Palmore, Wm.(X) to Margaret Burns July 23,1839 Bd:Nathaniel Cole

Palmore, Woodson(X) to Elizabeth Berks June 5,1834 Bd:Benjamin (X) Palmore

Pankey, Thomas A. to Susan Faircloth Aug. 7,1827 Thos.Peay,Bd.

Pankey, Thomas A. to Frances A. Taylor Apr.15,1846 Swanson Burch, Bd.

Parham, George W. to Eliza A. M. Bingham Oct.19,1848 Bd: John M. Byers

Parham, Thos. J. to Winneford L. Pope Feb.27,1823 Morris L.Bond

Parham, Williamson H. to Nancy A. Pigg Apr.22,1830 Elisha Dodson

Park, Wm. to Sarah Jane Crockett Apr.28,1836

Parker, Andrew W. to Nancy C. Matthews Nov.23,1849 Jas.N.Parks,Bd.

Parker, Asa to Nancy Buchanan May 15,1821 Thos. L. Robinson,Bd.

Parker, Geo. W. to Elizabeth B. Scott Oct. 31,1835 Jas. Hogan Jr.

Parker, Geo. W. to Nancy F. Ballow May 18,1836 by Jas.W. Rea.,MG

Parker, Gideon to Nancy Davis Oct. 28,1824 Nathaniel H.Thomas,Bd.

Parker, James W. C. to Mary A. Reynolds June 9,1834 Bd:Jas. A. McCrady

Parker, John M. to Emily G. Moss Aug. 24,1837

Parker, Robert T. to Mary D. Bomar June 15, 1837

Parker, Turman to Jane Hardison Sept. 8, 1850 Wiley Bradford, Bd.

Parker, Wm. W. to Artemisia Neal Apr. 18, 1833 Bd: Jesse H. McMahon

Parker, Zachariah to Christina Benthall Nov. 14, 1809 Jas. McGuire

Parkes, Thomas to Elizabeth Field Jan. 11, 1838 Bd: Michael Doyle
"Solemnized on Thursday evening Jan. 11th, 1838 at the house of J. Field before divers witnesses by Jas. S. Otey, Bp. of P.E. Church".

Parks, Andrew to Rhoda Neelly Apr. 31, 1821 Bd: John W. Neelly

Parks, Andrew to Elizabeth Barnett Nov. 23, 1845 Bd: Samuel S. House

Parks, Andrew W. to Martha J. Boyd Dec. 23, 1847 Bd: Jas. N. Parks

Parks, Benjamin to Nancy Alexander Nov. 19, 1810 Bd: Daniel Wilkes

Parks, James to Maria Ganter Jan. 23, 1818 Bd: Richard Parks

Parks, John to Susanna Neelly Oct. 28, 1817 Bd: Richard Parks

Parks (Parkes) Robert (X) to Celia Dial Apr. 19, 1838 Isaac W. P. West, Bd.

Parks, Theophelus to Polly Lyons Apr. 9, 1807 Ben Jarmin, Bd.

Parks, Wm. to Malinda Goodman Apr. 28, 1806 Bd: Abner Vaughn

Parks, Wm. C. to Elizabeth S. Beech Dec. 24, 1850 Bd: Chas. W. Smithson

Parrish, Abraham to Catharine Staggs May 29, 1821 Bd: Tilman F. Atkinson

Parrish, Arthur A. to Elizabeth Taylor Mar. 19, 1848 Bd: Alonza M. Tenison

Parrish, Charles D. to Mary Wood Oct. 5, 1833 Bd: Alex. F. McKinney

Parrish, Elijah R. to Catherine Gibson May 30, 1822 J. S. Robbins, Bd.

Parrish, Harvey D. to Hannah McCrory Jan. 28, 1823 Bd: Enos Pipkin

Parrish, James S. to Eleanor Wooten Sept. 12, 1833 Peter J. Walker

Parrish, Joel to Sophia Saunders Nov. 28, 1816 Bd: H. Petway

Parrish, John S. to Mary A. M. Crenshaw Dec. 14, 1848 Bd: C. W. Smithson

Parrish, Matthew F. U. to Priscilla E. North June 9, 1812 Bd: John Gholson

Parrish, Nathaniel to Mary Stanfield Apr. 14, 1829 Bd: John D. Stanfield

Parseley, Moses M. to Sarah E. Gault Dec. 23, 1841 Harvey W. Gault

Parsley, Drury W. to Rebecca Ivy Jany. 15, 1834 Wm. M. (X) Ray, Bd.

Parsley, Thomas C. to Monnica Ray Sept. 3, 1829 Sherwood K. Baty, Bd.

Parsley, Wm. to Susannah Jordan Dec. 30, 1822 John C. Alford, Bd.

Parsons, Thos. S. to Susanna Ingram Sept. 12, 1809 Bd: Rich. Puckett

Parsons, Vaden W. to Alcena Goodwin July 11, 1847 Bd: Henry Newton

Paschal, Jeptha R. to Mary Ann Roland Feb. 26, 1845 (Bond) Bd: James M. Larkins

Paschal, Robert A. to Mary A. Ham Feb. 3, 1842 James G. ham (spelled thus) Bd.

Pate, Charles O. (X) to Mary Rogers Dec. 23, 1843 Samuel L. C. Coleman, Bd. (Bond alone)

Pate, Charles O. (X) to Rosy Coleman Dec. 22, 1846 Thomas Wilson, Bd. (Bond alone).

Pate, Geo. M. to Sarah E. Ditto Oct. 13, 1842 Pleasant T. Joyce

Pate, Henry (X) to Camilla Boyd Sept. 6, 1825 Robert Pate, Bd.

Pate, Henry (X) to Betsey Covington Dec. 2, 1830 Jesse Pate, Bd.

Pate, James to Nancy Warren Nov. 29, 1834 John Covington, Bd.

Pate, Jesse to Elizabeth M. Ivy July 29, 1829 Littleberry Pate, Bd

Pate, Joseph Benjamin to Elizabeth F. Wood Oct. 17, 1850 Dooly Pate

Pate, Joshua A. to Polly B. Sharp Dec. 26, 1821 Robert Pate, Bd.

Pate, Kitchen to Polly Elam Jan. 31, 1812 Edward Elam, Bd.

Pate, Littleberry to Miranda Warren Nov. 19, 1829 Bd: Jesse Pate

Pate, Thos. to Polly Pate Nov. 5, 1822 Bd: Robert Pate (married in Dec. - no date - by H. Adams, J.P.)

Pate, Thomas (X) to Martha E. H. Betty Dec.20,1836 JohnD. Betty

Pate, Thomas(X) to Mary M. Hall Aug.7,1848 Henry(X)Pate, Bd.

Pate, Thomas R. to Mary Jane Smith Feb.24,1846 James Smith,Bd.

Pate, Thomas W. to Sarah A. F. Harrison Dec.20,1849 Wm. Parrish

Pate, Thompson W. to Louisa Tomlinson Nov.4,1841 Jos. P. Hunter

Pate, W. L. to Mary P. Pate Nov. 7,1844 James N. Carson, Bd.

Patrick, Daniel D. to Elizabeth Epsom Sept. 21,1827 Wm.XPatrick

Patterson, Arthur to Jane King Sept.20,1811 Aaron Alexander, Bd.

Patterson, David J. to Mary Ann Jamison Oct.29,1840 John B. Jamison

Patterson, David W. to Lucinda Dyer Dec.20,1821 Wm. McCrory,Bd.

Patterson, Duncan to Rebecca Armstrong Dec.22,1809 Kinchen Masengale, Bd.

Patterson, Everard M. to Eliza W. White Nov.7,1826

Patterson, Hillary to Ann Polk Apr.25,1819 John Polk, Bd.

Patterson, James to Ann Gardiner Oct. 1,1805 John Gardiner,Bd.

Patterson, James to Polly Herrin Apr.29,1814 Francis Jordan,Bd. Witness: William H. Stone

Patterson, John to Nancy Read May 17,1810 Josiah Read, Bd.

Patterson, John S. to Lucretia Carothers Oct.14,1815 Wm. Carothers, Bd.

Patterson, Luke to Hannah Westbrook Oct. 22,1807 Jacob McCollum

Patterson, Robert C. to Millinda Carsan Feb.20,1815

Patterson, Wm. to Elizabeth Mayfield Oct.1,1805 Jas. Mayfield,Bd

Patterson, Wm. Jenny Hodge Sept. 14,1818 James Hodge, Bd.

Patterson, Wm. to Mary Walker Mar. 13,1828 Isaac Wyatt, Bd.

Patton, Alexander I. to Lucinda A. Hughes Oct.13,1841 John Fitzgerald, Bd.

Patton, Jacob to Ann Curtis May 29,1806 by Tristram Patton

Patton, James to Narcissa T. Smith Ja.16,1823 David Youngman,Bd.

Patton, James to Susan C. Thompson Dec.25,1839

Patton, James E. to Polly C. Cowsart Oct.15,1817 Andrew Cowsart

Patton, Jason to Bethenia Bostick July 30,1811 Hampton Bostick

Patton, John D. to Margaret A. Patton July 5,1849 Jos.C. Patton

Patton, John W. to Malinda Pickens Oct.31,1827 John O.Patton,Bd.

Patton, Robert to Lucy Terry Dec. 6,1825 Wilford H. Rains, Bd.

Patton, Tristram to Martha Overton Apr.18,1868 John Overton,Bd.

Patton, Wm. A. to Ann Walker Feb. 1,1820 by Tristram Patton,J.P.

Patton, Wm. M. to Ann Walker Jan. 29,1820 Tristram Patton, Bd.
      Witn: Jno. P. McCutchan

Paul, Olivz to Sarah Vaughan Oct.8,1843 Bd: Edward Gocey

Paxton, Thompson to Cynthia Potts Mar.8,1810 David Squier,Bd.
    With bond letter from father to the Clk. of Williamson County: "Mr. Thompson Paxton intends to apply to the Court of Wmson. Co. for License of marriage between him and my daughter, Cynthia Potts. This is to certify that I have no lawful complaint to prevent him from obtaining a lisence". Given under my hand March 8, 1810. J. Potts"

Payne, Henry T. to Sarah S.Peay Oct.4,1832 Benjamin F. Roberts

Payne, James M. to Sarah R. Armstrong Apr.19,1842 AbsolomB.Scales

Payne, John to Susan Eaton Feb. 9,1809 David Mason, Bd.

Payne, Robert G. to Maria Y. Tulloss May 31,1829 Chas.B. Porter

Paynor, George(X) to Edy Corkett May 27,1828 John P. Dix, Bd.

Paynor, Stephen(Payner) to Sally Powell Nov.12,1821 David Rea

Peach, Archibald(X) to Dolly Humble Nov.3,1842 Bennett W. (X)
    Shelton (bond alone)

Peach, Charles(X) to Lucinda Little Dec. 31,1833 Wm. W. Robb,Bd.

Peach, Ellis(X) to Nancy Beasley Feb.4,1823 Neal Campbell, Bd.

Peach, James(X) to Sarah Williams Mar.23,1825 King D. Hudgans

Peach, James(X) to Nancy Sadler May 5,1840 Benjamin F. Holland

Peach, John to Sealey Trentham Feb.2,1816

Peach, John to Elizabeth King May 20,1835 Charles(X) Peach, Bd.

Peach, Johathan J. to Jane Little Ja.1,1835 Gassaway Peach,Bd.

Peach, Sterling B. to Susan Edes Dec. 28, 1848 Reuben R. Peach, Bd.
Peach, Wm. to Susannah Baucum July 18, 1833 James Hughes, Bd.
Peach, Wm. to Sarah Younger Mar. 31, 1847 Owen T. Craig, Bd.
Peache, John to Sealey Trencham Feb. 2, 1816 Archabald Peach, Bd.
Pearcy, Clement A. to Matilda Ann Shaffer Apr. 5, 1838 John Cramer
Pearre, Charles R. to Mary P. Ansley May 4, 1848 Franklin Herm
Pearre, Joshua to Milly Ann Arnold Oct. 30, 1828 Jesse Tarkington
Pearre, Joshua W. to Elizabeth Hulme Nov. 13, 1823 G. W. Hulme, Bd.
Pearson, Henry I. to Mary W. Matthews Dec. 24, 1829 Thos. P. Buchanan
Peay, Nathaniel to Jane Bowen July 12, 1812, William King, Bd.
Peay, Samuel to Mary Irion Dec. 19, 1825 Robert Grimmer, Bd.
Peay, Samuel to Eliza Jordan Oct. 20, 1827 Richard J. Hill, Bd.
Pedigo, Joshua(X) to Nancy Robinson Dec. 19, 1822 Wm. Adkins, Bd.
Peebles, James M. to Mary J. Tulloss Jan. 9, 1850 Sebastian C. King
Peebles, John W. to Mary E. Carothers Oct. 11, 1842 John Alston
Peebles, Robert to Mary C. Farrington June 27, 1825 Jacob Critz, Bd
Peebles, Thomas E.(X) to Emily E. Williamson Feb. 14, 1833 Bd: Ingram B. Peebles
Peebles, Thomas H. to Mary E. Paschal Feb. 15, 1845 Jas. N. Peebles
Pennington, Clement S. to Susan Smith Jan. 6, 1817 Jas. R. Tisdale
Pennington, Clement S. to Martha J. Gray Oct. 18, 1849 Bd: Charles W. Smithson
Pennington, Drury to Juda Fuqua Mar. 31, 1825 Joseph Fuqua, Bd.
Pennington, Wm. P. to Amanda Jane Young Feb. 6, 1845 Henry Lester
Pennington, Wm. S. to Sarah A. Gee Oct. 25, 1849 William Pate, Bd.
Perdue, John to Francus Mangham June 30, 1844 Thos. A. Graham, Bd.
Perkins, Daniel P. to Mary B. Camp Apr. 12, 1825 Manoah Bostick

Perkins, Eben to Patsey White June 15,1812 Meady White, Bd.

Perkins, Edward to Peggy Anglin Nov. 17,1819 John(X) Anglin,Bd.

Perkins, Nicholas to Polly H. Perkins Jan.22,1808 N. Perkins,Bd.

Perkins, Nicholas to Mary Cook June 18,1816 Thos. H. Perkins,Bd.

Perkins, Nicholas Edwin to Martha T. Maury Dec. 29,1848 Bd: Peter A. Perkins

Perkins, Peter to Sarah P. Camp Oct.6,1824 H. R. W. Hill, Bd.

Perkins, Peter to Lorinda V. Kirkham May 21,1834 Bd: Hardin P. Bostick,

Perkins, Powhatten to Catharine J. D. Defraffenreid Jan. 12, 1842 Zebulon M. P. Maury, Bd.

Perkins, Thomas Fearn to Leah America Cannon May 3,1832 Bd: Jas. M. Perkins

Perkins, Thomas H. to Mary N. Hardeman Mar. 12,1818 Bd: Constantine Perkins

Perkins, Thomas H. to Elizabeth Gustavia Salhad Hunt Aug.11, 1828 Bd: C. A. Harris

Perkins, Thos. H. Junior to Eliza Mildred Perkins Jan.5,1831 William E. Anderson, Bd.

Perkins, Thos. H. Jr. to Louisa J. Frost Sept.4,1833 Bd: Thos. Hardeman

Perkins, Wm. to Jane Vaughan Dec. 5,1833 Bd: Wm. J. Moody(X)

Perkins, Wright to Mary Brown Aug. 5,1834 Bd: John Norris

Perodian, Paul to Loretta Smith Apr. 17,1822 Bd:John Quigley

Perry, Lewis to Nancy Phipps Mar. 29,1821 Bd:Joel Kimmons

Perry, Martin to Anne Dixon Oct. 14,1808 Bd:Sam'l Fleming

Perry, Orion to Nancy Edney May 1,1828 Bd:A. Montgomery

Perry, Thornton to Polly White Apr. 16,1816 Bd:Robert Bates

Perry, Wiley to Betsey Gentry Aug. 28,1822 Bd: Wm. Wright

Perryman, Joshua to Nancy Loving Apr. 18,1809 Bd:Richard Polk

Petigo, XThomas Jefferson to Eliza Russell Oct.15,1844 Bd: Smith (X) Sampson

Pettus, Thomas W. to Elizabeth E. Jordan Oct.17,1829 Bd:Freeman W. Jordan

Petty, Edward to Margaret R. Sparkman Jan.28,1847 Wm.C.Sparkman

Petway, Ferdinand S. to Elizabeth Thweatt Dec.14,1836 Bd:Eben B. Staggs

Petway, Hinchey to Caroline Parrish Oct.23,1807 Thos. Masterson

Petway, John to Mary M. Stephens Dec.5,1827 Z. H. German, Bd.

Petway, Thomas M. to Susan D. Smith Feb.2,1832 Jas. Bradley,Bd.

Pewett, Hartwell(X) to Edney Gray Dec.12,1816 Thomas Gray,Bd.

Pewett, Thos. to Margaret Stobuck Sept.26,1810 Jno. C. Stobuck

Pewit, Joseph to Barbary Pewit Feb.17,1831 Frederick(X) Wright

Pewit, Malachi to Mary Inman Sept.28,1836 Bd:William Kirby

Pewitt, Adam to Barbary Smith Oct.4,1822 John(X)Yates, Bd.

Pewitt, Henry(X) to Rebecca Williamson Nov.16,1827 John(X)Smith

Pewitt, James to Sally Adams July28,1832 Zachariah Peasley,Bd.

Pewitt, John A.(X) to Elizabeth Gibbons Sept.11,1833 Bd:Isaac Hormal(X) Witn: W.H. Baily

Pewitt, Laban to Annis Inman Mar.2,1848 Wiley Pewitt,Bd.(Bond)

Pewitt, Mary W. to Mary E. Bucklew May2,1844 Benjamin Inman,Bd.

Pewitt, Thos. to Thania Smith Dec.18,1827 Wyatt Smith, Bd.

Phelps, John (X) to Caroline Lee Dec.7,1831 John Evans, Jr.,Bd.

Philips, Edward(X) to Drucilla Clark Feb.15,1822 HenryF.Clark(X)

Philips, Ivy(signed Phillips) to Nancy Edwards Oct.19,1816 Bd: Michael Hail

Philips, Isaac M.(signed Phillips) to Emily R. Nunn Nov.16,1833 Bd:Robt. A. Hill

Philips, Joel(X) to Jane Ager Jan.30,1838 Bd:George W. Marr

Philips, Joel to Malinda Edgar Aug. 16,1841 Jesse W. Ivy,Bd.

Philips, Wm. D. to Eliza Dwyer, June 3,1828 J.O. Wharton, Bd.

Phillips, Izrael to Martha Tillman Aug.28,1810 Bd:Hayden Tillman

Phillips, Joel to Ann Chambers June 8,1806 Bd:Wesley Witherspoon

Phlippin, Robert to Nancy Gunter Dec.9,1837 By James King

Pickard, Geo.M. to Margaret M. Orton Aug.1,1833 Samuel R.(X) Morton, Bd. By James W. Rea, M.G.

Pickens, John G. to Polly McKnight Dec.13,1809 Bd:Wm. Norton

Pickering, Wm. to Martha Whitby Dec.4,1832 Bd:John E. Crouch

Pierce, Arthur(signed Pearce) to Elizabeth Bizell Aug.14,1815 Bd:Edward Stevens

Pierce, Simon W. to Sarah H. Cox Nov.29,1848 H.W. Hitchcock,Bd.

Pigg, James to Jemima Dotson June21,1813 Bd:Jas. Neal

Pigg, John to Sally Berry Dec. 11,1815 Bd:James Pigg

Piggs, James M. to Margaret C. Hancock Dec.3,1835 Sam'lL.Graham

Pigott, Simon to Patsey Haley Mar.2,1820 Bd:George ---?

Pinkerton, Jas. F. to Catherine A. McMillen Mar.18,1819 Bd: Jas. McCutchan Note:"The within persons were carefully married Mar.18,1819" by Geo. Blackburn,Min.

Pinkerton, Joseph to Nancy Brewer Oct.29,1828 Bd:Henry McCluer

Pinkerton, Joseph to Louisa Sweeney May3,1840 Jas. McCutchen,Bd.

Pinkston, Matthew to Scina Smith Dec.8,1818 Bd: George Davis

Pinkerton, Sam'l M. to Elizabeth Smith Apr.18,1827 Thos.Betts

Pinkston, David to Francis Andrews Jan.25,1820 Bd:Geo.Poindexter

Pinkston, David to Mary Polk Jan.19,1841 Bd:Wm. Pinkston

Pinkston, Hugh to Polly McMullen May18,1808 Bd:John Howard

Pinkston, Hugh to Mary Pinkston Dec.24,1827 Alexander Pinkston

Pinkston, Matthew to Ann Stephens July 16,1811 Jas.Stephens,Bd.

Pinkston, Turner to Sally Jordan Feb.9,1818 Bd:George Davis

Pinkston, Wm. to Polly White July 25, 1825 Bd: Jas. C. Chute, Chas. McCall

Pinkston, Wm. to Hannah Polk Dec. 23, 1831 Bd: Wm. P. Lester

Pillow, Abner to Polly Thomas Mar. 30, 1808 Bd: John Sample

Pillow, Francis A. to Charlotte S. Rogers Jan. 2, 1840 Bd: William P. Brown

Pillow, John to Polly Fitzpatrick May 20, 1806 Bd: Morgan Fitzpatrick

Pillow, Samuel C. to Almira E. Clemons Aug. 19, 1849 Bd: Wm. Croson

Pillow, Wm. to Potcia Thomas Dec. 19, 1812 Bd: Stephen Childrep

Pinor, John(X) to Anna Gardner (Gardener in one place) Jan 10, 1836 Bd: Wm. (X) Pinor

Pistole, Abner to Susan Tisdale July 20, 1825 Bd: Banjamin Slayton

Pistole, Wm. R. to Polly Harris Oct. 12, 1815 Bd: Abner Vaughn, Gregory Wilson

Pitman, Samuel(X) to Catharine Hudgins Apr. 13, 1827 Bd: Daniel(X) Richardson

Plumber, Jonathan to Nelly Corbett Feb. 9, 1822 Solomon Plumber, Bd.

Plummer, Jacob(X) to Narcissa Brown Dec. 16, 1830 Bd: Titus Hale

Poe, John S. to Nancy Stanley Oct. 7, 1838 Bd: Thomas W. Little

Polk, Andrew(X) to Elizabeth Ozburn Dec. 10, 1846 Bd: John Waters

Polk, Armistead to Eliza Mary Stephens Aug. 7, 1828 A. H. Parter

Polk, Geo. W. to Sally S. (or L.) Hilliard Nov. 24, 1840 Bd: G.W. Polk by his sttorney in fact Edward French

Polk, John to Nancy Laymaster June 26, 1810 Jno. Willie Osburn, Bd.

Polk, Joseph to Mesemiah Green Dec. 25, 1836 by Thos. G. Porter, M.G.

Pogue, James(X) to Sarah Jane Patterson Dec. 15, 1840 Bennett Posey

Poindexter, Geo. T. to Polly Anderson Feb. 23, 1814 Jas. Gentry, Bd. With: William H. Stone

Pointer, Wm. H. to Sarah S. Buford Aug. 4, 1840 Bd: John T. Word

Polk, Richard to Elizabeth Lemasters Jan.4,1808 John Porter Jr.

Pollard, Geo. W. to Martha E. Mebane Mar.15,1842 Malachi W. Pollard, Bd.

Pollard, Joseph to Martha Nicholson Jan.28,1814 Elisha Madding

Pomeroy, Jas. to Mary Lynn (or Synn) Sept.12,1833 Bd: Peter P. Mayfield

Pouroy, John(X) (Pomeroy?) to Nancy C. Mullin Dec.24,1838 Bd: Silas Edmonson

Pomroy, Thomas(X) to Margaret Quinn Mar.27,1830 Bd: Francis W. Cunningham

Pomroy, Wm. (signed Pumoroy) to Delila Cochran May5,1839 Bd: Wm. S. Vernon

Ponder, Archibald to Sarah Kinsey Nov.26,1817 Bd: Thos. Kinsey

Pool, Colwell P. to Elizabeth W. Ragsdale Jan.8,1830 Bd: John Ashlin

Pope, Benjamin(signed Polk) to Peggy R. Moore Sept.26,1816 Bd: John Moore

Pope, Hardy to Sally Lewis Feb.25,1831 Bd: Jonathan Norman

Pope, James to Mary Reed July 17,1832 Bd: William Hill

Pope, Jeremiah to Polly Sims Apr. 5,1814 Bd: Sutherland Mayfield

Pope, Matthew to Susanna Walker Feb. 1,1816 Bd: John D. Pope

Pope, Quiny to Meome Haynes Feb. 1,1831 Bd: James C. Taylor

Pope, Wm. (X) to Thena Revel (Revil) Sept.23,1841 Bd: Charles (X) Pope

Porch, Wm. to Matilda Temple Jan. 31,1827 Bd: J. B. Allen

Porter, Abner D. to Phoebe E. Jordan Feb.3,1833 Wm. W. Parsley

Porter, Alexander to Elizabeth W. Hill Nov.2,1825 David P. Byers

Porter, Charles B. to Martha A. M. Old Jan.6,1829 Peter Perkins Witn: C. A. Harris

Porter, Elias D. to Minerva J. Hodge Nov. 5,1840 Robt. M. Crutcher

Porter, Geo. W.(or M.) to Margaret Edgar June8,1837

Porter, James to Jane Walthall Dec.21,1824 Bd: W. R. W. Hill

Porter, James B. to Frances W. Bond Mar.2,1821 Bd:Robert Davis

Porter, James H. to Elizabeth Cayce Sept.6,1824 Bd:Thos. J. Goff

Porter, John to Patsy Hobson June 1,1808 Bd:Robt. P. Currin

Porter, John (Lame) to Miram German June6,1812 Zacheus German

Porter, John Jr. to Polly Hamilton May 11,1812 Henry Swisher,Bd.

Porter, Thomas to Jane Brown Dec. 14,1809 Bd: John Goff

Porter, Thomas D. to Mary Sumner July 22,1820 Bd: T. Saunders

Porter, Wm. to Martha Love Jan. 14,1806 Bd: James Love

Porter, Wm. to Judith Owen May 30,1824 Bd: Peter Owen

Porter, Wm. C. to Martha Roy Apr. 18,1839 Bd:Daniel Williams

Posey, Benjamin to Catharine Kenada Dec. 23,1842 Bd:Wm. Holt

Poteat, John(X) (Peteete) to Nancy Tarpley May8,1819 Bd; Peter Hardeman

Poteet, Andrew to Jane Caudle Feb.25,1846 Bd:Thos. A. Graham

Poteet, James(X) to Betsey McLemore Nov.25,1830 Alexander M. Childress, Bd.

Poteete, Andrew to Mary A. Graham Oct. 20,1836 Bd:Edwin T. Childress

Poteete, James to Minerva Ann Fitz July 26,1833 Bd:Albert Poteete

Pootete, Isaac to Nancy Greer July 20,1807 Bd:Geo. Oldham

Potter, Henry D.(X) to Nancy M. Williams Aug.28,1839 Bd: Jones R. Coleman

Potter, Isaac to Frances Coleman July 25,1816 Bd:Joseph Meador

Potter, Robert D. to Sarah S. Neelly Oct.12,1835 Israel McCarroll, Bd.

Potts, Abner C. to Melinda Hotsted Jan.10,1833 Bd:Thos. S. Berry

Potts, Abner C. to Mary Simmons Mar. 11,1838 Wm. E. Ransom,Bd.

Potts, Geo. to Rebecca Gibson Jan.12,1826 by Daniel White, M.G.

Potts, James to Rebecca Fox Feb. 4,1826 by Mallachi Henley,J.P.

Potts, James M. to Margaret Fox Ja.24,1849 Geo. W. Thompson,Bd.

Potts, Joseph R. to Jane Williamson Aug.11,1834 John S. Morey,Bd.

Potts, Leroy D. to Mary Beard Aug.18,1842 Bd:Thomas Litton

Potts, Stringer(X) to Anne Winsett Apr.27,1816 Amos(X) Winsett

Potts, Westley to Betsey Barnett Jan.31,1822 John Barnett, Bd.

Potts, Willie to Catharine A. Floyd Jan.14,1829 Wesley Potts,Bd.

Powel, Charles L.(X) to Polly Stricklin Dec.12,1817 Bd:Zachariah Jackson

Powell, Ambrose to Lucy B. Chambers Mar.8,1824 Bd:Thos. Chambers

Powell, Braxton R. to Sarah Eliza Green Aug. 27,1839 Bd:Abraham (X) McLemore

Powell, Honour to Susannah Clark (Bond) Jan.11,1841 SquierPowell

Powell, John(X) to Martha Mitchell Oct.19,1820 Wm. Beasley,Bd.

Powell, John to Ellen E. Langdon Dec. 13,1849 Bd:Joshua J. Toon

Powers, Robert F. to Amanda Jones Jan.19,1843 Bd:A.J.(Andrew) Toon   By Joseph Carle, M. G.

Powers, Samuel to Lucy Quinn Jan.14,1846 Thos.J. Thompson(Bond)

Powers, Samuel H. to Myrah McCown Nov.22,1838 James M. Gault,Bd.

Powers, Wm. W. to Brunnetta Tiner Mar.28,1843 Bd: Young Clark

Poynor, Charles M. to Eliza Jane Burke Feb.10,1848 Wm. W. Neely, Bd. Bond alone filed

Poynor, James to Jane Warren Sept.29,1842 Wm. Gardner,Bd.

Poynor, John (Poynor) to Charlotte T. Stephens Oct.2,1828 Bd: L. S. Bateman

Poynor, Richard M. to Elizabeth Little Aug. 15,1847 Bd: R. W. Robison

Pognor (Poynor), Wm.(X) to Eliza Rice June 6,1839 Thomas (X) Chambers, Bd.

Prater, Eliphaz to Catharine Skelley Aug.1,1830 Wm.(X) Skelley

Pratt, Abner B. to Caroline T. Hamilton May 24,1849 Bd:Thos. Campbell

Pratt, Bailey to Sally Stewart Aug.7,1814 Bd:John Fitts

Pratt, James H. to Nancy Jane Mays July6,1843 J.(James)W.Boyd

Pratt, Samuel to Polly Boyd Sept.7,1814 Bd:James G. Swisher

Pratt, Wm. to Patsey Davis Jan. 4,1816 Bd:Jobe Louden

Preast, Thos. to Rachel Powel Nov. 6,1806 Bd:Joel Burns

Prewett, Geo. H. to Betsey Tarkington Sept.5,1807 Jas. Cose, Bd.

Prewitt, Joseph A. to Lettie Barnett Nov. 16,1848 Ephraim Jacobs

Prince, James to Hannah McCutchan Jan. 15,1813 Alexander Johnston, Bd.

Price, James to Elizabeth B. Mathews Jan.23,1823 Bd:Hartwell B. Hyde

Price, James to Susan Vaughn Jan. 5,1835 Bd: B. F. Roberts

Price, John to Betsey Coffee(Coffeey) Sept.30,1811 John Coffey

Price, Nathaniel M. to Mary Davis Sept.8,1831 Bd:Robert Davis

Price, Richard to Ramy Marchant Sept. 21,1823 Robt. Edmondson

Price, Wm. to Rachel J. Biggers Dec. 31,1844 Wm. V. Andrews,Bd.

Prichard, James W. to Joannah Ivy Jan.26,1833 David H. Walton

Prichard, Robt. to Selena Prichard July 2,1846 Bd:Samuel(X) Montgomery (Bond alone filed)

Prichard, Wm. G. to Gimimna Powers Dec. 15,1825 Benjamin Smith

Prichet, Thos. J. to Polly 6. Hudson Dec. 20,1817 Bd: David (X) Hudson

Prichett, Henry to Martha Ozburn Jan. 10,1833 Thos. Carmichael

Prichett, Thos. J. to Mary A. Degraffenreid Apr.17,1850 F. G. Irvin, Bd. By A. N. Cunningham, M. G.

Priest, Abram to Nancy M. Padgett Sept. 16,1829 Thos.(X) Priest

Priest, Jas. to Nancy Shannon Nov. 13,1817 John Mays, Bd.

Priest, James M. to Mary Jane Padgett July 29,1829 Wm. Harrell

Priest, Jas. C. A. to Panthea F. Edmonson Jan.5,1830 John Edmonson

Priest, John (X) to Lithe Black July 5,1821 Bd:Geo. Long Witn: Thos. G. Ballow

Priest, John A. to Lucy Andrews Oct.9,1818 Bd: Jas. Merritt

Priest, John M. to Martha Vaughter Jan. 5,1842 Jas. M. Priest,Bd.

Priest, Leonard to Susan Long May 30,1822 Eli Dyall, Bd.

Priest, Moses(X) to Elizabeth Long May 2,1816 Milton O. Hiter,Bd.

Priest, Thos. H. to Nancy Merritt Sept. 3,1835 Moses G. Gocey

Prim, John(X) to Ely Brodway Jan. 17, 1816 Bd:Thos. Lashby

Primm, Charles H. to Jane Wilson Apr. 3,1835 Bd: Wm. C. Hunt

Primm, Jeremiah W. to Rebekah Hamer Sept.21,1805 John Primm,Bd.

Primm, Shadrack W. to Mary S. Hampton Nov.20,1838 Bd:Richard D. (X) Vaughan

Primm, William to Nancy C. Vaughan Mar.13,1834 Smith Truter,Bd.

Prince, Chaney to Rilley W. Winsett Oct. 22,1845 (Bond alone) John M. Burns, Bd.

Prince, Owen J. to Martha Buch Jan. 17,1846 Wm. J. Buckingham

Pritchett, Christopher C.(X) to Martha L. Tucker Sept.7,1849 Bd: Levon E. Rhodes

Prowell, Calvin H. to Mary A. Prowell Aug. 7,1849 C. C. Mayhew

Prynor, Robt. to Jinnetta Benton Aug. 24,1826

Pryor, Tapley B. to Martha M. Peay Dec. 9,1830 Wm. M. Wilson,Bd.

Puckett, Benjamin F. to Martha Ann Waters Nov. 26,1843 Bd: Richard Berry

Puckett, Edward to Mary Ann King Mar. 27,1838 Mordecai Newport

Puckett, Harvey to Calhoun(Catherine on license) Braden June 19, 1816 Daniel German, Bd.

Puckett, Jared to Anne Collins Aug. 1,1815 H. P. Holt, Bd.

Pulley, Wm. to Sarah Bragg Jan. 23,1823 Alexander McCown, Bd.

Pumroy, Abraham to Nancy Jones Dec. 27,1821 Bd:Wm. Pumroy Witn: E. L. Hall & Cary White

Pumroy, Willis to Catharine McCanles July 24,1823 Jas.(X)McCanles

Puryear, Mordecai C. H. to Sarah Ann Reese Feb.10,1830 John I. Watson, Bd.

Putman, Amos(X) to Sarah Cook Oct. 21,1840 John B. Cowsey, Bd.

Putman, Jabel to Luraney Lamb Mar. 12,1840 James (X) Melton, Bd.

Putman, James(X) to Polly Barrett Nov.28,1834 Wm. Putman, Bd.

Putman, James D. to Sarah Ann Morris June 18,1840 Amos(X)Putman

Putman, William(X) to Delila Richardson May 22,1832 Geo. Hopkins

Pyson, Azariah (Pyron?) to Nancy M. Rickett July 27,1835 Bd: Wm. Boman

Pyron, Charles to Martha Deson Apr. 28,1839 Anthony Lavender,Bd.

Quin, Isham O. to Elizabeth Moody Aug. 23,1827 Robt. T. Currin

Quinn, David to Clarkey Lovet Aug. 30,1817 Bd: John Bell

Quinn, David to Elizabeth Cahoon Feb. 20, 1826

Quinn,XJohn C. to Sarah Long July 15,1829 Richard Steele

Quinn, Luke to Elizabeth Ham Feb. 12,1839 (license alone filed)

Rabey, Wm. to Mary Downey Nov. 25,1829 Bd: Wm. Span

Radcliffe, Francis G. to Martha P. Reams Aug. 23,1842 Bd:Thos. L. Radcliffe

Radford, James to Julian Hay June 7,1817 David Lancaster, Bd.

Radford, Samuel S. to Lettis Lamb Nov. 29,1838 Edwin(X)W.Overton

Ragan, James(X) to Mary Bateman Dec. 15,1840 Bd:Wm. J. Bateman

Ragan, Joseph(X) to Eleanor Bateman Jan.18,1838 Wm. J. Bateman

Ragan, Thomas(X) to Nancy McPherson May 15,1827 Jas.B.McPherson

Ragsdale, Abel(X) to Ancy Standley July 29,1819 Andrew(X)Ragsdale

Ragsdale, Alfred(X) to Elizabeth Ragsdale July 8,1845 Bd: Elcany (X) Johnson

Ragsdale, Andrew(X) to Elizabeth Stanley June 26,1821 Abel(X) Ragsdale, Bd.

Ragsdale, Daniel to Margaret Hewton Mar. 1,1811 James Hewton,Bd.

Ragsdale, Demsey(X) to Polly Montgomery Feb.21,1823 Eli Lunn,Bd.

Ragsdale, Edward to Penelope White Dec. 24,1808 Edw'd Buford,Bd.

Ragsdale, Edward to Sarah Barns Apr. 4,1815 Geo. Andrews, Bd.

Ragsdale, Edward to Elizabeth Hargrove Jan. 4,1823 Bennett (X) Hargrove, Bd.

Ragsdale, Eli to Celia Ragsdale Apr. 24,1839 Thomas (X) House

Ragsdale, Henry to Cynthia Hamilton Feb. 5,1846 J.A. Ragsdale Bd. Bond alone filed

Ragsdale, Hiram(X) to Mary Johnson Feb. 22,1834 Thos. T. Peay

Ragsdale, James to Sally Ragsdale Nov. 30,1823 Sam'l Ragsdale

Ragsdale, Jamison M. to Emily Bressee Nov. 24,1830 E. A. Ragsdale, Bd.

Ragsdale, Jesse L. to Margaret E. A. Ragsdale Nov. 9,1843 John (X) C.Montgomery, Bd.

Ragsdale, John to Nancy Andrews Jan. 2,1809 Tapley Andrews,Bd.

Ragsdale, John to Polly Davis Aug. 18,1826

Ragsdale, John to Elizabeth Ragsdale Sept. 12,1836 Riley Ragsdale, Bd.

Ragsdale, John (X) to Sarah Dowdy Apr. 28,1849 Porter Montgomery

Ragsdale, Lancaster to Elizabeth Randolph Feb. 2,1819 Bd: John C. Randolph

Ragsdale, Levi C. (X) to Finetta or Tinetta P. White Nov. 28, 1847 Bd: M. A. White

Ragsdale, Mark W. to Betsey Ann Robertson June 2,1836 Thos. Ragsdale, Bd.

Ragsdale, Mark W. to Polly Robinson Oct. 28, 1838 Bd: Benj.Brown

Ragsdale, Micajah (X) to Elizabeth Montgomery Oct. 1,1829 Bd: Samuel Ragsdale

Ragsdale, Peter to Mary Mitchell Jan. 26,1807 Alex Mebane, Bd;

Ragsdale, Richard to Elizabeth Roberson Aug. 30,1836 Micajah(X) Ragsdale, Bd.

Ragsdale, Richard(X) to Mary Jane Atkinson Oct. 29,1846 Bd: M. P. Montgomery

Ragsdale, Riley to Elizabeth Houston July 1,1826

Ragsdale, Robert to Sally Andrews Dec.27,1806 Lapley Andrews,Bd.

Ragsdale, Robert to Emily Sommerville May 23,1843 Wm.Ragsdale,Bd.

Ragsdale, Samuel to Jane Montgomery Dec.27,1825 Swanson(X)Johnston

Ragsdale, Thos. to Dicey Ragsdale May 4,1842 Robert D. Potter, Bd.

Ragsdale, Wm. N. to Martha J. Montgomery Oct.26,1848 Geo.White,Bd.

Raiford, Wm. to Eliza Cramer May 18,1846 (license only found)

Rainey, John to Mary Giles Mar.20,1833 Claburne Johnson, Bd.

Raleigh, Armstrong(signed John A. Rylie) Jan.5,1836 Thos.XBrittain

Ralston, Alexander to Sally Jordan Jan.31,1818 Joseph Love,Bd.

Ralston, Andrew to Mary Ann Woods Feb.22,1850 J. G. Reid, Bd.

Ralston, Joseph to Ann Hill Jan. 31,1828 Nathan L. Novell,Bd.

Ralston, Robert to Minerva Manire Jan.21,1845 Bd: John Webb

Ralston, Robert L. to Mary M. Stevens Dec.20,1848 Americus B.Buch

Ramsey, Henry(X) to Amy Plumlee May 13,1829 Marshall Haile,Bd.

Ramsey, Robert to Betsey Wilson Feb.7,1811 Zacheus Wilson,Bd.

Randolph, John C. to Dicy Ragsdale June8,1819 John Lunn, Bd.

Raney, John(X) to Jane Patterson Oct. 14,1841 Abram Glum,Bd.

Raney, Wm. to Catharine Thomas July 29,1822 Bd:John Raney

Rankin, George L.(X) to Martha Fields Nov.1,1821 Wm. Fields,Bd.

Rankin, Sam. K. to Rebecca S. Whitworth Apr.24,1839 David G.Deason Bd. Witn: Sam B. Robinson

Rankin, Bluford B. to Elizabeth Hicks Nov.19,1842 Enoch J. Hunt

Ransom, Benjamin F. Ransom to Nancy Livonia Jordan Oct.31,1848 A. J. Wood, Bd.

Ransom, Whitmill to Martha J. Williams Jan.24,1849 B.F. Ransom

221.

Rash, Stephen H. to Sarah I. McMurray Aug.3,1841 John P.Still J:

Ratcliffe, John W. to Sarah F. Reams Nov. 4, 1845 by F. G.
    Pitts, MG. Isaac C. Nicholson, Bd. Bond dated Nov.7
    (Several bonds dated after the Minister says he mar-
    ried the couple. However this is probably the case
    of the absent-minded Preacher, who marries several
    couples before he gets back to the Court House to
    record them, and forgets the exact dates.)

Ray, Alexander to Rachel Simpkins Aug.22,1806 William Henry,BD.

Ray, Alexander to Zylpha Garrett   June 17,1818. Sampson Lea-
    ford signs the bond for the groom with John B.Cunningham
    Wit: Thos. Hardeman

Ray, Alexander to Charlotte Ooton Oct.12,1836 Wm.J.Moody, Bd.

Ray, Collin (X) to Elizabeth Jackson Oct. 15, 1825
    John L. (X) Walker, Bd.

Ray, David to Polly Robertson Jan. 24, 1818 Wm. Robertson,Bd.

Ray, Elsey (X(to Ibba Ray Dec.4,1833 Jeremiah (X)Williamson,BD.

Ray, John (Signed Wray) to Lucy Thomas Dec. 29, 1821 by
    James Whitsitt. Edward Thomas, Bd.

Ray, Thomas to Susan Hill Sept. 24, 1823 by G. Hunt
    George W. Alford, Bd.

Ray, Thomas to Mary Ogilvie Nov. 12, 1829 James Robinson, BD

Ray, Thomas to Elizabeth Jackson Oct.6,1836 Wm.K. Ransom,Bd.

Ray, Thomas to Julia Crocker Apr 1, 1837 bond only

Ray, Wiley (Willie) to Mary Humphreys Jan 25,1821 by G. Hunt
    Teste: Elisha L. Hall   John C. Smith, Bd.

Ray, William (X) to Sally Featherstone Aug. 29,1839
    Robert (X) Garrett, Bd. Test: R. Davis

Ray, William A.(Signed Wray) to Mary E. Lofton Oct. 4, 1843
    by Matthew Marable, JP. Harvey J. Haynes, Bd.

Ray, William M. (X) to Elizabeth Jane Jackson Dec. 17, 1833
    by Robert Pate, J. P. Drury W. Parsley, Bd.

Rayburn, William (X) to Mary Hargrove Mar. 7, 1829 by M. L.
    Andrews, MG. David A. Gillespie, Bd.

Read, Alexander (signed Reid) to Sarah Fisabee Jan 31, 1850
      by Lycurgus McCall, JP and Bd. Wit: Chesley Williams

Read, J. G. to Catharine Ralston Jan 17,1850 Wm. M. Lamb,Bd.

Read, James to Sally Pearre Dec. 27, 1812 James Cox, Bd.

Read, Robert to Alvira Carson Mar. 27, 1842 by John Landrum,
      Baptist Minister. Wit:C. Williams. Clement T.Read,Bd.

Ready, William F. to Isabella C. Berkley Dec. 12, 1832 by
      Jas. H. Otey, Rector,St. Paul's Church. Andrew J.Hooven,Bd.

Reams, Edwin A. to Margaret A. Mayfield July 24,1834 Mastin Clay B

Reams, Henry to Sally North Mar 15, 1817 Erastus T. Collins,Bd

Reams, Henry B. to Amelia M. Bateman Dec.17,1846 Joel D.Roper,BD

Reams, John to Iona Jackson May 1, 1817 Joshua Reams, Bd.

Reams, Joshua to Polly Winslow Dec 5, 1812 Henry B. Jackson,Bd

Reams, Oscar to Martha S. Dodson, Jan.29,1847 Austin W.Potter,Bd

Reams, Robert to Mary F. Womack Jan.10,1833 Wm. Peach, Bd.

Reams, Robert Jr. to Elizabeth F. North Oct. 7, 1847 R.M.Crutcher

Reams, William R. to Sarah Jane Allen Dec. 25,1846 Wm.E.Green,Bd

Reavis, Henry W. to Eliza Baker Mar 7,1835 John Jordan, Bd.

Reavis, Lewis W. to Osia Jordan Feb 3,1828 Robertson Heaton,Bd

Redd, Robert S. to Rispas Wilson June 9,1830 Sam.S.Haile,Bd.

Redford, James to Sally Shelburne Mar 18,1819 Mack Roberts,Bd.

Redford, John to Sally Roberts Jan.1,1810 Sam'l Shelburn,Bd.
      Wit. Wm. P. Harrison (Quote-Back of license -"I
      selebrated the Rights of Maridy between the within
      cople on 29 day Dec 1809 -given under my hand 1 Jan
      1810." Sam'l Shelburn JP.)

Redford, William H. to Sarah Nichols Sept 1 , 1837 By J.Anderson

Redmon, Robert T. (X) to Sarah Johnson Dec.29,1850 Geo.L.Neely,Bd

Redmond, John to Betsey Stokes April 3, 1826 bond

Redmond, John F. (X) to Malvina Scott Jan 21, 1849 by G.W.
      Pollard, J. P. at 3 O'c. S. S. Mayfield, Wit and Test.

Redmond, Josiah T. to Jane Wheeler Nov. 3,1848 J. H. Achey, Bd.

Redmond, Sidenn to Nancy Hampton Oct. 5,1837

Reed, Caleb to Hannah Reed Dec. 18,1815 Andrew Reed, Bd.

Reed, James L. to Catherine C. Wells Nov. 11,1815 David Kaigler, Robert G. McKnight, Bd.

Reed, Jesse(X) to Mary Allen Oct. 5,1822 Reuben Wright, Bd.

Reed, John to Betsey Taylor Aug. 4,1815 James(X) Taylor, Bd.

Reed, John C. to Sarah R. Wallace Nov. 26,1833 Shadrack W. Reed

Reed, Leander J. to Emeline Tucker Oct. 8,1844 Jas. A. McElhany

Reed, Robert(signed Read) to Elizabeth Gentry Jan. 16,1817 Bd: James Patterson

Reed, Shadrack W. to Elizabeth Ragan Mar. 8,1843 John E. Reed

Reed, Wm. to Thankful Lovett Sept. 8,1830 Joseph Lovett, Bd.

Reese, Francis M.(X) to Rebecca Ferguson Apr. 27,1848 Bd: Arthur A. Parrish

Reese, Jordan M. to Mary Virginia Martin May 9,1835 Turner L. Green, Bd.

Reese, Joseph T. to Nancy Belcher Feb. 25,1845 Peyton H. Witt

Reese, Patrick to Sally North Dec. 2,1816 Bd: John Watson

Reese, Robert to Eliza Jane McCollum July 25,1850 Bd: Austin McCollum

Reeves, John to Nancy Kenny June 30,1809 Bd: Jno. Edgar

Reeves, John C. to Rebecca Pinkston Sept. 19,1819 Alexander Wood, Bd.

Reeves, John H. (signed Rives) to Louisa J. McCrory July 8, 1832 Bd: William McCrory

Reeves, Ozburn to Esther H. Osteen May 5,1812 Bd: Jese Osteen

Region, Joel(X) to Lauretta Bateman Nov. 11,1816 Robt. McLemore

Reid, Andrew to Polly C. Adams Feb. 10,1817 Jacob Critz, Bd.

Reid, Clemmon to Elizabeth Taylor Feb. 11,1830 Jas. C. Taylor

Reid, David Y. to Elizabeth Bennett Dec. 24,1811 Cooper Bennett

Reid, George W. to Catherine Legate Jan. 17,1821 Jacob J. Cahoon

Reid, James to Hannah Legate Dec.20,1819 William Legate, Bd.

Reid, John to Elizabeth B. Maury Sept.6,1809 John B. Hogg

Reid, John to Agatha Johnston Jan. 3,1813 Terry Bradley, Bd.

Reid, Thomas to Louisiana D. Banks Mar.2,1837

Reid, Wm. J. to Sarah C. Maury June 5,1849 Jas. P. Maury, Bd.

Reynolds, Geo. A. to Mary E. Cook Oct.16,1845 Charles F. Wall, Bd.

Reynolds, Henry C. to Sarah C. Gutherie Dec.22,1844 John R. Marshall

Reynolds, James M. to Nancy Dunlap Dec.12,1836 Sam'l S. Graham

Reynolds, John to Mary Lawrence Dec.4,1806 Wm. Connelly, Bd.

Reynolds, Reuben to Miriam Fisher Oct. 2,1815 Elijah Mayfield

Reynolds, Reuben to Polly T. Gillaspie July 22,1816 Sam'l Brooks

Reynolds, Richard to Mary Stone June 21,1820 Samuel Cox, Bd.

Reynolds, Spencer to Sally Parker Apr. 6,1812 Michael Burroughs

Reynolds, Thomas to Mary Carter Sept. 13,1815 Henry Cook

Rhea, Septimus to Milly Alexander July 25,1822 John Landrum, Bd.

Rhoads, Joseph to Serenah Denton Feb.20,1807 Rob't Cartwright,
    Joseph McPherson, Bd.

Rhodes, James to Sally Edwards Aug. 30,1823 Jas. Edwards, Bd.

Rhodes, Jarris(X) to Priscilla Fox Aug.28,1850 Elijah R. Davis

Rhodes, Josiah(X) to Nancy Cummins Mar.20,1822 Lambert Forehand

Rhodes, Levin E. to Louisa V. Roper Apr.4,1850 Henry C. Lazenby

Rhodes, Wm. to James Mayfield Dec. 25,1805 Samuel Mayfield, Bd.

Rice, Ebenezer to Caty Baldridge June 12,1809 John Baldridge, Bd.

Richardson, Coonrod to Elizabeth Fuqua Oct. 16,1811 Benj. Roberts

Richardson, Daniel to Mary Campbell July 24,1823 Neil Campbell

Richardson, Daniel to Elizabeth Quinn Dec. 22,1850 Jacob Vanderslice, Bd.

Richardson, John to Mary C. Marable Sept.9,1828 Peter Owen,Bd.

Richardson, John to Ann Wright Aug. 10,1831 Andrew B. Ewing,Bd.

Richardson, John W. to Malvina Perkins Sept. 12,1850 Henry S. Crutcher, Bd.

Richardson, Martin W. to Nancy Harper Apr.20,1816 Phineas Thomas

Richardson, Robert G. to Elizabeth Ann McKay Dec.18,1842 Bd: Jonathan Rothrock

Richmond, Isaac to Betsey Carroll Dec.6,1822 James G. Jones,Bd.

Riddle, Henry to Cyntha Short Oct. 1,1830 Wm. Harrison, Bd.

Ridge, Thomas to Sally Martin Aug. 20,1814 Thomas Ridge, Bd. Witn: Wm. B. Eaton

Ridger, Wm. (or Ridgen) to Catharine Mairs Dec.23,1809 Jos.Mairs

Ridgway, Joseph to Mary Henderson Mar.4,1816 James Ridgway,Bd.

Ridley, Beverly to Elizabeth Gooch June 12,1828 R. Ridley,Bd.

Ridley, Geo. G. to Rebecca B. McEwin Jan. 14,1841 Lumsford P. Black, Bd.

Ridley, Henry to Elizabeth Allison Jan. 4,1815 Josiah Knight,Bd.

Ridley, Robert to Sally Houston Mar.26,1820 Geo. Ridley, Bd.

Ridley, Samuel J. to Sarah C. McEwen Sept.8,1846 Richard H. Ogilvie, Bd. By An. N. Cunningham, M. G.

Ridley, Thomas to Elizabeth Hood Nov. 13,1819 Bunwell Brack,Bd.

Ridley, Wm. A. to Sarah C. Anthony Mar.16,1842 Walter Kibble,Bd.

Riggins, Daniel(X) to Ann N. Sudberry Feb.29,1832 Joseph Yates

Riggins, John to Rebecca Stone Dec. 30,1835 Oran (X) Hopkins, Bd.

Riggs, Gideon to Polly Reynolds May 16,1816 Aaron Boyd, Bd.

Riggs, James B. to Martha Ezell Nov.6,1828 Thomas P. Norton,Bd.

Right, Dincalian to Patsy Roberts Aug.4,1842 John(X) Roberts,Bd.

Ring, Hiram E. to Emma T. Motheral Jan. 12,1840 Jas. H. Mallory

Rivers, Joel F. to Sarah B. Lane Sept. 10,1840 Spivy Stanfield

Rivers, Thomas E. to Martha Turner Jan. 12,1832 John J. Roberts

Rives, Albert P. Elizabeth Wilds Oct. 23,1833 Everett Owen, Bd.

Roach, John A. to Martha I. Fou Apr. 19,1828 F. A. Stone(Sten)

Roach, Simon to Ann H. Moore May 3,1843 John T. Church, Bd.

Roads, James to Nancy Forehand June 25,1815 Thos. Forehand, Bd.

Robb, Wm. D. to Diademna Catharine Inman Mar. 18,1840 AugustusDoe

Robb, Wm. W. to Ann Little Nov. 30,1825 Loving H. Wooldridge, Bd.

Roberds, Thomas (X) to Polly Burnett Nov. 28,1816 Bird Dodson, Bd.

Roberts, Anderson G. (X) to Celia Tatum May 26,1831 SamuelS. Radford, Bd.

Roberts, Benjamin F. to Margarett Halfacre Mar. 10,1836 Thos. Edmondson, Bd.

Roberts, Clement S. to Mary Ann Young Sept. 14,1842 Daniel Morton

Roberts, Francis(X) to Nancy Moran Feb. 15,1849 Richard(X) Thompson, Bd. By J. C. Anderson, M. G.

Roberts, Howard to Vinah Pinkston July 9,1818 Everett Creech, Bd.

Roberts, Howard to Nancy Ray June 19,1823 Alexander Wood, Bd.

Roberts, Jesse(X) to Nancy Tremble Nov. 10,1832 Wm. W. Inscome

Roberts, John to Sally Smithson June 30,1821 Mack C. Roberts, Bd.

Roberts, John to Ann Giles Jan. 18,1827 M. Kinnard, Bd.

Roberts, John B. to Polly Petty Mar. 2,1820 James Merritt, Bd.

Roberts, John D. to Elizabeth Tisdale Nov. 19,1829 Luke(X) Williams, Bd. By Andrew Craig, M. G.

Roberts, Joseph to Susannah Brown Oct. 21,1806 Wiley Brown, Bd.

Roberts, Joseph(X) to Elizabeth A. Fletcher Mar. 8,1838 Newton Roberts, Bd. By L. Powell, M. G.

Roberts, Mack to Lucy Radford Oct. 9,1818 Henry Walker, Bd.

Roberts, Mack C. to Frances Robinson Oct. 28,1840 Pettus S. Hay

Roberts, Newton to Sarah Giles Aug. 3,1838 Richard(X) Giles,Bd.

Roberts, Thos. H. to Jane J. Crockett Nov.28,1839 JohnE.Tulloss

Roberts, William to Mary Orton Aug. 17,1826 by G. Hunt,J.P.

Roberts, Wm. M. to Eveline Marshall Dec.23,1824 N. Warren,Bd.

Roberts, Wm. R. to Charity Dunneber(illegible) Jan. 27,1841
    Robert H. McNail, Bd. By Pet Ownes, J. P.

Roberson, Wm.(X) to Amanda Vaughan Nov.6,1842 John B. Barnes,Bd.

Robertson, Burges to Elizabeth Paynor Dec. 13,1827 John(X)Paynor

Robertson, David to Sally Rubottam Dec.9,1819 Martin(X)Trantham

Robertson, Edward(X) to Mary Ann Barnes Sept.2,1841 John B.Barnes

Robertson, Henry(X) to Nancy Williams Mar.10,1816 Alexander(X)
    McDaniel, Bd.

Robertson, Henry to Elizabeth C. Applewhite Sept.5,1830 Wm. D.
    Taylor, Bd. By Robert Davis, M. G.

Robertson, Henry V. to Rebecca B. Oldham Dec. 27,1828 Owen T.
    Watkins, Bd.

Robertson, Jesse(X) to Elly Vernon July 24,1828 Leonard Vernon

Robertson, John to Pheobe Reed(or Reid) Dec. 13,1823 HughB.Reid

Robertson, Levi(X) to Betscy Anglin May 3,1823 Wm. (X) White,Bd.

Robinson, Alexander to Frances Ogilvie Nov.17,1817 Benj.B.Lanier

Robinson, Alexander M. to Malinda B. Ragsdale Feb.6,1844 Bd:
    Jesse H. Sparkman By J. Burnett, J. P.

Robinson, Andrew to Polly Hays Jan.17,1828 Gray W. Barker,Bd.

Robinson, Charles to Edney Bizzle Sept.8,1825 Humphrey Hardison

Robinson, Charles W. to Sarah E. Skelly July 27,1848 Jesse H.
    Sparkman, Bd. By W. F. A. Shaw, J. P.

Robinson, David to Nancy Burgess Sept. 28,1848 Joseph Brice,Bd.

Robinson, David J. to Ester Moore Nov.12,1816 James Brittain,Bd.

Robinson, George R.(X) to Susannah B. Wilson July 23,1835 Samuel Brown, Bd. By J. Wall, J. P.

Robinson, Hardy(X) to Matilda Cato Feb. 19,1832 Ezekiel Wall,Bd.

Robinson, Henderson D.(X) to Nancy Chambers Apr.7,1831 Bd:Joseph P. (X) Harrison By Andrew Craig, M. G.

Robinson, James to Elizabeth A. Bumpass May 21,1839 AndrewKennedy

Robinson, James E. to Elizabeth C. Carter Oct. 9,1850 Bd:Green Colquitt By John Hay, J. P.

Robinson, James M.(X) to Milly Hoggard Sept. 21,1848 IsaacXLong

Robinson, James S. to Parthenia Evans Oct. 21,1849 Bd:John H. Hay

Robinson, John(X) to Nancy Williams Nov. 11,1818 John Smith,Bd.

Robinson, John to Ann M. Donnelson Nov. 21,1829 Jas. Robinson,Bd.

Robinson, John J. to Elizabeth Cato Nov. 4,1841 Wm. H. Cato,Bd.

Robinson, Michael to Matilda Akins Sept. 12,1808 Mitchell Robinson

Robinson, Nathan P. to Virginia Scruggs Nov.28,1850 Sanford G. Allen, Bd. By Bird Swanson, J. P.

Robinson, Nicholas T. to Rebecca Robinson Feb. 11,1841 Chas. W. Robinson, Bd. By J. Burnett, J. P.

Robinson, Nicholas T. to Jane Cowen Oct. 20,1846 Jesse H. Sparkman

Robinson, Richard W. to Martha Merritt Mar. 31,1820 Daniel R. Merritt, Bd.

Robinson, Shadrack J. to Sarah Jane Robinson Oct.31,1850 John S. Robinson, Bd. By W. F. A. Shaw, J. P.

Robinson, Thos. L. to Elizabeth S. Jones Nov.5,1844 By J.Carle,MG

Robinson, Thos. S. to Elizabeth S. Jones Nov. 4,1843 (Bond)

Robinson, Wm. to Eliza Hay Dec. 11,1827 Albert(X) Madden, Bd.

Robinson, Wm.(X) to Ann Madden Jan.11,1841 David Forehand,Bd. (Bond alone filed)

Robinson, Wm. P. to Nancy Stephens Sept.6,1848 Jas. Williams Jr.

Robison, David M. to Mary Ann Shannon Dec.3,1846 Thos. J. Griggs

Robison, Edward (X) to Susan Clark Dec.17,1846 Clement W. Williams

Robison, Richard W. to Elizabeth King Aug.11,1835 Zebulon C. Nolen, Bd.

Rogers, Andrew to Roche M. Carter Oct. 22,1840 Samuel S. Morton

Rogers, James A. S. to Elizabeth B. Hughes Dec.31,1846 George W. Parham, Bd.

Rogers, Lemuel to Martha Hilliard Sept.19,1833 Wm. D. Taylor,Bd.

Rogers, McDaniel(X) to Martha Belcher Dec.6,1843 Samuel L. Z.(X) Coleman, Bd.

Rogers,(X) Park to Mary Haley Oct.6,1838 John (X) Maupen, Bd.

Rogers, Robert to Polly Gentry June 9,1812 Watson Gentry, Bd.

Rogers, Samuel M. to Harriet E. Hancock May 3,1842 Coatsworth P. Logan

Rogers, Wm. A. to Mary R. Seatte Feb.9,1843 Samuel Vernon, Bd.

Roland, Abraham to Nancy Whitley Mar.18,1819 Mansfield House,Bd.

Roland, Isaac to Martha Wrenn Dec. 2,1824 John Mays, Bd.

Roland, John to Sarah H. Carter Sept.4,1814 Thos. Hiter, Bd. Witn: Wm. B. Eaton

Roland, John to Elizabeth Bryant Aug.17,1848 Wm. A. Graham,Bd.

Roland (Rolland), Thos. to Nancy Christley Nov.27,1828 Bd:Alfred (X) Reeder

Roller, Geo. A. to Susan Ann Halfacre Mar.4,1849 Wesley House,Bd.

Roper, Geo. W.(X) to Nancy Scott July 5,1844 John McDaniel, Bd.

Rosald, Asia to Mary Ann Cary Feb. 2,1826 by G. L. Nolen,J.P.

Rosenbum, Alexander(X) to Patsey Luty Feb.26,1820 Drury (X)Wall

Ross, James F. to Elizabeth M. Sharp Dec.18,1832 Wm.P. Sharp,Bd.

Ross, Wm. to Barthmy Morton Sept.28,1823 Charles Robinson,Bd.

Ross, Wm. B. to Polly Witherspoon Feb.6,1823 Daniel Perkins,Bd.

Rosson, Roswell J. to Judith R. Owen Sept.27,1848 Nashville J. Wright, Bd.

Roswell(signed Rozell), Ashley B. to Margaret M. Ralston Sept.16, 1828   Bd: Wm. Johnson   By German Baker, M. G.

Roundtree, Joseph T. to Frances Odell Aug.5,1825 Duncan Campbell

Rounselville, Amos to Susan F. Walker Aug.15,1833 Sydney Walters

Rountree, Chas. S. to Ann O. Crutcher Dec. 1,1842 Jas. B. Porter

Rountree, Wm. to Susan W. H. Rhoades Sept. 3,1829 Jesse Jacobs,Bd.

Rowland, John to Eliza Tuter June 4,1840 James(X) Morris

Rowland, Nathaniel H. to Jane Blankinship Nov.30,1815 Bd:Richard W. Hicks

Rowlett, John J. to Lucy Ann Matthews Jan.7,1830 Sherwood W.Beaty

Rowlett, Martin to Ann Rivers Aug. 13,1840 Robert Rivers Jr.,Bd.

Rowlett, Wm. to Elizabeth Glenn Jan.29,1829 Jasan Winsett,Bd.

Rowlett, Wm. P. to Mary Culberson Aug.23,1837 By H.B. Hyde,J.P.

Roy, John to Nancy Stone Nov. 21,1812 Andrew Montgomery, Bd.

Roy, John to Delila Wooton Jun.17,1816 Geo. W. Wooton,Bd. "Married few days after date of license" by G. Hunt

Roy, Thomas to Perlina Fitz Mar.14,1841 James(X) Poteete, Bd.

Roy, Wm. to Jane Shumate July 22,1811 Bd: Walter Hill

Rubottom, Dixon to Cynthia Nicholson July 21,1830 Wm. Burns,Bd.

Rucker, John to Myra Boyd Nov. 1,1824 B. A. Rucker, Bd.

Rucker, Joseph B. to Rebecca Champion Jan. 11,1844 Benjamin Seward, Bd. By Jno. Landrum, M. G.

Rucker, Wm. to Mary J. Pillow Sept. 25,1827 Wm. Burns, Bd.

Rudder, Richard H. to Mary Bostick Jan. 1,1822 Abner McCord,Bd.

Rumage, John to Ann Striplan Oct. 30,1826 by J. Farrington

Ruperd(Rupard), Erasmus to Nancy Nall Mar.23,1820 James(X)Glass

Russell, Baxter S. to Mary Jane Vaughan Aug.24,1848 A.B. Morton

Russell, Daniel W. to Kathron A. Toon Dec.19,1850 Carter H. Witt

Russell, Elam(X) to Elizabeth Gates Jan.14,1817 James(X) Gates

Russell, Elijah(X) to Lila Garrett July2,1829 Jesse Pate, Bd.

Russell, Geo. T. to Ann D. Jowitt Jan. 25,1840 Moses D. Castery

Russell, Geo. W.(X) to Nancy Burnett June24,1839 Robt.McCuistain

Russell, Geo. W. to Elizabeth A. Cromer Feb.3,1842 StephenBennett
    Bd. Witn: Blount Jordan

Russell, Haley to Mary Thweatt Jan.7,1835 Wm. B. Barker, Bd.

Russell, Haley W. to Mary Ann Floyd Feb.24,1841 James A. Shaw

Russell, James to Sally Garrett(or Garnett) May 15,1824 Bd:
    James Stirk

Russell, James W.(X) to Elizabeth Hall Jan. 28,1847 Hugh(X)
    Sherwood, Bd. By John King, M. G.

Russell, John to Phoebe Gates Jan.18,1812 Robert Featherson,Bd.

Russell, John H. to Mary W. Old July 16, 1820 Samuel D. Read,Bd.

Russell, John J. to Sarah Sires Dec. 18,1844 Samuel Gillorton,Bd.

Russell, Josephus to Ann M. E. Davidson Nov.1,1844 Stephen D.
    Fields, Bd. By H. H. Horton, M. G.

Russell, Thomas to Nancy Fields Mar. 21,1836 John McMurray,Bd.

Russell, Thomas to Emeline Langley Dec.28,1848 Wm. H. Spratt, Bd.

Russell, Wm. T. to Margaret T. Ingram Feb.28,1850 Geo.W. Allen

Russworm, John to Sarah Clark Dec. 20,1817 Bd:Nich. Scales

Rustin, Samuel to Mary Godwin Apr. 2,1822 Wm. Sparkman, Bd.

Rutherford, Benjamin D. to Susan Brown June 18,1812 EphraimBrown

Rutherford, Stephen T.(X) to Sally Tatum Aug.5,1825 DavidPinkston

Rutledge,Alexander to Nancy McLemore Mar.12,1808 Elijah Rutledge

Rutledge, Robert to Fanny G. Cahoon Oct.12,1809 George Cahoon,Bd.
    Witn: Solomon Stone

Ryan, Peter(X) to Hetty Ray July 9,1843 Martin(X) Davis,Bd.

Ryan, Reuben to Rachel Harper June 14,1815 Zacheriah Smith(X),Bd.

Rylie, James to Mary Snow July 15,1828 Bd: James Martin

Sadler, John to America Nance Mar.20,1834 Nathan Newsom, Bd.

Saddler, John to Elizabeth Griggs Nov. 4,1849 Henry Green, Bd.

Sage, Rufus W. to Martha J. Hughes Dec. 4,1833 John Layne, Bd.

Sage, Travis to Rachael Potts Sept. 30,1822 Bd: Basil Trail

Salmon, John(X) to Polly Blair Dec. 26,1817 Bd:Walter(X) Salmon

Salsberry, James to Mary Long(Lang) Oct.25,1815 James Prist, Bd.

Sammons, Baxter to Nancy Pate Jan. 21,1812 Jones Glover, Bd.

Sammons, John to Dice Whitlock Aug. 20,1814 Bd:Edward Russell,
    Robert W. Crafton   Witn: Wm. B. Eaton

Sempkins, James H. to Anna C. Roberts May 10,1837

Sample, Smith to Margaret Ann Buchannan Feb. 24,1825 Bd: Thomas
    Sample

Sampson, Emanuel to Elizabeth Chrisman Sept. 6,1849 A.W.Chrisman

Sampson, Smith(X) to Miscinda Rozzell July 22,1830 Isaac G. Haile

Samuel, James M. to Louisa V. Perry Mar. 31,1830 Richard Alexander

Samuel, Wm. S. to Dorinda Anderson Aug.6,1835 Bd: Wm. Anderson

Sandefur(Sandifer) John S. to Angelina C. Bond Jan. 12,1843 Bd:
    W. H. (Wm.) Trimble By M. L. Andrews, M. G.

Sandels, John to Catherine M. Hines Nov.10,1846 Wm. Hines, Bd.

Sanders, John S. to Lucy Ann Russell Jan. 1,1829 John(X)Russell

Sanders, Joseph to Mary A. Rogers Oct. 11,1841 Joseph Bunch,Bd.

Sanders, Wm. R. to Susan E. Dillin Feb.2,1845 Chas. P. Dillin,Bd.

Sanderson, Robt. to Mary Ann Owen Mar.8,1841(Bond)Andrew I.Sellers

Sandford, Archer W. to Sarah C. Brown Oct.2,1849 Dooly Pate, Bd.
    (date of ceremony omitted)

Sanford, Archer W. to Mary Ann Wood Jan. 16,1850 Stephen K. Wood

Sanford, James to Fanny Wood July 20,1824 Reuben Sanford, Bd.

Sanford, Joseph to Nancy S. Lane Nov. 28,1839 Benjamin Sandling

Sandford, Joseph to Elizabeth Prichett Mar. 12,1829 Isaiah Dyer

Sanford, Peyton to Clarinda Morton Dec. 3,1837 By W. B. Hall,C.C.

Sanford, Robert to Jane H. Burns Dec. 21,1818 John Matthews,Bd.

Sanford, Wm. to Elizabeth Manerva Elliott Jan.27,1834 Samuel Jackson, Bd. By John Richardson

Sandford, Wm. to Elizabeth E. Adams Jan. 3,1836 Bd:Wm. L. Pate

Sandling, Benjamin to Isabella(Elizabeth one place) C. Turner June 8,1840 Bd: James Sandford

Sanson, Dorrell N. to Jannette White Feb. 2,1815 John Sample,Bd.

Sapar, Stephen to Elizabeth Wilson July 25,1823 Bd:J. Wilson

Saper, Stephen to Tabitha Coor Dec. 23,1820 Bd: Wm. Coor

Sanford, Reuben to Mary Wood July 6,1820 Bd: H. B. Hyde

Sappington, Thomas to Elizabeth Gibson Mar. 16,1826

Sappington, Thos. S. to Sophronia Barnett Sept. 14,1831 Brice M. Hughes, Bd.

Sassum, Peter to Mary Ann Taylor Oct.8,1829 Jno. P. J. Sassum, Jno. L. Moray, Bd.

Satterfield, Joseph to Martha J. Jacobs Jan. 31,1850(Maury Co. license) By Henry B. North, M. G.

Saunders, Alfred to Parmelia J. Lipscomb Dec.23,1850 Bd:Robert S. Chambers

Saunders, Ezekiel to Polly Stephens May 5,1821 Charles Stephens

Saunders, Henson to Sally Childrup July 4,1825 Bd:Luamma Bateman

Saunders, Nathan to Nelly Stewart Mar. 30,1815 Bd: John Fitts

Sawyer, James to Martha Jane McDowell Oct. 4,1838 Wm.(X)Sawyer

Sawyer, John to Harriet McDowel Sept. 9,1830 Harvey(X) Haley

Sawyer, Willis to Elizabeth Ferrell Mar. 5,1834 Geo. W. Graham

Sawyers, Edmund(X) to Sally Bonds Oct. 5,1835 Stephen Foley,Bd.

Sawyers, James to Louisa Tarkinton Dec. 14,1845 Geo. White, Bd.

Sawyers, Lemuel to Mary E. T. Drake Nov.8,1849 Jas. W. White,Bd.

Sayers, Abner to Nancy Jane Scales Aug. 15,1844 Baldwin D. Taliaferro, Bd.   By John Rushing, M. G.

Sayers, Andrew C. to Ann D. Scales July 25,1844 Wm. G. Ozburn,Bd.

Sayers, David to Nancy K. Scales Dec. 9,1830 Bd: Noah Scales

Sayers, James J. to Ann M. Taliafero Jan.26,1835 Wm. Johnson,Bd.

Sayers, Sampson to Virginia Clark Dec. 13,1809 Cleyton Talbott

Sayers, Wm. (X) to Olly McDowd Apr. 14,1827 James Prichett,Bd.

Sayre, Henry to Elizabeth Underwood Nov. 23,1831 Bd:Henry Wyme

Scales, Absalom G. to Martha E. Lavender Oct.15,1845 Sam'l Webb

Scales, Absolom R. Eliza B. Morton Nov. 18,1830 Wm. Jordan,Bd.

Scales, Ellsworth P. to Lucy E. King Dec. 22,1823 Theo. L.Gentry

Scales, Henry to Ann Scales Dec. 7,1813 Thos. Manefer, Bd.

Scales, Joab to Mary G. Scales Sept. 3,1835 Samuel Scales, Bd.

Scales, John to Sarah E. Sawyers July 24,1823 Bd:Thos. Ridley

Scales, John to Rebecca D. Ladd July 28,1846 Bd:Laban Hartley

Scales, John A. to Euphamia Johnston Sept. 13,1838 Jas. V. Snell

Scales, Joseph G. to Fanny G. Webb Feb. 22,1819 Samuel Scales,Bd.

Scales, Joseph W. to Tabitha G. Scales Oct. 20,1847 Jas. Morton

Scales, Nathaniel F. to Mildred A. Webb Oct. 12,1837

Scales, Noah to Mary Sayers Aug. 11,1836 John W. Allen, Bd.

Scales, Robert Jr. to Nancy Young June 4,1829 Wm. S. S. Harris

Scales, Samuel to Melissa Ann Wilson Apr. 3,1838 Spencer Bobo,Bd.

Scales, Thomas H. P. to Charlotte H. Dalton June 24,1818 Bd: Andrew L. Martin

Scales, Wm. to Elizabeth Wilson Sept. 18,1832 Robt. W. Calhoon

Scholl, Milton to Jeretia Alexander Aug. 30,1815 Bd:John N. Chaster

Scipell, Zachariah to Suhany Armstrong Apr. 9,1812 Sam'l Hemphill

Schooler, Samuel to Priscilla Williamson Sept.7,1817 Lazarus Dodson, Bd.

Sconce, Green H. to Matilda Boyd Feb. 23,1830 John W.F. Boxley

Scott, Arthur to Hannah Porter Jan. 5,1816 Bd: John Scott

Scott, Charles M. to Nancy Hodge May 4,1837 By Robt. Davis, M.G.

Scott, David to Mary Wilson Nov.6,1816 James McEwen, Bd.

Scott, Eli D. to Cornelia A. Slaughter Mar. 4,1845 Wm.O.N.Perkins

Scott, Henry(X) to Matilda Roller Apr.29,1841 Asa (X) Harper,Bd.

Scott, Isaac to Tempy Wells Nov. 8,1813 Briant, Wells, Henry Avery

Scott, Jacob Jr. to Mary Dyer Aug. 19,1833 Bolen C. Barnes,Bd.

Scott, James M. to Matilda I. Wells (Bond) Aug.4,1840 Jas.B.Scott

Scott, John to Ferriby Martin Nov. 25,1807 Wm. Crunk, Bd.

Scott, John L.(X) to Margaret Canada Dec. 6,1845 John(X)McCandlass

Scott, John W. to Polly Whitby Jan. 19,1848 Bd: Wm. F. Carter,

Scott,(X)Malachi to Ann Givens Aug. 10,1843 Benjamin Inman, Bd.

Scott, Samuel(X) to Maria Guinn July 24,1842 Literal Guinn, Bd.

Scott, Thos. H.(X) to Sarah P. Smithson Jan. 15,1839 Wm. P. Stevens

Scott, William to Eunice Reid Dec. 9,1819 Bd: James Hughes

Scott, William to Jane Patton Aug. 20,1829 James B. Scott, Bd.

Scnuggs, Edward to Alpha Hassell Aug. 1,1818 John Scruggs, Bd.

Scruggs, John to Polly Hassell Sept. 7,1818 Joseph Hassell,Bd.

Scruggs, John to Sarah Carl Sept. 20,1832 Samuel F. Glass, Bd.

Scruggs, John B. to Martha Walton June 29,1819 Bd:Wm. H. Wells

Scruggs, Jos. to Angeline Bennett Oct.8,1844 Jerome R. Tenison

Scruggs, Langon T. to Kiziah Walton Sept. 24,1848 A. M. W.Kelly

Scruggs, Wm. to Lucinda A. Battle Oct. 3,1819 Geo. Everly, Bd.

Scruggs, Wm. A. to Lettie E. White July 31,1850 Sam'l P. Allen

Sea(or Lea), Eli (X) to Polly Hotstead(Holstead?) July 25,1829
    Travis Windrow, Bd.

Searcy, Wm. W. to Emeline R. Johnson May 30,1833 Jas. M. Green

Searight, Geo. to Matilda P. Nichol Apr. 13,1842 Wm. S. Campbell

Sears, Starkes B. to Mary Peach May 23,1839 Reuben R. Peach,Bd.

Seay, Wm. B. to Mary Ann Fletcher(Bond only) Aug.11,1846 Bd:
    Stephen A. Jordan

Secrest, Abraham to Nancy Gray Feb. 28,1811 Bd:Benjamin Deane

Secrest, John to Elizabeth Lock May 10,1817 Bd: Wm. Wallker

Secrest, Wm. to Betsy Pigg Feb. 24,1816 Bd: James Shelby

Secris, Francis to Elizabeth Gray Apr. 16,1814 Sampson Gray,Bd.

Seedberry(Sudberry?), James A.(X) to Sarah E. Gray May 16,1850
    George W. Seedbury, Bd.

Seedbury(Sudbury?), John B. to Susan E. Jackson Dec. 17,1846
    J. W. Seedbury, Bd. (Bond alone)

Seedbury(Sudbury), Madrack R. to Susan Pognor Oct. 31,1839 Bd:
    Jesse W. Williams

Seedberry (Sudberry), Patrick H. to Minerva Smithson Sept.30,
    1846 John J. Lagron, Bd.

Seigfrait, Frederick to Malinda Hicks June 21,1838 Stephen(X) W.
    Hicks, Bd.

Selph, James P. to Catharine Atkinson Feb. 15,1841 Jas. Hogan Jr.

Sessions, James P. to Anna G. Hardeman July 9,1846 Thos.N.Figures

Sessums, Blount N. to Mary Ann Cayce Nov. 13,1824 Thos. Cayce,Bd.

Sesums, George W. to Delila Sparkman June 12,1827 Jesse Sparkman

Sevel(Level?), Harel to Elizabeth Reddle Aug. 23,1838 CalebDodson

Sevier, John to Elizabeth Ridley Aug.11,1807 Beverly Ridley,Bd.

Sevit(or Sewett-illegible), Samuel to Nancy Hall Feb. 3,1843

Seward, Benjamin to Sarah M. P. Scales Oct. 20,1836 Jos.H.Nelson

Seward, John C.(S.?) to Sarah P. Caldwell Dec. 19,1843 John B. Crichlow, Bd.

Seward, John C. to Joana M. Crockett July 4,1849 James H. Scales

Sexton, Alexander to Lucy Stockett Oct.9,1843 John(X) Edds, Bd.

Shadden, Martin to Ailcey Dodson July 10,1807 Jas. Swanson, Bd.

Shakelford, Thos. to Elizabeth C. Pullam Apr.24,1817 Gibbs G. Washington, Bd.

Shall, John to Nancy Williams Aug. 19,1830 Bd: D. J. Williamson

Shannon, David to Anne Pickens Dec. 10,1808 Jas. Shannon, Bd.

Shannon, James to Polly Kaigler(Keglar?) Oct. 24,1807 Woodson Hailey, Bd.

Shannon, James to Mary Gray June 9,1825 Bd: Thomas Holt

Shannon, Jefferson to Rachel Dowdy July 8,1849 John S.McKnight

Shannon, John D. to Polly Goode Sept. 24,1817 Alexander S.McKnight, Bd.

Shannon, Samuel R. to Elizabeth Cosson(Coural?) Mar. 15,1829 Samuel C. Peay, Bd.

Shannon, Stephen M. to Ann Eliza Crutcher (Bond) May 13,1839 David M. Odil, Bd.

Shannon, Thos. to Eziriah Pickens Feb. 23,1807 James Shannon,Bd.

Sharber, Jehu to Julia W. Taylor Jan. 29,1840 Wm. R. Ransom,Bd.

Sharbar, John to Phene Jones Aug.10,1812 Bd: Jarvis Jones

Sharp, James B. to M. Miranda Horton June 4,1842 Thos.R. Pate,Bd.

Sharp, John to Betsey Bolen Dec. 24,1816 Bd: Robert Sayers

Sharp, John to Sally F. Price Oct. 5,1823 Bd: Richard Price

Sharp, John M. to Mary Martin Dec. 2,1835 Bd: Joel Walker

Sharp, Joseph(X) to Mary Caskey Dec. 17,1844 Moses D. Caskey,Bd.

Sharp, Nehemiah to Milly Clayton Sept. 15, 1807 Robt. Clayton,Bd.

Sharp, Sumner to Ann P. Henderson July 26,1827 R. H. Campbell

Sharp, Wm. to Lavinia Mason Dec. 19,1823 Thomas Pritchett, Bd.

Sharp, Wm. P. to Julia Ann Southall Oct.22,1835 Wm. W. Ross,Bd.

Shaw, Banister W. Minerva Ann Harper 1830(no date) W.B. Barker

Shaw, Calvin J. to Mary Ann Stephens Oct.15,1840 Wm. D. Ladd,Bd.

Shaw, Isaac to Sarah Gatlin Nov.8,1832 Samuel T. Patton, Bd.

Shaw, John A. to Emily C. Wilson Jan.8,1838 Thos. A. Pope, Bd.

Shaw, John A. to Charlette E. Neelly May 2,1840(Bond) JohnBaugh

Shaw, John M. to Eliza Seaton Feb.17,1841 John P. Charter,Bd.

Shaw, Timothy to Polly Garrett Nov.11,1812 Sam'l Edmiston,Bd.

Shearwood, Hugh(X) to Mary Jackson Oct.13,1829 DennisW. Howlett

Shearwood, John H. to Milly Robertson June9,1813 DanielShearwood

Sheffield, John(X) to Celia Vaughan Dec.17,1846 Jas. H. Wells,Bd.

Shelburn, John P. to Nancy Duncan July 15,1814 Wm. Williams,Bd.

Shelburn, Samuel to Polly Browder Jan.13,1806 H. Childrep,Bd.

Shelburn, Samuel to Peggy Hardin Sept. 25,1812 Nathaniel Smithers

Shelburne, James to Susan S. Sappington Aug.26,1824 Samuel P. Shelburne, Bd.

Shelburne, Jas. to Parmelia W. Lester Apr.12,1838 Beverly Toon

Shell, George(X) to Mary Corlett Aug.29,1822 George Chrisman,Bd.

Shell, John to Peniza Ford Aug. 25,1847 William(X) Ellis, Bd.

Shelton, Edward(X) to Zilpha Glenn Jan.1,1837 Samuel(X)Shelton

Shelton, George W.(X) to Margaret White June29,1845 Samuel W. McMahan, Bd. By J. G. McMahan, J.P.

Shelton, Jese(X) to Polly Johnson Jan. 7,1815 Samuel Cox, Bd.

Shelton, Thos. to Susan W. Thompson Oct.11,1828 Wm. B.McClellan

Shelton, Thomas Jr.(X) to Elizabeth Ezell Oct.13,1842 Jesse
    Shelton,Bd. Witn:J. Rothrock, M. L. Chapman

Shelton, Washington to Mary M. Fields Nov.27,1827 JohnSouthall

Shepard, Lewis to Elizabeth Norris Nov.26,1810 Peter Steele,Bd.

Shepherd, James(signed Sheppard) to Nancy Alfred Dec.12,1822
    J. K. Spear, Bd.

Shepherd, John to Eliza Mandley Nov.6,1819 John W. Cooke, Bd.

Shepherd, Thomas(signed Sheppard) to Mary Sullivan Nov.4,1835
    John Sullivan, Bd.

Sherwood, Hugh(X) to Eliza Pennington Mar.8,1847 Jas.(X)Rupett

Sherwood, Wm.(X) to America C. Pope(Bond) May6,1840 Wm.Landrum

Short, John I. to Malissa McGan July 5,1837 By T. Fanning

Short, Monroe to Lucinda Harrison Oct.4,1838 Richard A.Graham

Short, Thos. to Unice Y. Brown July 25,1833 Wm. A. Boyd, Bd.

Short, Wm. H. to Judith Atkinson Aug. 15,1822 Wm. Atkinson,Bd.

Short, Willis D. to Martha Jane Cloud June9,1846 J. H. Allen,Bd.

Shumate, Berryman to Lucy Tarpley May 10,1819 Richard(X) York

Shumate, Fielden(Fielding)(X) to Milly Vaughn Sept.12,1827
    Wm. J. Shumate, Ed.

Shumate, Wm. J. to Rachel Smith Feb. 3,1816 Wily Roy, Bd.

Shumate, Wm. J. to Eliza Smith June 26,1828 Joshua W. McCown,Bd.

Sills, Wyatt(X) to Nancy Smith Oct. 14,1819 Benjamin Roberts,Bd.

Simmes, Joseph to Agnes I. Rutherford June 23,1817 Thos. Hiter

Simmonds, Wm. H. to Martha Sneed Aug. 14,1815 Hardan Perkins,
    Phil G. Mallory, Bd.

Simmons, Alexander Y. to Eliza Y. Heter Jan. 14,1830 Theodrick
    Carter, Bd.

Simmons, Garrett(X) to Susan Wade Nov. 4,1823 Wm. H. Cullum,Bd.

Simmons, Hardy(X) to Patsey Seay Feb. 17,1825 Wm. H. Cullum,Bd.

Simmons, Hawkins(X) to Mary F. Jackson Aug.11,1831 John M. Gant

Simmons, James H. to Rebecca E. Hill (Bond) Feb. 27,1849 Bd: William Floyd

Simmons, John C. to Catherine L. W. Irion Sept. 27,1825 Bd:Thos. S. Anthony

Simmons, Thomas A. to Eliza A. German Aug. 7,1827 Jas. Marshall

Simms, Joshua G. to Betsey Carroll Jan.14,1829 Bd:Wm. Mebane

Simms, Millenton to Annie Estes Dec. 25,1821 Bd:Wm. Roberts

Simons, Andrew H.(X) to Sarah K. Smith Mar.30,1820 Jas. Johnson

Simons(Lemons?), John W. to Elizabeth A. Brimm Dec.10,1827 Bd: Thos. S. Brimm

Simpson, Jeremiah to Elizabeth Horner Dec.18,1809 Wm. Hail,Bd.

Simpson, Matthew P. to Nancy Kerr Nov.13,1821 John Potter,Bd.

Sims, John to Asenath Hightower Nov.7,1814 Bd:John H. Eaton, Oliver B. Hayes

Sims, Thomas to Mary S. Yeargain Apr.26,1832 Theodprick North

Sinclair, Henry C. to Sarah Haynes May 22,1845 Wm. Anderson,Bd.

Sinclair, John P. to Priscilla A. McAlister Jan.27,1846 Bd: Harrison H. Merritt

Singleton, Edward to Martha Ann Kirks June 13,1833 John Hudgins

Sires, Bennett to Jane Haley Jan.23,1848 Bd: W. L. McConnico,Bd. (Also see Cyrus, Bennett)

Sires, James to Sara Ann Waller Mar. 13,1839 Joseph(X) Sires,Bd.

Sires, Joseph H. to Sarah Brewer Apr.18,1843 Bd:James S. Owen

Skelly, Pryor(signed Prier Shelby)to Ritta Ragsdale Dec.14,1824 Bd: H. (X) Pigg

Skelly, Samuel to Mary Gardner Mar.8,1842 Vardy (X) McAlpin

Skelly, Sparkman to Rebecca Dungan Oct. 15,1828 Bd:Allen Dungan

Skelly, William to Mary Ann Beasley May 4,1842 Seth Sparkman,Bd.

Skiles, Jacob to Nelly Graham Apr.15,1815 Bd: James Short

Skillington, John A. to Lucinda McCall Oct.17,1833 Sydney(X) McCall, Bd.

Skinner, Gilly I.(X) to Mary M. Crouch June 16,1846 John M. Skinner

Skinner, Griffin T. to Jane Hartly Dec.30,1847 Wm. Goodwin,Bd.

Skinner, John M. to Drucilla R. Hargrove Feb.10,1840 Jas.Hargrove

Skinner, Spencer H.. to Priscilla Hartley Nov.2,1842 John W. Goodwin, Bd. (Bond alone)

Slade,Bennajah to Hannah Hobbs Oct. 5,1814 Bd: Wm. Hobbs

Slater, Benjamin to Eliza C. Smithson Mar.2,1837 By L.Powell,M.G.

Slaughter, Wm. E. H. to Hannah G. Crump Oct.12,1825 W.F.Guthrie

Sledge, Daniel(X) to Celia Kennedy Dec.15,1824 John (X) McKinney

Sledge, Elihu to Catharine Wall May 4,1848 Joseph Gentry, Bd.

Sledge, Henry to Betsey Pate Aug. 29,1814 John B . Salmons,Bd.

Sledge, John to Mary Ann Kennedy Dec.4,1823 James Gray, Bd.

Sledge, John to Mary P. Allen Apr. 20,1848 Bd: B. M. Hatcher

Sledge, Robert to Catherine K. Smithson Mar.28,1833 Wm.P.Campbell

Sledge, Sterling to Elizabeth Skillington Dec.20,1829 Bd:Wm. P. Campbell

Sledge, Timothy to Charlotte Smithson Apr.3,1824 Daniel Crenshaw

Sledge, Zebulon S.(signed Zeblin) to Sarah O. N. Warren Dec.4, 1834 Bd: Benjamin F. Roberts

Sleeker, George to Patsey Hay Aug. 24,1808 Bd: John Hay

Sleeker, George Jr. to Ede Sampson Dec. 22,1824 Joshua G. Simms

Sloan, Ferguson W.(Fargonson) to Peggy Murrey July 26,1825 Bd: Stephen Chapman

Sloan, Ryleigh D. L. to Matilda O. Vernon Sept. 23,1849 Bd:Wm. T. Ferguson

Sloan, Samuel(X) to Eliza Tucker Aug. 12,1827 Samuel Dotson,Bd.

Slocumb, Riley to Nancy Potts Dec. 21,1813 Bd:Zachariah Jackson

Sluder, Aaron B. of Davidson County to Mary B. Hill Jan. 28, 1836
    Bd: Robt. W. Walker of Davidson County

Smiley, Alexander to Terressa Wilkinson Nov. 14, 1818 Alfred M.
    Osburn, Bd.

Smith, Alexander to Mary Adeline Chadwell Aug. 30, 1837-8? Bd:
    Wm. H. Elliott

Smith, Andrew G.(X) to Sarah Fox July 22, 1830 Stephen(X) Potts

Smith, Anthony to Elizabeth Johnston Aug. 5, 1811 Joel Patterson

Smith, Bartlett(X) to Elizabeth Gray Aug. 6, 1821 John H.(X) Smith

Smith, Daniel F. to Martha A. T. Ragsdale Apr. 2, 1840 John W.(X)
    Hawk, Bd.

Smith, Edward to Polly Brown Feb. 13, 1821 Thompson Brown, Bd.
    "Married at the house of Ruffin Brown in Williamson Co."

Smith, Gabrial(X) to Elizabeth Snellgrove Aug. 10, 1815 Adam Taylor

Smith, Harmon W. to Sarah Jane Rolland Feb. 20, 1838 Thos. E. Wol-
    dridge, Bd. By R. W. Morris, Elder M. E. Church

Smith, Henry to Sally Sledge July 9, 1835 Sylvanus W. Smithson

Smith, Isaac to Polly Wilson June 28, 1814 Zacheus Wilson, Bd.

Smith, James to Lavina Breese Nov. 28, 1812 Bd: Richard Smith

Smith, James to Phebe Cayce Oct. 10, 1820 Neal Little, Bd.

Smith, James L. to Mary Wootan Mar. 16, 1820 Thos. Roundtree, Bd.

Smith, James M. to Martha Page June 18, 1825 Thos. Hardeman, Bd.

Smith, James S. to Rachel S. Dickson Jan. 26, 1825 Cyrus McEwen

Smith, James S. to Lucy Matthews Aug. 16, 1832 Wm. Matthews, Bd.

Smith, James S. to Mary Jones June 20, 1837

Smith, James Jr. to Malinda W. McGavock Oct. 3, 1833 J.L.F. Hill

Smith, John to Charity Wilson Oct. 27, 1806 James Ramsey, Bd.

Smith, John to Dianna Yates Jan. 20, 1810 Fortunease Dodson, Bd.

Smith, John to Rebecca Boswell Aug. 7, 1822 Mathias M. Stokes, Bd.

Smith, John(X) to Betsey Kirby Nov. 27,1827 Thomas(X)Pewett,Bd.

Smith, John High to Rosey Taylor May 22,1819 James Pewitt, Bd.

Smith, John J. to Mary A. Wray Feb. 16,1847 Burwell Lazenby,Bd.

Smith, John M. to Martha E. Swanson Oct. 26,1843 James M.Critz

Smith, John P. to Catherine S. Robinson Apr.20,1819 Nicholas P. Smith, Bd.

Smith, John W.(X) to Mary E. Carter Feb. 18,1823 John(X) Carter

Smith, Joseph(X) to Elizabeth Kelly Dec.26,1818 Thomas Kelly,B d.

Smith, Joseph to Ann P. McAlpin Jan. 12,1849 Wm. C. Stephenson

Smith, Joseph D. to Jane A. Bradley Mar. 6,1814 Page Bond, Bd.

Smith, Josiah B . to Lucy A. Pate Jan. 25,1844 Thomas R. Pate

Smith, Seanah to Margaret B . West June 29,1825 Isaac (X)West

Smith, Lemuel to Agness W. Perkins Jan.22,1822 Robt. McLemore

Smith, Luke to Sidney Cole Jan. 21,1808 James Dial, Bd.

Smith, Luke L. to Elizabeth Allen July 23,1843 John W. Allen,Bd.

Smith, Martin to Jane Wilson Oct. 10,1824 James Williams, Bd.

Smith, Nathaniel to Martha H. Smith Mar.17,1817 Wm. Carr, Bd.

Smith, Nicholas P. to Polly(Mary)O'Neal Perkins Nov.6,1816
    Thos. H. Perkins, Bd.

Smith, Patrick to Rosey Rhodes Dec. 20,1841 John(X)C.McDowell

Smith, Peter N. to Mary A. E. Parrish Nov. 13,1827 Nicholas P. Perkins, Bd. By Jas. H.Otey, Rector St. Pauls,Franklin

Smith, Samuel to Sena Nolen Apr. 2,1816 Stephen Nolen, Bd.

Smith, Samuel to Polly H artly Nov. 14,1847 Jonas Sutton,Bd.

Smith, Samuel D. to Margaret Jane Williamson July 23,1839
    H enderson McMahan, Bd. By Robt. Davis, M.G.

Smith, Samuel W. to Deborah Warren Sept. 28,1837

Smith, Stephen to Joicy Burton Aug. 30,1821 Neal Campbell,Bd.

Smith, Sydney Prior to Julia Ann Hunter Nov. 19, 1840 John D. Bond

Smith, Thomas to Phebe W. Reynolds Aug. 2, 1849 A. B. Morton, Bd.

Smith, Thomas H. to Susan J. Caperton June 10, 1846 Jas. B.
    Caperton, Bd. By M. B. Molloy, G. M.

Smith, Thomas S. to Lucinda Blackwell Nov. 18, 1833 Mansfield House

Smith, Turner to Amanda M. McGavock Aug. 8, 1839 (license only)

Smith, Washington G. to Elizabeth Davis June 25, 1841 Turner Davis
    Bd. (Bond alone filed)

Smith, Wm. M. to Margaret M. Wilson Dec. 24, 1834 Samuel C. Wilson

Smith, Wm. N. to Martha A. Giles June 8, 1842 Philip H. Warren

Smith, Wm. P. to Martha H. Taylor Aug. 19, 1830 Thos. B. Smith

Smith, Williamson to Camilla R. Starnes Oct. 28, 1830 Miles H.
    Owen, Bd. By German Baker, M. G.

Smith, Zacheriah to Sally Jackson Feb. 3, 1816 Wm. Taylor, Bd.

Smithson, Charles to Jane Giles Dec. 20, 1827 Andrew Thomas, Bd.

Smithson, Charles W. to Drucilla W. Pennington Oct. 15, 1836
    Sylvanus W. Smithson, Bd.

Smithson, Charles W. to Sarah A. Pennington Oct. 7, 1847
    Wm. J. Smithson, Bd.

Smithson, Coleman G. to Celia Lester Dec. 21, 1843 John Lester, Bd.

Smithson, Horatio S. to Lydia Andrews Dec. 6, 1832 Clement Smithson, Bd.

Smithson, John G. to Ann V. Ladd Feb. 18, 1841 Isaac English, Bd.

Smithson, Nathaniel B. to Sarah A. Smithson Dec. 6, 1838 Bd:
    James S. Gibson By M. L. Andrews, M. G.

Smithson, Richard K. to Sarah O. P. Holloway July 24, 1833 Bd:
    Jno. A. (X) Elmore By Andrew Craig, M. G.

Smithson, Samuel to Matilda Secrest Dec. 5, 1818 James Tisdale

Smithson, Sylvanus W. to Louisa Smithson May 10, 1821 Bd: Clement
    L. Pennington

Smithson, Sylvanus W. to Mary Jane Gibson June 8, 1837

Smithson, Wm. O. to Lucy W. Giles Dec.18,1834 Chas.W.Smithson,Bd.

Smuthuman, John(X) to Polly Edwards Apr.2,1822 Thos. H. Edwards

Smyth, Mack to Mary Ann Ferguson Nov.26,1837

Sneed, James to Mary Hunt Feb.25,1823 Constantine P. Sneed, Bd.

Sneed, James P. to Julia C. Herbert Mar. 10,1836

Sneed, Mark A. to Mary A. Sneed July 27,1837

Snellgrove, Benjamin(X) to Sally Coward June 11,1816 GabrielSmit.

Snow, Charles of Tuscaloosa, Ala. to Sarah Myra Perkins Oct. 7, 1828   Bd: Thos. Hardeman

Solomon, Jordan to Sally Wisner Mar. 25,1809 Francis Gunter, Bd.

Somerville, Wm. to Emily Cody July 3,1840 Mark L. Andrews, Bd.

Southall, James to Nancy D. Bond Feb. 2,1837 by H.B. North, M.G.

Southall, John to Elizabeth Campbell Jan. 4,1842 Wm. H. Crouch

Southall, Joseph J. B. to Mary C. K. McGavock Sept. 22,1836
        Charles D. Parrish, Bd.

Southall, Mack W. to Nancy Cummins Sept. 11,1845 Bd:JosephR.Hunte

Spalding, Ulyses to Jane A. Smith Sept. 4,1827 C. A. Harris, Bd.

Spann, Hartwell(X) to Mariah Bonds Mar. 25,1846 Young(X)Tatum

Spann, James to Lucy A. Matthews Feb. 3,1842 Thos.(X) Spann, Bd.

Spann, Moses I. to Jane Carsan Feb.6,1816 Jeremiah Spann, Bd.

Spann, Wm. to Peggy Carson Sept. 19,1817 Moses T. Spann, Bd.

Spann, Wm. F. to Susanna P. Johnson July 29,1834 Henry W. Smith

Spann, Wm. to Anna Myers Dec. 22,1834 Bd: William Spann

Sparkman, Charles R. to Jane Lattey Mar. 17,1828 LawrenceXSmith

Sparkman, Humphreys to Seally Wirthington Feb.16,1818 Kinchen
        Sparkman, Bd.

Sparkman, James G. to Delamy M. Sparkman Feb. 15,1838 Wm. C.
        Sparkman, Bd.

Sparkman, Kitchen(Kinchen?) to Eliza Ann Simpson Nov. 29,1813 Wm. Sparkman, Bd.

Sparkman, Matthew P. to Mary A. Robinson Dec. 28,1837

Sparkman, Wm. to Elizabeth Vestal May 4,1820 Jay Vestal, Bd.

Sparkman, Wm. L. to Luc inda Wakefield Dec.6,1849(Bond alone) John L. Robinson, Bd.

Sparkman, Wm. S. to Martha M. Roberson Oct.13,1836 Richard Ragsdale, Bd.

Speer, Joshua to Phebe Sheppard Dec.9,1816 L. W. Marbury, B d.

Speers, James(X) to Rebecca Watkins Oct. 25,1832 John(X)Hutcheson

Spence, Alson to Mary Ann Revel Dec. 23,1840 Bd:Jas. Williams

Spence, Daniel(X) to Polly Ann Pewitt Dec.9,1828 Wm.K.XSteepleton

Spencer, Bartholomew(X) to Eliza Ann Moppin Aug.22,1839 Thomas H . Roberts, Bd.

Spencer, Wm. to Elizabeth Jones Sept. 23,1830 Richard Berry,Bd.

Spratt, Blythe to Rachel Blythe Oct. 14,1811 John Spratt,bd.

Spratt, Joseph to Elisabeth Padgett Nov. 23,1820 Bryant Crow,Bd.

Spratt, Joseph to Martha Jones Oct.15,1846 Miles R. Hudson,Bd.

Sprott, James A. to Susan Shaw Feb. 12,1843 John Fitzgerald, Bd.

Sprott, John B. to Sarah E. Crutcher May 24,1849 Thos. N. Pettus

Sprott, Samuel to Mary Ann Jones Feb. 22,1843 Geo. Lavender Jr.

Sprouse, Philip to Sarah Attekison Oct. 12,1830 Jos. H.Corzine(X)

Squier, David to Sarah Pryor Nov. 13,1816 Matthew D. Cooper, Bd.

Squier, Gurdon to Mary Maury Aug. 5,1812 Robert P. Curren, Bd.

Stacy, Abner to Eliza Jane Morgan Oct. 3,1833 Andrew G. Porter

Stacy, John to Nancy Braden July 23,1812 Gurdon Squier, Bd.

Stacy, Thomas to Patcy Brown Nov. 25,1817 Robert Lynch, Bd.

Staggs, Ebben B. to Mary Winstead Feb. 8,1828 L. S. Bateman,Bd.

Staggs, Pleasant(X) to Polly Jackson Feb. 6,1821 John P. McCutchan, Bd.

Staggs, Thomas to Dolly Lock Apr. 18,1818 Bennett Phillips, Bd.

Stainback, Robert to Drucilla Patton Sept. 17,1808 Lawrence Bass

Stallions, David(X) to Betsey Waller Sept.21,1819 John Smith

Stamps, Miles to Amanda Jane Horton Dec.21,1835 Claiborne Jackson

Standley, Thomas E. to Holland W. Gatlin Sept. 22,1825 Thosmas Matthews, Bd.

Stanfield, Carter to Nancy Bennett Jan.6,1842 John(X) Hampton

Stanfield, George to Dolly Lane June6,1813 John Shores, B d.

Stanfield, Hosea to Mary Griggs Jan. 8,1835 James H. Lampkin,Bd.

Stanfield, John Q. to Elizabeth Mayberry Mar.21,1847 James Cunningham, B d.

Stanfield, Spiry to Nancy Tisdale Aug.19,1841 William P.Stevens

Stanfield, Wm.X to Elizabeth Griggs Jan. 11,1842 Wm. B. Orton,Bd.

Stanley, James to Elizabeth Dunham Mar.13,1806 Abraham Truit,B d.

Stanley, John to Nancy Jones Dec. 17,1829 Benton Jones, Bd.

Stanley, Martin to Eliza Little Dec.28,1828 Martin S. Little,Bd.

Starnes, Jas. W. to Mary C. Rudder Apr.19,1849 Peter A. Perkins

State, Hiram R. to Lucy R. Rudder Dec. 23,1841 Obadiah Jones,Bd.

Stavin, Alexander to Matilda Gillaspie Nov.15,1821 Sam'l A. Gillespie, Matthew P. Wallis, Bd.

Steagall, Henry W. to Elizabeth C. Gee Dec.19,1850 Robt. Waller

Steel, Moses to Indah Lambert Oct.16,1813 John L. Davis, Bd.

Steel, Moses to Fanny H. Allen Sept. 28,1816 Wm. Scott, Bd.

Steel, Richard to Margaret Grayham Nov.12,1805 D. Squier,Bd.

Steele, Ephraim to Frances Morton Aug.26,1819 Charles E. Woods

Steele, Richard to Elizabeth H. Walters Feb.27,1831 Wm.H. Crouch

Steele, Wm. A. to Mary E. Steele Oct. 15,1850 Wm. Y. Bennett,Bd.

Stephen, German to Charlotte Mitchell Jan.26,1807 Frederick Joy

Stephens, Albert G. to Luvinia A. Hill Sept.13,1849 Hiram State

Stevens, Arthur to Nancy Stanfield Nov.24,1842 John D. Wood,Bd.

Stevens, Benjamin to Lucy Ann Griggs Mar.9,1837

Stephens, Calvin to Edline D. Woods Apr.28,1831 Frederick Halfacre, Bd.

Stephens, Charles(X) to Eliza A. Burge Dec.14,1830 Benjamin
Stephens, Bd.

Stephens, Curtis(signed Stevens) to Mary T. Watkins Feb.25,1834
John T. Watson, B d.

Stephens, Dennis to Jane Hutson Aug. 1,1822 John Hutson, Bd.

Stephens, Edward to Nancy Pearce Dec. 30,1806 Henry Stephens

Stevens, Edward (X) to Paulina Lamb Feb.16,1832 Andrew Halfacre

Stevens, Edward M. to Elizabeth Tindall Feb. 24,1847 Jacob T.
Stevens, B d.

Stephens, George(X) to Polly Hamblin Aug.10,1820 BenjaminHamblin

Stephens, Henry to Elizabeth Page Sept. 1,1809 Charles Stephens

Stephens, Henry to Eleanor C. McEwen Mar.24,1824 R. M. Ewing

Stephens, James to Harriett Goodwin Aug.5,1833 Warren T. Goodwin

Stevens, Jas. C. to Rebecca J. Glenn Nov.28,1838 Lawrence O'Bryan

Stevens, Jas. W. to Nancy Westbrooks Feb.9,1848 B . A. Johnson

Stevens, Jeremiah to Emeline Ezell Nov.6,1833 Jepthah Ezell

Stevens, Jeremiah to Elizabeth Graham May18,1843 Johothan R.
(X) Graham, Bd. (Bond alone)

Stevens, John P. to Hannah T. Lamb Feb.1,1844 Isaac S. Pope,Bd.

Stephens, John S. to Matilda W. Chrisman June 13,1833 Wm. D.
Taylor, Bd.

Stevens, Lewis B . to Cyntha J. Bateman Apr.1,1835 Jas.P.Stevens

Stephens, Lovett to Olive Davis July 24,1820 Moses(X) Davis, Bd.

Stevens, Milton H. (Signed Stephens) to Mary H. Osburn Nov 2,1848 Jacob T. Page, Bd.

Stephens, Silas to Caty Waddel Jan. 3,1818 Wm. E. Owen, Bd.

Stephens, Thos.(X) to Polly Walters Dec. 6,1825 H azh(X)B atts

Stephens, Wm. to Sally Page May 8,1810 Theophilus Fulgham, Bd.

Stephens, Wm. to Martha Chrisman Aug. 24,1834 Benjamin Stephens

Stephens, Wm. to Lovey Page Mar. 6,1811 David Stephens, Bd.

Stevens, Wm. P. to Jane E. Green Mar. 30,1842 John Wood, Bd.

Stevens, Wm. P. to Louisa Nolen June 17,1849 Jas. P. Stevens, H. S. Bateman, Bd.

Stephenson, Benjamin C. to Emily Ferguson Mar. 6,1845 Thos. A. Stricklin, Bd.

Stephenson, Jas. G. to Anne Dyer Mar. 31,1816 Jas. Hardgraves, Bd.

Stepehenson, Jas. G. to Rachel Curtis Jan. 31,1818 Moses Curtis

Stevanson, Jas. H. to Mary A. Dudley Oct. 10,1838 Anderson(X) Potts, Bd.

Stephenson, James W. to Jemima Stephenson Apr. 22,1826

Stephenson, John G. to Martha Lester Aug. 13,1828 Whitehead Lester

Stephenson, Moses D. to Eliza Ann Stephenson Feb. 16,1848 James C. Stephenson, Bd. (Bond alone)

Stephenson, Wm. to Matilda Saperton Jan. 11,1819 Francis Gordon

Stewart, Alex to Jenny McKinney Aug. 4,1810 Noble Osburn, Bd.

Stewart, Arthur to Rachel Sprott July 25,1811 Sam'l Sprott, Bd.

Stewart, Elijah to Eve Warren Dec. 3,1840 Washington (X) Clark

Stewart, Elisha F. to Elizabeth S. Gatlin Sept. 16,1824 John Gatlin

Stewart, James to Emmily R. Deaderick Aug. 26,1817 Wm. G. Childrep

Stewart, James to Frances Warren Mar. 7,1833 John Williams, Bd.

Stewart, Jas. to Louisa Wray July 5,1842 Christian G. Miller, Bd.

Stewart, John M. to Britania Fitz June 19,1849 P.W. Moss, Bd.
Stewart, Marcus to Rachel Herrin Sept. 22,1814 John Spratt,Bd.
Stewart, Marcus to Jane Herron Feb. 19,1823 James Herron, Bd.
Stewart, Wm. K. to Polly Gillespie Nov.23,1813 David Gillespie
Stigall, John R. to Mary Ann King June 10,1841 Wm. M. Nunn, Bd.
Still, John P. to Rebecca Copeland June 8,1828 Wilson Davis,Bd.
Still, John P. Jr. to Mariah F. Rash July 25,1839 Thos. Carmicha'
Stobaugh, John to Betsey Roads June 5,1809 Jno. Fitzhugh, Bd.
Stockett, John B. to Barbara Ann Mitchell Nov.11,1847 Charles R. Pearce, Bd.
Stockett, Stephen to Nancy Armstrong Feb. 5,1817 Jno.Armstrong
Stokes, Berry to Tuzza Patton.Dec.29,1810 Jas. Stephenson,Bd.
Stokes, Edward(X) to Mary Tatum Nov.30,1832 Young Tatum
Stokes, John to Peggy Tatum Dec.21,1821 Benjamin Tatum, Bd.
Stokes, Josiah E. to Isabella M. Cherry Nov.17,1843 Daniel D. Russell, Bd.
Stokes, Josiah E.(X) to Minerva Edmonds Nov.18,1850 R.A. Wilson
Stokes, Wm. to Polly Denton Jan. 13,1842 Wm. A. Jarrat, Bd.
Stone, John (X) to Nancy Dotson Aug.6,1807 Fortune Dotson,Bd.
Stone, John H. to Unity S. Reynolds July 27,1842 John H. Hunter
Strambler, Reuben to Sarah A. Speed Nov.3,1819 Wm. Johnson,Bd.
Stratton, Henry to Elizabeth Field Dec.17,1828 John Field, Bd.
Strickland, Joseph to Celia Ann Bateman June 29,1820 John Smith
Strong, Alexander S. to Lavinia E. Morton Feb. 13,1844 Sam Peay
Stuart, Andrew K. to Rebecca A. Bennett Apr. 19,1843 John M. Stewart, Bd.
Stuart, Henry to Ann Wilson Mar.23,1839 James Hogan, Jr. Bd.
Stuart, Thos. to Maria M. Mayfield Sept. 30,1824 A. Vaughan,Bd.

Stuart, Thomas to Tabitha Boxley Sept.17,1840 James Hogan Jr.

Sulivan, John to Sintha Gibson Dec. 15,1818 Simon Myers, Bd.

Sullivan, Caleb W. to Elizabeth Roper Apr.19,1837

Sullivan, Thomas(X) to Ruth Worley Aug. 21,1819 Neilly Brown,Bd.

Sullivan, Uriah(X) to Martha Campbell Dec.7,1819 Daniel(X)Sulliva

Sullivan, Wm. to Artimesa E. Green May 4,1848 Wm. J. Walker, Bd.

Summers, Thos. M. C. to Mary Nipper Jan. 28,1827 M. Stanfield,Bd.

Sumner, John a free man of color to Polly Sumner, a free woman of color Jan. 12,1837 by T. D. Porter, M. G.

Sumners, Abraham to Nancy Seagler Sept. 20,1814 Nathan McDaniel, Andrew Thomas, Bd.

Sutton, Alexander to Ann Ham Sept. 24,1829 John B. Sutton, Bd.

Sutton, Charles(X) to Eliza Malone Sept. 13,1849 Moses E. Cator Jr.

Sutton, John A. to Fanny Ann White Aug.20,1837

Sutton, John A. to Tisitah Russell Dec. 15,1841 John J.(X)Russell

Sutton, Jonas to Charlotte Baucom Nov. 13,1833 Aaron A. Wilson

Sutton, Thos. J. to Caroline E. Dennis Jan.12,1850 Jas. V. King

Sutton, Uriah to Mary Ann Rudder Jan.11,1846 D. D. Russell, Bd.

Swaim, John to Polly M. Ormes July 15,1819 Evan B.Ormes, Bd.

Swancy(Swaney?) James to Sarah R. Johnston Dec.15,1819 Thos. Hardeman, Bd.

Swanson, Edward to Polly Allen July 21,1823 John Swanson, Bd.

Swanson, Ira to Mary E. Myrick Sept. 3,1846 L. B. Beech, Bd.

Swanson, John to Rhahab Lankford Dec. 17,1822 Edward Swanson,Bd.

Swanson, Peter to Milly Tarkington Jan. 8,1809 Arch Potter, Bd.

Sweeny, Chas. P. to Sarah Ann Huggins Mar.19,1835 John Z. Wrenn

Sweeny, Geo. to Eveline T. Hughes Nov.5,1840 Chas. P. Sweeny,Bd.

Sweeney, Henry to Rebecca Ritchil Nov.9,1831 Patrick Reese, Bd.

Sweeney, Henry W. to Mary Brooks Jan.14,1836 Wm. Harrison, Bd.

Sweny, John to Mary C. S. Marshall June 21,1848 Jacob Sweeny

Sweeney, Silas M. to Sarah Ann Williams Dec.6,1848 Wm. McCann,Bd.
    Bond alone

Sweet, David(X) to Mary Allen Jan. 23,1838 Wm. Stevens, Bd.

Sweet, Samuel(X) to Nancy Hall Feb.1,1842 Wm. Tucker, Bd.(Bond)

Sweet, Wm.(X) to Frances Jane Wells Dec. 22,1848 Samuel(X)Sweet

Sweete, Dennis(X) to Rebecca Hall May 23,1843 Lewis Ogilvie,Bd.

Swisher, Green H. to Caroline Cox Nov. 23,1830 Wm. M. House,Bd.

Swisher, Henry Harry to Lina Boyd June 6,1820 Wm. S. Hamilton,Bd.

Swisher, James G. to Elizabeth Boyd Sept. 13,1815 John C.Hulme

Swisher, Michael to Anna Bateman Jan.28,1823 B. W. Lane, Bd.

Swisher, Samuel to Sally Cox Nov. 21,1822 Thos. A. Thompson,Bd.

Talbitt(Tillett?), Wm. to Polly Wright Dec.30,1818 Jas. Cox,Bd.

Taliaferro, John A. to Mary A. Taliaferro Sept. 28,1837

Tally, Allen to Fanny Tucker Oct. 14,1813 Joseph Tucker, Bd.

Tally, James M. to Polly Crenshaw Dec. 18,1827 Henry(X)Thweatt

Tally, John(X) to Susan Rupard(Rusard) July 1,1823 MicajahDowdy

Tally, John P. to Julia Ann Miller Oct.5,1843 Jefferson Martin

Tally, Samuel to Lilly Ann Short Dec.5,1833 John Goodrich, Bd.

Tankersley, Benjamin to Polly Corbit Nov. 5,1816 Wm. Logan,Bd.

Tankersley, John R. to Sarah Brooks Aug. 24,1816 J. Hubbard,Bd.

Tanner, Joseph to Alsey Harrison Mar.19,1814 Murrill Bressea

Tanner, Robert(X) to Ruthy Gray Oct. 1,1846 Thos. S. Tanner,Bd.

Tanner, Samuel to Susan Andrews Mar.9,1820 Francis Andrews,Bd.

Tanner, Thomas to Sarah Andrews Oct. 20,1821 Wm. Andrew,Bd.

Tanner, Wm. to Matilda Tucker Dec. 24,1844 Leander J. Reed,Bd.

Tappan, Benjamin S. to Margaret B. Camp May 1,1823 Robt.C.Foster

Tappan, Benjamin S. to Margaret B. Wood Mar.23,1832 Jos.J.Pugh

Tarkington, Asbury(X) to Louisa McDowel Jan.5,1832 Homer McDowel

Tarkington, Isaac to Jane Cox Sept. 25,1809 James Cox,Bd.

Tarkington, Jesse to Milly Simmons Oct.9,1817 Wm. Tillett, Bd.

Tarkington, John G. to Rebecca Hunter Oct.15,1827 Wm. Duty, Bd.

Tarkington, Joseph to Amelia Owen June 6,1818 Edward W. Tignor

Tarkington, Sylvenus to Patsey Alexander June 8,1814 Jeremiah Tranum, B d.

Tarkington, Thomas J. to Rosannah Midgett Nov.30,1843 B.H. Harrison, B d.(Letter attached to Bond:"I, Thomas J. Tarkington, do hereby nominate and appoint B. H. Harrison my attorney in fact to sign and seal my name in execution of a bond to obtain a marriage license from the county court clerk of Williamson County for the purpose of giving authority to an person legally authorized to solemnize the bonds of matrimony between myself and Miss Rosannah Midgett. Hereby granting to my said attorney my full authority in signing and sealing my name to the above mentioned bond in as full and complete a manner as if I myself were personally present. In witness whereof I here set my hand and seal this 30th day of November 1843". Thomas J. Tarkington. A test: G. L. Leigh

Tarkinton, Whitten N. to Betsey Cox Apr. 19,1823 Jesse Tarkinton

Tarpley, John to Mary Legate Feb. 11,1812 David Lancaster, Bd.

Tate, James to Margaret Mebane May 13,1830 Nathan H. Mebane, Bd.

Tate, John G. to Priscilla McLemore Dec. 31,1829 Henry McClure

Tatom, Alfred(X) to Fanny Roberts Feb. 18,1824 Silas Camender

Chumm(or Climm?), J. Tatom to Charlotte Baucom Aug.4,1827 Edward Ragsdale, Jr. Bd.

Tatom, Clem J.(X) to Mary Young Nov.1,1827 Nathan Haley, Bd.

Tatum, Benjamin L. to Philadelphia Stokes Mar.22,1832 Michael Cody, Bd.

Tatum, John to Sally Gates Oct. 11,1821 John Redmond, Bd.

Tatum, Riley D. to Sarah A. Smith Oct.18,1849 N. J. Calhoon,Bd.

Tatum(signed Tatone),Young to Malissa Pickron Dec.23,1840 Josiah E. Stokes, Bd.

Taylor, Abraham to Milley Mitchell Dec.12,1812 Alston Winton,Bd.

Taylor, Alston J. to Mary Alford Dec.20,1841 Wm. Taylor, Bd.

Taylor, Benj. B. to Minerva A. Elam Dec.7,1837

Taylor, Cornelius(X) to Nancy Trout Dec.30,1824 Chas.X Hutchison

Taylor, Goodwyn to Polly Williams Dec.19,1817 Richard Tanner,Bd.

Taylor, Henry(X) to Cynthia Biggars Jan.26,1830 James Biggars,Bd.

Taylor, James to Nancy Bond Apr.14,1812 William Dodson,Bd.

Taylor, James(X) to Peggy Grimes July 19,1821 Shimmey Merritt,Bd.

Taylor, James(X) to Frances Glymph Oct.11,1827 John Williams,Bd.

Taylor, James to Elizabeth Maury Nov.20,1835 Thomas W. Haddick

Taylor, James H. to Sarah Ann Atkinson July16,1842 Richard A. Graham, Bd.

Taylor, James M. to Jenetta Jackson Oct.22,1841 Wm. A. Ransom,Bd.

Taylor, James S. to Susan Barnett Nov.17,1849 Morris L. Bond,Bd.

Taylor, John to Rachel Evans Jan.24,1809 John Evans, Bd.

Taylor, John(X) to Jane Lambert Apr.1,1829 Moses Steele, Bd.

Taylor, John to Letty Givens Feb.17,1837 By Thos. Prowell, J.P.

Taylor, John to Tabitha Nolen Dec. 16,1837 By R. W. Robinson,JP

Taylor, John(X) to Julia Ann Hay July 16,1838 Frederick Taylor

Taylor, John P.(X) to Lucinda C. Durdon Feb.19,1846 Thos.Taylor

Taylor, Johnson J. to Mary Hill Feb.22,1837 By James Rea,M.G.

Taylor, Jonathan to Irena Winsett Sept.12,1830 Joseph Ralston,Bd.

Taylor, Joseph to Lydda W. Laughlin (or McLaughlin) Feb.17,1808 James Cox, Bd.

Taylor, Merritt(X) to Nancy Roberts Oct.28,1820 James Edwards,Bd.

Taylor, Nathan to Angeline Prince Sept.23,1844 Henry(X)Stenson

Taylor, Nehemiah to Nancy G. Gilliam Sept.12,1822 Robt.Grimmer

Taylor, Peter to Betsey Dawson June2,1806 Joseph Dawson,Bd.

Taylor, Raney M. to Mary Ray Nov.13,1845 Wm.S.(X) Taylor,Bd.

Taylor, Robert to Phebe M. Cheatam Jan.18,1838 Wm.K. Ransom,Bd.

Taylor, Samuel to Rebecca Frost Feb.10,1841 Jas.C.Bailey(bondon1

Taylor, Stephen to Jenny Wade Jan.3,1809 Stephen Wade, Obadiah Wade, Bd.

Taylor, Thomas to Patsey Kidd Dec.4,1810 Elisha Kidd, Bd.

Taylor, Thomas to Louisa Lamb Feb.2,1832 Burton Jordan, Bd.

Taylor, Thomas L. to Louisa J. Pate Oct.22,1833 Uriah(X) Call,Bd

Taylor, Vincent to Margaret Cheatham Feb. 22,1847 F. S. Brown,Bd

Taylor, Waller(X) to Elizabeth Camp Jan.17,1839 Thomas Green,Bd.

Taylor, William to Fanny Hughs June20,1815 Joseph(X) Davis,Bd.

Taylor, William to Emeline Cole Dec. 22,1825 Thomas(X)Pate, Bd.

Taylor, William(X) to Nancy Taylor Jan.16,1827 Larkin Burch,Bd.

Taylor, William to Elizabeth Dowdy Nov. 2,1836 Charles P. Ansley

Taylor, Wm. D. to Elisabeth White June 29,1821 Elisha L. Hall,Bd.

Taylor, Wm. G.(X) to Mary H . Smith Aug.19,1830 Joseph Taylor,Bd.

Taylor, Wm. P. to Minerva D. Stephens July6,1841 TurnerS. Green (bond alone)

Teague, Isaac to Milley Pumroy Aug.2,1831 Wm. (X) Pumroy,Bd.

Temple, Lewallen A. to Susan T. Hughes Feb.14,1833 Jos.L.F.Hill

Temple, Roderick to Mary Lee Sept.27,1817 Edward Smith, Bd.

Tenison, Alonzo M. to Rebecca A. S. Hamilton Aug.7,1849 Thos. F. P. Allison, Bd.

Tennison, Absolom C. to Mary Ham June16,1826 Elijah Ham, Bd.

Tennison, Joseph to Sally Gholson Nov.30,1819 James Johnson,Bd.

Tennison, Joseph to Elizabeth Shelburne Jan.3,1833 Hartwell H. Hobbs, Bd. By Andrew Craig, M.G.

Terrell, Hezeziah to Margaret S. Dabney Dec.20,1838 John J. Watson

Terrell, Timothy to Nancy W. Dotson Apr. 22,1835 Jas.S.McCrady

Terrell, Wm. to Sally Tyner Jan. 1,1835 Charles Scott, Bd.

Terrill, James to Amanda Malvina Edwards Dec.20,1827 Perkins Hunter, Bd.

Terrill, Joseph R. to Harriet M. Buttry Feb. 1,1848 W.B.White

Terry, David to Catharine Lavender Feb.23,1837

Terry, Henry B. to Ursey Allen July 1,1830 Allen N. McCord,Bd.

Terry, Jeremiah to Polly Sloan Feb. 1,1813 John Sloan,Bd.

Terry, Robert to Elizabeth N. Pate Dec. 31,1829 Elijah Adams,Bd.

Thomas, Andrew to Elizabeth Radford May 14,1817 Geo.(X)Roper,Bd.

Thomas, Charles J.(X) to Mary Caffrey Sept. 27,1848 Sam'l S.Thomas

Thomas, Elijah to Thursey Stokes Jan.26,1826 By C. McDaniel,JP

Thomas, James I. to Nancy Garrett Oct.6,1810 Dempsey Nash,Bd.

Thomas, James M.(X) to Nancy Jane Daugherty Mar.7,1845 JohnLBurch

Thomas, Jesse to Mira L. Boyd Feb.27,1834 Boling C. North, Bd.

Thomas, John to Polly Dilliard Oct. 10,1810 Phineas Thomas,Bd.

Thomas, Jonas E. to Martha Atkinson July 13,1829 John H. Vaughn

Thomas, Nathaniel H. to Martha Crenshaw Jan. 24,1819 Pettus Shelburne, Bd.

Thomas, Samuel N. to Mary B. Hyde Nov. 30, 1848 Wm. Harrison,Bd.

Thomas, Wesley(X) to Elizabeth Sudberry Jan. 30,1840 Wm. T. Sudberry, Bd.

Thomas, Woodson to Eliza Watson Aug. 8,1844 John (X) Lamb, Bd.

Thompson, Alexander to Rebecca Robinson July 26,1840 Littleberry Beasley, Bd.

Thompson, Benjamin D. to Mariann Anderson Feb.18,1822 Wm.Montgomery, Bd.

Thompson, Charles H. to Elizabeth Curtis July 25,1832 Beverly (X) Gordon, Bd.

Thompson, David T. to Susan E. Aden Aug. 29,1844 Wm. Anderson

Thompson, Ebenezer E. to Sarah Burnett Aug.19,1828 John Howard

Thompson, Ebenezer E. to Catharine Pomroy Mar.31,1845 Wm. Pomroy

Thompson(signed Thomson), George to Rachael Ratcliffe May 9,1832 John McDaniel, Bd.

Thompson, Henry R. to Mary Madden Dec.8,1838 Henry Ragsdale,Bdd.

Thompson, Hugh D.(X) to Polly Ragsdale Nov.29,1840 Daniel S. Gardner, Bd.

Thompson, Hugh D.(X) to Sarah Baker May 22,1845 DanielS.Gardner

Thompson, John to Nancy Bridges Dec. 2,1807 Wm.Kennedy,Thos. Herring, Bd.

Thompson, John to Nancy Ferguson Oct.16,1823 John(X)Burnett,Bd.

Thompson, John B.T.(X) to Mahala D. Walker Feb.28,1850 John J. Sparkman, Bd. (Bond alone)

Thompson, John M. C. to Emeline Cunningham June 3,1833 John Cunningham, Bd.

Thompson, Joseph to Fanny Berry Mar. 8,1842 David S. Gardner,Bd.

Thompson, Joseph C. to Bethynia H. Patton Jan.3,1839 Jas.Hogan Jr

Thompson, Joseph S. to Sally Adams Jan.15,1821 Thomas H. Word

Thompson, Phillip to Susannah German Nov.15,1813 Jas. Jordan,Bd.

Thompson, Samuel to Charity Bonner Dec. 29,1812 Edwin Austin,Bd.

Thompson, Samuel to Susan Ann Meacham Dec. 21,1848 Josiah M. Meacham, Bd.

Thompson, Samuel G. to Tennessee A. Pinkston Jan.30,1845 Thomas N. Pinkston, Bd.

Thompson, Solomon K.X to Anna Terry May 24,1849 Alexander M. Thompson, Bd.

Thompson, Thomas to Milly Walker Feb. 13,1816 James Thompson,Bd.

Thompson, Thos. A. to Susan Potts Aug. 3,1824 Felix Ewing, Bd.

Thompson, Thomas W. to Elizabeth M. Tucker July 4,1841 Henry G. Tucker, Bd.

Thompson, Wm. to Martha Ann Hudgens Dec. 24,1816 Duncan H. Campbell, Bd.

Thompson, Wm. to Mary Jane Fox May 3,1845 John Neelly, Bd.

Thompson, Wm. C. to Alvira Buttery Jan. 28,1844 David T. Thompson

Thornberry, Hiram to Martha White Oct.13,1835 Thomas Lovett, Bd.

Thornbrough, Allen to Rachel White Sept.17,1829 Wm. Smith, Bd.

Thornborough, Wilson to Martha Ann Martin July9,1845 Thos. Carson

Thornsberry, Allen to Rebecca White Aug. 2,1827 Samuel Brown, Bd.

Thornton, John to Catharine Kirk Oct. 6,1808 David Russell, Bd.

Thornton, Kinion M. to Jane Boatwright Nov.25,1830 Joseph (X) Haynes, Bd.

Thornton, Reuben S. to Mrs. Mary Owen Apr. 3,1823 Nathan Owen, Bd.

Thornton, Sterling to Mary C. Owen Jan.6,1842 Richard H. Owen, Bd.

Thurman, Graves to Christian Terry Oct.8,1812 Joseph Terry, Bd.

Thurman, Jeremiah M. to Lucy Roberts Sept. 1,1850 Wm. Lunn, Bd.

Thurston, John J. to Amanda Jefferson Jan. 12,1846 Samuel Veach

Thweatt, Harwood to Elizabeth Acholes Dec. 2,1815 Daniel Gill, Bd.

Thweatt, Isaac J. to Emily A. Parham July 20,1847 John Christley

Thweat, Isham to Sarah David Dec. 24,1816 W. R. Hill, Bd.

Thweatt, John E. to Martha M. A.E. Reese Mar.2,1841 John E. Wall

Thweatt, Martin S. to Mary Laramore Nov.26,1835

Thweatt, Peter B. to Frances D. Thweatt May 15,1833 Cary White

Thweatt, Peyton L. to Frances E. Coleman June 21,1837

Thweatt, Wm. H. to Mary Allen Aug.16,1832 (license alone)

Thweatt, Wm. H. to Amelia T. Pigott Oct.18,1843 W.M. Bingham

Tidwell, Francis R.(X) to Etaline Powell July 31,1841 James(X) Anglin, Bd.

Tignor, Edward W. to Martha Mandley Feb. 11,1822 Bird H ill, Bd.

Tignor, James to Susannah Cooper Oct. 24,1816 Henry Oliver, Bd.

Tignor, John to Mildred Walton Aug. 30,1826

Tignor, Wiley to Sarah Elizabeth Walker Apr.17,1828 Alexander Caudle, Bd.

Tignor, Wm. to Martha Morton Jan. 16,1833 Edward Morris, Bd.

Tillett, Wm.(Talbitt?) to Polly Wright Dec.30,1818 James Cox,Bd.

Tillett, Wm. to Elizabeth Granger Apr. 1,1823 Jesse Tarkinton,Bd.

Tindill, Henry to Mary Holland Dec. 4,1823 John T. Shanks, Bd.

Tinnin, Lawrence W. to Louise Mebane Feb. 27,1834 Richard Alexander, Bd.

Tinsley, Coleman to Margaret Henderson Jan.15,1827 J.T. Herron

Tippet, Addison W. to Caledonia H . R$_e$ynolds Dec.24,1841 Coatesworth P. Logan, Bd.

Tisail, R. J. to Polly Merritt Nov. 14,1816 James Parks, Bd.

Tisdale, Francis M.(X) to Emeline Crafton Mar.2,1848 Wm.H.McClaran, Bd.

Tisdale, James R. to Harriet Clay Feb. 16,1834 Thomas(X)Scott

Tisdale, John to Betsey Burge May 3,1821 Taswell J. Burge,Bd.

Tisdale, Shirley(X) to Rachel Owen Sept.23,1829 John(X)Tisdale

Tisdale, Washington G. to Maria B urgs Apr.16,1828 JohnD.Roberts

Tison, Jesse(X) to Rachel Wallace Mar.6,1828 John Holt, Bd.

Tiver, Wm.(X) to Martha Venable Dec. 12,1825 John B . Miles,Bd.

Todd, James B. to Eleanor F. Loften Oct.19,1848 Wm. H. Dodson,Bd.

Todd, John to.Elizabeth G. Smithson Oct.27,1846 John J. Lagron

Toller(signed Toler), John to Martha Irvin June29,1821 Siria Montgomery, Bd.

Tombs, John H.(X) to Sarah Jackson Oct.15,1845 Richardson Davidson, Bd.

Tomlin, David to Aley Graham Oct.22,1816 George Glascock, Bd.

Tomlin, James to Nancy Bragg Mar.6,1809 David Campbell, Bd.

Tomlin, John to Parkey or Purkey Lester July 5,1815 Milton P.
    Hiter, George Everly, Bd.

Tomlin, John A. to Mary Wade Apr.18,1850 Robert (X) Jackson,Bd.

Tomlin, Nicholas to Elizabeth Blackman Dec.16,1814 John Tomlin

Tomlin, Nicholas(X) to Nancy Black Sept.4,1844 Yancy Cody,Bd.

Tomlinson, Charles(X) to Martha Mangrum May 11,1844 Thos.A.Graham

Tomlinson, Henry W. to Elizabeth Little Dec.24,1840 Josiah E.(X)
    Stokes, Bd.

Tomlinson, Henry W. to Dosia Townson Sept.11,1845 Wm. J. Moss,Bd.

Tomlinson, Richard to Elizabeth Short Apr.4,1839 RichardG.Cowan

Tompkins, John G. to Catharine S. Fall Feb.23,1838 Jas. H.
    Charlton, Bd.

Toney, John to Elvy Wilson Oct. 21,1819 A. A. Wilson, Bd.

Toney, Littleberry to Mary E. Wilson Feb. 26,1826

Toon, Andrew J. to Susan A. Vaughan July 20,1843 JohnJ. Short

Toon, Beverly B. to Sarah D. Nolen July 27,1848 Mark L.Andrews

Townsend, Richard to Mary Jordan Dec.2,1825 John W.M. Hill,Bd.

Trail, James(X) to Mary Trail Aug.8,1850 Travis A.(X)Williams

Trail, Valentine(X) to Rachel Lamb Nov.10,1827 Thos. Hendrix,Bd.

Traile,(X) Wm. to Mary Amanda Morgan Mar.26,1838 W.K. Ransom,Bd.

Tranthan(signed Trenthen),Wm. to Amanda R. Estis July 29,1842
    Hunphrey H.(X) Gardner, Bd.

Tranum, Jeremiah to Elizabeth I. Wilson Jan.22,1810 John Wilson

Travis, George to Matilda Dobson Dec. 7,1812 George Burnett,Bd.

Tremble, George W. to Elizabeth E. Dyer Sept.9,1815 John Little

Trent, Edward A.(H?) to Salley P. Cavender Nov.12,1835 William
    Anderson, Bd.

Trigg, John to Elizabeth Bradley Aug.13,1821 David Mason, Bd.

Trimble, David to Martha G. Foster Mar.23,1834 Jas. Hogan Jr.

Trimble, James D. to Artemisia Chaney Jan.27,1841 Wm.H.Trimble

Trimble, Jas. D. to Antinusa Chaney Jan.27,1841 (license only)

Trimble, John D. to Adelia Ann Neal June 7,1840 Granville A. Cameron, Bd.

Trimble, Wm. to Penny Ivey Jan.20,1808 James White, Bd.

Trimble, Wm. H.(or W.) to Catharine W. Bond May 30,1844 Robert B. Trimble, Bd.

Trint, Steven to Milly Jackson Feb. 11,1826

Tripp, Samuel to Mary Pinkston May 26,1814 Ebenezer Darby,Bd.

Trotter, Isham R. to Sally P. Old Mar. 28,1809 Elisha North,Bd.
    Note accompanying license: "This is to certify that Isham R. Trotter hath my consent to marry my daughter Sally P. Old. Please issue license for that purpose given under my hand this 27th March 1809" Thos. Old

Trout, Jacob(X) to Maryan McMillin Jan. 6,1818 Robert McMillen

Tucker, Allen C. to Elizabeth I. B ugg Oct.19,1837

Tucker, Bartley(X) to Harriet Betty July 1,1830 Chas. M. Scott

Tucker, Benjamin to Melissa Jane Pritchett Dec. 2,1847 Joseph F. Roach, Bd.

Tucker, Daniel to Mary Alexander Graham June 29,1830 Samuel Graham, Bd.

Tucker, Henry G. to Mary L. Wilson Feb. 17,1834 Edwin A. Reams

Tucker, Henry G. to Mary Greer June 9,1842 James Wiggins, Bd.

Tucker, Jacob to Nancy Anglin Sept. 5,1818 Thos. Kinsey, Bd.

Tucker, James to Polly Butt Oct. 20,1824 John Davidson, Bd.

Tucker, James H. to Addeline Chrichlow Sept. 13,1849 Jno.L.Hill

Tucker, John(X) to Martha Taylor June 23,1839 Wm. Taylor, Bd.

Tucker, Joseph to Sarah Tucker Dec. 29, 1812 Wm. Tucker, Bd.

Tucker, Orsborn to Sarah Wallace Dec. 11,1828 Thos.H. Hayner,Bd.

Tucker, Richard(X) to Margaret McElhaney June10,1834 JohnDowdy

Tucker, Wm.(X) to Patsey Bugg Nov.12,1833 Wm. Zachery, Bd.

Tucker, Wm. C. to Eliza Ann Whitehead Aug. 24,1844 Josiah(X) Caudle, Bd.

Tucker, Wm. M. to Susan C. Crichlow Aug. 23,1849 Charles C. Crowder, Bd.

Tulloss, Thornton Carnes to Eliza Buchanan Jan.30,1826

Tulloss, Robert C. to Parthenia Starnes Oct.8,1850 JohnE.Tulloss

Turbeville, Jefferson(X) to Nancy Corbitt Jan.10,1824 Wm. (X) Stotraugh, Bd.

Turbeville, Wm.(X) to Jane Mirchant Jan.1,1818 Samuel Thompson

Turbeville, Wm.(X) to Sally Broom Feb.28,1822 Francis(X)Gunter

Turman(X)Garrett to Nancy Bradford Mar. 2,1822 Ephraim (X)Kelly

Turman, Wm. to Elizabeth Tompkins Apr. 12,1810 Wm. McMillen,Bd.

Turmey, Morris D. to Harriet N. Terrell Dec. 29,1841 John A. Graves, Bd.

Turnage, Wm. to Polly McLattan June 5,1815 Mansfield House, Bd.

Turner, Drury to Mary Vaughn Apr. 29,1850 D. D. Russell, Bd.

Turner, Elisha Wright to Mary Little Feb. 9,1831 Presley(X) Trinkard, Bd.

Turner, George(X) to Betsey Watkins Sept. 11,1820 Joel Watkins

Turner, James to Easther Ewing Sept. 2,1806 Thos. Herron, Bd.

Turner, James to Catharine S. White Sept. 2,1811 W. W. Watson

Turner, James(X) to Margaret E. Fields June 19,1842 JohnC.Reed

Turner, Jesse to Alcy Carmichael July 7,1807 John Fly, Bd.

Turner, John(X) to Jane Brown June 20,1832 Thos. (X) Owen,Bd.

Turner, John(X) to Sally Richardson May 25,1824 Stephen Turner

Turner, Joseph R. to Betsey Marshall Dec.2,1830 Thos.(X) Pate

Turner, Spratley to Martha Boyt Mar. 1,1809 John Thompson,Bd.

Turner, Stephen(X) to Polly Corzine Apr. 3,1824 Lewis Corzine,Bd.

Turner, Stephen(X) to Polly Betty Sept. 6,1836 John W. Crunk,Bd.

Tweedy, Wm. to Amelia Tarkington Nov. 28,1833 Wm. M. Wright, Bd.

Twinage, Thomas to Sally Hadley Nov. 4,1815 George Everly,Bd.

Tyner, James to Anna Hollis Jan.2,1811 James Dyal, Bd.

Tyner, Wm. to Brimitta Hall July 6, 1826

Underwood, John(X) to Eliza Bryant Mar. 7,1822 Jeremiah Underwood(X), Bd.

Ury, Joseph to Mary L. Rutherford July 6,1820 Dudley S. Jennings

Uttey(Utley?), John to Agnes Long Jan.27,1825 Edward Anderson

Utley, Samuel to Mary Adams Jan. 29,1828 Thomas Layne, Bd.

Vaden, Joseph A. to Catharine G. Wilson Sept. 27,1838 Jas. S. Gibson, Bd.

Vaden, Stephen H. to Nancy Smithson Jan.22,1825 James L.Crawford

Vaden, Wm. H. to Martha Smithson Apr.27,1832 Joseph A. Vaden,Bd.

VanGleeve(Cleeve?), Ebenezer to Elizabeth Carrick Dec.30,1819 James Corson, Bd.

Van Hook, Hiram to Frances Reams Sept. 5,1848 W. E. Carter, Bd.

Van Pitt, Henry to Ann Hickman Smith Aug.13,1819 Thos.Hardeman

Vanderslice, Jacob to Terisea A. R. Johnson Oct.19,1847 Michael M. Leath, Bd.

Vannatta, Christopher to Nancy Lowder Apr.27,1808 Terry Bridges

Vaughan, Asa N. to Araminta Craig Jan.11,1832 Wm. Vaughan,Bd.

Vaughan, Charles to Mary Bozley Sept. 21,1840 Robert(X)Vaughan

Vaughan, Daniel to Polly H. Short Dec. 11,1817 Silas Stephens

Vaughan, Daniel to Rebecca Coleman July 3,1824 John Atkinson,Bd.

Vaughan, Geo. W. to Sarah Ann Poynor Dec. 21,1848 Jesse W.(X) Warren, Bd.

Vaughan, Isaac S. to Susan M. Bateman Jan. 11, 1837 by James King. S. B. McConnico, Clerk Wmson Co. Court

Vaughan, James H. to Mary Oldham Dec. 31, 1833 by A. Adams, M.G. Bondsman: Davis Hardgrave

Vaughan, James to Louisa Fisher July 3, 1841 by Vance M. Green, J.P. Bondsman: Henry W. Foster Clerk of Court, Lemuel B. McConnico, by W. Lafayette McConnico.

Vaughan, James (signed Vaughn) to Martha Ann Brooks (Bond Only) May 15, 1849 Bondsman: Israel McCarroll

Vaughan, John to Jane Phillips June 24, 1819 Joseph Vaughan, BD.

Vaughan, John (X) to Catharine W. Walton July 18, 1839 by C. T. Owen, J.P. Bondsman: William Floyd

Vaughan, Joseph to Elizabeth Philips Aug 7, 1819 John Vaughan, BD

Vaughan, Lemuel to Mary Wall Jan 7, 1835 by D. C. McLeod or McLod, Minister. Bondsman: Samuel (X) Shelton

Vaughan, Lemuel to Elizabeth Bragg Aug. 14, 1841 by J. W. Hatcher, J. P. Bondsman: Stephen (X) Turner

Vaughan, Lewis B. to Mary E. Brown Oct 3, 1848 by John Hay Bondsman: John (X) Sadler

Vaughan, Robert to Celia Kellow Dec. 21, 1836 by J. A. Holland, J.P. Bondsman: Thomas Wilson

Vaughan, Spencer C. to Nancy Wisenor March 6, 1820 by G. Hunt. Bondsman: Israel McCarrell Jr.

Vaughan, Thomas (X) to Mary A. E. Young July 23, 1845 by Thos. Thomson, J. P. Bond: Lewis C. Waggoner Attest: Jonas L. Ronel

Vaughan, Thomas F. (X) to Eliza L. Redman Nov. 11, 1833 by Geo. Shannon, J.P. Bondsman: Richard D. (X) Vaughan

Vaughan, Thomas T. or G. to Caroline B. Johnson Dec. 1, 1836 By T. D. Porter, M.G.

Vaughan, William to Melissa Craig March 20, 1832 by W. Maney, J.P. Bondsman: Abner Vaughan

Vaughan, William (X) to Lucy Poynor March 9, 1834 by Geo. Shannon, J.P. Bondsman: Henry Gl. Cliner

Vaughan, William to Mary C. Vernon April 24, 1850 by B.R. Gant, M.G. Bondsman: William T. Vernon

Vaughan, William L.(or S) to Harriet Davis Nov. 16, 1837 by
      William Lanier, J. P.

Vaughn, Abner to Polly Wilson Mar. 16, 1806 (Bond Only)
      Test: Peter Hardeman Bondsman: Abraham Secrest

Vaughn, Abner/W(signed Vaughan) to Harriet E. Craig Jan.25,1832
      By E. R. Parrish, M.G. David C. Montgomery, Bdsm.

Vaughn, Archibald (X) to Mapy Mortane October 3, 1818
      Bdsm: Wm. P. Edds Wit: Thos. Hardeman and Thos.Miller Jr.

Vaughn, Hartwell (X) to Elizabeth Walker Nov. 20, 1816
      Bds: James Salisbury Rev. Garner McConnico, M.G.

Vaughn, James to Dorothy C. Owen Sept. 10, 1818 Joseph Vaughn,Bl

Vaughn, John H. to Sarah Atkinson Aug 8, 1827 Banister W.Shaw,BD

Vaughn, Richard to Jane Wilks July 24, 1834 Robt.A.Craig,Bd.

Vaughn, Richard D. to Elizabeth Hampton Dec 30, 1836 by J.A.
      Holland, J. P.

Vaughn, Samuel (X) to Myra Martin Jan 14, 1841 by Peter
      Owen, J.P. Bondsman: Samuel (X) Davis (Note attached)
      "This day came Samuel C. Davis before me Peter Owen,
      acting Magistrate in and for said county, and made
      oath in due form that there has been stolen from
      him or he lost the marriage license before the
      rites of matrimony were solemnized, that they were
      stolen or lost without any design on his part to
      prevent the solemnization of the same."

Vawter, Asa S. to Martha Madden Oct. 27, 1835 by D. Baugh
      J.P. Jacob Dunn, Bds. Thos. N. Figures, D.C.

Veatch, Landers to Ibby Simpkins Dec 18,1816 Richard Polk,Bd.

Venable, David to Mary M. Neal Jan 9, 1849 by Minus C. Jor-
      dan, J.P. Daniel D. Russell, Bd. Chesley Williams,Wit.

Venable, Larkin to Fanny Brown May 14, 1825 Wm.(X) Teaver,Bd.

Venable, Richard to Darcas Marchant Aug. 9, 1808
      Bondsman: Josiah Henry Wit: A. Potter

Vernon, John C. to Mary Peay Feb. 4, 1826 (Bond Only)

Vernon, Leonard, to Jenneth (Jemeth) Robinson May 14, 1831
      Bennett Sirus, Bds. Geo. Shannon, J. P.

Vernon, Obediah (X) to Ellen Cyrus Feb. 29, 1828 by John P. Irion, J. P. Leonard (X) Vernon, BD. Will Hardeman Wit. Thos. Hardeman, Clerk by J. W. McCown, D.C.

Vernon, Robert (X) to Sarah Robinson Mar. 20, 1830 by Geo. Shannon, JP Nathaniel Barnes, Bd. John G. Hay, Wit.

Vernon, Thomas to Rhoda Woods Dec. 31, 1847 by L. B. Johnson, JP Augustus S. Tindall, Bd.

Vernon, William A. to Nancy Carmichael Oct. 26, 1840 J. P. Stite, JP David A. Hampton, Bds.

Vernon, William A. to Sarah Ann Chadwell Aug. 9, 1846 by Martin Clark, Elder in M.E.C. Lewis C. Waggoner, Bd. "Not to be published til license returned" on bond.

Vestal, Aaron to Elizabeth Sparkman April 10, 1827 Andrew Craig, M.G. Robertson Sparkman, Bondsman

Vickery, Absolem (X) to Lavinia Putnam Feb. 23, 1820 by Franc Johnson, J. P. John Starnes (X) Witness & Bds.

Vickery, Richard (X) to Polly Barnes June 14, 1834 by Thos. Prowell, J.P. Patrick Reese, Bds.

Vickory, Isaac to Nancy Francis Hall Mar. 22, 1842 by J.R. Pearcy, JP John J. Pennington, Bds.

Vickory, Owen (signed Vickrey)-Nancy Smith Jan. 17, 1847 John Richardson, JP Isaac Vickrey, Bondsman

Vicory, Azel (X) to Elizabeth Carroll Jan. 31, 1838 by Sam. B. Robison, JP Owen (X) Vicory, Bondsman

Vicory, Jonathan (sgn Vickory) to Elizabeth Smith Feb. 13, 1839 by John Landrum, Bapt.M. James Jackson, Bds.

Vinsent, Orrin to Mary Ezell Nov. 6, 1828 Abner Vinsent, Bd

Vitteto, Stokley T. to Rebecca Ferguson May 18, 1826 (Bond)

Voorhies, Wm. M. to Catharine H. Roy Jan 12, 1848 Robt. G. Irvine

Vowell, Thomas (X) to Harriet Jane Hawk Mar. 28, 1844 by. J.J. Bingham, JP Richard (X) Godwin, Bds.

Vowell, William to Isabel Gardner May 23, 1846 Richard (X) Thompson, Bondsman

Vowell, William (X) to Isabel Gardner Oct. 25, 1849 by W.F. A. Shaw, JP Shadrack J. Robinson, Bondsman

Waddall, Joseph to Frances T. Nolen Jan. 9, 1840 by
    Philip P. Neely, MG Beverly B. Toon, Bondsman

Waddell, Samuel D. to Betsey Browder Feb. 20, 1807
    Frederick Browder, Bds. N. P. Hardeman, Wit.

Waddy, Elliott P. to Sarah L. Andrews Dec. 19, 1835
    Samuel Henderson, Bondsman

Waddy, Spence to Mary C. Lavender Aug. 26, 1846 by Robert
    L. Andrews William T. Fleming, Bondsman

Wade, Austin M. to Michy Bizzle Feb. 13, 1825 Stephen (X)
    Bizzle, Bondsman M. L. Crutcher, JP.

Wade, George to Polly Kinny Sept. 9, 1817 Thos. Craig, Bd.
    Robert Davis, Witness

Wade, John to Leah Bateman Apr 14, 1806 Benj. White, Bds.

Wade, Mastin to Mary Smith Nov. 19, 1829 Jos. W. Davis, Bds.

Wade, Middleton to Rachael Alexander June 14, 1824 by
    Lewis Loyd, Jp Benj. Inman, Bds. E. L. Hall, Wit.

Wadkins, Owen to Nancy Davis Dec. 18, 1806 James Davis, Bds.
    N. P. Hardeman, Witness

Wadley, Gillman to Emily R. Phillips Nov. 25, 1841 by
    E. W. Hendrix, M.G. Wm. A. Ransom, Bds.

Waggoner, James to Atlantick M. Bittich Feb. 1, 1848
    Wm. A. Whitsitt, MG Samuel Hopkins, Bondsman

Waggoner, Jessee to Sarah Shanks Feb. 9, 1825 by G. Hunt
    Daniel (X) Ireland, Bondsman

Waggoner, John to Sally Stevens Nov. 10, 1817 Wm. Stevens, Bd.

Waggoner, Lewis C. to Mary A. Walker Aug. 29, 1839 by
    Jesse Cox, MG John I. Watson, Bondsman

Wakefield, Charles to Margaret Thompson Feb. 13, 1838 by
    Thos. Prowell, JP John W. Wakefield, Bondsman

Wakefield, John W. to Mary M. Fose Dec. 6, 1836 Jas. Fox, JP

Wakefield, Joseph to Mary E. Younger Jan 3, 1844 Jno. T. Church, BD

Wakefield, Thomas to Elizabeth Fox Sept. 26, 1837 Thos. Prowell, JI

Waldron, William to Rebecca Shannon Feb. 2, 1836 by Jesse Cox,
    MG. Ralph S. McFadden, Bondsman

Walker, Addison H. to Jane C. Carothers Dec. 22, 1836 J. Cox, MG

Walker, Benjamin F. to Sarah Jane Jordan Nov. 15, 1849 by
    Jesse Cox, MG   Thomas Peay, Bondsman

Walker, Clayton to Polly Dunagan Oct 12, 1812 Sam Andrews, Bds.

Walker, Clement T. to Jane Champ Mar. 20, 1823 by C. Mc-
    Daniel, J.P. Levi Gardner, Bondsman

Walker, Daniel M. (or David M.) to Mary G. Rook Oct. 15, 1846
    Pettus Shelburne, JP Damascus Layne, Bondsman

Walker, Elisha to Jincy Cavinder Dec. 14, 1808 John Walker, Bd
    (Bond only) (Wonder if this was Lavinder?)

Walker, Freeman Jr. (X) to Susan Radford July 14, 1824
    James E. Dupree, Bondsman

Walker, George E. to Susan J. Layne Feb. 24, 1842 by Cowden
    McCord, JP Wm. G. Ozburn, Bondsman

Walker, Henry Jr. to Sally Radford Aug 17, 1821 J.R. Alexander, Bd

Walker, Henry J. to Elizabeth R. Owen Dec. 25, 1833 by
    Jas. King, MG. Robert S. Thomas, Bondsman

Walker, Henry S. to Elizabeth Roberts Sept. 23, 1810
    Elisha Walker, Bondsman Wm. P. Harrison, Wit.

Walker, James to Polly Thompson Mar. 8, 1821 by Geo.
    Blackburn, V.D.M. William Amis, Bondsman

Walker, James to Sally Phelps Jan 28, 1835 Davis Hardgrave, Bd

Walker, James to Rebecca Cathey May 20, 1845 by Jno. Wall,
    J.P. Thomas Cathey, Bondsman

Walker, James (X) to Mary S. Wells Mar. 3, 1847 Wm. Gray, Bds. *

Walker, Joel to Mary Motheral April 20, 1830 by Wm. Hume,
    V.D.M. Bowling Walker of Hickman, Bondsman

Walker, John to Nancy Bridges Dec. 2, 1807
    George H. Prewett, Bds. N. P. Hardeman, Test.

Walker, John to Nancy McKinney June 10, 1825 by Nichs. Scales
    Randal (X) McKinney, Bondsman

Walker, John to Mary Walker Feb. 21, 1837 by Jeremiah Stephen

    * Bond Alone Filed

Walker, John to Malinda Tucker Nov. 25, 1841 by John
    Wall, JP Aaron (X) Stevens, Bondsman

Walker, John F. to Mary Warren July 3, 1834 by Jesse Cox,
    M.G. Isaac W. P. West, Bondsman

Walker, John H. to Edy B. Tucker Dec. 29, 1842 by John
    Wall, JP Robert T. Parker, Bondsman

Walker, John L (X) to Barbary Jackson Oct 17, 1816 by Owen
    T. Watkins, JP. James (X) Stanly, Bondsman

Walker, Noah to Polly Sparkman Oct. 13, 1814
    Noah Walker, Bondsman N.P. Hardeman, Wit.

Walker, Peter J. to Elizabeth M. Crockett April 14, 1822 by
    Nich. Scales Constantine P. Sneed, Bs. R.W. Lane, Wit.

Walker, Warren W. to Elizabeth Ann Gee June 26, 1819
    Thomas Miller Jr., Bds. J. Farrington says he
    married them, but no date given.

Walker, Wiley to Lucinda Alexander June 27, 1837 by F.P.
    Bingham

Walker, William to Polly Andrews July 13, 1812 Benjamin
    Gholson, Bondsman (Bond Only) *

Walker, William (X) to Nancy Anglin Feb. 27, 1824 Jas. Walker, Bd

Walker, William (X) to Betsey Robertson Dec. 24, 1835 by
    Jas. Fox, JP. William H. Baldridge, Bondsman

Walker, William J. to Martha Jane Church Jan 7, 1849 by
    Rev. C. C. Mayhew William T. Younger, Bondsman

Walker, Woodson to Sally McClaran June 8, 1819 by Horatio
    Burns Hartwell B. Hyde, Bondsman

Walkup, James to Ann Cross Mar. 6, 1849 by Wm. W. Wright, JP
    Henry W. Sweeney, Bondsman

Wall, Braxton J. to Rebecca A. Wiggs June 26, 1850 Green Wiggs*

Wall, Charles to Catharine Hoskins May 3, 1827 by M.L. Andrews,
    M.G. Harvey B. McCord, Bondsman

Wall, Charles F. to Elizabeth T. Shannon April 29, 1847 by
    M.L. Andrews, M.G. Jake H. Cowley, Bondsman

Wall, John to Patsey Wilson Dec. 23, 1819-44th year of our
    Independence, W.M. Logan, JP. James C. Hill, Bds.
  (*Bond Alone Filed)

Wall, John (X) to Charlotte Bittick August 5, 1824 by
        N. Scales   Bondsman: Newton (X) Wall

Wall, Newton to Sally Wilson Oct. 28, 1819 James Walker, Bd.

Wall, Peter P. to Christenia Wall June 15, 1850 by Matt
        Dobson, JP. James W. Griffin, Bd. Chesley Williams, Wit.

Wall, Scoggin (X) to Elizabeth Berry 31 Dec. 1818
        Richard Rudder, Bondsman Thos. Mebane Jr., Wit.

Wall, William to Caty Martin Aug. 16, 1810 John Brim, Bd.

Wall, William to Rutha H. Maddox, Dec. 6, 1846
        A. Hughes, Bondsman R. D. Jordan, J. P.

Wallace, Harrison T. to Myra McCord Feb. 12, 1840
        John Glenn, Bondsman James King, M. G.

Wallace, John (X) to Jane Bailey 3 August 1827
        Joseph L. Bailey, B ds. Tristram Patton, J.P.

Wallace, Joseph to Lucinda M. White 1 November 1825
        John H. Smith, Bondsman Thos. L. Douglas

Wallace, Mortimer R. to Elizabeth Heaton Jan 11, 1837
        N. P. Modrall, M. G.

Wallard, Curchel (X) to Mary Fox Nov. 13, 1815
        William (X) Sparkman, Bondsman

Waller, Alfred to Martha Ann Cartwright Jan 21, 1840
        C. B. Boxley, Bds. W. B. Carpenter

Waller, Alfred to America S. Anderson Jan. 28, 1847
        Charles W. Crowder, Bds. J.C. Anderson, M.G.

Waller, Benjamin (X) to Martha Kelly July 23, 1828
        Joseph Barnes, Bds. P. Green, J.P.

Waller, Ferdinand to Sarah E. Smith Aug. 20, 1846
        Thomas S. Taylor, Bds. L.B. Johnson, J.P.

Waller, Francis (X) to Catharine Hamlett Sept 13, 1840
        John Waters, Bds. Name of Minister not given

Waller, Joel H. S. and Charlotte R. Robertson Dec. 28, 1836
        By Robert Davis, M.G.

Waller, John P. and Mary Cartwright Jan 15, 1837 by S.S.
        Bartlett, J.P.

Waller, John G. to Elizabeth S. Moore Mar. 23, 1837 by J.P.

Waller, John P. to Mary Eliza Reid   Oct. 17, 1850
    Wiley B. White, Bds. Philip Ball, M.G.

Waller, Joseph S. to Nancy T. C. Dotson   Oct 30, 1832 by
    Bird Dodson   Bondsman: Presley Dodson

Waller, P. to Emily Laura Matthews   June 6, 1844
    Sutherland S. Mayfield, Bds. By, W. B. Carpenter

Waller, Pierce to Elizabeth A. Cannon   Aug. 2, 1843 by
    M. L. Andrews, M.G. Wm. H. S. Hill, Bds.

Wallis, Bogan C. to Lavinia Read   December -, 1827
    William T. North, Bondsman - No return

Wallis, James H. to Rebecca F. Jones   Sept. 3, 1846 by
    Jas. B. Porter, M.G. Joseph Sprott, Bondsman

Wallis, Matthew P. to Sarah Wilson   Nov. 22, 1821 by W.R.
    Nunn. Alexander Stairn and Sam'l A. Gillespie, Bds

Wallis, William to Sophia Gillaspie   Sept. 19, 1820 by
    W. M. Regan Richard T. Long, Bds. E. L. Wall, Wit.

Walls, Drury (X) to Mary Berry   Aug. 10, 1816 by N. Scales
    Wm. (X) Dermunber (?), Bondsman

Walter, Drury S. (X) to Elizabeth A. Mangrum   Mar. 2, 1850
    Henry J. Merritt, Bds. Geo. Andrews, J.P.

Walters, Edward to Sarah E. Crockett   Sept. 28, 1843
    Lancelot Johnston, Bds. M. L. Andrews, M.G.

Walters, Laban L. to Martha A. Marshall   Jan 12, 1834 by
    M. M. Marshall.   Richard Steele Jr., Bds.

Walters, Laban S. to Martha S. Carsey   Nov. 17, 1836 by
    Robert Davis, M.G. Robert Charter, Bds.

Walton, James L. (X) to Mary D. Sims   Mar. 7, 1850 by
    Geo. Andrews, J.P. Thos. A. Graham, Bds.

Walton, Jesse to Nancy Swisher   Nov. 26, 1817   Thos. Walton Bds.*

Walton, John to Elizabeth Hood   Jan. 17, 1843 by Monroe
    Short, J.P. Thomas A. Graham, Bds.

Walton, John B. to Elizabeth N. Alston   Sept. 22, 1847
    James N. Hamilton, Bondsman Bond Alone Filed

Walton, John W. to Adeline Thompson   Oct. 13, 1821 by
    G. Hunt. Daniel German, Bondsman

*No Return given

Walton, Josiah S. to Lettia Caton Feb. 25, 1816
    William Moore, Bondsman Robert Davis, Test.

Walton, Thomas to Nancy L. Utley Aug. 16, 1817
    Abner Boyd, Bondsman Robert Davis, Test.

Walton, Thomas to Sally Scruggs July 11, 1818 Wm. Kavenaugh, Bd.*

Walton, Thomas (X) to Peggy Montgomery July 21, 1847 Jas. Davis, Bd.*

Walton, Wm. to Hannah Hughes Feb. 12, 1828 Thos. Williams, Bd.*

Walton, William (X) to Nancy Hay May 14, 1839 by Henry Walker,
    Minister. Joseph Gibson, Bondsman

Walton, William A. to Mildred A. Adams Dec. 26, 1843
    George M. Pate, Bondsman (Bond Alone Filed)

Walton, William E. (X) to Sarah Sims April 12, 1849 by
    George Andrews, J.P. Thomas P. Anderson, Bds.

Wamack, John to Elizabeth Elliott Feb. 11, 1830 by
    Abner M. Dowell Walter T. Elliott, Bondsman

Ward, John (X)(Signed Wart -written on license Warf)? to
    Betsy Hood Dec. 25, 1816 by Tristam Pattan, J.P.
    Peter (X) Hood, Bondsman L. H. Hardeman, Test.

Ward, Joseph to Susanna Engleman Sept 11, 1813 James McCombs, Bd.*

Ward, William C. to Lucinda Patterson Feb. 2, 1837 by Sam
    B. Robinson, J.P.

Warran, Archibald to Nancy Ortan Aug 9, 1806 David Ortan, Bd.

Warren, Barrel (X) to Mary Redford Nov. 12, 1832
    James Shelburne, Bondsman; Will Hardeman, Wit.

Warren, Burwell to Keziah Fields Dec. 3, 1835 by Wm. B.
    Carpenter. Samuel Burk, Bondsman

Warren, Drury to Narcissa Ann Stevens Dec. 9, 1840 by
    G. Marshall, J.P. William (X) Warren, Bds.

Warren, Edward A. to Rhoda North Jan. 27, 1825 by
    D. Brown, V.D.M. John House, Bondsman

Warren, Fielden to Elizabeth Maupin March 24, 1818
    Paul H. Neely, Bondsman Thos. Hardeman, Jr. Wit.

Warren, James (X) to Lucy Singleton Feb. 21, 1818
    Wm. Stone, Bondsman Robert Davis, Test.

* Return not filed.

Warren, James M. to Martha O. Walton July 23, 1840 by
H. B. Hyde, J. P.   Wm. J. Hill, Bondsman

Warren, Jesse W. (X) to Mary A. Field Mar. 1, 1849 by
Jas. S. Owen, J.P. John C. Nelly, Bondsman

Warren, John to Polly Mayfield Sept 20, 1822
Ambrose Mayfield, Bondsman (No Return)

Warren, John to Frances G. Buckingham Jan 21, 1840 by
N. B. Owen, J.P. Burrell Warren, Bondsman

Warren, John (X) to Susan J. Bazdel Oct. 12, 1845 by
C. M. Pognor, J. P. George W. Moppin, Bds.

Warren, John D. to Polly W. Crouch Nov. 28, 1817
John House, Bondsman Robert Davis, Test.

Warren, Joseph to Parmelia Hill Jan 12, 1816 Wm. Coor, Bds.
Thos. Hardeman Jr., Wit.

Warren, Middleton F. to Minerva Ann Bazell Sept. 27, 1849
G. W. Rolland, J.P. M. H. Nicholson, Bondsman

Warren, Munford to Ann H. Roberts Mar. 14, 1826 by G. Shannon

Warren, Philip H. to Sarah Wood Oct 28, 1842 by H. B. Hyde,
J.P.   John E. Raney, Bondsman ("Not to be published under 2 weeks" written on license.)

Warren, Quilla M. to Mary Ann Moppin June 30, 1844 by
T. H. Roberts, J. P. William W. Neely, Bds.

Warren, Stewart to Sarah Willett Apr. 3, 1831 by Wright
Stanley, J.P. Reuben Littleton, Bondsman

Warren, Thomas (X) to Sally McKinney May 23, 1827 by
Nich^s Scales   Thomas Parsley, Bondsman

Warren, William to Lucy Bizziel Jan 17, 1831 by
George Shannon, J.P. Ennis Murrey, Bondsman

Warren, William (X) to Martha J. Moppin Nov. 17, 1844 by
Charles M. Poynor, JP. William W. Neelly, Bds.

Warren, William to Caroline M. Glenn Sept 16, 1847 by
E. P. Scales, J.P.   John E. Raney, Bondsman

Warren, William M. to Matilda Hanks June 22, 1849
Thomas C. Parsley, Bondsman (Bond Alone Filed)

Warrington, Elijah to Rosanna Dillen Nov. 24, 1825
William Hopewell, Bondsman - no return given.

Washington, Frances W. to Elixa U. Hall Oct. 13, 1820
   "Merred by me, Geo. Blackbum, Minister"
   Wm. G. Dickinson, Bondsman

Waters, John to Leah Ozburn Nov. 10, 1836 by Wm. B.
   Carpenter.   Thos. B. Smith, Bondsman

Waters, Samuel to Jane Berry Dec. 28, 1823 by
   Thomas Nelson   James Wisener, Bondsman

Watkins, Alexander to Lucy Connel (Caunel) June 26, 1815
   William Caunel, Bondsman

Watkins, Benjamin (X) to Elizabeth D. Henley Jan 1, 1829
   By Wm. B. Carpenter   Wm. H. Johnson, Bondsman

Watkins, Isaac to Rebecca Evans Sept. 12, 1809
   James Jackson, Bondsman Wm. P. Harrison, Wit.

Watkins, John to Lucinda Brown Jan 16, 1839 by
   R. White, JP.   W. B. White, Bondsman

Watkins, Owen T. to Mary C. Kinnard Apr 19, 1849 by
   Jesse Cox, M. G.   Wm. F. Watkins, Bondsman

Watkins, Samuel G. to Martha Jane Foster July 7, 1846 by
   Phil P. Neely, M.G.   Alexander W. Bentley, Bds.

Watkins, William (X) to Ritta Perkins No. 19, 1831 by
   Daniel White, M. G.   John Norris, Bondsman

Watkins, Williamson (X) to Sarah Jane McGee Aug. 4, 1848
   George Andrews, J.P.   William Epps, Bondsman

Watkins, Willis to Dolley Staggs June 22, 1819 Thos(X)Staggs*

Watson, George to Fanny Dowdy Nov. 12, 1828 by Hartwell
   B. Hyde, J.P.   William Span, Bondsman

Watson, George W. to Pauthia Elliott Dec. 27, 1838 by
   H. B. Hyde, JP.   James D. Culbertson, Bds.

Watson, Isaac N. to Sarah Jane Hulme Dec. 30, 1847 by
   R. M. McDaniel, J.P.   William Hughes, Bondsman

Watson, James (X) to Nancy Andrews Jan 21, 1835 by
   John Allison, J. P., who was also Bondsman

Watson, John M. to Tabitha W. Gentry Feb. 15, 1827 by
   Andrew Craig, MG. John Page, and Milton H. Page, Bds.

*No return given

275

Watson, Stephen to Ellen McCollum Aug. 26, 1847 by
    H. B. North, M. G.   Bondsman: Reese Lamb

Weakley, Benjamin F. to Mary E. Porter   July 26, 1838
    Bondsman: Alexander Winbourne

Weatherford, Lewis (X) to Susan Edwards   Dec. 30, 1819 by
    W. M. Logan   Bondsman: Doctor F. Fuqua

Weatherford, William W. to Martha Featherston   Jan 30, 1845
    Bds,: Daniel L. Weatherford   J.B. Boyd, J.P.

Weatherford, Willis to Martha Fuqua   Feb. 16, 1827
    Bds: James Price   D.C. Kinnard, J.P.

Weatherington, Joshua to Martha Gardner   Mar. 28, 1819
    Bds: Thomas Gardner   Wm. Dunnesan, J.P.

Weathers, Edmund to Barbary Shumate   Sept. 10, 1823
    Bds: Jas. Williams   Wit: Joshua M. McCown

Weaver, Absalem to Betty Ruperd (Ruserd)   July 3, 1819
    Bondsman: John Lynch

Weaver, Shaderick to Julia Ann Tucker   Feb. 24, 1833
    Bds: Thos. Early   J. Wall, J.P.

Weaver, Thomas to Nancy Dowdy   Feb. 10, 1831 by Isaac Jones MG
    Bds: James Edwards   Clerk: Thos. Hardeman

Webb, Amasa to Mary S. Love   Dec. 23, 1824   John W. Love, Bds.

Webb, Andrew to Elizabeth Woldridge   Nov. 25, 1834
    Bds: John E. Crouch   John W. Hanner, MG

Webb, Edmund (X) to Mary Jane Floyd   Oct. 25, 1848 by
    Lent Brown, M.G.   Bds: Benjamin Floyd

Webb, Henry Y. to Martha Jane Hughes   May 29, 1834 by
    T. D. Porter,   Bds: Meredith P. Gentry

Webb, Hugh - see Wood, Hugh

Webb, James to Rebecca C. Gault   Oct 4, 1843
    Bds: Hugh M. Gault   J. Dyer, J.P.

Webb, James S. to Margaret A. E. T. Ewing   Sept. 18, 1849
    Bds: Wm. W. Hunt   M. L. Andrews, M. G.

Webb, John to Patsey Landrum   Jan 15, 1811   Thos. Landrum, BDs.*

Webb, John to Nancy Buckley   Dec. 25, 1815 by W. P. Turn
    Bds: John Jackson   Thos. H. Perkins, Deputy Clerk

*Bond alone filed

Webb, Joseph (X) to Sally Pope Feb. 9, 1823
        Bds: Wm. Pope   Wm. Dollar, J. P.

Webb, Samuel M. to Elizabeth L. Webb Sept. 6, 1847
        Bondsman: William W. Kimbro (Bond along filed)*

Webb, William to Sarah Elam Aug. 6, 1827 Hugh M. Gault *Bds.

Webb, William to Mary M. Hughes Feb. 2, 1837 Solemnized

Webster, Thomas to Rhoda (Rhody) Burke June 3, 1820
        Sylvester Jones, Bds. H. L. Tilman, Wit.

Weddell, George to Isabella Primm Oct. 4, 1824 by
        G. Hunt.   Jeremiah Primm, Bondsman

Weeks, Abraham (X) to Betsey Hutchison Oct 28, 1824
        John M. Hutton, Bds. Lewis Loyd, J.P.

Weems, Joseph to Mary A. Brewer August 27, 1850 by
        A. L. S. Green, M.G. Patrick H. Otey, Bds.

Wells, Banks C. to Eliza Caperton April 14, 1840 by
        Daniel Baugh, J.P. Thompson Caperton, Bds.

Wells, Edward P. to Elizabeth Greer Nov. 23, 1844 by
        W. B. Carpenter   John (X) Lazenby, Bds.

Wells, George W. to Hannah D. Vaughan Dec. 19, 1832 by
        Wilford H. Rains, JP. Wm. J. Moody, Bds.

Wells, John B. to Mary B. Epps Aug. 29, 1850 by
        M. B. Molloy, M.G. Robert A. Erskine, Bds

Wells, Thomas to Polly Staggs, Sept. 4, 1816 by
        A. Mebane, JP. Thos (X) Staggs, Bds.

Wells, (Wills) Thomas to Elizabeth M. Garrett Dec. 10, 1838
        Bds: J. Thos. Parrish H.F. Leacock, Rector, PEC

Wills, Thomas P. to Susan S. Smith Dec. 26, 1833 by
        Michael Finney, J.P. Jesse N. White, Bds.

Wells, William to Lucinda Alford Jane 12, 1834 by
        Michael Finney, J.P. Joseph W. Baugh, Bds.

Wells, William to Dolly P. Hood March 6, 1814 by
        Tristram Patton, JP. D. Dunn, Bds.

West, Daniel W. (X) to Franky Wild May 7, 1825
        John Reed, Bondsman (Bond only filed)

(or L.)
West, Marcus S. to Martha A. R. Newsom   Feb. 24, 1841 by
    C. M. McDaniel   William K. Peebles, Bds.

West, Stephen to Elisabeth Childrep   Dec. 22, 1821 Jacob Critz

West, Thomas to Nancy Blackman   July 3, 1809
    John West, Bds.   Wm. P. Harrison, Wit.

West, William C. to Sarah Nevils   July 30, 1846 by
    Jesse Cox, MG.   Moses G. Gocey, Bds.

West, Willoughby S. to Marcaney Yarbrough   Oct. 17, 1822 by
    Joel Anderson   John Dial and Richard.S.Yarbrough,Bds.

Westbrook, Ridley R. (X) to Susannah West   April 14, 1825
    Elijah West, Bds.   J. W. McCown, Wit.

Whaly, William to Nancy Jackson   Mar. 1, 1819 by
    A. Mebane, J.P.   Joseph Epps, Bds.

Wharton, C. J. Fox to Amanda E. Criddle   Nov. 3, 1834
    John W. Campbell, Bds.   (Bond alone filed.)

Wheat, John Junior to Sally Sturdivant   May 25, 1820 by
    Edward Ragsdale, J.P.   Squire (X) Williams, Bds.

Wheatt, William (Maury Co. Resident) to Martha Pistole
    Nov. 8, 1822   Ennis (X)Duffel,Bds.
    Rites solemnized Nov. 10, 1822 Samuel Merritt,JP

Wheeler, Benjamin M. to Malinda Johnson   May 13, 1841
    James Williams, Bds.   (Bond Alone Filed)

Wheeler, Elijah J. to Eliza W. Ferguson   Dec. 20, 1845
    Parson M. Brogden, Bds.   (Bond alone Filed)

Wheeler, James to Mary Murrey   Aug. 11, 1831 by S. Green
    Thomas Glymph, Bondsman

Wheeler, Williamson A. to Louisa Williams   Dec. 9, 1843 by
    Jas. M. Green, J.P.   Simeon Venable, Bds.

Whitaker, John to Sally Hammond   Apr 28, 1807
    Robert Steel, Bds.   N. B. Hardeman, Wit.

Whitby, Ederson to Elizabeth F. Palmer   April 18, 1842 by
    Thos. H. Roberts   Donald Cameron, Bds.

Whitby, Richard H. to Senora M. Pickering   Dec. 27, 1832 by
    C. M. Johnston, JP.   Asa Ham, Bds.

Whitby, Seth (X) to Polly Long   May 5, 1829   Harwood(X)Cartwright*

*Bond along

Whitby, William to Rhoda M. Burke Mar. 3, 1847 by
    E. D. Matthews, MG. George P. Brimm, Bds.

White, Adam to Mary Ann Andrews Nov. 22, 1842 by
    A. Burns. Jesse N. White, Bds.

White, Alexander to Jane E. H. Rudder, Jan 19, 1843 by
    Cowden McCord, J.P. Napoleon B. Neal, Bds.
    Blount Jordan, Witness

White, Benjamin to Eliza Kinny Aug 5, 1822 Thos. Thompson, Bds. *

White, Benj. R. to Diadema Alexander June 25, 1822 Henry Edbeck *

White, Daniel(X) to Mahala Ann White Oct. 8, 1843 by
    M. L. Andrews, MG. John White, Bondsman

White, Daniel S. to Sarah Shepherd Nov. 28, 1834 by
    Daniel White, M.G. Reuben White, Wit.

White, Ealihu (X) to Cloe Johnson June 20, 1823 by
    John Moore, J.P. James M. Talley, Bds.

White, Elisha to Jane Walker Mar 1, 1806 Thomas Wood, Bds. *

White, Franklin P. to Martha M. Ashlin Oct 2, 1834 by
    Robert Davis, MG. Tilman F. Atkinson, Bds.

White, George to Maria Potts May 3, 1827 by Thos. L. Douglas
    Bd: William Young and Wit: J. W. McCown

White, George M. to Elizabeth White Dec. 22, 1834 by
    J. Wall, JP. Nelson (X) Lavender, Bondsman

White, George W. to Margaret L. Word June 20, 1842 by W. H.
    Wharton, of Nashville, Tenn. Henry P. Pointer, Bds.

White, Hiram A. to Prudence Hewston Dec. 7, 1829 by Andrew
    McCrady. Samuel Reeves, Bds.

White, Holland L. to Catherine Echols Dec. 27, 1816 by
    Garner McConnico. James W. McComb, Bds.

White, James to Catharine Hufstetler Jan 4, 1808
    Abram Sharp, Bds. A. Potter, Wit.

White, James to Polley Flemmons Aug. 22, 1811 by Nick
    Scales. Stephen White, Bds. Wm. P. Harrison, Wit.

White, James A. to Eleanor Kincaid Dec. 20, 1827 by Geo. J.
    Poindexter. James Hargrove, Bds.

White, Jesse N. to Mary T. McMaury Nov 10, 1843 by W. Burns,
    MG. Blount Jordan, Bds. Chesley Williams, Wit.

* Bond alone filed

White, John to Minerva Green Jan 27, 1839 by R. White
    Philip (X) Anglin, Bondsman

White, John H. to Lavinia McClain Sept 29, 1827 Jos.(X)Willett*

White, John McC. to Anna Champ July 31, 1821 by C. McDaniel
    Levi Gardner, Bondsman

White, John W. to Sarah C. Cannon Nov. 17, 1841 by Philip
    P. Neely, MG. Wm. H. Hill, Bondsman

White, John W. to Caroline Glenn Dec 7, 1846 Archer W. Sanford*

White, Joseph to Nancy Horseford Jan. 20, 1833 by William
    Carson, J.P. Robert Redd, Bondsman

White, Joshua to Polly P. Holt July 6, 1813 John Hardeman, Bds *

White, Meady to Rachel Roberts Oct 29, 1845, by J. J. Bingham
    Wiley B. White, Bds. L.B. McConnico, Clerk

White, Needy to Anna Worley Jan 2, 1812 (Bond alone filed)
    Jonathan Barfoot and James Norris, Bondsmen

White, Parker A. to Martha A. Downing Aug. 24, 1843 by (Wit.
    Wm. J. Garrett, M.G. Wm. S. White, Bds. Blount Jordan,

White, Reuben to Polly Kerby Ja 24, 1828 by Daniel White
    John Norris, Bondsman

White, Robert to Evarilla Lavender July 15, 1829 by M. L.
    Andrews, M. G. Allen Thornbrough, Bondsman

White, Robert (X) to Jane Plumlee Dec. 23, 1832 by
    J. Wall, Jp. Wm. Anderson, Bds. Will Hardeman, Wit.

White, Robert B. to Mary Lunn, Feb. 11, 1842 Jesse N. White, Bd*

White, Seaborn to Fanny Anglin Nov. 2, 1829 by Thos B.
    Brown, J. P. Daniel Anglin, Bds.

White, Stephen (X) to Catherine Johnston Aug. 4, 1831 by
    Wm. Moor, JP. Michael Page, Bds

White, Thomas to Nancy D. Chriswell Oct 28, 1823 by
    Jas. Reid, J.P. Laben Chriswell (Criswell) Bds.

White, Thomas B. to Sally Chester Dec. 1, 1813 Edward Hood, Bd*

White, Thomas L. to Martha Blythe Feb. 10, 1819 by John
    Thompson, J.P. John Blythe, Bds.

* Bond alone filed

White, Wiley B. to Nancy Sherrin Dec. 26, 1829 by
    Daniel White, MG. Reuben White, Bondsman

White, Wiley B. to Sarah E. Terrell April 11, 1844 by
    R. White. William H. Coleman, Bondsman

White, William to Eliza Taylor Dec. 15, 1836 by
    S. B. Robison, JP Nathan A. Boyd, Bondsman

White, William to Mary M. Bennett Sept. 10, 1840 by
    J. C. Anderson, MG. Samuel F. Glass, Jr. Bds.

White, William H. to Cinthia C. Baily Feb. 22, 1844 by
    C. William, JP. Charles Calhoon, Bondsman

White, William M. to Mary S. Wells July 11, 1840 by
    Jno. P. McKay, JP. William D. Ferguson, Bds.

White, William S. to Phebe Ann White March 26, 1842
    Jesse N. White, Bondsman (Bond Alone Filed)

White, Wilson J. (X) to Milly Ann Johnson Sept. 26, 11850
    W. F. A. Shaw, JP. Franklin (X) Reese, Bds.

Whitehead, Jacob to Harriett McCall June 24, 1807
    Jacob Whitehead, Bds. Wm. P. Harrison, Wit.

Whitehead, John S. to Eliza Powell Jan. 29, 1850 by
    L. McCall, J.P. Lycurgus McCall, Bds.

Whitehead, Milton F. to Jamie S. (L. Wilson Sept. 13, 1840 by
    J. Wall. J.P.

Whitehurst, James (X) to Martha Wilkinson Mar 26, 1825
    James Wilkinson, Bdsman. (Bond only filed)

Whitfield, Felix to Minerva Williamson Jan 3, 1837 by
    Robert Davis, M.G. S. B. McConnico, Clerk Ct.

Whitfield, George W. to Sarah Bond Mar. 5, 1849 by
    M. L. Andrews, MG. Harrison Whitfield, Bds.

Whitfield, Harrison to Sophronia M. Conn Sept. 16, 1845 by
    M. L. Andrews, M.G. James S. DeMoss, Bds.

Whitfield, James M. to Rebecca A. Newsom May 16, 1845 by
    J. L. Andrews, M.G. William Ewing, Bds.

Whitfield, Thomas J. to Eliza J. Nolen Feb. 6, 1829 by
    G. Marshall JP. A. H. Evans, Bds.

Whitfield, Wilkins, to Elizabeth Ridley Sept. 3, 1846 by
    Robert Davis, MG. Wm. H. Hill, Bds.

See page 165 for additional "W"'s

Whitley, Elisha M. to Candace Burnett Jan 10, 1843 by
    R. B. B. Cannon, J.P. B. Boswell T. Gray, Bds.

Whitley, Jesse (X) to Mary Bridgeman June 7, 1827 by
    W. B. Carpenter James Watson, Bds.

Whitley, James (X) to Cloe Alford Apr 12, 1823 Winfield Pope*

Whitlock, Baldin R. to Nancy G. Berry Aug. 24, 1825
    David W. Gee, Bds. J. W. McCown, Wit.

Whitman, Samuel to Mary Young Aug 6, 1816 by Samuel
    Merritt, J.P. Solomon Whitman, Bondsman

Whitman, Solomon to Catherine (Laygroon (Lagroan) Feb. 15, 1816
    Samuel Whitman, Bondsman. Rites by Owen T. Watkins

Whitney, Joseph A. to Permelia E. Shell Jan . 14, 1850 by
    James M. Reed, JP. George (X) Roper, Bds.

Whitsett, James M. to Martha Anthony Aug. 8, 1815
    John Sappington, Bds. (Attached was a note by
    George Tilman certifying he married these two on
    8th of Aug. 1815 but license was lost and not
    found until Apr. 5, 1818 and found agreeable to
    assembly.)

Whitsett, William A. to Nancy Jane Morton Sept 24, 1839 by
    Jas. Whitsett Wm. Anthony, Bds.

Whitson, William to Harriett Witherspoon Nov. 11, 1817 Jas.
                                                      Witherspoon*

Whitter, Richard (X) to Nancy Elliott June 7, 1828 by
    George J. Poindexter, JP. Wm. T. Haynes, Bds.

Whitthorne, George M. to Ellen W. Johnson June 5, 1850 by
    M. L. Andrews, MG. Sam. H. Whitthorne, Bds.

Whitus, Richard (X) to Martha Virginia Sutton Mar. 4, 1849 by
    James M. Reid, JP Thomas D. (X) Cartwright, BDs.

Whitus, Tullus (X) to Martha E. Sutton by Wm. Walgreen on
    April 2, 1849 Robert S. Ballow, Bds.

Whitworth, Harmon C. to Mary Quinn July 15, 1830 by
    G. Hunt. Mortimer R. Walliz, Bds.

Wiggins, Archibald (X) to Jane Haynes Oct 14, 1825 T.K. Haynes*

Wiggins, James (X) to Susan German Dec. 31, 1822 by
    Sion Hunt John W. Walton, Bds.

Wiggs, William (X) to Abby Allen Sept. 10, 1824
    Thomas Beasley and Thomas Fly, Bds. *

Wilburn, Samuel G. to Mary E. Starnes Dec. 18, 1842 by
    B. D. Neal, MG. Lycurgus H. Moseley, Bds.

Wilkes, Thomas A. to Mary A. Ellis   Oct. 15, 1843 by
    M. L. Andrews, MG.   Robert B. Trimble, Bds.

Wilkes, William to Martha A. White   Dec. 13, 1848 by
    John King.   D. A. Elmore, Bondsman

Wilkins, Alexander to Sally Kirk   Oct. 13, 1814 Jas. Wilkins*

Wilkins, James to Martha Hill July 20, 1813
    David Dunn, Bds.   Thos. T. Hardeman, Wit.

Wilkins, James to Clarissa Ann Fisher   July 5, 1847 by
    Wm. A. Whitsitt, Baptist MG.   Thos Fowler, Bds.

Wilkins, John to Rachel Thompson   Dec. 21, 1807 John White*

Wilkins, John to Betsey Butt   Aug. 26, 1829 by
    M. Kinley, JP.   Edward Campbell, Bondsman

Wilkins, John A. to Elizabeth J. Hughes   Apr 4, 1844 by
    M. L. Andrews, MG.   Morris L. Bond, Bds.

Wilkins, John H. to Lucinda Prichard   Dec. 29, 1846 by
    J C. Anderson, MG.   George M. Long. Bds.

Wilkinson, James to Lydia Bowers   Jan. 19, 1822
    Benjamin (X) Wilkerson, Bds.   E. L. Hall, Wit.

Wilkinson, John F. to Ann Swisher   Sept 4, 1828 Theoderic Carter

Wilkinson, Thomas H. to Phereby T. Bateman   June 8, 1829 by
    C. E. McEwen, JP.   John F. Wilkinson, Bds.

Wilkinson, William to Sarah Norfleet Wilson Feb 5, 1819 Joh. Wilson*

Wilks, Daniel to Elisabeth Craig Sept 30, 1816 Joseph Cole, Bds*

Wilks, John C. to Mary A. H. Cromer   Oct. 27, 1836 by
    James W. Carson, JP   James Shelburne, Bds.

Williams, Alfred (X) to Patsey Alford   Feb. 6, 1825 by
    H. Bailey, JP.   Wm. H. Alford, Bds.

Williams, Allen to Jincy McClaran   Oct 24, 1825 Wm. H. Downing, Bd*

Williams, Alvis to Eliza Jane Henderson Feb. 4, 1834 by
    Andrew Craig, MG.   James Anderson, Bds.

Williams, Annion (X) to Delpha Hutchison Sept 30, 1815
    Spencer (X) Hutchison, Bds.   N. P. Hardeman, Wit.

Williams, Benjamin W. to Eliza M. Perkins Dec. 25, 1839 by
    Benj. F. Weakley, MG.   Joel A. Battle, Bds. and
    Attorney for B. Williams.

*Bond alone filed.

Williams, Chesley to Elizabeth Jordan Dec. 10, 1830 by
    R. W. Morris, (E.A.M.E.), Grant F. Allen, Bds.

Williams, Christopher H. to Jane Allison Dec. 7, 1819
    Jesse Bugg, Bondsman Thos Hardeman, Wit.

Williams, Clem W. to Tabitha Barnes Dec. 23, 1847 by
    L. B. Johnson, JP. William (X) Barnes, Bds.

Williams, Clement W. to Adaline Barnes Nov. 27, 1840
    N. B. Owan, JP. William (X) Fish, Bds.

Williams, Daniel to Sarah E. Hill Nov. 24, 1831 by
    Andrew Craig, MG. Thomas T. Wyatt, Bds.

Williams, David to Nancy Ann Brock Mar. 13, 1828 by
    John Witherspoon. Thomas Short, Bds.

Williams, David to Mary T. Rogers Mar. 10, 1844 by
    John Nichols. James W. Fitts, Bds.

Williams, Elmer W. to Susan A. Hamilton Oct. 22, 1840
    Jas. W. Rea, M.G. Isaac H. Gray, Bondsman

Williams, Franan (X) to Martha D. Vault Nov. 15, 1842 by
    T. W. Haynes, M.G. Elias M. Vaught, Bds.

Williams, Harbart (X) to Martha Williams Oct 9, 1830
    John Guthrie, Bds. John G. Hay, Wit.

Williams, Henry to Mary Ann Chrisman Oct. 20, 1818
    Samuel (X) Williams, Bds. Thos. H. Hardeman, Wit.

Williams, Henry to Ann Still Nov. 21, 1839 by
    James M. Greer, JP. Jacob M. Twigg, Bds.

Williams, James to Polley C. Johnson Nov. 19, 1811
    Andrew Johnson, Bondsman Wm. P. Harrison, Wit.

Williams, James (X) to Frances Nicholson May 24, 1819
    Guilford Dudley Jr., Bds. Thos Hardeman, Wit.

Williams, James to Mary Wilson Nov. 7, 1824 by
    Andrew Craig, MG. John Secrest, Bds.

Williams, James to Catharine M. Moss Dec. 24, 1830 by
    M. L. Andrews, MG. Jos. H. Fry, Bds.

Williams, James to Elizabeth Johnson Jan 16, 1838
    L. Crosley, J. P. Thomas Harris, Bds.

Williams, James to Ann Terry June 11, 1844 by B. D.
    Neal, M.G. Hiram Murdock, Bondsman

*Bond alone filed.

Williams, James E. to Elizabeth A. T. Jordan Oct. 16, 1847
	Joseph McPeak, Bds. Chesley Williams, Wit.

Williams, James M. to Mary F. Kirk Jan 25, 1844 by
	G. W. Sneed, M.G. John G. Roberts, Bds.

Williams, James S. to Maria E. Wilson Nov. 7, 1824 by
	Andrew Craig, M.G. Alexander Moore, Bds.

Williams, James W. to Mary A. Crosby Dec. 18, 1845 by
	B. D. Neal, M.G. C. J. Wood, Bondsman

Williams, John to Jean Williams June 1, 1807 Rush Williams, Bds.*

Williams, John to Mahala Singletary March 28, 1823
	B. M. Nicholson, Bds. W. McCown, Wit.

Williams, John to Emmaritta Appleton July 27, 1825 by
	Joel Anderson. James Williams, Bondsman

Williams, John (X) to Elizabeth Younger Dec. 17, 1828
	Abraham Church, JP. John Brooks, Bds.

Williams, John to Sarah Wilson Nov. 25, 1830
	E. R. Reddick, JP. James Williams, Bds.

Williams, John C. (X) to Catharine Dugger July 23, 1834
	S. B. McConnico, JP. John McDaniel, Bds.

Williams, John C. to Sarah N. Sneed Sept. 26, 1848
	G. W. Sneed, MG. Nicholas T. Sneed, Bds.

Williams, John H. to Mary Jane Biggar Solemized about
	midnight on the night between 29th and 30th of
	April 1848 by Lycurgus McCall, JP. Wm. Terry, Bds.

Williams, John T. to Sarah Jane McCord Oct 3, 1849
	M. L. Andrews, M.G. James M. Zachary, Bds.

Williams, John W. to Elvira Brock Nov. 26, 1829 David Williams*

Williams, Johnson D. to Nancy L. Ruder Feb. 9, 1832
	Robert Davis, M.G. John Moore, Bds.

Williams, Johnson D. to Susan Ann Wells Sept 22, 1842
	Daniel Baugh, JP. Jacob H. Crowley, Bds.

Williams, Luke (X) to Kitura Parrish Oct. 31, 1825
	Richard Bishop, Bds. J. W. McCown, Wit.

Williams, Morris P. to Nancy P. Neal July 6, 1832 Ezek. Baxter, Bd*

Williams, Owen to Polly Lancaster May 30, 1806
	Benjamin Lancaster, Bds. H. Childrep, Test.

*Bond alone filed.

Williams, Robert A. to Elizabeth A. Field Nov. 7, 1844
    Joseph Sprott, Bds. M. L. Andrews, M.G.

Williams, Samuel (X) to Eleanor (Nelly) Taylor Sept 15, 1817.
    James (X) Taylor, Bds. Robert Davis, Test.

Williams, Squire (X) to Martha Hemphill Nov. 19, 1823
    Joel Anderson, J.P. Robert Reed, Bds.

Williams, Thomas to Eleanor Robertson Sept 13, 1821
    Sam'l Merritt, J.P. Jere Hardin, Bds.

Williams, Thomas to Martha Ann Lane Aug. 29, 1828
    Geo. J. Poindexter, JP. William Williams, Bds.

Williams, Thomas J. to Frances E. Glymp Jan 28, 1848
    L. B. Johnson, JP. Parson M. Brogden, Bds.

Williams, William to Elizabeth Gray Aug. 3, 1807 John Love, Bd*

Williams, William to Mary McCall July 21, 1810
    John Hardin, Bds. Wm. P. Harrison, Witness

Williams, William to Mary Hendley Oct. 18, 1824
    H. Bailey, JP. John Atkinson, Bds.

Williams, William to Rachel Sloane July 15, 1842
    J. M. Green, JP. Thomas Williams, Bds.

Williams, William to Frances Toombs July 31, 1850 by
    John Hay   George Chrisman, Bds.(Signed Wm.W.W.)

Williams, William A. to(S)or Luraney B. Owen Mar. 25, 1846 by
    W. B. Carpenter   James S. Owen, Bds.

Williams, William D. to Mary Ann Howlet Mar. 9, 1830
    C. McDaniel, J. P. Harrison B. Hinton, Bds.

Williams, William D. to Susan B. Hill Feb. 17, 1838 by
    W. D. F. Sawrie   David W. Peeler, Bds.

Williams, William F. to Mary A.E. Magee Sept 4, 1833
    Fieldin Helm, JP. James W. Carson, Bds.

Williamson, Benjamin to Cyntha M. Hope Jan 18, 1815
    Robert Harper, Bds. N. P. Hardeman, Test.

Williamson, George A. (X) to Emily Cosby Dec. 16, 1829
    John Nichols, JP. Stephen West, Bds.

Williamson, John (X) to Cyntha Montgomery Sept. 12, 1820
    Robert Foster and James T. Stewart, Bds. E.L.Hall, Wit.

*Bond alone filed.

Williamson, John G. to Nancy D. Key   Jan. 27, 1820 by
    Robert Davis, MG.   Bondsman: James Merritt

Williamson, John H. to Zorilda P. McCurdy   Sept. 18, 1838 by
    John McCurdy, MG.   Bondsman: William D. Andrews

Williamson, Richard W. to Sarah Glum   Aug. 19, 1841 by
    James McEwen, J.P.   Bondsman: Henry S. Crichlow

Williamson, Richard W. to Mary A. House   Dec. 25, 1849 by
    John M. Gault, J.P.   Bds: Thomas Williamson, Wit: C. Williams

Williamson, Rush (Rut)? to Nancy Critchlow   April 4, 1807
    Bds: Lancaster Glover and Richard Williamson
    Witness: N. P. Hardeman

Williamson, Thomas S. to James M. Jordan (Must be Jane) Dec. 19,
    1843 by Jesse Cox, JG.   Bds. John B. Crichlow

Williford, William R. to Angelina Arnold Oct. 13, 1838
    Bondsman: Joel Parrish.   Bond alone filed

Wilson, Aaron A. to Selica Webb   Nov. 1, 1821 by W. M. Hogan
    Bondsman: L. B. Tony

Wilson, Alexander to Nancy Fuzell   Sept. 30, 1815 John Wilson, BDS*

Wilson, Gregory to Sally Harden Aug. 17, 1815 David Hewstin (Huston)

Wilson, Henry to Nancy Steel Jan. 10, 1830 by Joseph Carl, EMEC.
    Bondsman: Thos. Hughes

Wilson, Henry to Sarah McCrory Heiter   June 4, 1839 by
    Robert Davis MG in the Evening.   Bds: James Hogan Jr.

Wilson, Henry to Mary E. Childress   Jan. 24, 1850 by A. N.
    Cunningham, MG.   Bondsman: Robert P. Moss.

Wilson, Isaac B. to Mary A. Jordan   Sept 8, 1834 by T. D. Porter
    Bondsman: Wm. Webb

Wilson, James to Malinda Wilson Dec. 2, 1805 (Date torn but I
    believe it is 1805 instead of 1835) Bds: George E. Julen*

Wilson, James to Jenny Wilson   Aug. 6, 1807   Robert Clark, Bds. *

Wilson, James to Sally McClellan   Jan. 17, 1811 Witness: N. P.
    Hardeman   Executed by Nick Scales

Wilson, James to Mary Ann Kee Sept. 16, 1816   James Alston, Bds.*

Wilson, James to Scinthia (Sinthy) Wilson   July 16, 1817
    Test: Robert Davis   Bondsman: Wm. E. Clardwell

* Bond alone found filed

Wilson, James to Sally McLellan Jan. 12, 1820
    Bondsman: William McKnight Wit: Wm. P. Harrison

Wilson, James to Mary Christopher Mar. 12, 1823 by Henry
    Bailey, J.P. Bds.: Willis Baucom

Wilson, James (X) to Susannah Nall Jan 5, 1841
    Bondsman: Lynden (X) Laughlin (Bond only found)

Wilson, James H. to Emeline Wilson Mar. 20, 1821
    Samuel Houston, Bondsman Wit: Elisha L. Hall

Wilson, James S. to Nancy Vaughan Oct. 6, 1832 Thos. M. Sconce, Bds.*

Wilson, Jason C. to Jane Bostick Sept 29, 1815 Executed by
    N. Scales Samuel N. Martin, Bondsman

Wilson, John to Celia Campbell Feb. 27, 1810
    Bondsman: Hiram Campbell Wit: Wm. P. Harrison

Wilson, John to Ann Williams Mar. 5, 1835 Samuel Brooks, Bds.*

Wilson, John to Mahala McPherson Oct. 8, 1836 Joseph McBride, Bds.*

Wilson, John A. to Mary Wilson April 14, 1825 by M. L.
    Andrews, JP. Bondsman: John Baucom

Wilson, John S. to Mary M. Wilson Nov. 4, 1841 Executed by
    Thos. Douglass Bondsman: Robert P. Currin

Wilson, Joseph (X) to Parmelia A. Duncan Mar. 22, 1838 by
    Stephen Nolen, JP. Bondsman: Benjamin A. Hicks

Wilson, Joseph W. (X) to Ann White July 3, 1821 by
    Edward Ragsdale, JP. Bondsman: Samuel C. Brook

Wilson, Joseph W. to Frances Dowdy Aug. 4, 1833 by
    Lewis Heath, JP. Joseph D. Ezell, Bondsman

Wilson, Josiah to Rexina Wilson May 25, 1813
    Bondsman: Joseph Wilson Wit: Thos. Hardeman

Wilson, Josiah to Mary Coble Nov. 8, 1832 by J. Wall
    Bondsman: Isaac Smith

Wilson, Josiah to Julia Ann Moseley Dec. 23, 1845 by
    Lycurgus McCall, Jp. Wit: L.B. McConnico, CWCCourt.
    Bondsman: John T. (X) Wilson

Wilson, Josiah F. and Nancy Baucom July 28, 1831 by
    M.L. Andrews, M.G. Bondsman: Josiah Wilson Jr.

Wilson, Lemuel A. to Nancy Taylor May 4, 1826 *

*Bond alone filed

Wilson, Matthew to Elizabeth Russell Nov. 28, 1832 by
    J. Wall, JP   Bondsman: Robert Wilson

Wilson, Robert to Anna P. Reid Oct. 8, 1816 George W. Reid, Bds.*

Wilson, Robert to Nancy Haley Jan. 4, 1833 Robert Calhoon, Bds.*

Wilson, Samuel to Milley Brown July 18, 1810
    Bondsman: Aaron Wilson Wit: Wm. P. Harrison

Wilson, Samuel to Rosey Bateman Feb. 18, 1835 by G. L. Nolen,
    J.P.   Bondsman: Thos. H. Wilkinson

Wilson, Samuel to Ann Coble Feb. 23, 1843 by J. B. Boyd, JP
    Bondsman: Milas N. Wilson Wit: Chesley Williams

Wilson, Samuel C. to Ruth Whitlock May 31, 1832 by
    J. Wall, JP. Bondsman: Robert W. Calhoon

Wilson, Samuel D. to Eliza Herbert Dec. 18, 1828 by
    T. D. Porter Bondsman: J. G. Wheaton

Wilson, Thomas to Peggy Wilson Mar. 7, 1805
    Bondsman: Russ Porter Wit: John Hardeman

Wilson, Thomas D. to Ann H. Sims Oct. 27, 1836 by
    M. Marshall Bondsman: Charles D. Parrish

Wilson, Thomas S. to Charity M. Smith May 6, 1841 by
    John Wall, JP. Bondsman: John S. Wilson

Wilson, Thomas W. to Mary Banks April 30, 1834 by
    Peter S. Gayle   Bondsman: Hamon Critz

Wilson, William to Rebecca Berry July 9, 1817 Bondsman: Thos.* ___ ?

Wilson, William (X) to Elizabeth Cummins Oct. 12, 1825
    Bondsman: John Berry Wit: J. W. McCown

Wilson, William M. to Rebecca Wilson Jan. 25, 1822 Robert Crosby, Bds.*

Wilson, Zacheus to Eliza Wilson Apr. 25, 1822 by Edward Ragsdale,
    J.P. Bondsman: Zacheus Wilson (same name as groom)

Wilson, Zacheus to Naomi Gillaspie July 16, 1822 by
    Henry Bailey, JP. James Wilson, Bds. Elisha L. Hall

Wilson, Zacheus to Nancy White Sept. 1, 1831 by
    Wm. Allison, J.P.   Bondsman: James G. Wilson

Winfree, Robert to Sally Burns July 22, 1819 by
    Horatio Burns Bondsman: John Smith

* Bond Alone filed

Wingo, James T. to Sarah M. Warren Feb. 10, 1848 by
    Wm. Y. Carter, JP. Bds: Fielden (X) Warren

Winn, Ebenezer P. to Celia Freeman May 5, 1831 by
    Robert Pate, JP. Bondsman: Alexander McClaran

Winset, Williams (X) to Arabella Welburn Jan. 7, 1824
    Bondsman: Amas (X) Winset

Winsett, Asa to Elizabeth Benson Nov. 7, 1809 by N. Scales
    Bondsman: Daniel Brown Wit: Wm. P. Harrison

Winsett, Elijah D. to Lurana Kelly Aug. 26, 1836 Executed
    by N. Patterson Modrall, MG. Bds: Felix G. Kelly

Winsett, German to Sally Clark May 23, 1807
    Bondsman: Sterling Brown Wit: N.P. Hardeman

Winsett, Jason (X) to Anne Glenn Dec. 17, 1816
    Bondsman: Amos (X) Winsett Test: N.P. Hardeman

Winsett, Silas to Sally Freeman Mar. 18, 1812
    Bondsman: John Freeman Wit: Wm. P. Harrison

Winsett, Wiley to Edy Chapman June 1, 1818
    Bondsman: Jason Winsett Wit: Thos. Hardeman

Winstead, John M. to Nancy Whitfield Mar. 8, 1827 by
    John C. Hicks, L.D. in M.E. Church.
    Bondsman: John Edmondson

Winston, John J. to Polly Jones Jan. 17, 1807
    Bondsman: William Jones Attest: Peter Hardeman

Winyard, George to Polly Night June 24, 1814 Joshua Winyard, Bds

Wisdom, Frances N. (His Mark) to Cynthia M. Brown Mar. 11, 1846
    By R. White, JP. Bds: James Brown

Wise, John to Sally Core Feb. 1, 1817
    Bondsman: Jonathan Core Test: Robert Davis

Wisener, Henry to Nancy Low Feb. 13, 1810
    Bondsman: Luke Pryor Wit: Wm. P. Harrison

Wisenor, Alexander to Elizabeth Williams Sept. 8, 1825 by
    G. Hunt Bondsman: Archibald Carmicheal

Wisenor, James to Mary Jane Barnes Oct. 24, 1848 by
    Wm. A. Whitsitt, MG. David J. Gray, Bds.

Wisenor, Robert to Jane Cochran Aug. 4, 1825 by G. L.
    Nolen, JP. Bondsman: G. L. Nolen

* Bond alone filed.

Wisenor, William to Polly Taylor   Nov. 10, 1812
    Bondsman: John Hardin   Wit: Wm. P. Harrison

Wisner, Martin to Edith Chapman   Aug. 7, 1805
    Bondsman: Robert Chapman   Test: Peter Hardeman

Witherington, William to Celia Sparkman   July 2, 1812
    Bondsman: Noel Walker   Wit: Wm. P. Harrison

Witherspoon, David to Penelope Gee   Nov. 1, 1809
    Bondsman: Jones Gee   Wit: Wm. P. Harrison

Witt, William M. to Cleopatra Ann Grigsby   Dec. 29, 1841 by
    Jas. King, M.G.   Bondsman: William H. Trimble

Woldridge, Aldolphus W. to Amanda Ellen Dodson   Nov. 30, 1848
    By Jas. King, M.G.   Bondsman: C.T. Stone

Woldridge, Ferdinand S. to Tennessee Parrish   Jan 16, 1850
    By M. L. Andrews, M.G.   Bondsman: John L. McEwen, Jr.

Wolf, Thomas to Edney Boling   Dec. 29, 1829 by Wm. McTee, JP
    Bondsman: Benjamin (X) Williams   Wit: Will Hardeman

Wolfe, William to Elizabeth McCalpin   July 26, 1813
    Bondsman: Thomas Goff   (Bond alone filed)

Wollard, Churchel to Nancy Fulks   Sept. 17, 1833 by
    Thos. Prowell, JP.   Bondsman: Henry Fulks

Wollard, Washington M. to Sarah Rosanna Walker   Feb. 11, 1836
    Executed by S. S. McKinn, JP.
            (X)   *
Wood, Alexander to Polly Pinkston   Nov. 19, 1813 Samuel Trip, Bds.
                                                                *
Wood, Alexander (X) to Polly Littleton   Jan. 12, 1825 Wm. Trimble, BDS

Wood, Allen to Sally Wood   Oct 15, 1820 by H. Adams, JP.
    Bondsman: Stephen Wood

Wood, Edmund to Lavinia Reid   July 19, 1820 by W. R. Nunn
    Bondsman: John Wood   Wit: Jno. P. McCutchan

Wood, Hugh see Word, Hugh

Wood, James (X) to Polly Stanfield   April 14, 1821
    Bondsman: Benjamin Evans

Wood, John to Milly Stanfield   Sept. 2, 1816   Thos. Fouler
    Bondsman signed by Ann Hardeman (Probably wife of Clerk)

Wood, John D. to Rebecca G. Ladd   May 10, 1843 by R. B.B.
    Cannon, J.P.   Bondsman: William P. Ladd

*Bond alone filed

Wood, Johnson to Susan Jordan Nov. 30, 1815 Thompson Wood, Bds.*

Wood, Johnson to Martha Ann Sledge Nov. 3, 1847 by
    W. Burns, MG. Bondsman: James K. Knott

Wood, Johnson C. to Margaret S. Downing Dec. 4, 1845 by
    Wm. Hatcher, JP. Bondsman: Archer W. Sanford

Wood, Josiah to Susanna Hill Sept. 5, 1810 by N. Scales
    Bondsman: Joshua Jordan Wit: Wm. P. Harrison

Wood, Josiah to Martha Johnston Dec. 30, 1828 by
    Franklin McClaran, JP. William Crenshaw, BDs.

Wood, Reuben to Jane Curry Nov. 13, 1810
    Bondsman: Isaiah Curry Wit: Wm. P. Harrison

Wood, Richard J. to Nancy R. Polk Jan. 22, 1846 by
    L.B. Jones Bondsman: Jesse(X) B. Morton

Wood, Richard M. to Almira Stevens July 8, 1840 by
    Jesse Cox, M.G. Bondsman: John Wood

Wood, Stephen to Martha Evans July 1, 1828 by Thos D.
    Porter, MG. Frederick Page, Bds. J.W. McCown, Wit.

Wood, Stephen K. to Elizabeth M. Warren Oct. 16, 1850 by
    E. P. Scales, JP. Bondsman: Dooly Pate

Wood, Thompson to Elizabeth Carter Sept. 10, 1817
    Bondsman: Hartwell B. Hyde Teste: Robert Davis

Wood, William W. to Nancy A. Russell Jan 31, 1850 by
    W. Burns, M.G. Bondsman: Garner M. Cox

Woodall, John C. to Mary E. Crutcher Oct. 1, 1839 by
    H. H. Horton, MG. Bondsman: William Park

Woodall, John C. to Emeline Blackwell Sept. 14, 1846 J.S. Park BD*

Woodall, William P. to Elizabeth J. Joslin July 19, 1850
    Bondsman: J.G. Neely (July 19th date license was
    issued, date of marriage was omitted.)

Woodruff, Aaron, to Sarah White Jan. 18, 1823 John P. Irion, Bds.*

Woodruff, George to Julia Ann Bryan Nov. 2, 1842 by
    M. L. Andrews, MG. Bondsman: Benjamin Seward

Woodruff, Howel to Mary Malone Dec. 11, 1827 by
    C. McDaniel, JP. Bondsman: James Brewer

Woodruff, Howell S. (X) to Elizabeth Laughlin June 5, 1820
    Bondsman: Robert W. (X) Woodruff *

* Bond alone filed

Woodruff, William W. to Mary Ann Hamilton Jan. 1, 1835 by
    James W. Rea, M.G. Bondsman: Washington Shelton

Woods, Alfred (X) to Narcissa Clarkson Jan. 7, 1848 by
    John Nichols, JP. Bondsman: N. P. Gilbert

Woods, James (X) to Polly Potts Mar. 31, 1816
    Wit: N.P. Hardeman Bondsman: Rushass (X) Reynolds ?.

Woods, Joseph to Nancy Fox Feb. 2, 1843 by Thos.
    Prowell, J.P. Bondsman: Addison Satterfield

Woods, Oliver to Nancy Haynes Dec. 1, 1807
    Bondsman: James Haynes Test: A. Potter

Woods, Richmond to Elizabeth Eggleston Aug. 29, 1836 by
    John Landrum, JP. Bondsman: James W. Felts

Woodside, Henry B. (X) to Selina Jane Kirkpatrick Sept 6,
    1849 Bondsman: Alonzo M. Tenison (Bond alone filed)

Woolridge, John H. to Elizabeth Stephens July 6, 1826
    Solemnized by Gilbert Marshall, JP. Thos. Hardeman, Clk.

Wooldridge, Loving to Elizabeth Williams May 29, 1822 by
    Robert Davis, MG. Bondsman: Joseph W. Camp

Wooldridge, Sam'l C. to Elizabeth Ann McDaniel Dec. 4, 1819
    Bondsman: M.D. Cooper Wit: Thos. Hardeman

Wooldridge, William F. (Groom signed Wm. J.) to Susan
    Ingram Dec. 3, 1823 Rites performed by Joel Anderson
    Bondsman: Thos. Hardeman who was also Clerk of the Ct.

Wooten, Henry to Elizabeth Ray Jan. 5, 1818 Wm. McCalpin, Bds.*

Wooten, James to Fanny Gill Feb. 9, 1814 Benj. Henderson, Bds.*

Wooton, George W. (X) to Jane Gray May 21, 1816 by W. R.
    Nunn, JP. James Carothers, Bds. Thos. H. Perkins, Wit.

Wooton, John to Ellenor Garner Nov. 6, 1807
    Bondsman: Morris Chennault Test: A. Potter

Word, Hugh to Mary Ann Hague Jan. 11, 1821 by Wm. Hogan, JP.
    Bondsman: William Webb. (Groom's signature reads:
    Hugh Webb and one place on bond name looks like Wood)
    Indexed under all three names - pick your ancestor.

Word, John T. to Margaret W. McLemore April 6, 1843 by
    A. L. P. Green, M.G. Bondsman: Henry Pointer

* Bond alone filed

Word, Samuel to Nancy Giddens Dec. 15, 1816 by
    Garner McConnico, MG. Bondsman: M. L. Bond

Worley, Moses to Elizabeth Davis Jan. 28, 1811
    Gabriel Worley, Bds. Wm. P. Harrison, Wit.

Worsham, John B. to Caroline R. Roland July 16, 1838
    Bondsman: Isaac M. Foster Only bond here, see below.

Worsham, John B. to Caroline Rebecca Roland, the daughter
    of John Roland who applied for license and signed
    Worsham's name July 18, 1839. Bds: John Roland
    Rites celebrated by R. W. Norriss, MG. M.E.E.P.Church

Wray, John M. to Nancy W. Neal May 23, 1848
    Bondsman: John T. McBride Wit: Chesley Williams

Wray, Joseph (X) to Susan Williams July 1, 1845 by
    W. H. Adams, M.G. Bondsman: George W. Williams

Wray, William (X) to Mary Ann Poynor June 12, 1850 by
    C. C. Church, JP. Bondsman: Francis M. Lavender

Wren, Cicero A. to Arrazine C. White July 2, 1848 by
    M. L. Andrews, M. G. Bondsman: James Hughes

Wren, John Z. to Elizabeth Shaderick Jan. 19, 1825 by
    Sam'l Merritt Bondsman: Joshua G. Sims

Wrenn, Peter to Clary Sparkman Nov. 7, 1822 by
    John Moore, J.P. Bondsman: Wm. Wrenn

Wrenn, William to Winey Sparkman Dec. 9, 1818
    Bondsman: David Hamilton (Bond alone)

Wright, Daniel to Myria Alexander April 19, 1821 by
    Wm. Dunnegan, JP. George (X) Wright, BDS. E.L.Walls, Test.

Wright, Edward M. H. to Alamannah Stockett Feb. 19, 1844
    Bondsman: Wm. F. Gray (Bond alone)

Wright, Francis (X) to Fanny Givvins Sept 6, 1836 by
    Lewis Magee, JP. Bondsman: Malachi Pewitt

Wright, Frederick to Amelia Ann Smith April 30, 1847
    Bondsman: W. B. White (or Wiley) (Bond alone)

Wright, George (X) to Milly Campbell July 20, 1820
    Bondsman: Daniel (X) Wright (Bond alone)

Wright, George P.(X) to Eliza Ann Martha Brooks Aug. 26, 1829
    Bondsman: John E. Crouch (Bond alone)

Wright, John H. to Elizabeth Sherrin   Sept. 23, 1830 by
    James Brown, J.P.   Bondsman: Mijamin (Benjamin?)Kinsey

Wright, Reuben(X) to Sally Wood   Mar. 3, 1830 by
    F. Ivy, J.P. Bondsman: Isaac (X) Hommel

Wright, William to Nancy Tillett   Jan. 21, 1822 by
    Wm. Smith, JP. John Charter, Bds. Elish L. Hall, Wit.

Wright, William to Sarah Fitts   Aug. 17, 1847 by
    John Nichols, JP. Bondsman: Harrison Nichols

Wright, William B. to Mary Marshall   Dec. 13, 1821 by
    Jno. N. Blackburn, M.G. Bondsman: R. B. Marshall

Wyatt, Joseph to Martha Walton   Jan. 27, 1821 by
    Levin Edney, M.G. Bondsman: Thomas Cooper

Wyatt, Thomas S. to Jane Phelps   Nov. 29, 1840 by
    Wm. Moor, JP.   Bondsman: John E. Crouch

Wynn, Thomas (X) to Nancy Gray   Oct. 5, 1819 by
    Levin Edney, MG. John (X) Alexander, Bds.

Wynne (Wyme), Henry to Susan Neal   July 11, 1833 by
    Wm. Allison, JP.   Bondsman: John H. Bullock

Wynne, (Wyme), John to Cesila Neal   Feb. 9, 1840 by
    J. R. Pearcy, JP. Bondsman: James Carson

Wynne, Samuel (X) to Elizabeth McGay (McGuy) May 21, 1821 by
    Daniel White, MG. Thomas (X) Wynne, Bds. Elisha Hall, Wit.

Wyzenberry, George to Louisa M. Adams July 11, 1850 by
    S. S. Smith, JP. Bondsman: Andrew J. Lampkins
    Witness Present: Young Minfunberger (?)

"Y"

Yarborough, George to Polly Manire June 2, 1817 Thos G. Gentry, Bds.*

Yates, Daniel(X) to Ailey Lamb Aug. 11, 1815 Aquilla(X)Lamb, Bds.*

Yates, Elijah (x) to Charlotte Casey July 15, 1819 by
    Wren Dunnesan, JP Bondsman: John D. (X) Alexander

Yates, Henderson H. to Martha T. Hopson Apr 2, 1845 John(X)Baugh, Bd*

Yates, John to Betsey Riggins Sept 10, 1823 Nathan (X) Lane, Bds*

Yates, John to Elizabeth Wells Aug. 20, 1824 Bond signed for
    groom by his Attorney-in-fact Walter B. Richardson who
    was also the other bondsman.*
Bond alone filed.

Word, Samuel to Nancy Giddens   Dec. 15, 1816 by
    Garner McConnico, MG. Bondsman: M. L. Bond

Worley, Moses to Elizabeth Davis   Jan. 28, 1811
    Gabriel Worley, Bds. Wm. P. Harrison, Wit.

Worsham, John B. to Caroline R. Roland   July 16, 1838
    Bondsman: Isaac M. Foster   Only bond here, see below.

Worsham, John B. to Caroline Rebecca Roland, the daughter
    of John Roland who applied for license and signed
    Worsham's name July 18, 1839. Bds: John Roland
    Rites celebrated by R. W. Norriss,MG. M.E.E.P.Church

Wray, John M. to Nancy W. Neal   May 23, 1848
    Bondsman: John T. McBride   Wit: Chesley Williams

Wray, Joseph (X) to Susan Williams   July 1, 1845 by
    W. H. Adams, M.G.   Bondsman: George W. Williams

Wray, William (X) to Mary Ann Poynor   June 12, 1850 by
    C. C. Church, JP.   Bondsman: Francis M. Lavender

Wren, Cicero A. to Arrazine C. White   July 2, 1848 by
    M. L. Andrews, M. G.   Bondsman: James Hughes

Wren, John Z. to Elizabeth Shaderick   Jan. 19, 1825 by
    Sam'l Merritt   Bondsman: Joshua G. Sims

Wrenn, Peter to Clary Sparkman   Nov. 7, 1822 by
    John Moore, J.P.   Bondsman: Wm. Wrenn

Wrenn, William to Winey Sparkman   Dec. 9, 1818
    Bondsman: David Hamilton   (Bond alone)

Wright, Daniel to Myria Alexander   April 19, 1821 by
    Wm. Dunnegan,JP. George (X) Wright,BDS. E.L.Walls,Test.

Wright, Edward M. H. to Alamannah Stockett   Feb. 19, 1844
    Bondsman: Wm. F. Gray   (Bond alone)

Wright, Francis (X) to Fanny Givvins   Sept 6, 1836 by
    Lewis Magee, JP.   Bondsman: Malachi Pewitt

Wright, Frederick to Amelia Ann Smith   April 30, 1847
    Bondsman: W. B. White (or Wiley) (Bond alone)

Wright, George (X) to Milly Campbell   July 20, 1820
    Bondsman: Daniel (X) Wright (Bond alone)

Wright, George P.(X) to Eliza Ann Martha Brooks   Aug.26,1829
    Bondsman: John E. Crouch (Bond alone)

Wright, John H. to Elizabeth Sherrin   Sept. 23, 1830 by
       James Brown, J.P. Bondsman: Mijamin (Benjamin?)Kinsey

Wright, Reuben(X) to Sally Wood   Mar. 3, 1830 by
       F. Ivy, J.P. Bondsman: Isaac (X) Hommel

Wright, William to Nancy Tillett   Jan. 21, 1822 by
       Wm. Smith,JP. John Charter, Bds. Elish L. Hall, Wit.

Wright, William to Sarah Fitts   Aug. 17, 1847 by
       John Nichols, JP. Bondsman: Harrison Nichols

Wright, William B. to Mary Marshall   Dec. 13, 1821 by
       Jno. N. Blackburn, M.G. Bondsman: R. B. Marshall

Wyatt, Joseph to Martha Walton   Jan. 27, 1821 by
       Levin Edney, M.G. Bondsman: Thomas Cooper

Wyatt, Thomas S. to Jane Phelps   Nov. 29, 1840 by
       Wm. Moor, JP.   Bondsman: John E. Crouch

Wynn, Thomas (X) to Nancy Gray   Oct. 5, 1819 by
       Levin Edney, MG. John (X) Alexander, Bds.

Wynne (Wyme), Henry to Susan Neal   July 11, 1833 by
       Wm. Allison, JP.   Bondsman: John H. Bullock

Wynne, (Wyme), John to Cesila Neal   Feb. 9, 1840 by
       J. R. Pearcy, JP. Bondsman: James Carson

Wynne, Samuel (X) to Elizabeth McGay (McGuy) May 21, 1821 by
       Daniel White, MG. Thomas (X) Wynne, Bds. Elisha Hall,Wit.

Wyzenberry, George to Louisa M. Adams July 11, 1850 by
       S. S. Smith, JP. Bondsman: Andrew J. Lampkins
       Witness Present: Young Minfunberger (?)

                           "Y"

Yarborough, George to Polly Manire June 2, 1817 Thos G.Gentry,Bds.*

Yates, Daniel (X) to Ailey Lamb Aug. 11, 1815 Aquilla(X)Lamb, Bds.*

Yates, Elijah (x) to Charlotte Casey   July 15, 1819 by
       Wren Dunnesan, JP Bondsman: John D. (X) Alexander

Yates, Henderson H. to Martha T. Hopson Apr 2,1845 John(X)Baugh,Bd*

Yates, John to Betsey Riggins Sept 10,1823 Nathan (X) Lane,Bds*

Yates, John to Elizabeth Wells Aug. 20, 1824 Bond signed for
       groom by his Attorney-in-fact Walter B. Richardson who
       was also the other bondsman.*
Bond alone filed.

Yates, John to Nancy Russell Mar. 21, 1836 Bird Fitzgerald, Bds.*

Yates, Jonathan to Lucinda Cook Aug. 14, 1827 by J. W.
    McCown, D.C. Bondsman: Thomas (X) Pewitt
    (Aug. 14 date license issued, marriage date torn)

Yates, Joseph to Polly Mays July 14, 1832 John Yates, Bds.*

Yates, Joseph to Mary Ann Clardy Nov. 28, 1841 by
    Jas. King, M.G. Bondsman: William P. Peace

Yates, Joshua (X) to Nancy Ann Inman Feb. 20, 1832 John Smith*

Yeargin, Bartlett to Maryan Lawrence Aug. 18, 1813
    Bondsman: Edmond Lawrence *

York, James (X) to Eliza Merritt Nov. 30, 1830 by
    Nichs Scales, JP. Bondsman: James Rice

York, Joel to Litha Jackson July 2, 1810
    Bondsman: John Marr Wit: Wm. P. Harrison

York, Richard to Barbara Shumate Dec. 26, 1812
    Bondsman: Fielden Shumate Wit: Wm. P. Harrison

Young, Acton to Elizabeth P. Lavender Aug. 23, 1842
    Bondsman: Benjamin Williams

Young, Alvin J. to Mary McLavin (McLaurin) April 21, 1821
    Bondsman: William T. Haynes

Young, Andrew J. (X) to Amanda F. Bailey July 21, 1846 by
    J. J. Bingham, JP Bondsman: John R. Bailey

Young, David to Elizabeth Reed (Read) Jan. 22, 1829 by
    L. Manvil, JP. Bondsman: William Young

Young, Ephraim to Polly Bugg May 14, 1817
    Bondsman: Tapley Andrews Test: Robert Davis

Young, George W. (X) to Emeline Haithcock Jan. 28, 1847 by
    H. Thomson, JP. Bondsman: Lemuel G. Haithcock

Young, Isaac to Martha Walton Jan 12, 1835 by L. H. Wolange,
    JP. Bondsmen: Wm. Wright and John McDaniel

Young, Isham to Elizabeth Luallen Nov. 27, 1818
    Bondsman: Daniel (X) Young also Attorney for groom
    Witness: Thos. Hardeman Jr.

* Bond alone filed

Young, James to Emeline McAlpin Feb. 26, 1839 by
W. B. Carpenter Bondsman: William Seabury

Young, Lawrence to Susan Wilkins Oct. 17, 1811
Bondsman: Joseph T. Ellison Wit: Wm. P. Harrison

Young, Nathan to Susannah Cunningham Aug. 29, 1816 by
A. Mebane, JP. Bondsman: Samuel Breden

Young, Peter to Polly Lagrone May 5, 1813
Bondsman: Wm. Lagrone Wit: Wm. P. Harrison

Young, William to Rebeckah Bugg March 12, 1809 Teste: A. Potter
Bondsmen: John Ragsdale and Robert Ragsdale

Young, William H. (X) to Martha A. Fore (or Fou) July 29,
1841 by Gilbert Marshall JP. Bds: Jacob H alfacre Jr.

Younger, Henry N. to Lucy Ann Younger Nov. '5, 1846 by
Thos. Prowell, JP Bondsman: Thomas Wakefield

Younger, John W. to Mary E. Church Mar. 4, 1846 by
Thos. Prowell, JP Bondsman: Joseph Wakefield

Younger, Thomas to Sally Church Sept. 6, 1823
Bondsman: David Fly Wit: Joshua W. McCown

Younger, William to Elizabeth Wakefield Jan. 13, 1829 by
Abram Church, JP. Bondsman: Thomas Younger

Youngman, David to Nancy McMahon April 4, 1833 by
Robert Hardin, M.G. Bondsman: Andrew Crockett

Youree, James to Dorothy Hardeman July 11, 1822
Bondsman: Alfred P. Gowan (Bond alone filed)

"Z"

Zachary, Elisha to Amanda F. Porter Dec. 13, 1825
Bondsman: Isaac Wyatt (bond alone filed)

Zachary, James J. to Eliza Jane Vaught Sept. 16, 1848 by
Rev. C. C. Mayhew Bondsman: Benjamin F. Brown

Zolicoffer, George to Abbigale Nicholson Dec. 18, 1810
Bondsman: Thomas H. Holland Wit: Wm. P. Harrison

BRIDE'S INDEX

ACHOLES, Elizabeth 258
ADAMS, Amanda J. 18, Ann Eliza 156
  Catherine 4, Elisabeth 105,
  Eliza S. 72, Elizabeth E. 145,
  233, Ellen 117, Frances 98,
  Louisa M. 294, Marina 2, Mary
  263, Mildred A. 272, Mary D. 1,
  Mary H. 183, Matilda Jane 48,
  Nancy 18, Polly C. 223, Sally
  131, 257, 210, Sarah P. 148
ADDAMS, Polly 69.
ADEN, Josephine 67, Susan E. 257
ADKINS, Lewvania 78, Patsey 148
AGER, Jane 210
AIKIN, Dorcas 87, Edith 2, Rebecca
  H. 195, Ellen 166, Matilda 228
  Polly 41
AKRIDGE, Elizabeth 16
ALDRIDGE, Elizabeth 160, Mary 1
ALEXANDER, Diadema 278, Eleanor
  164, Elizabeth 75, Eliza W. 174,
  Elizabeth L. 71, Jane 62, 137,
  Jeretia 235, Lucinda 269, Margaret S. 37, Mariah 7, Milly
  224, Myria 293, Nancy 204, Parmelia 138, Patsey 253, Peggy
  136, Rachael 267, Ruth 150
ALFORD, Cloe 281, Lucinda 276,
  Malinda 65, Mary 254, Nancy D.
  111, Patsey 282
ALFRED, Nancy 239
ALKINSON, Martha 256
ALLEN, Abby 281, Amelia 50, Angeline 171, Barbara 139, Catharine
  77, Diana B. 23, Elizabeth 243,
  Elizabeth Ann 3, Elizabeth M.K.
  5, Fanny H. 247, Ferrily 61,
  Hannah 28, Jane 82, 53, Mady D.
  112, Margarite 147, Martha 155,
  Martha B. 61, Martha Jane 31,
  Martha M. 195, 159, Mary 223, 54
  258, 252, Mary P. 241, Nancy 145
  4, 73, Nancy Ann 108, Nancy T. 4
  Polly 251, Priscy 174, Sally 145
  Sarah 169, Sarah Jane 222, Sophronia M. 3, Tabitha 18, Tabitha
  M. 134, Tenesse 5, Ursey 256
ALLISON, Elizabeth 225, Jane 283,
  Mary Jane 197, Polly 170
ALSTON, Annie R. 8, Elizabeth N.
  271, Elizabeth P. 137, Jane 79,
  Jane D. 170, Lucy Ann 152, Luraney S. 52, Mary M. 171, Nancy
  203, Sarah K. 145

ALSUP, Nancy 122.
AMIS, Elizabeth, 49
ANDERSON, America S. 270, Betsey 180,
  Catharine 154, Dorinda 232, Eliza 21,
  Elizabeth 160, Frances M. 140, Harriett
  96, 190, Henrietta N. 7, Laura 164,
  Mariann 256, Nancy C. 41, Nancy W. 134,
  Polly 212, 7, 25, Rebecca 164, Rosanna
  107, Ruth 63, Sarah 131, Sophia W. 77
ANDREWS, Adeline J. 184, Avelina 74,
  Betsey 109, Caroline 9, Delia Ann 96,
  Elisabeth 187, Eliza 72, Elizabeth 162,
  147, Elizabeth H. 8, 23, 120, Emily M.
  F. 89, Faney 129, Francis 211, Jane C.
  5, Josephine 62, Leannah 158, Letitia
  C. 167, Lucy 217, Lucy R. 88, Lydia
  244, Madaline 9, Mariah S.A. 9, Mary
  Ann 278, Mary W. 202, Nancy 219, 164,
  274, Nancy R. 62, Pamelia M. 122, Polly
  76, 269, Rebecca 187, Ruth 185, Sally
  220, Sarah 252, Sarah L. 267, Sarah P.
  L. 9, Susan 252, Susan R. 162, Teresa
  185, Virginia S. 121
ANGLIN, Betsey 227, Fanny 279, Nancy 261,
  269, Peggy 209
ANTHONY, Martha 281, Mary B. 185, Sarah C
  225
APPLETON, Emmaritta 284, Susanna 115
APPLEWHITE, Elizabeth C. 227
ARMSTRONG, Betsey 11, Dida Mira 75, Elizabeth 16, Frances 194, Harriott 110,
  Lucy 189, Mary 197, Nancy 250, Naomy
  176, Rebecca 206, Sarah R. 207, Suhany
  235
ARNOLD, Angelina 286, Milly Ann 208
ASHLIN, Francis 178, Martha M. 278, Mary
  178, Virginia L. 172
ATKERSON, Nancy Jane 120
ATKINS, Martha 177
ATKINSON, Catharine 236, Frances S. 127,
  Frances T. 140, Jane 62, Judith 239,
  Julia F. 154, Lucy 131, Mary 21, Mary
  Jane 220, Mary W. 178, Nancy B. 127,
  Polly 31, 3, Polly A. 45, Sally 112,
  Sarah 201, 265, Sarah Ann 254, Sarah
  Jane 128, Sinderilla 57
ATTIKISON, Sarah 246
AUSLEY, Mary P. 208
AUSTIN, Nancy 72
AXEM, Rebecca 163
AXUM, Nancy 163

BAGBY, Mary 81
BAILEY, Amanda F. 295, Cinthia
  C. 280, Elizabeth A. 141, El-
  lender 161, Hannah 14, Jane
  270, Martha 1, Mary A. 97
BAIRD, Mary C. 41
BAKER, Catharine 19, Eliza 222,
  Elizabeth 37, Sarah 257, Sid-
  ney 57
BALDRIDGE, Caty 224, Jane 122,
  Jane B. 134
BALLARD, Ally 24
BALLOW, Eliza 78, Elizabeth 199,
  Mary Jane 2, Nancy F. 203,
  Sarah Ann 14
BANKS, Elizabeth 27, Louisiana D
  224, Mary 288
BARCLIFT, Ann 16
BARFIELD, Harrett 144, Mary Jane
  32, Penelope H. 43, Tabitha
  189
BARHAM, Caroline M. 143, Mary
  Jane 182
BARKER, Eliza 55, Martha Jane 162
  Mary Ann 162, Polly 186
BARLETT, Patsey 158 (see Bartlett
BARMAN, Louisa 91
BARNES, Adaline 283, Ann Eliza
  119, Anna 158, Caroline 189,
  Emeline 91, Frances 49, Jemi-
  ma 87, Margaret 103, Martha
  64 (see Barus), Mary Ann 227,
  Mary D. 85, Mary Jane 289,
  Mary W. 111, Polly 125, 266,
  Rachel 104, 72, Sarah E. 9,
  Susan 36, Tabitha 283
BARNETT, Angelina 49, Betsey
  215, Elizabeth 175, 204, Let-
  tie 216, Sophronia 233, Susan
  254
BARNS, Martha 64, Sarah 219
BARNWELL, Drucilla 131
BARRETT, Polly 218
BARTLIFF, Patsey 158
BARTON, Charlotte 24
BASS, Nancy 168, 196, Polly 147
BATEMAN, Amelia M. 222, Amy 185,
  Anna 252, Celia Ann 250, Cyn-
  thia J. 248, Eleanor 218,
  Eunice 168, Frances A. 141,
  Harriett S. 34, Lauretta 223,
  Leah 267, Lewe or Lena 31,
  Mary 218, Olly 34, Phereby 282
  Rosanna 13, Rosey 288, Susan
  264
BATES, Arrena 154, Martha Ann 83
  Polly 18

BATEY, Isabella 69
BATTLE, Lucinda A. 236
BAUCOM, Charlotte 253, 251, Eliza-
  beth 94, Nancy 287, Susannah 208
BAUGH, Ann L. 10, Frances H. 135,
  Mary 58
BAZDEL, Susan J. 273,
BAZDELL, Elizabeth 179
BAZELL, Minerva Ann 273
BAZWELL, Sarah 172
BAZZELL, Nicy 23
BEACH, Mary Bays 76, Sarah Ann E.
  165, Sarah B. 195
BEALE, Frances A. 60, Mary Eliza
  122, Susan A.G. 24
BEARD, Catherine 108, Comfort 36,
  Jane 28, Mary 215, Nancy A. 72,
  Rhoda 190
BEASLEY, Betsey 4, Elizabeth 150,
  Mary Ann 240, Nancy 149, 207,
  Nancy Jane 51, Susan 102,
  Tilitha A. 120
BEATY, Isabella Boyd 130
BEAVENS, Polly 127
BEAVERS, Sally 114
BEECH, Addeline V. 19, Elizabeth
  S. 204, Jane 112
BELCHER, Frances 91, Frances A.
  171, Martha 229, Nancy 223
BELL, Eliza Ann 188, Elizabeth 79
  Elizabeth Jane 6, Mary E. 88,
  Mary H. 149, Mary M. 64, Sally
  162
BELLENFENT, Mouren (Morney) 185
BENNET, America 85
BENNETT, Angeline 235, Bethenia S.
  67, Dorothy 29, Elizabeth 224,
  41, Elizabeth P. 151, Mary M.
  280, Nancy 84, 247, Rebecca A.
  250
BENNETS, Jane 136
BENSON, Elizabeth 289
BENTHAL, Nancy 10
BENTHALL, Christina 204
BENTON, Jinnetta 217
BEREY, Fanny 257
BERKLEY, Isabella C. 222, Mary 49
BERKS, Elizabeth 203
BERRY, Elizabeth 270, Jane 274,
  Martha 30, Mary 271, Nancy 112,
  Nancy G. 281, Polly 36, Rebecca
  288, 110, 148, Sally 211
BERRYMAN, Jane 143
BERSON, Harriet E. 127, Juliet 151
BEST, Polly 130
BETTY, Harriet 261, Lucy Jane 4,
  Martha E.H. 206, Nancy R. 113
  Polly 263

BIGGAR, Mary Jane 284
BIGGARS, Cynthia 254, Nancy 77
BIGGER, Anna 99, Rachel J. 216
BINGHAM, Eliza A.M. 39, 203, Elizabeth 174
BIRD, Eliza L. 96, Jane 138
BIRDWELL, Adaline 161
BITTICK, Atlantick M. 267, Charlotte 270
BIZELL, Elizabeth 211, Nancy 58
BIZZELL, Sarah J. 8, Lucy 273
BIZZLE, Edney 227, Michy 267
BLACK, Ellenor 194, Lithe 217, Nancy 260
BLACKBURN, Bethenia B. 69, Elizabeth H. 113, Jane M. 187, Mary Ann 5, Martha M. 162, Mary E. 53, Narcissa J. 115, Rachel 175
BLACKMAN, Elizabeth 260, Martha 99, Nancy 277, Susan 105, 76, Tilpha 106
BLACKSHORE, Hannah 166
BLACKWELL, Catharine P. 66, Elizabeth 195, Emeline 291, Lucinda 244, Martha 202
BLAIR, Elizabeth 176, Polly 232
BLAKE, Abigail 157, Sarah 29, Sleaty 29
BLANKINSHIP, Jane 230
BLYTHE, Eleanor 186, Elizabeth K 58, Martha 279, Nancy 16, Patsey, 186, Rachel 246, 16
BOATWRIGHT, Jane 258, Sally 120
BOBBITT, Mary 82
BOELMUS, Mary Jane 97
BOLEN, Betsey 237
BOLING, Edney 290
BOMAR, Lucy 109, Mary D. 204
BOND, Angelina C. 232, Bethenia 85, Catharine B. 73, Catharine W. 261, Elizabeth P. 192, Frances W. 214, Lucy 200, Lucy Ann 94, Lucy Henry 128, Lucy M. 134, Margaret A. 172, Margaret L. 180, Maria B. 124, Martha A 49, Mary 13, Mary E. 122, 134, Nancy 254, Nancy D. 245, 155, Sarah 280
BONDS, Mariah 245, Parallee 162, Polly 91, Sally 233
BONE, Mary 33
BONNER, Charity 257
BOON, Elizabeth 184, Fanny 130
BOONE, Mary A. 157
BOREN, Lela 78
BOSELEY, Lucy Ann 75
BOSLEY, Emeline 193

BOSTICK, Bethenia 207, Christiana 56, Elizabeth 19, Jane 287, Mary 270, Parthenia 7
BOSWELL, Rebecca 242
BOVEN, Lela 78
BOWDEN, Elizabeth E. 38
BOWEN, Jane 208
BOWERS, Lydia 282
BOWLIN, Polly 194
BOWMAN, Letty N. 192
BOXLEY, Tabitha 251
BOYD, Ann 195, Camilla 205, Caroline 113, Elizabeth 252, Elizabeth E. 149, Lina 252, Louisa E 83, Martha A. 134, 135, Martha J. 204, Mary E. 43, Matilda 235, Medy 149, Mira L. 256, Myra 230, Nancy 7, Polly 216, Wilmoth 86
BOYT, Martha 263
BOZLEY, Mary 263
BRACEY, Mary L. 154
BRACK, Latitia 55
BRADEN, Catherine 217, Nancy 246
BRADEY, Fanny 69
BRADFORD, Elizabeth 12, Nancy 262, 17
BRADLEY, Catharine 141, Elizabeth 261, Jane A. 243, Masdrey 142, Polley 21, Rebecca 6, Sally 44
BRADY, Penny 16
BRAGG, Elizabeth 264, Nancy 260, Sarah 217
BRANCH, Eliza 137
BRANDON, Elizabeth W. 35, Sarah 177
BRANTLEY, Harriett 7
BREAST, Caroline E. 150
BREESE, Cassa 11, Lavina 242
BRESSEE, Emily 219
BREWER, Mary 59, Mary A. 276, Nancy 211, Sarah 240
BRIANT, Elizabeth 10, Tiersey 175
BRICE, Susan 23
BRIDGEMAN, Mary 281
BRIDGES, Celia 199, Martha Ann 44, Nancy 268, 257
BRIGHT, Narcissa 65
BRILEY, Luvicy 168
BRIMM, Elizabeth A. 240
BROADEN, Mary 78
BROADMORE, Margaret 175
BROCK, Elvira 284, Nancy Ann 283
BROCKS, Eliza Ann 293
BRODNAX, Frances 175
BRODWAY, Ely 217
BROGDON, Susan 144, Unity 13
BROOKS, Ann D. 201, Ann M.M. 166, Anna 105, Catherine 140,

BROOKS, Elizabeth A. 30, Elizabeth S. 6, Martha Ann 75, 264, Mary 252, Matilda T. 201, Nancy 21, 173, Rebecca Simons 124, Sarah 252, Susan 4, Susan P. 106
BROOM, Sally 262
BROOMFIELD, Cynthia M. 181
BROUGHTON, Nancy L. 36
BROWDER, Betsey 267, Polly 238, Sally 97
BROWN, Ann 112, Ann M. 193, Anna 8, Caledonia 97, Caroline 5, Catharine 7, Cynthia M. 289, Delila 195, 2, Elizabeth 202, 61, 195, Elizabeth R. 134, Ellen Jane 116, Fanny 265, Henrietta 107, Jane 214, 262, Judy 101, Lavinia 179, Louisa 2, Lucinda 274, Mary 209, Mary A. 139, Mary A.E. 113, Mary E. 264, Mary P. 128, Michael E. 107, Milley 288, Nancy 73, Narcissa 212, Patcy 246, Patsey 93, Peggy 197, Polly 112, 242, 182, Sarah C. 232, 20, Sarah Jane 169, Susan 231, Susannah 226, Tabitha 6, Unice 239
BROWNLEE, Sarah 178
BROYDAN, Eliza 147
BRUMLEY, Martha Ann 53
BRYAN, America N. 189, Julia Ann 291, Rebecca 165
BRYANT, Eliza 263, Elizabeth 229, Elizabeth 134, Susan 136
BUCH, Martha 217
BUCHANAN, Anna 183, Eliza 262, Mary B. 103, Mary E. 5, Nancy 203, Rebecca W. 153
BUCHANNAN, Elizabeth 21, Margaret Ann 232
BUCK, Sarah 36, Sarah Ann 39
BUCKINGHAM, Frances G. 273
BUCKLEW, Mary E. 210
BUCKLEY, Nancy 275
BUFORD, Amanda W. 35, Elizabeth 35, Harriett A. 35, Katharine 175, Mary F. 197, Mary W. 35, Priscilla 98, Sarah S. 212, Susan S. 35
BUGG, Angelina 94, Catherine 131, Elizabeth 7, Elizabeth A. 94, Elizabeth I. 261, Louise 65, Lucy A. 81, Mahala 166, Pamelia P. 97, Patsey 262, Polly 295, Rebeckah 296, Sarah Ann 19, Susan C. 13
BULLOCK, Betsey 119, Elizabeth 101 Nancy 164

BUMPASS, Elizabeth A. 228, Judith 57
BURCH, Elizabeth 192, Malvena 74, 10, Parthenia 33
BURFORD, Francis 89
BURGE, Betsey 259, Eliza A. 248, Elizabeth D. 181, Rebecca 116,
BURGES, Christiana E. 83, Jane 44, Peggy 45
BURGESS, Letitia 48, Nancy 227, Sarah A.E. 30
BURGS, Maria 259
BURK, Sarah 194
BURKE, Eliza Jane 215, Mary J. 40, Rhoda 276, Rhoda M. 278
BURNETT, Ann E. 75, Candace 281, Emeline 163, Margaret 136, Nancy 231, Polly 226, Sarah 257, Susanna 37
BURNHAM, Nancy 160, Sarah H. 77
BURNS, Jane H. 233, Margaret 203, Sally 288
BURTON, Ann 175, Jane 59, Joicy 243, Nicky 175, Rebecca G. 148
BUTT, Bersheba 22, Betsey 282, Nancy C. 37, Polly 261, Selina P. 178
BUTTER, Mary 23, Sophronia 160
BUTTERY, Alvira 258
BUTTICKS, Margaret 128
BUTTREY, Cassy 200
BUTTRY, Harriet M. 256
BUTTS, Mary Ann 115

CAFFREY, Mary 256
CAHOON, Ann 178, 194, Elizabeth 218, Margaret 178
CAIN, Elizabeth 170
CALDWELL, Catharine B. 167, Elizabeth 1, Sarah P. 237
CALHOON, Anna M. 122, Fanny G. 231
CALHOUN, Margaret 47, Tabitha 50
CALVERT, Rachel 179
CAMERON, Eliza A. 47
CAMP, Elizabeth 255, Margaret B. 253, Mary B. 208, Pamelia 191, Sarah P. 209, Susan 73
CAMPBELL, Ann A. 202, Ann L. 180, Caty 28, Celia 287, Cynthia 197, Cynthia Ann 190, Elizabeth 125, 51, 179, 245, Jane 152, Margaret M. 42, Margaret P. 169, Margaret W. 152, Martha 251, Martha C. 19, Mary 87, 224, Mary A. 87, Milly 293, Purity 187, Rachel 193, Rebecca 123
CANADA, Margaret 235

CANNADY, Rhoda 48
CANNON, Elizabeth A. 271, Leah America 209, Leticia 181, Livinia T.C. 51, Polly 33, R. Adeline 168, Sarah C. 279
CAPERTON, B etsey 103, Eliza 276, Laetitia A. 132, Matilda 249, Polly 196, Susan J. 244, Susan M. 103
CARDEN, Anna Eliza 23
CARL, Elizabeth 122, Sarah 235
CARLE, Nancy 173
CARLILE, Nancy 39
CARLISLE, Polly 20, Susan 124
CARLIN, Nancy 103
CARMICHAEL, Alcy 262, Nancy 266
CAROTHERS, Jane 127, 268, Lucretia 206, Martha Ann 148, Mary 149, Mary E. 208, Nancy H. 66, Patsey 162, Polly 43, Sally 44, Volantia I 57
CARPENTER, Elizabeth 116
CARREL, Debotha 58
CARRICK, Elizabeth 263
CARROLL, Betsey 225, 240, Elizabeth 266, William 152
CARSLY, Isadora M. 43, Martha S. 271, Sarah A. 138
CARSAN, Jane 245
CARSON, Alvira 222, Anna 203, Elizabeth 172, 32, Jane 24, Margaret 53, Martha 179, Millinda 206, Nancy 109, 100, Patsey 97, Peggy 245, Sarah 141
CARTER, Elizabeth 291, 82, 228, Mary 224, 59, Mary E. 243, Mary R. 203, Prumett or Pruett E. 47, Roche M. 229, Sally V. 109, Sarah 193, Sarah A.E. 102, Sarah H. 229
CARTRIGHT, Elizabeth 58, Hannah 193, Martha Ann 270, Mary 34
CARTWRIGHT, Margaret Ann 94, Mary 270, 188
CARY, Mary Ann 229
CASEY, Charlotte 294, Ruth 193
CASH, Louisianna D. 13, Virginia 193
CASKEY, Elemina M. 186, Mary 237, Mary Jane 192
CASON, Nancy 117
CASTLEMAN, Jane 56
CATES, Susan 84
CATHEY, Rebecca 268
CATO, Elizabeth 228, Matilda 228
CATON, Lettia 272
CATOR, Martha 183

CATTERY, Frances C. 46
CAUDLE, Jane 214
CAUSEY, Ann Rebecca 123
CAUSLEY, Mary C. 196
CAVANNAUGH, Polly 56
CAVENDAR, Julisey 47
CAVENDER, Nancy 269, Rebecca 47, Sally P. 260
CAVINDER, Jincy 268
CAYCE, Elizabeth 214, Mary Ann 236, Nancy 59, Phebe 242, Sarah 47
CHADWELL, Mary Adeline 242, Nancy 8 Sarah Ann 266
CHAMBERLAIN, Polly 28
CHAMBERS, Ann 211, Frances 166, Julianah 57, Lucy B. 215, Nancy 228
CHAMP, Anna 279, Jane 268
CHAMPION, Rebecca 230
CHANLY, Artemisia 261, Sally 76
CHAPMAN, Catherine 26, Edith 290, Edy 289, Elizabeth 1, Nancy 116, Sarah 25
CHATHAN, Franky 70
CHEATHAM, Elizabeth 187, Margaret 255, Phebe M. 255
CHERRY, Isabella M. 90, 250
CHESSER, Tabitha Ann 69
CHESTER, Sally 279
CHILDRESS, Elizabeth 135, Elisabeth C. 277, Polly 21, Sally 81, 233, 182, Susan 135
CHILDRESS, Ann E. 28, Elizabeth 78, Margaret, J. 170, Mary E. 286, Polly 42, Betsey 182
CHILES, Mary M. 171
CHITWOOD, Susannah 5
CHOWNING, Ann 56
CHRICHLOW, Addeline 261
CHRISMAN, Elizabeth 232, Lydia Ann 86, Martha 249, 49, Mary Ann 283, Matilda W. 248, Nancy 139, Polly Ann 59, Ruth 59
CHRISTLEY, Nancy 229
CHRISTLY. Margaret 58, Milly 114
CHRISTMAS, Drucilla 166
CHRISTOPHER, Jane 180, Mary 287, Ruth A. 102, Sarah E. 30, Susannah 117
CHRISTY, Anna 184
CHRISWELL, Martha 116, Nancy D. 279 Sally 135
CHURCH, Flora 38, Hannah E. 17, Martha Jane 269, Mary E. 296, Sally 296
CIRKLES, Eve 116
CLAND, Susan 180
CLARDY, Henrietta 65, Mary Ann 295

CLARK, Adeline 66, Ann R. 154,
  Catharine D. 152, Drucilla 210,
  Elizabeth 88, Mahala 196, Martha 177, Martha B. 158, Mary S.
  126, Nancy Jane 129, Sally 289,
  Sarah 231, Susan 229, Susannah
  111, 215, Virginia 234, 40
CLARKSON, Narcissa 292
CLAY, Harriet 259, Polly 139
CLAYTON, Milly 238
CLEMM, Catharine J.A. 33
CLEMONS, Almira E. 212
CLOUD, Caroline F. 186, Frances
  W. 186, Martha Jane 239, Mary
  70, Nancy Ellen 27, Priscilla
  W. 136, Susan 71
CLOYD, Charollotta 31, Fanny 31
  Matilda 85
CLYNARD, Rosannah 62
COATNEY, Nancy 18
COBLE, Ann 288, Martha 112,
  Mary 287
COCHRAN, Delila 213, Eunice 173,
  Jane 289, Louisa 142, Peggy 138
  Polly 182, Sally 95
CODY, Elizabeth Jane 23, Emily
  245
COFFEE, Betsey 216
COLE, Elizabeth 72, 9, 165, Emeline 255, Sidney 243
COLEMAN, Charlotta 73, Frances
  214, Frances E. 258, Martha 19,
  Mary Ann 37, 133, Mary S. 80,
  Rebecca 263, Rosy 205
COLLIER, Elizabeth S. 48
COLLINS, Anna 199, Anne 217, Caroline K. 27, Mary Ann 27, Matilda 188
COMER, Pauline C. 174
CON, Frances A. 141
CONN, Sophronia M. 280
CONNEL, Lucy 274
COOK, Jemima 126, Lucinda 295,
  Mary 209, Mary E. 224, Polly 27
  Rebecca 39, Sarah 218
COOPER, Jane 186, Lucy 178, Mary 7
  Minerva R. 89, Nancy 98, Susannah 259, Sydney 135, Terrissa P.
  135
COOR, Tabitha 233
COORE, Milley 160
COPELAND, Cynthia 130, Jane 48,
  Rebecca 250, Sally 72
CORBIT, Polly 252
CORBITT, Nancy 262
CORDD, Sally 53
CORE, Sally 289, Sarah E. 104

CORKETT, Edy 207
CORLETT, Mary 238, Nelly 212
CORSBY, Harriet 95
CORZIN Jane 27
CORZINE, Ascennatta M. 65, Jurusha
  65, Mary 179, Polly 263, Rachael
  M. 144, Rachel Mihale 11
COSBY, Emily 285
COSE, Elizabeth P. 133, Susan A.
  126
COSSON, Elizabeth 237
COTTON, Sarah Ann 138
COULEY, Catharine M. 61, Rachel 33
COVINGTON, Betsey 205, Mary 21
COWAN, Elisabeth 84, Mary Ann 174
  Susan 37
COWARD, Sally 245
COWEN, Eleanor 17, Jane 228, Rosanna 174
COWLES, Eliza Goodwin 100, Mary
  Frances 8
COWSART, Polly C. 207
COWSERT, Jane 86, Mary Ann 42,
  Nancy A. 151
COX, Betsey 253, Caroline 252,
  Jane 253, Martha O. 74, Rachel
  47, Sally 252, Sarah H. 211
CRAFTON, Emeline 259, Jemima 61,
  Sally 54
CRAIG, Araminta 263, Clarissa 130
  Elisabeth 282, Eveline 74, Harriet E. 265, Jane C. 74, Malinda
  178, Margaret 177, Malissa 264,
  Polly 190, Susan 179
CRAMER, Eliza 220
CRANE, Susan 22
CRAWFORD, Elizabeth 63
CREEK, Crissy 16, Elizabeth 130
CRENSHAW, Anna 96, Martha 256,
  Mary A.M. 204, Patsey 118, Polly
  252, Sarah 63, Susanna 129
CRICHLOW, Susan C. 262
CRICK, Elizabeth 156, Elizabeth
  Ann 170, Nancy 156, Sarah 176
CRIDDLE, Amanda E. 277, Mary A. 12,
  Sally 164
CRISMAN, Elizabeth 111
CRISWELL, Hannah Jane 170, Mary
  147
CRITCHLOW, Nancy 286
CROCKER, Elizabeth 132, Julia 221,
  Louisa Jane 55
CROCKETT, Elizabeth M. 269, 64,
  Frances 169, Jane 101, 227, Joana M. 237, Louisa 145, Margaret
  J. 43, Mary 40, 28, Matilda 165,
  Nancy 202, Polly 64, Sally 167,

CROCKETT, Sarah Ann 194, Sarah E. 271, Sarah Jane 203
CROMER, Elizabeth A. 231, Julia Ann 148, Letitia 163, Mary A.H. 282, Nancy Ann 61
CROSBY, Caroline 117, Mary A. 284
CROSIN, Sarah E. 175
CROSLEY, Oliva, E. 95
CROSS, Ann 269
CROUCH, Mary M. 241, Polly W. 273 Susannah 32
CROUSE, Anna 23, Sally 132
CROW, Mary 46
CROWDER, Lucy A. 84, Mary C. 111, Polly 105
CRUMP, Hannah G. 241, Sarah Ann 197
CRUNK, Susan W. 199
CRUTCHER, Ann Eliza 237, Ann O. 230, Elizabeth J. 194, Mary E. 291, Sarah E. 246, Sinai 152
CULBERSON, Mary 230
CULBERTSON, Elizabeth 126
CULLOM, Elizabeth 190
CUMMINS, Amanda 134, Elizabeth 288 41, Elizabeth L. 123, Emily 129, Jane A. 75, Martha 151, Mary 80, Nancy 224, 245, Polly Ann 200
CUNNINGHAM, Emeline 257, Susannah 296
CURRY, Elizabeth S. 1, Henrietta Mariah 88, Jane 291, Patsey 171
CURTIS, Anne 206, Catharine 87, Elizabeth 257, Rachel 249, 81, Rebecca 87, 186
CUTCHEN, Elizabeth 90
CYRUS, Ellen 266, Mourning 66

DABNEY, Ann P. 181, Bethenia 191, Elizabeth 152, Mary 98, Margaret S. 256, Nancy 26, Polly M. 131, Peggy S. 191
DAIZLY, Amanda 1
DALEY, Nancy 152
DALTON, Charlotte H. 234, Elizabeth S. 195, Susan 140
DANCY, Rebecca 174
DANIEL, Gennett 183
DANIELS, Sarah S. 187
DARDEN, Clotilda 61
DAUGHERTY, Nancy Jane 256
DAVENPORT, Martha 139
DAVIDSON, Ann M.E. 231, Hannah 138 Margaret W.C. 6, Mary Jane 198
DAVIS, Abba 95, Anna 161, Catharine J. 75, Catherine Jane 109, Delaney 103, Eliza H. 171,

DAVIS, Eliza R. 69, Eliza R.B. 63, Elizabeth 12, 293, 244, 180, 70, Francis A. 196, Harriet 265, Jane 71, Julia 146, Savenia 174, (Lavenia) Louisa M. 44, Martha A.E. 198, Mary 197, 216, Mary A. 161, Mary Jane 73, 140, Milley 65, Nancy 267, 81, 203, 161, 16, Nancy A. 13, Nancy W. 33, Olive 249, Patsey 216, Peggy 78, Polly 219, Polly W. 121, Sally Jones 74, Sarah 258, Sarah E. 149, Sarah Jane 161, Sarah J. 176
DAWSON, Betsey 255, Drucinda 102
DLADERICK, Emmily R. 249
DEAL, Polly 54,
DEAN, Caroline A. 9, Elizabeth 185, Mary 69, 6, Nancy 86, 51, Parthenia 72
DEANS, Abby 108
DEAVENPORT, Nancy 177
DEBNAM, Elizabeth B. 191, Dorothy 54
DEENS, Elizabeth 36
DEGRAFFENREID, Catharine J.D. 209, Mary A. 216
DELLENDER, Polly 74
DEMOS, Annie 69, Joannah 177
DEMOSS, Polly 125
DEMSEY, Sally K. 151
DEMUMBREN, Margaret W. 60
DENNIS, Caroline E. 251
DENNY, Matilda 183
DENSON, Rebecca 103, Matilda C.G. L. 50, Martha L. 106
DENTON, Barbary 18, Deborah 185, Polly 250, Rhoda 68, 188, Sarah 54, S (L)erenah 224, Susan 59
DERRIBERRY, Elizabeth 13, Caty 10
DERRYBERRY, Christina 78
DESHAZO, Tabitha 170
DESON, Martha 218
DEVILING, Eley 93
DEVORE, Martha 164
DIAL, Celia 204, Margaret A. 197
DICKSON, Eliza A. 173, Isabella E. 58, Mary 145, Polly 103, Rachel 242, Sarah 92
DILLIARD, Branchy 51, Polly 256
DILLEN, Rosanna 273
DILLENDER, Jenny Hamilton 202
DILLIN, Susan E. 232
DITTO, Sarah E. 205
DIXON, Anne 209
DOBBINS, Aley 189, Anna 154, Jane 154, 101, Nancy 200, Polly 84, Rachael 66, Rachel 41

DOBBS, Polly 73
DODD, Addeline 199, Elizabeth 85
  Martha E. 70, Polly 85
DODGE, Martha 50
DOBSON, Isabel 24, Martha P. 134,
  Mary 161, Matilda 260, Nancy 24
  Sarah 99, Sally 122
DODSON, Ailcey 237, Amanda Ellen
  290, Elizabeth M. 173, Martha
  222, Mary 136, Rosena 3, Tab-
  itha 23
DOHERTY, Polly 199, Susanna 199
DOLLAR, Dicey 95
DONALDSON, Jane 194
DONELSON, Leah 85, Mary 157
DONLY, Priscilla 159
DONNELSON, Ann M. 228
DOOLEY, Caty 20
DOOLIN, Louisa E. 119
DORREL, Mary 114
DOTSON, Ellen 14, Jemima 211,
  Jane 202, Margaret 14, 28,
  Mary H. 72, Nancy 250, Nancy T.
  C. 271, Nancy W. 256, Sally 76
DOUGLASS, Frances 163, Jane G. 151
DOWDY, Catherine 7, Elizabeth 255
  Fanny 274, Frances 287, Hannah
  81, Nancy 275, Polly 145,
  Rachel 237, Sarah 219
DOWNEY, Judah 175, Mary 218
DOWNIE, Sally 35
DOWNING, Margaret 291, Martha A.
  279
DOYLE, Nancy 169, Sally 137
DRAKE, Lila 64, Mary E.T. 234,
  Susan 186
DRANNAN, Ann 114
DRINKARD, Mourning 82
DUDLEY, Betsey 67, India Ann 124,
  Judith R. 163, Mary 125, Mary
  A. 249, 75, Virginia 46
DUFF, Ann 41, Mary Ann 49
DUFFEL, Peggy 88
DUFFER, Martha Ann 108
DUFFILL, Elizabeth 58
DUFFY, Virginia W. 56
DUGGER, Catharine 285
DUKE, Nancy 58
DUMMUBER, Elizabeth N. 199
DUNAGAN, Polly 268
DUNCAN, Nancy 238, Parmelia 287,
  Peggy 184
DUNGAN, Parthenia 191, Rebecca 240
  Sarah 176
DUNHAM, Elizabeth 247
DUNLAP, Eliza 202, Nancy 224
DUNN, Martha 168

DUNNAGAN, Kitty 9
DUNNEBER, Charity 227, Sarah 133
DURDEN, Martha W. 29
DURDON, Elizabeth H. 162, Lucinda
  C. 254
DURHAM, Matilda 26
DUTY, Manerva 134, Mary Ann 77,
  Priscilla 196
DWYER, Eliza 211, Sarah 86
DYER, Anne 249, Elizabeth 260, Lu-
  cinda 206, Mary 235, Nancy 87,
  Tabitha 87

EARLY, Caroline 163, Catharine 183
  Sarah 183
EASTEYS, Sarah 36
EATON, Paulina 28, Susan 207
ECHOLS, Catherine 278
EDDINGTON, Polly 187
EDES, Susan 208
EDGAR, Lillie 137, Malinda 210,
  Margaret 213, Mary 41
EDMINSTON, Elizabeth 19, Eleanor 187
EDMISTAN, Anne 192, Margaret 182
  Mary E. 14, Mary R. 188, Mary 81
  Martha G. 188, Martha 34
EDMONDSON, Emeline 138, Frances 183
EDMONSON, Eveline 81, Julia 90,
  Malissa 61, Margaret 188, Mary 128
  Mary J. 176, Narcissa 142, Pan-
  thea F. 216, Parthenia P. 68
EDNEY, Emily 189, Mary A. 49,
  Nancy 209
EDMONDS, Minerva 250
EDWARDS, Amanda Malvina 256, Ann
  148, Celia 17, Eliza E. 76,
  Elizabeth 77, 118, Louisa 49,
  Mary Thomas 177, Mintha 11,
  Minthy 10, Nancy 104, 210, 17,
  Narcissa 197, Polly 245, Sally
  224, Sarah 153, 146, 195,
  Susan 275
EGGLESTON, Elizabeth W. 292
ELAM, America R. 15, Elizabeth 140,
  48, Minerva 254, Nancy 183,
  Polly 205, 110, Sarah 276
ELLIOTT, Anna 66, Elizabeth 272,
  Elizabeth Manerva 233, Lucy Ann
  165, Nancy 281, Panthia 274,
  Polley 82, Sarah E. 167
ELLIS, Mary A. 282
ELMORE, Nancy 144
ELY, Nancy 76
ENGLEMAN, Susanna 272
ENSLEY, Permelia 38
EPPS, Harriet 199, Mary B. 276
EPSON, Elizabeth 206

ESTES, Annie 240, Polly 189
ESTIES, Ellen 25
ESTIS, Amanda R. 260
EVANS, Charity 202, Charity S.P. 66, Elizabeth 138, Eveline 71, Fanny 89, Levicy 96, Martha 291, Mary 50, 140, Parthenia 228, Rachel 254, Rebecca 274, Susan A. 99
EVERLY, Louisiana 175
EWING, Easther 262, Margaret 275
EZELL, Bethenia 119
EZBERN, Betsey 126
EZZELL, Elizabeth 130, 239
EZELL, Emeline 248, Julia 17, Malvira 113, Martha 225, Mary 266

FAIRCLOTH, Susan 203
FALL, Catharine S. 260
FARMER, Eliza P. 166, Martha C. 182, Mary Ann 166
FARRINGTON, Mary C. 208
FAUER, Patsey 83
FEATHERSTON, Gilly 121, Julia Farmer 50, Margaret 164, Martha 275
FEATHERSTONE, Eliza Ann 160, Sally 221
FERGUSON, Betsey 178, Eliza 277, Emily 249, Jane 46, Mary Ann 245, Narcissa 52, Nancy 257, 87 Rebecca 266, 223
FENNY, Zilpha 45
FERES, Peggy 76
FERREL, Mary Ann 199
FERRELL, Elizabeth 233
FERRILL, Annis 151
FIELD, Dosha 136, Elizabeth 250, 204, 285, Maacha 79, Mary 158, 190, Matilda 60, Sarah 58
FIELDS, Ann Eliza 114, Jane 72, Keziah 272, Maacha 120, Margaret E. 262, Martha 220, Mary M. 239, Mary A. 273, Nancy 231
FIELDER, Betsey 1, Mirah 22, Nancy 46, Susanna 1
FIGURES, Harriet 191, Louisa Ann 12
FINDLEY, Polly P. 163
FISABEE, Sarah 222
Fish, Elizabeth 132
FISHER, Clarissa Ann 282, Louisa 264, Mary F. 92, Miriam 224, Nancy 92, Parmelia 106, Polly 124
FISK, Dilly 158, Sally 78
FITZ, Britania 250, Elizabeth 190 Minerva Ann 214, Perlina 230

FITTS, Sarah 294
FITZGERALD, Elizabeth 76, Mary 75, Nancy 4
FITZPATRICK, Polly 212, Rebecca 199
FLEMING, Elizabeth 153, 154, Jenny 173, Margaret 80, Susan E. 133
FLEMONONS, Polley 278
FLETCHER, Elizabeth A. 226, Emily A. 149, Mary Ann 236
FLIPPIN, Nancy 4
FLOURNOY, Mary 68
FLOYD, Amy C. 93, Catharine 215, Elizabeth N. 97, Jane 150, Lurena 17, Martha 96, Mary Ann 231, Mary Jane 275, Nancy 202, Priscilla 70, Raney 17
FLY, Anna 42, Elizabeth 14, Lucy 42, Matilda 155, 125, Rebecca 53
FORD, Catherine 91, Elizabeth 23, Ellendor 91, Peniza 238, Polly 130, Sarah Ann 5
FORE, Martha 296, Sarah B. 12, Martha 226
FOREHAND, Emeline 193, Margaret 178 Nancy 226, 193, Prudence 80, Sarah Jane 132, Wealthy 84
FOSE, Mary M. 267
FORGERSON, Diana 201
FOU, Martha I. 226
FOSTER, Ann E. 125, Martha G. 261 Martha Jane 274, Mary Ann 174, Patcy 92, Sara E. 77
FOX, Cynthia 190, Elizabeth 267, 18, Jane 190, Margaret 130, 215 Mary 270, Mary Jane 258, Nancy 292, Priscilla 224, Rebecca 215 Sally 46, Sarah 242, Susan 92
FRANCIS, Manerva 64, Permelia 82 *
FRANKLIN, Lorinda 142, Marinda Catherine 74
FRANTHAM, Jane 180, Sally 128
*FRANCIS, Sarah 188
FRAZIER, Anna 147
FREEMAN, Celia 289, Elizabeth 42, Henrietta 121, Lovey 116, Lucy 89, Martha 4, Mary W. 106, Nancy 119, Sally 289
FRITH, Parmelia 111
FROST, Louisa J. 209, Mary E. 79, Rebecca 255
FRY, Elizabeth 27
FRYETTE, Julia 198
FUQUA, Elizabeth 224, Juda 208, Martha 275, Nancy 121, Polly 159
FULKS, Nancy 290
FUZELL, Nancy 286

GALYSAN, Rhoda 165
GANT, Hester Ann 178
GANTER, Maria 204
GAMBLE, Polly 36
GARDINER, Ann 206, Charlotte 92, Mary 94, Mary Ann 172
GARDNER, Anna 212, Eleanor 143, Elizabeth 184, Isabel 266, Martha 275, 95, Mary 240
GARLAND, Mary 26
G ARNER, Elizabeth 20, Ellenor 292 Hannah 200
Garrett, Cincy 76, Dorothy 147, Elizabeth 41, 276, Lila 231, Louisa 64, Lucy 194, Mary 190, Melita Ann 66, Nancy 256, Nancy M. 25, Patsey 107, Polly 238, Sally 188, 231, Sara 32, 127, Zilpha 221
GATES, Elizabeth 231, Mary Ann 172, Phoebe 231, Rebecca 121, Sally 253
GATLIN, Elizabeth 249, Holland W. 247, Mary 137, Sarah 238, Sidney 104, Susan 172
GAULT, Gracy 144, Mary E. 110, Mary H. 38, Rebecca C. 275, Sarah E. 205, Susannah 187
GEE, Elizabeth 38, Elizabeth Ann 269, Elizabeth C. 247, Lucy C. 73, Martha 83, Mary W. 175, Penelope 290, Sarah 208, Susannah 137
GENTRY, Elizabeth 223, 107, Faney 49, Letsey 209, Nancy 163, Polly 229, Sinia 163, Tabitha W 274
GERMAIN, Eley 137, Nancy 174
GERMAN, Eliza A. 240, Mahala D. 10 Miram 214, Susan 281, Susannah 257
GHOLSON, Sally 255
GIBBONS, Elizabeth 210
GIBSON, Betsey 37, Emeline 4, Calista 103, Catherine 204, Elizabeth 233, 86, Jincy 134, Mary 99, Mary Jane 244, Peggy 15, Priscilla 184, Rebecca 214, Sintha 251
GIDDENS, Amanda 93, Louesa 182, Margaret 79, 198, Nancy 293, Polly 35, Rachael 185, Sarah 181
GIDEON, Mary W. 182, Priscilla 45
GILES, Ann 226, Arminta 104, Frances Jane 99, Jane 244, Lucy 245 Martha 104, 244, Mary 220, Sarah 227
GILL, Fanny 292

GILLAN (GILLIAN) Sally 132
GILLASPIE, Amelia 173, Matilda 247, Nancy 44, Naomi 288, Polly 224, Sally 42, Sophia 271
GILLESPIE, Mary 170, Naoma 6, Polly 250
GILLIAM, Nancy G. 255
GILLISPIE, Frances 57, Jane 80, Margaret 87
GILBERT, Amey 2, Martha Jane 52, Patsey 95, Sally 90
GIVENS, Ann 137, 235, Letty 254, Nancy 136
GIVVINS, Fanny 293
GLASCOCK, Eliza 164
GLASS, Sally 62, 193
GLEAVES, Sarah E.A. 71
GLEEVES, Marietta 100
GLENN, Anne 289, Caroline 279, 273 Elizabeth 230, Martha 24, Mary E. 159, Rebecca J. 248, Susan Anne 158, Zilpha 238
GLOVER, Elizabeth 7
GLUM, Sarah 286
GLYMP, Elizabeth 108, Frances 285
GLYMPH, Frances 254, Sally 141
GLYMPLE, Louise 107
GOCEY, Elizabeth 163, Polly 59
GODWIN, Mary 231
GOFF, Elizabeth 113, Jane 192, Mary 151, 44, Nancy M. 138
GOLLY, Sally 185
GOOCH, Elizabeth 225, Frances 151, Lucinda 152, Martha 64, Nancy 95, Polly 173, Sicily 181
GOODE, Polly 237
GOODMAN, Malinda 204, Peggy 103
GOODRUM, Elizabeth 22, Jane 202
GOODWIN, Alcena 205, Elizabeth 39 Harriett 248, Mary Jane 132, Sarah B. 181, Susan 81
GOPETT, Polly 87
GORDON, Jane 29, Lockey 104, Nelly 74
GORE, Delilah 125
GOSAGE, Sarah 70
GOSEY, Catharine 56
GRAHAM, Abegail 123, Aley 260, Altamyra 18, Cynthia 189, Elisabeth 101, Eliza 77, Elizabeth 248, Eleanor 164, Ester 164, Jane 74, Jane Cowan 60, Lucinda 105, Mary 133, 214, Mary Alexander 261, Nancy 27, Naomy 144, Nelly 240, Sarah E. 165
GRANGER, Elizabeth 259
GRAVES, Frances 83, Polly 82,

GRAVES, Theodosia 167, Zerilda 176
GRAY, Anna 201, Edney 210, Elizabeth 285, 236, 242, 23, Frances 56, Harriott 162, Jane 292, Lucinda 133, Martha J. 208, Martha 129, Mary 237, Mary Ann 69, 146, Nancy 236, 294, Nicey 31, Ruthy 252, Sally 159, 157, Sarah 128, 236, Susan Ann 87, Susannah 26, Tabitha 100, Temperess 120
GRAYHAM, Margaret 247
GREEN, Artemissa E. 251, Jane E. 249, Louisiana J. 102, Lucinda 123, Mahala 17, Martha 195, Mary Ann 124, Mary O. 119, Mesemiah 212, Minerva 279, Polly 147, Sarah Eliza 215, Sarah H. 181, Tabitha 17
GREER, Elizabeth 276, Malvira D. 117, Mary 261, Nancy 214
GREMMER, Margaret 26, Sarah 179, Susan 181
GRENNIER, Lucinda 186
GRIFFIN, Charlotte 33, Delila 24, Ibby 18
GRIGGS, Amanda 39, Elizabeth 247, 232, Lucy Ann 248, Mary 247, 124, Quinny 36, Sally 107, Susan 131, Virginia 189
GRIGSBY, Cleopatra Ann 290
GRIM, Susan A. 36
GRIMES, Elizabeth 91, Nancy 9, Peggy 254, Sarah 40
GRIMMER, Elizabeth 36
GUINN, Maria 235, Mary 4
GULLY, Lucy 99
GUNTER, Betsey 92, Eliza W. 120, Martha Ann 47, Matilda 10, Nancy 78, 211, Frances 72, Sarah 174
GUTHRIE, Harriett S. 200, Polly 158, Sarah C. 224
GUY, Elizabeth 114, Jane W. 114, Nancy 148, Susan 132
GWINN, Marion 11

HADLEY, Evelina 23, Martha 74, Sally 263
HAETHCOCK, Edrey 15
HAGUE, Mary Ann 292 (Hayne?)
Haile, Betsey 100
HAILEY, Elizabeth 31, Harriet 56, Sally M. 42
HAILY, Fanny 117
HAIRGRAVE, Susannah 138
HAITHCOCK, Emeline 295
HALE, Elizabeth 155, Sarah 171

HALEY, Amelia H. 42, Elizabeth Ann 22, Emeline 70, Emilia 22, Jane 240, Mary 229, 69, Nancy 22, 288, 25, Patsey 211, Polly 46, Sarah 194
HALFACRE, Barbara 63, Barbary 52, Catharine 167, Emily 52, Margaret 226, Mary 155, 112, Susan Ann 229
HALL, Amanda Jane 1, Amanda 5, Brimetta 263, Elizabeth 231, Elizabeth A. 58, Elixa 274, Delpha 156, Frances 73, Harriet 48, Martha A. 142, Mary F. 11, Martha J. 198, Mary M. 206, Nancy 237, 15, 252, Nancy Frances 266, Polly 291, Rebecca 252
HALY, Ann Elizabeth 147
HAM, Ann 251, Elizabeth 51, 218, Fanny 145, Lotty 198, Martha 96 Mary 255, 205, Susan Ann 179
HAMBEE, Sally 43
HAMBLET, Kesiah 88
HAMBLETON, Elizabeth 95
HAMDLIN, Polly 248
HAMER, Charoltte N. 112, Louiza 15 Rebekah 217, Sarah Ann 19
HAMILTON, Caroline T. 216, Cynthia 219, Eliza 27, Elizabeth 95, Emily S. 126, Martha S. 196, Mary 62, Mary Ann 292, Polly 214, Rebecca A.S. 255, Rebecca S. 188, Sarah 93, Sina H. 41, Susan A. 283
HAMLET, Catharine 113, Nancy 68, Sally 88
HAMLETT, Catharine 270, Elizabeth 106, Frances 110
HAMMOND, Barbary 61, Sally 277
HAMMONS, Elizabeth 56
HAMPTON, Ann 108, Elizabeth 265, Harriett 57, Julia Ann 37, Mary 117, Mary S. 217, Nancy 223, Peggy 178, Rebecca 70, 27, Sally 34, Sarah 145
HANCOCK, Harriet E. 229, Margaret 211
HANKS, Fanny 89, Matilda 273
HARDCASTLE, Edy 96
HARDEMAN, Anna 236, Bethenia 88, Betsey 201, Dorothy 296, Lucretia Nash 115, Martha D. 61, Mary M. 86, Mary N. 209, Nancy L. 65, Susan 76,
HARDEN, Sally 286
HARDESON, Elizabeth 141
HARDIN, Peggy 238

HARDISON, Jane 204, Polly 115
HARFORD, Elizabeth 11
HARLIN, Peggy 68
HARPER, Ann 75, Delinda 29, Mary
 Jane 47, Minerva Ann 238, Nan-
 cy 225, 191, Pachel 231, Rebecca
 90, Sarah E. 38, Selina J. 34,
 Susan 147
HARTGRAVE, Amy 189, Lettisia 128
HARDGRAVES, Celia 100, Nancy M. 116
HARGRAVE, Sarah 13
HARRIS, Annis 49, Dynitia 58, Edy
 178, Elizabeth 174, 56, Eve 28,
 Mary M. 117, Polly 212, Sintha
 124, Susan 76
HARRISON, Alsey 252, Eliza 146,
 Lucinda 239, Lucy 177, Malvira
 131, Mary Jane 202, Milly Ann
 146, Sarah A.F. 206
HARTGROVES, Ann 71
HARGROVE, Drucilla R. 241, Eliza-
 beth 219, Mary 221, Sarah Ann 32
HARREL, Sarah 64
HARTLEY, Elizabeth 147, Malinda
 22, Martha 116, Martha Ann 50,
 Priscilla 241
HARTLY, Eveline 184, Jane 241,
 Nancy 8, Polly 243, Ruthy 155
HARVEY, Sarah 200, Martha 86
HASKIN, Marthena 127
HASSELL, Alpha 235, Nancy 23,
 Polly 235
HASTING, Jane 138
HAY, Barbara 182, Eliza 228, Ju-
 lian 218, Julia Ann 254, Lusetta
 70, Nancy 272, Patsey 241
HAYNE, Narcisa 144
HAYNES, Betsey 47, Drucilla 40,
 Eliza J. 60, Jane 281, Julia A.
 150, Mary 177, Meome 213, Nancy
 292, Sarah 120, 176, 240
HAYS, Agnes 163, Emily 194, Mary
 35, Polly 227, Portia 121,
 Sarah 36
HATCHER, Catharine 80, Celina 108,
 Margaret 80, Sarah 103
HAWK, Harriet Jane 266
HAWKINS, Martha 141, Nancy 118,
HAWKS, Nancy 179
HAZELWOOD, Gilley 177
HAZLETT, Margaret 135
Hazzlewood, Sabra 79
HEATH, Emily 193
HEATHCOCK, Lurana 15
HEATON, Elizabeth 270
HEEMAN, Priscilla 53
HEITER, Sarah McCrory 286

HELM, Mary Zerilda 197
HELTON, Sarah 43, 131
HEMPHILL, Catharine 16, Jane 19,
 Martha 285
HENDERSON, Ann Elizar 123, Ann P.
 238, Eliza Jane 282, Levicy 30,
 Lucy 108, Maria 114, Margaret
 259, 72, Mary 225, Methilda 22,
 Sally 199
HENDLEY, Mary 285,
HENDRICKS, Nancy 126, Ruth 140
HENDRISE, Polly Ann 9
HENDRIX, Elizabeth 94, Mary 167
HENLEY, Elizabeth D. 274
HENNING, Mary Jane 135
HERBERT, Eliza 288, Julia 245,
 Thursey 43
HERRIN, Elizabeth 187, Margaret 10,
 Polly 206, Rachel 250, Hannah 117
 Jane 250, Mary 154, Rebecca 162
HESTER, Lucy 87
HETER (Hiter) Eliza 239
HEWSTON, Prudence 278
HEWTON, Margaret 219
HEYLAR, Peggy 129
HICKMAN, Nancy 37, 158
HICKS, Betsy 151, Eliza 68, Eliz-
 abeth 220, 81, Malinda 236, Nan-
 cy 185, 128, 114, Polly 83, Sal-
 ly 46, 144, Sarah 155
HIGHTOWER, Asenath 240, Eliza 33,
 Jincy 201, Lucinda 33, Mary
 Smith 109, Sally C. 121
HILBURN, Polly 41
HILES, Mary 62
HILL, Ann 220, Asenette 54, Betsy
 85, Eliza 42, Eliza Ann 70,
 Eliza Elizabeth 178, Eliza M.
 121, Elizabeth 6, 32, 213, Eme-
 lia 26, Fanny 23, Frances 156,
 Isabella 21, 91, Lavinia 39, Lu-
 vinia A. 248, Margaret 39, Mar-
 tha 282, Mary 254, 242, 38, 25,
 Mary Jane 127, Nancy 62, 53, 170,
 38, 26, Parmelia 273, Polly 3,
 Rachael 149, Rebecca 240, Sarah
 283, Susan 221, 285, Susanna 291
HILLIARD, Martha 229, Sally 212
HINES, Catherine 232
HITER, Mary 178, Polly 108
HOBBS, Eliza Jane 187, Hannah 241,
 Mary 91, 11, Nancy Ellen 26
HOBSON, Patsy 214
HODGE, Jenny 206, Margaret 66,
 Mary 106, Minerva 213, Nancy 235
 Priscilla 183, 44
HODGES, Annis 125

HOGAN, Elizabeth 60, 57, Lucy 158
  Nancy 10
HOGGARD, Milley 228
HOGWOOD, Eliza 179, Nancy 158 14
HOLLIDAY, Rachel 92, Sally 92, Mary/
HOLLAND, Elizabeth 90*   126
*HOLT, Polly 145, Edith 117, Eliz./
*HOLLAND, Nancy 122, Elizabeth 119
  Rosanna 134, Elizabeth 30, Jane
  25, Judith 75, Mary 259, Patsey
  106, Sarah Jane 80
HOLLOWAY, Nancy 124, Sally 170,
  Sarah A. 106, Sarah O.P. 244,
  Seniza 30
HOLLIS, Anna 262
*HOLT, Dorothy B. 66, Polly P. 279
  Telitha C. 55
HOMBLE, Caroline 192, Sally 43
HOOD, Amanda 55, Betsy 272, Dolly
  276, Elizabeth 225, 271, 89,
  Rebecca 55, Sally 175
HOPE, Cyntha 285
HOPKINS, Elizabeth 165, Evelind
  142
HOPSON, Martha 294
HORNER, Elizabeth 240
HORSEFORD, Nancy 279
HORTON, Amanda Jane 247, Arcadia
  157, Elizabeth 88, Jane 131,
  Margaret 162, Martha 180, Mary
  9, M. Miranda 237, Polly 119,
  Sarah Ann 142, 99, Susan 162
HOSKINS, Catharine 269
HOTSTEAD (HOLSTEAD), Polly 236
HOTSTED, Melinda 214
HOUSDEN, Polly 48, Rebecca Jane 33
  Sarah 109
HOUSE, Elizabeth 131, Jane 195,
  Lucinda 195, Margaret 148, Martha 155, Martha 185, Mary 286,
  Rhoda Ann 194
HOUSTON, Anna Swisher 112, Elizabeth 220, Nancy 113, 19, Sally
  225
HOWARD, Nancy 65, Polly 91
HOWELL, Sarah 15
HOWELL, Nancy 29, Patsey Adaline
  23, Tempey 94
HOWLET, Mary Ann 285
HOWLETT, Mahala 5
HUBBARD, Susannah 122
HUDGENS, Martha Ann 258
HUDGINS, Catharine 212, Eliza 71
HUDLOW, Catherine 118, Polly 124,
  Sally 118
HUDSON, Polly 216
HUFSTUTLER, Catharine 278

HUGGINS, Eliza 59, Jane 111, Mary
  179, Sarah Ann 251
HUGHES, Christiana 201, Elizabeth
  179, 229, 282, Eveline 251,
  Frances 158, Hannah 272, Letitia
  75, Lucinda 206, Martha J. 232,
  Martha Jane 275, Mary M. 276, 34,
  Mary R. 20, Nancy 167, 72, Narcisia 125, Rachel Jane 123, Sarah E. 105, Sarah W. 19, Susan 126,
  255, Talitha 129
HUGHS, Fanny 255, Jane 163
HULME, Elizabeth 208, Matilda 28,
  Mary 147, Nancy 178, Rebecca 21,
  Rebekah 133, Sarah Jane 274
HUMBLE, Catharine 132, Dolly 207
HUMPHREYS, Ann 125, Harriett 200,
  Jane 200, Mary 221, Sally 81
HUNGARFORD, Martha 175, Nancy 78
HUNT, Cintha 132, Elizabeth Gustavia S. 209, Mary 245, Rebecca 146,
  Sarah 39, Temperance 123
HUNTER, Agnes 101, Arrabella 191,
  Catharine 31, Elizabeth 88, 87,
  Juan E.C. 25, Julia Ann 244, Margaret 88, 33, Martha 66, Mary 21,
  36, Narcissa R. 68, Peggy 130,
  Rebecca 253, Sarah 25, Sophronia 173
HUTCHENS, Elizabeth 55
HUTCHERSON, Casander 56, Polly 146,
  Rebecca 101
HUTCHINSON, Nancy 123
HUTCHISON, Betsey 276, Delpha 282,
  Nancy 12
HUTSON, Elizabeth 34, Frances 16,
  Jane 248, Lucy W. 80, Mary 18,
  Nancy 180, Sally 166
HUTTON, Mary Ann 91
HYDE, Elizabeth 27, Ferreby 143,
  Jency 93, Mary B. 256, Polly 26,
  Presellar 92

INGRAM, Charlotte 1, Margaret 231
  Mary 113, Peggy 187, Rebecca 157
  Roma 28, Sarah Ann 4, Susan 292
  Susanna 205
INMAN, Annis 210, Catharine 87,
  Diademma Catharine 226, Decenda
  101, Elizabeth 130, Hannah 46,
  Jane 76, Mary 101, 210, Nancy Ann
  295, Racheal 100, Sarah 124,
  Sarah Jane 2,
IRION, Adaline 97, Catherine 240,
  Mary 208, Sarah 82
IRVIN, Elizabeth 138, Hannah 70,
  Jane 32, Malinda 59, Margaret 3

IRVIN, Martha 259, Mary 3, Nancy 160, Rebecca 69
ISLAND, Elizabeth 117
ISOM, Rosetta 130
ISRIEL, Eliza Jane 100
IVEY, Mary Ann 119, Penny 261
IVIE, Eliza 139
IVY, Elizabeth 205, Joannah 216, Mary 112, 177, Rebecca 205, 182

JACKSON, Barbary 269, Elizabeth 221, 221, 167, Elizabeth Jane 221, Iona 222, Jenetta 254, Litha 295, Martha 40, Mary 238, Mary A. 6, Mary F. 240, Milly 261, Nancy 82, 140, 277, 126, 10, Nina 196, Polly 123, 247, Sally 188, 244, Sarah 259, Susan 236, Susannah 167, Tincy 47
JACOES, Martha J. 233
JAMES, Catherine P. 202
JAMISON, Elizabeth 196, Mary Ann 206
JARRETT, Jane 129
JARROTT, Nancy 119
JEFFERSON, Amanda 258, Michy 143
JENKINS, Elizabeth 67, Mary Ann Nancy 140
JETER, Elizabeth 142
JOHNSON, Amanda 119, Ann C. 12, Brittania 147, Caroline B. 264, Cloe 278, Elizabeth 283, 59, Ellen 83, 281, Emeline 236, Frances 119, Julia 88, Malinda 277, Margaret 120, Martha 90, Mary 18, 219, 202, 20, 55, Milly Ann 143, 280, Parthenia 82, Polley 283, 238, Rachel 142, Sarah 90, 222, Sarah Jane 99, Serissicy 63, Susanna P. 245, Tabitha C. 200, Terissa A.R. 263 Zerinah 75, Ferriby 148
JOHNSTON, Agatha 224, America 60, Anne 178, Catherine 279, Cynthia 184, Elizabeth 242, Euphamia 234 Hannah 171, Margaret A. 85, Martha 291, 175, Mary Ozburn 106 Milly 99, Nancy 144, 93, Polly 18, Sally 187, Sarah 30, 95, 113 Sarah R. 251, Susan H. 201, Susan H. 3, Tennessee 62
JOICE, Dolly E. 28, Mary Jane 94, Susan 173
JONES, Abigail 193, Amanda 215, Anna 68, Debby 53, Dicey 191, Eleanor 150, Elizabeth 48, 246, 87, 174, 228, Jackey 199,

JONES, Jane B. 157, Jane M. 198, Julia 147, Julia Ann 54, Martha 246, Mary 242, Mary Ann 164, 246 Matilda 79, Nancy 217, 247, 42, Penelope 106, Phene 237, Polly 289, Rebecca 271, Rhoda Boyd 162 Sarah A. 53, Sarah Ann 162, 24, Sarah C. 4, Susan 86, Susannah 169
JORDAN, Eliza 208, Elizabeth 149, 283, Elizabeth A.T. 284, Elizabeth Ann 137, Elizabeth E. 210, Fanney 100, Jane 186, James 286, Jane W. 178, Lethe 89, Manerva 146, Martha 30, 3, Mary 61, 260, Mary A. 153, 286, 90, 152, Mary G. 149, Meda 126, Minerva 143, Miry P. 200, Nancy Livonia 220, Osia 222, Patsey 143, Phoebe 213, Sally 187, 211, 220, Sarah 111, Sarah F. 148, Sarah Jane 268, Susan 291, Susannah 205
JOSLIN, Elizabeth J. 291
JOWITT, Ann D. 231
JOYCE, Louisa 30
JUDKINS, Mary Adeline 26

JOHNSON, Letitia 165

KAIGLER, Polly 237
KAVANAUGH, Patsey 190
KEARBY, Sarah 138
KEE, Mary Ann 206
KEFFER, Henrietta P. 195
KELLOW, Celia 264, Susan 133
KELLY, Eliza 137, Elizabeth 243, Martha 270, Polly 108, Lurana 289
KENADA, Catharine 214
KENNAD, Dinah 150
KENNEDY, Betsey 110, Celia 241, Chloe 180, Elizabeth 80, Mary Ann 241, Rhoda 48, Sally 109, Sarah 17, Virginia 120
KENNEY, Jane 156, Nancy 223
KERBY, Polly 279
KERFMAN, Elizabeth 88
KERR, Nancy 240, Polly 198
KEY, Martha W. 1, Nancy D. 286, Onah 49, Rebecca 92
KEYLAR, Peggy 129
KIDD, Eliza Jane 43, Jane (Patsey) 181, Mary 168, Nancy 114, Patsey 255
KILES, Patsey 188
KIMBROUGH, Mary 192, Zelpha 152
KINCAID, Elianor 278, Hannah 34
KING, Elizabeth 229, 207, Jane 206

KING, Jenny 190, Louisa E. 26,
 Lucy E. 234, Martha 193, Mary
 60, Mary Ann 217, 250, 161,
 Nancy W. 26, Sarah E. 144,
 Virginia 162
KINGSTON, Elizabeth 140
KINNARD, Adaline B. 75, Catharine
 186, Charlotte 132, Elizabeth 42
 Henritta 186, Mary C. 274, Mary
 T. 65, Sally 59, Susan 188
KINNEY, Peggy 107
KINNY, Eliza 278, Polly 267
KINSEY, Annis 180, Sarah 213
KIRBY, Betsey 243, Nancy 105,
 Rachel 138, Rebecca 2
KIRK, Catharine 258, Elizabeth 23,
 Mary F. 284, Rebecca C. 78,
 Sally 282
KIRKHAM, Lorinda 209
KIRKPATRICK, Martha Ann 125, Se-
 lina Jane 292, Salina P. 112,
KIRKS, Martha Ann 240
KIRZER, Mary 12
KNIGHT, Christianna 117, Elizabeth
 5, 113, Mary 161, Rhoda 96
KNOT, Mary 156
KNOTT, Sarah Ann 186

LACY, Mary 2, Sarah Ann 200,
 Winny Ann Eliza 91
LADD, Ann V. 244, Rebecca 231, 290
LAGOOCH, Marilla 14
LAGRONE, Polly 296
LAGROON, Catharine 281
LAMB, Ailey 294, Ann 176, Cathar-
 ine 110, Elizabeth 83, Hannah
 248, Lettis 218, Louisa 255,
 Luraney 218, Mary 68, Nancy 81,
 Paulina 248, Susan 155, Rachel
 260
LAMBERT, Indah 247, Jane 254,
 Lucinda 11
LAMPKINS, Eliza 150
LAMMONS, Polly 54
LANCASTER, Polly 284
LANDFORD, Sarah 69
LANDRAM, Esther 155
LANDRUM, Elizabeth C. 58, Harriett
 3, Nancy 63, Patsey 275
LANE, Dolly 247, Grizzell 191,
 Martha Ann 285, Nancy S. 233,
 Sarah B. 226
LANGDON, Ellen E. 215
LANGLEY, Emeline 231
LANGSTON, Margaret 185
LANIER, Lemiza 126, Lucy 9, Nancy
 200, Patsey 35, Penizer 181

LANKFORD, Rhahab 251
LANSOM, Mary W. 49
LARAMORE, Mary 258
LARIMORE, Martha 161
LATTEY, Jane 245
LAUGHLIN, Elizabeth 291, Lydda W.
 254
LAVENDER, Catharine 256, Elizabeth
 P. 295, Evarilla 279, Maria 83,
 Martha E. 234, Mary C. 267,
 Nancy 83, Wincy W. 111
LAWRENCE, Mary 224, Maryan 295
LAYNE, Elizabeth W. 125, Louisa 14,
 Mary 88, Susan J. 268
LAYMASTER, Nancy 212
LAZENBERRY, Frances 168
LEAHORN, Mirah 173
LEAK, Miram 14
LEATON, Rachael 2
LECK, Sally 69
LEE, Caroline 210, Elizabeth 38,
 Frances J. 167, Mary 255
LEGATE, Catherine 224, Hannah 224,
 Mary 253
LEIGH, Elizabeth 10, Lavinia 93,
 Mary 135
LEMASTERS, Elizabeth 213
LEMONS, Elizabeth 16, Polly 174
LESTER, Celia 244, Elizabeth 49,
 Louisa 94, Martha 249, 98, Nancy
 14, 102, Parmelia 238, Parkey 260
LEWIS, Ailsey 33, Caty 80, Lucre-
 tia 129, Mary 124, 159, Sally 140,
 213
LIGGETT, Mary Jane 50
LIGHTFOOT, Elizabeth 196
LILLARD, Sarah E. 181
LIMON, Jane 125
LINDSLY, Eliza 176, Rebecca 199
LIPSCOMB, Parmelia 233
LITTLE, Ann 226, Cyntha 47, Eliza
 247, Elizabeth 108, 163, 260, 215,
 Hannah 138, Jane 207, Lucinda 207,
 Mary 114, 262, Sally 108, Susan
 192
LITTLETON, Nancy 130, Polly 290,
 Sally 68, 114, Susan 24
LIZEMBURY, Betsey 188
LOATEY,(Looty) (Loatey), Betsey 102
LOCK, Dolly 247, Elizabeth 236,
 Matilda 147
LOCKE, Nancy 161
LOFLIN, Nancy 193
LOFTEN, Eleanor 259
LOFTIN, Lydia 92, Sarah 99
LOFTON, Mary 221
LOGAN, Betsey 90, Mary 165

LOGSDON, Nancy 202
LONG, Agnes 263, Anna 120, Elizabeth 217, Lavinia 151, Louisa 136, Margaret 74, Martha 63, Mary 232, 195, Matilda 56, Polly 277, Rebecca 78, Sarah 156, 218, Susan 217
LOUDER, Olive 183
LOVE, Flora Ann 199, Martha 214, Mary 158, 275, Nancy 58
LOVET, Clarkey 218
LOVETT, Thankful 223
LOVING, Nancy 209
LOW, Nancy 289
LOWDER, Nancy 263, Sabry 196
LOWRY, Susannah 168
LOYD, Mary 155, 88, Sarah 80
LUALLEN, Elizabeth 295
LUKE, Hannah 131
LUNN, Elizabeth 58, 87, Mary 279
LUTY, Nancy 44, Patsey 229
LYNN, Mary 213
LYONS, Betsey 59, Polly 204
LYTLE, Jane 153
LYTTLE, Elenor 96

MABERRY, Sarah 67
MACK, Sally 193
MADDEN, Ann 228, Frances 85, Martha 265, Mary 257
MADDOX, Rutha 270
MAGEE, Mary A.E. 285
MAGNESS, Susan 1, Zilpah 102
MAIRS, Catharine 225, Polly 166, Rachel 29
MALONE, Bridget 127, Eliza 251, Elizabeth 25, Malinda 27, Mary 291, Sarah 25
MALLORY, Margaret 4
MANDLEY, Betsey 127, Eliza 239, Mahala 152, Martha 259
MANGHAM, Frances 208
MANGRUM, Elizabeth 271, Martha 260
MANGUM, Cynthia 121
MANIER, Elizabeth 20, Matilda 60
MANIRE, Anna 90, Eliza Jane 153, Malinda 60, Minerva 220, Polly 294
MANLEY, Dicey 52
MANNING, Emily 126
MANSCO, Polly 176
MANSKA, Susan 140
MARABLE, Eliza Haywood 145, Mary 225, Nancy 185, Parmelia 159
MARCHANT, Dorcas 265, Nancy 19, Ramy 216
MARIM, Rebecca 153

MARLIN, Ann 193, Betsey 91, Jane 16, Mary 145, Rhoda 146
MARLING, Jane 96, Mary J. 157
MARTIN, Barbara 196, Caty 270, Ferriby 235, Jane 111, Martha Ann 258, Mary 237, 58, Mary Virginia 223, Myra 265, Nancy 149, Polly 31, Rebecca 34, Sally 225
MARSHALL, Betsey 262, Eveline 227, Martha 271, Mary 294, 252
MASON, Lavinia 238, Martha 194
MATTHEWS, Chloe 196, Elizabeth 216 Emily Laura 271, Lucy 242, 245, Lucy Ann 230, Martha 148, Mary P. 9, Mary W. 208, Minerva 9, Nancy 203, Sally 81, Susan 152, Winnefred 8
MAUPIN, Elizabeth 272
MAURY, Elizabeth 254, 224, 201, 128, 27, Martha 76, 116, 209, Mary 246, Matilda 109, Peggy 27, Sabrina 191, Sarah, 224
MAXWELL, Elizabeth 181
MAY, Frankey 108
MAYBERRY, Elizabeth 247, Elizabeth Jane 66, Susan P. 181
MAYFIELD, Elizabeth 206, Elizabeth Ann 40, James 224, Margaret 222, Maria 250, Polly 273
MAYO, Tabitha 103
MAYS, Frances 89, Judy 52, Martha 89, Micha 52, Nancy 106, 2, Nancy Jane 216, Polly 295
MEACHAM, Frances 145, Martha 17, Susan Ann 257
MEADOW, Charlotte 63, Lucinda 5, Sally 109,
MEADOWS, Lockey 104, Mary 55, Priscilla 159
MEBANE, Louise 259, Margaret 253, Martha E. 213, Mary 10
MELONE, Sarah 101
MELTON, Polly Ann 198, Sarah 175
MERCHANT, Betsey 7, Jane 262
MERRIN, Sophia 67
MERRITT, Amanda 182, Eliza 295, Jane 144, Martha 228, Nancy 178, 217, Narcissa 142, Polly 259, Rhodda 143, Sarah 116, Susan 145, Wincey 143
MIDGETT, Elizabeth 64, Rosanna 253
MILES, Nancy 150
MILLER, Anne 20, Avalin 71, Christiana B. 176, Hannah 153, Jane 190, Julia Ann 252, Susan 184
MILTON, Rebecca 155, Sarah 63, Winneford 176

MINCY, Mary Ann 39
MITCHELL, Barbara 250, Charity 69
 Charlotte 248, Eliza 203, Martha 215, Mary 219, Mary E.F. 114
 Mary R. 170, Milley 254, Polly 37
MITCHUM, Mary Ann 23
MIZELL, Elizabeth 200
MODLIN, Cynthia Ann 46, Elizabeth 108
MOODY, Elizabeth 218
MOON, Mary 196, Mary A.V. 17, Sarah 31
MOORE, Amanda 63, 144, Ann 226, Elizabeth 184, 110, 57, 185, 59 Eliza F. 29, Elizabeth 270, Ester 227, Harriet 63, Jane 74, Joannah 18, Julia 21, Lucinda 26, Mava 93, Mecca 110, Nancy 103, Patsey 51, Peggy 213, Rebecca 86, Sally 19
MONCRIEF, Ann 151
MONT, Elizabeth 136
MONTGOMERY, Cyntha 285, Elizabeth 219, 181, 137, Jane 220, 165, 49, Louisa 84, Malinda 16, Martha 98, 220, Mary 32, Peggy 272 Polly 219
MOPPIN, Eliza Ann 246, Frances 133 Martha 273, Mary Ann 273
MORAN, Nancy 226
MORFET, Sally 90
MORGAN, Louisa 101, Mary Amanda 260, Milly 73, Nancy 11, 180, Polly 51
MORIN, Susanna 46
MORRIS, Amy 169, Ann Eliza 180, Casandrew 66, Catharine 172, Eliza Jane 246, 45, Mary 184, Nancy 29, Ruth 52, Sarah Ann 218 Sarah E. 158
MORTANE, Mapy 265
MORTON, Barthmy 229, Clarinda 233 Dicy 192, Eliza B. 234, Elizabeth 21, 13, Frances 247, 100, 197, Lavinia 250, Levithey 45, Lucinda 55, Martha 259, Mary 17 Nancy Jane 281, Polly 192, Tabitha 68, Suvicey 68
MOSELLY, Julia Ann 287
MOSES, Martha 199
MOSS, Catharine 283, Emily 203, Lucy 80, Rebecca 112, Ruth 124, Sarah 136
MOTHEREL, Cynthia 115, Emma 226, Mary 268

Mowry, Ellen 55
MYRICK, Mary 251
MUCHUM, Elizabeth 184
MULLEN, Eliza 103, Elvira 71, Martha 12, Nancy 84, Sarah 151
MULLIN, Nancy 213, Sally 81
MUMFORD, Mary 202
MURFREE, Elizabeth 93, Sally 74
MURPHY, Elizabeth 45, Rebecca 161 Sally 46
MURREY, Mary 277, Peggy 241
MUSGRAVE, Zilpah
MYERS, Anna 245

MC ADOO, Sarah 132
MC AFEE, Patsey 56, Penny 44
MC AFFEE, Susan 147
MC ALISTER, Elizabeth 199, Frances 169, Margaret 125, Priscilla 240
MC ALPIN, Ann 243, Elizabeth 25, Emeline 296
MC BRIDE, Martha 77, Polly 104, Priscilla 111
MC CABE, Caroline 78, Cena 53, Nancy 178
MC CALL, Elizabeth 192, Harriett 280, 118, Hulda 114, Lucinda 241 Mary 285, Milly Emeline 116, Polly 116
MC CALPIN, Elizabeth 290
MC CLAIN, Lavinia 279, Darcass 184
MC CANDLESO, Jean 98
MC CANLES, Catharine 218
MC CARREL, Fanny 198, Susan 78
MC CARROLL, Jane 72
MC CASLIN, Nancy 192, Susanna 192
MC CLARAN, Jincy 282, Sally 269
MC CLARY, Esther 54
MC CLELLAN, Ann 100, Mary 35, 40, Nancy 191, Polly 30, Sally 286
MC CLURE, Edith 171
MC COLLUM, Ellen 275, Fanny 186, Eliza Jane 223, Mary 102
MC CONICO, Nancy H. 75
MC CORNICO, Adeline 154, Angelina 53, Ann 84, Mary 159, Nancy 189
MC CORD, Martha 35, Martha Jane 110 Mary 83, Nancy 189, Myra 270, Sarah Jane 284
MC CORMICK, Elizabeth 202, Margaret 201
MC COWN, Elizabeth 196, Helen Mary 13, Myrah 215, Susan 39
MC COY, Catharine 6, Sarah 80
MC CRACKEN, Jane 66
MC CRADY, Cecilia 105, Dorcas 32

MC CRADY, Martha 105, Sally 8
MC CRORY, Hannah 204, Louisa 223,
  Mary A.C. 42, Rachel S.L.C.M. 85
  Sally 126
MC CULLUM, Ruth 155
MC CURDY, Elizabeth 93, Rebecca 88
  Zorilda 286
MC CUTCHAN, Hannah 216, Rachel
  Cannada 190
MC CUTCHEN, Catharine 124, Mary 40
  Margaret 31, Mary 201, Sally 115
MC DANIEL, Charlotte 32, Elizabeth
  Ann 292, Harriet 104, Martha 202
  Mary Ann 105, Mary Jane 95,
  Susan 161
MC DOWD, Olly 234
MC DOWEL, Harriet 233, Louisa 253
MC DOWELL, Martha Jane 233
MC ELHANEY, Margaret 262
MC EWEN, Eleanor 248, Eliza 169,
  Emeline 98, Ibby 103, Margaret
  190, 156, Sally 102, Sarah 225
MC EWIN, Rebecca 225
MC FADDEN, Catharine 187, Eliza
  Lucinda 189, Elizabeth 83,
  Ginny 203, Hannah 72, Roseanna
  72
MC FARLAN, Matilda 50
MC FAWL, Jane 152
MC GAN, Malissa 239, Merinda 86
MC GAVOCK, Amanda 244, Elizabeth
  115, Eliza Jane 10, Lucinda 104
  Malinda 242, Mary C.K. 245,
  Nancy K. 52, Sally M.S. 15
MC GAY (MC GUY), Elizabeth 294
MC GEE, Cessey O.F. 20, Elizabeth
  20, Martha 71, 20, Mary 12,
  Nancy 152, Roseana 54, Sarah
  Jane 274
MC GUIRE, Margaret 187, Sarah 142
MC LATTAN, Polly 262
MC INTIRE, Elizabeth 70
MC INTOSH, Peggy 157
MC KAY, Elizabeth Ann 225, Malinda
  200
MC KENLEY, Isabella 133
MC KENNY, Margaret 150
MC KEY, Anne 48
MC KIFEE, Nancy 192
MC KINLEY, Martha 107
MC KINNEY, Jenny 249, Nancy 268,
  Sally 273
MC KINNY, Sally 82
MC KNABB, Adaline 97
MC KNIGHT, Polly 211
MC LAIN, Elizabeth 38, Lena 94
MC LANE, Nancy 191

MC LAUGHLIN, Alzada 29, Hester Per-
  ry 148, Martha 155
MC LAVIN (MCLAURIN), Mary 295
MC LELLAN, Sally 287
MC LEMON, Frances Elizabeth 191
MC LEMORE, Barbara 26, Bethenia
  Ann 191, Betsey 214, Elizabeth
  102, Margaret 73, 167, 292,
  Nancy 231, Priscilla 253, Sarah
  73
MC MAHAN, Diana 24, Louisa 134,
  Nancy 296, Rachel 86
MC MAURY, Mary 278
MC MEAN, Nancy 176
MC MILLEN, Catherine 211
MC MILLIN, Maryan 261
MC MULLEN, Polly 211
MC MULLIN, Susan 115
MC MURRAY, Mary 30, Sarah 221
MC NABB, Amanda 91, Eliza 36,
  Sarah 18
MC NEAL, Mary Ann 133
MC NEIL, Elizabeth 100, Permelia
  124
MC PHAIL, Sarah 196
MC PHERSON, Hanna 37, Lucretia 45
  Mahala 287, Margaret 57, Matilda
  97, Mary Ann 158, Mourning 85,
  Nancy 218, Patsey 129, Rebecca
  156, Sally 91
MC RAY, Lucy Ann 13
MC WHERTER, Jenny 29

NAIL, Matilda 17
NALL, Caroline 157, Elizabeth 7,
  Nancy 230, Polly 145, Susannah
  287
NALLS, Minerva 171
NANCE, America 232
NASH, Louisa 169
NEAL, Adelia Ann 261, Arthmisia
  204, Cesila 294, Elizabeth 128,
  Mary Ann 62, Mary E.S. 54,
  Mary 265, Nancy 284, 293, Rebec-
  ca 61, Susan 294
NEELY, Arman, 150, Elizabeth 195,
  Frances 41, Nancy Jane 132, Cath-
  arine 24,
NELLY, Charlotte 238, Eliza 131,
  Fanny 131, Frances 150, Jane 89,
  NELLLY, Mary 89, Rhoda 204,
  Sally 195, Sarah 214, 18, Sus-
  anna 204
NEIL, Polly 110
NELSON, Nancy 201, Sarah 193
NEVILS, Mary 102, Sarah 277
NEVILLS, Ann 28, Mary Addeline 14

NEWCOMB, Harriet 34
NEWCORN, Sarah 179
NEWMAN, Mildred 120
NEWSOM, Charlotte 183, Jane 198,
  Martha A.R. 277, Mary 197,
  Rebecca A. 280, Sarah 126
NICHOL, Matilda 236
NICHOLS, Elizabeth 181, Sarah 222
  Susan Ann 135
NICHOLSON, Abbigale 296, Betsey 50
  Cynthia 230, Frances 283, Louisa
  196, Martha 213, 24, Mary E. 108
  Mary M. 200, Matilda 24, Sarah
  202, Sophia 136, Susan 42
NIGHT, Polly 289
NIPPER, Mary 251
NOBLE, Parmelia S. 43
NOBLES, Nancy 32
NOLEN, Adelia 144, Ann 145, Belinda 195, Caroline 142, Delia 105,
  Delia C. 153, Eliza 80, 280,
  Emily 14, Frances 143, 267,
  Hardemia 101, Harriet 44, Jane
  123, Louisa 249, Lucy 115, Mary
  25, Michal 197, Nancy 148, 89,
  Peggy 147, Polly 70, Sarah 101,
  260, 196, Sena (Lena) 243,
  Tabitha 254
NORMAN, Betsey 3
NORRIS, Cinthia 98, Elizabeth 239,
  136, Martha Ann 100, Rachel 37
NORTH, Elisabeth 135, 222, Martha
  55, Mary A.R. 200, Priscilla
  205, Rhoda 272, Sally 223, 222
NORWOOD, Hannah 175
NUNN, Emily R. 210, Minerva 94,
  Polly 97, Sally 173

O BRIANT, Inda 48
ODELL, Frances 230
ODEN, Catharine 31, Elizabeth 199,
  Sarah 73
ODUM, Mary 88
OGILVIE, Amy 186, Elizabeth 191,
  Frances 227, Mary 221, Mary Jane
  186, Nancy 6, 153, Penelope 15,
  Piety 40, Sarah 153
OLD, Blanche P. 113, Elizabeth H.
  190, Martha A.M. 213, Mary 231,
  Polly 12, Sally P. 261
OLDHAM, Eliza 79, Elizabeth 151,
  Judith 116, Manerva 189, Martha
  10, Mary 264, Rebecca 227, Sally
  43
OLIVER, Dorcas 108, Elizabeth 33
  Nancy 142
OOTOIN Adeline 39, Charlotte 221

ORMAN, Adeline 179, Eliza 86,
  Martha 29, Mary E. 66
ORMES, Elizabeth 106, Harriett 175
  Polly M. 251
ORMS, Charlotte 118, Jane 188, Jane
  H. 1, Louisa C. 127
ORR, Elizabeth 174, Jenet 41,
  Polly 44
ORTAN, Nancy 272
ORTEN, Margaret M. 211
ORTON, Mary M. 60, Lucy 173, Narcissa 185, Mary 227
ORWIN, Tabitha 99
ORUM, Tabitha 99
OSBURN, Jane 30, Mary H. 249
OSLIN, Nancy 40
OSTEAN, Elizabeth 96
OSTEEN, Esther H. 223, Joanna 67,
  Masa 38
OTEY, Florence R. 45
OTT, Eliza A. 122
OUSBURN, Sina 39
OUTTRY, Polly 135
OVERTON, Casy 39, Martha 207
OWEN, Agnes 168, Amelia 253, Ascenatti S. 123, Delilah 17, Dorothy
  265, Eliza 118, Eliza Ann 201, 5
  Elizabeth 59, 202, 139, 268,
  Jane 154, Judith 214, 229, 71,
  Louesa 175, Lucinda 105, Margaret
  57, Martha 80, Mary 5, 258, 55,
  Mary Ann 232, 258, 37, Rachel 259,
  Sarah 105, 201, Luraney 285
OWENS, Elizabeth 68, Nancy 46
OXFORD, Polly 28
OZBORN, Elizabeth 212, Leah 274,
  Martha 216

PACE, Ann 133, Rachael 143,
PADGETT, Eliza 199, 246, Lucy 8
  Mary Jane 216, Nancy M. 216
PAGE, Elizabeth 248, Jean 94,
  Lovey 249, Martha 242, Nancy 74,
  Sally 249
PALMER, Elizabeth 277, Nancy 172
PALMON, Elizabeth 160, Joanna 258
PARHAM, Emily 258, Mary A.G.M.J.
  194, Rebecca 174, Zilleam 76
PARK, Elizabeth 180, 114, Frances
  41
PARKS, Elizabeth 171, Sally 173,
  Sarah Jane 132
PARKER, Artemisia 40, Margaret 59,
  Nancy 33, Sally 224, Susan 171
PARRISH, Caroline 210, Kitura 284,
  Mary A.E. 243, Rachel 40, Susannah 124, Tennessee 290

PARSONS, Hannah Bush 202, Martha 102
PASCHALL, Caroline 123, Elinor 2, Mary 208
PATE, Betsey 241, Elizabeth 256, Louisa 255, Lucy 243, Lucy Ann 144, Matilda 50, Minerva 60, Mary 206, Nancy 232, 143, Polly 205, Susan 60
PATTERSON, Catherine 195, Celia 56, Elizabeth 29, Jane 220, Lucinda 272, Margaret 192, Mary 15, 123 168, Sarah Jane 212, Susanna 184
PATTON, Bethynia 257, Drucilla 247, Eliza 15, Emeline 107, Jane 235, Margaret 11, 207, 181, 14, Martha Jane 62, Mary Ann 11 26, Rebecca 123, Sarah 200, Tuzza 250
PAYNE, Mary Louisa 67
PAYNOR, Catherine 124, Elizabeth 227
PEACH, Eliza 143, Elizabeth 38, Mary 236, Nancy Jane 2, Peggy 92, Susan 12
PEARCE, Clarissa 107, Nancy 248, Sarah 200
PEARSE, Elizabeth 16, Margaret 155 Sally 222 (Pearre)
PEAY, Betsey 5, Elizabeth 169, Manerva 186, Martha 217, Mary 14, 265, Nancy 149, Sarah 207
PEEBLES, Mary 120, Mary E.S. 6, Nancy 188, Susan 120
PEELER, Anne 152
PENNINGTON, Drucilla 244, Eliza 239, Sarah 244
PERKINS, Agatha 42, Agness 243, Ann Green 115, Bethunia 115, Cary 137, Eliza 126, 282, Eliza Mildred 209, Elizabeth 76, Elvira 109, Leah P. 191, Malvina 225, Marietta 148, Mary Ann 52, Mary E. 28, Nancy 169, Mary T. 179, Patience 198, Polly 209, Polly O'Neal 243, Rachel 192, Ritta 274, Sarah Myra 245
PERRY, Louisa 232, Malinda 70
PETERSON, Elisabeth 110
PETTUS, Elizabeth 149
PETWAY, Mary 190
PETTY, Polly 226
PEWETT, Nancy 105
PEWIT, Barbary 210, Nancy 78
PEWITT, Barbara 138, Margaret 91

PEWITT, Parallee 136, Polly Ann 246, Sarah 165, Susannah 176
PHAGAN, Lydia 180
PHELPS, Caroline 38, Elizabeth 66, Jane 294, Nancy 21, Sally 268
PHILIPS, Catherine 158, Elizabeth 264
PHILLIPS, Emily 267, Jane 264, Polly 126, 14, Sarah 94, Rebecca 12
PHIPPS, Nancy 209, Nelly 81, Patsy 81
PICKENS, Ann 237, Eziriah 237, Malinda 207
PICKERING, Senora 277
PICKRON, Malissa 254
PIGG, Betsy 236, Dicey 70, Nancy 203
PIGOTT, Amelia 258
PILLOW, Caledonia 119, Mary 230
PILLOWS, Polly 181
PINKARD, Mary Ann 169
PINKERTON, Betsey 169, Isabela 65, Jane 144
PINKLETON, Sarah 96
PINKSTON, Elizabeth 19, Fanny 132, Lavinia 5, Mary 261, 211, 35, Nancy 8, Polly 290, Rebecca 223, 92, 159, Sarah Angelia 141, Tennessee 257, Vinah 226
PIPSKIN, Harriet 11
PISTOLE, Martha 277
PITTS, Sally 177
PLUMLEE, Amy 220, Jane 279
PLUMLEY, Dorothy 48
POARCH, Nancy 157
POGNOR, Lucy 15, Susan 236
POINTER, Eleanor 35, Harriet 19, Susan 49
POLK, Ann 206, Elizabeth 190, Hannah 107, 212, Mary 127, 211, Nancy 291, Polly 163, Sarah 25
POLLARD, Martha 93
POMEROY, Elizabeth 177
POMROY, Catharine 257, Mary 177, Temperance 81
POPE, Amarillar 16, America 239, Ann 93, Candice 73, Cyntha 62, Elizabeth 156, Martha 65, 160, Missouri 161, Oney 13, Denny 13, Ruthy 63, Sally 276, Sarah 195, Winneford 203, Winnefred 167, Winney 156
PORTER, Amanda 296, Hannah 235, Mary 275, 46, Minerva 189, Nancy 40, Rebecca 187, Sally 82, Serena 135

POTTER, FRANCES ANN 73, Salina 196
  Sally Lark 84
POTTS, Cynthia 207, Elizabeth 166,
  Lucy 185, Maria 278, Mary 130,
  Nancy 241, 69, 81, Peggy 22,
  Polly 292, Rachael 232, Sarah A.
  160, Susan 257, 98
POWEL, Rachel 216
POWELL, Eliza 280, Elizabeth Ann
  11, 146, Etaline 258, Jean 77,
  Lavinia 101, Nancy 118, Polly
  192, Sally 207
POWERS, Elizabeth 104, Gimimna 216
  Martha Ann 67, Parmelia 128
POYNOR, Lucy 264, Mary Ann 293,
  Sarah Ann 263, Sarah 95
PRATT, Julia 65, Lavinia 65
PREAST, Fanny 18
PRICE, Ann 104, Betsy 129, Elizabeth 22, Isabell 94, Jane 48,
  Lucy 109, Mary 191, Mary Ann 12
  Sally 237, Susan 156
PRICHARD, Lucinda 282, Selena 216
PRICHETT, Elizabeth 233
PRITCHETT, Elizabeth 193, Melissa Jane 261
PRIEST, Elizabeth 195, Polly 137,
  Rebekah 157, Rhoda 194, Susan 7
  Tenny 187
PRIMM, Elizabeth 67, Isabella 276
  Mary 162, Polly 175
PRINCE, Angeline 255, Elizabeth
  123, 155, Viney 35
PROWELL, Annis 53, Mary 73, 70,
  217
PRUET, Ann 154
PRYOR, Sarah 246, Virginia 126
PUCKETT, Fanny 98, Sally 148
PUGH, Emily 122, Mary 98
PULLAM, Elizabeth 237
PUMROY, Milley 255, Nancy 185
PUTMAN, Canzady 140, Elizabeth 57
  Hannah 156, Holly 40, Jane 43,
  Janetta 63, Sarah 43, Susan 63
PUTNAM, Lavinia 266, Parry 156,

QUARLES, Matilda 48
QUINN, Eleanor 150, Elizabeth 225
  Lucy 215, Margaret 213, Martha
  202, Mary 281, Sally 20

RADFORD, Elizabeth 256, Lucy 226,
  Martha 119, Nancy 156, Ruth 45,
  164, Sally 268, Susan 268
RAGAN, Elizabeth 223, Emeline 171
RAGANS, Catherine 12

RAGINS, Hannah 46
RAGSDALE, Betsey 196, Celia 219,
  Dicey Jane 170, Dicy 220, Dicey
  220, 177, Elizabeth 63, 219, 132,
  57, 218, 213, Frances 166,
  Keziah 110, Mahala 144, Malinda
  227, Margaret 219, Martha 136,
  Martha A.T. 242, Nancy 132, 9,
  Polly 257, Rhoda 177, Ritta 240,
  Sally 219, Sarah 142
RAINS, Sally 51
RALSTON, Catharine 222, Margaret
  230, Martha 172, Mary 171
RANDOLPH, Elizabeth 219
RANEA, Prudence 99
RANEY, Louisa 82, Lucinda 162,
  Mary 97, Mary Ann 131, Nancy 101,
  Susan 101
RANSOM, Elizabeth 60, Sarah 166
RASH, Mariah 250, Rebecca 153,
  Sarah 97, Susan F. 192
RATCLIFFE, Ann 22, Rachael 257
RAY, Ann 169, Ann Matilda 6, Elizabeth 157, 122, 292, Hetty 231,
  Ibba 221, Martha Ann 167, Mary
  255, Monnica 205, Nancy 226,
  Rachel 110
REA, Nancy Jane 67
READ, Fanny 79, Lavinia 115, 271,
  Nancy 206
REAMS, Amanda 139, Amelia Ann 138,
  Frances 263, Louisa 172, Lucy
  Ann 173, Martha 82, 218, Mary
  60, Patsey 199, Rebecca 198,
  Sarah F. 221, Sarah M. 62, Vituria 198
REATRAW, Cintha 22
RED, Arissha 182, Louiza 176,
  Mary 196
REDD, Catherine 72
REDDLE, Elizabeth 236
REDFORD, Mary 272, Hannah 182
REDMAN, Eliza 264, Margaret 136,
  Saluda 111
REED (RUD), Catharine 159, Cynthia
  38, Elizabeth 295, Hannah 223,
  Mary 213, Nelly 54, Pheobe 227,
  Sarah 79
REESE, Elizabeth 67, Martha M.A.E.
  258, Sarah Ann 218
REEVES, Martha 42, Mary 201,
  Susan 123
REGION, Celia Ann 14
REID, Anna 288, Elisabeth 84,
  Eunice 235, Lavinia 290, Mary
  Eliza 271, Priscilla 80

REILLY, Harriett 89, Susan 109
REVEL, Mary Ann 246, Sally 139, Thena 213
REVIS, Nancy A.J. 171
REYNOLDS, Bethenia 110, Caledonia 259, Elizabeth 61, Harriet 114, Jincy 20, Mary A. 203, 93, Mary M. 17, Nancy 143, Phebe 244, Pheby 72, Polly 61, 225, Sarah 139, Sally 85, Susan 61, Unity 250
RHOADES, Susan W.H. 230
RHOADS, Elizabeth 112
RHODES, Betsey 101, Mary 194, Rosey 243, Sally 220
RICE, Eliza 215
RICHARDSON, Delila 218, Sally 262
RICKETTS, Margaret 25, Nancy 218
RIDDLE, Susan 147
RIDGE, McCandles 161, Sally 3
RIDLEY, Ann 82, Elizabeth 236, 280 Martha 129, 6, Rebecca 141, 41
RIELY, Sarah 168
RIGAR, Nancy 128
RIGGINS, Betsey 294, Edy 138
RIGGS, Mary 111, Mira 198, Nancy 79
RINES, Mary 201 (Rives?)
RITCHIL, Rebecca 251
RITTER, Love 31
RIVERS, Ann 230, Sarah 89
RIVES, Mary 201
ROACH, Mary 46, Nancy 198
ROADS, Betsey 250
ROAR, Frankey 125
ROBBINS, Nancy 41, Rebecca 38
ROBERSON, Elizabeth 219, Martha 246, 108, Matilda 46
ROBERTS, Ann 160, 273, Anna 232, Betsey 159, Charlotte 112, Elizabeth 268, Fanny 253, Icy 74, Lucy 258, Marjory 13, Maranda 112, Mary F. 33, Nancy 254, 17, 2, Nancy Owen 99, Patsy 225, Rachel 279, Sally 222, Sarah Ann 170, Susanah 112
ROBINSON, Catherine 243, Elizabeth 122, Frances 227, Jemeth 265, Martha 41, Martha A.E. 62, Mary 14, Mary A. 246, Nancy 208, Polly 22, 219, Rebecca 256, 228 Sarah 266, Sarah Ann 64, Sarah Jane 228, Margaret 194, Sally 8
ROBISON, Martha J. 142
ROBERTSON, Betsey 269, Betsey Ann 219, Catharine 98, Charlotte 270 Eleanor 285, Elizabeth 107,

ROBERTSON, Judah 127, Maria 22, Martha A.P.T. 107, Mary 32, Milly 238, Nancy 190, Patsey 127, Polly 221.
ROBINS, Elizabeth 133
RODDERY, Norry 199
RODGERS, Nancy 4
ROGERS, Charlotte 212, Frances 8, Mary 205, 232, 283, Nancy 179, Ruth 97, Zane 111
ROLAND, Caroline R. 293, Caroline Rebecca 293, Margaret 130, Mary Ann 104, 205
ROLLAND, Sarah Jane 242
ROLLER, Esther 185, Matilda 235
ROOK, Mary 268
ROPER, Elizabeth 251, Louisa 224, Mary 51, Sally 64
ROSENBUM, Charity 179
ROSS, Jenny 169
ROUNSEVALL, Elizabeth 98
ROUNSWALL, Polly 20
ROUNSAVALL, Scina 95
ROWLAND, Rebecca 60
ROWLETT, Ann 90, Lucy 101
ROY, Catharine H. 266, Eliza 178, Martha 214
ROYSTER, Elizabeth 120
ROZELL, Sophia 50
ROZZELL, Sarah 110, Miscinda 232
RUBOTTOM, Sally 227
RUCKER, Keturah 38, Mary E. 97, Myra 172, Sarah 77
RUCKS, Elizabeth 111
RUD, Catherine 159
RUDDER, Jane E.H. 278, Lucy 247, Mary 186, Mary Ann 251, Mary C. 247
RUDER, Catharine 157, Nancy 284
RUFFIN, Mildred 178
RUPARD (RESARD), Susan 252
RUSELL (RUPELL), Bitsey 70
RUPERD (RUSERD), Betty 275
RUSE (REESE), Nancy Ann 47
RUSEL, Patsey 96
RUSEL, Rebecca 118
RUSSELL, Amelia 52, Ann 85, Clarissa 61, Eliza 210, Elizabeth 288, Helen 72, Lucy Ann 232, Mary 49, Nancy 295, 291, Tisitah 251
RUSTIN, Mesina 102
RUTHERFORD, Agnes 239, Clarissa 95, Elizabeth 62, Jane 183, Margaret 183, Mary 263
RUTLEDGE, Fanny 184, Margaret 24, Susannah 185

SADLER, Judy 106, Mary 174, Nancy 207
SAMMONS, Margaret 127, 54
SAMPKINS (LAMPKINS) Lucinda 129, Susan A. 125
SAMPLE, Sarah Ann 160
SAMPSON, Ede, Elizabeth 62, Mary 154, Rebecca 117
SANDERS, Louisa 86
SANFORD, Elizabeth 19, Lucy 129, Mary Jane 71, Polley 79
SAPPINGTON, Ann B. 149, Rebecca B. 97, Susan 238
SARMONS, Sally 52
SATTERFIELD, Susan 51
SAUCER, Elizabeth 112
SAUNDERS, Fanny 164, Sophia 204
SAWYERS, Catherine 188, Keziah 47, Sally 154, Sarah 234
SAYERS, Mary 234
SCALES, Ann B. 52, Ann D. 234, Anne 234, Eliza B. 6, Elizabeth 42, 140, Jane 20, Jemima 76, Leah P.P. 164, Mary 185, 234, 202, 123, Mildred 88, Nancy 64, Nancy Jane 234, Nancy K. 234, Tabitha 234, Theodicia 122
*SCRUGGS, Sally 272, Sarah 237
SCONCE, Cynthia 141
SCOTT, Elizabeth 137, 128, 203, Ibby 156, Malvina 222, Margaret 190, Nancy 229, Polly 158, Viney 116
* SCRUGGS, Augusta Ann 146, Elizabeth 170, Jane 74, Mary 47, Nancy P. 66, Virginia 228
SCURLOCK, Nancy 43
SEA (LEA), Polly Ann 86
SEAGLER, Nancy 251
SEATON, Eliza 238, Rachael 2, Susan 3
SEATTE, Mary R. 229
SEAY, Louisiana 79, Patsey 239
SECREST, Jane 160, Matilda 244
SEWELL, Oney 51
SHADERICK, Elizabeth 293, Sarah 157
SHAFFER, Matilda Ann 208
SHANKS, Sarah 267
SHANNON, Elizabeth 85
SHANNON, Elizabeth 269, Jane 191, Mary Ann 228, Nancy 216, Rebecca 267, Rebecca Jane 34
SHARBER, Elizabeth 3, Mary Jane 42 Nancy 168
SHARP, Amanda 129, Ann B. 29,

SHARP, Barbary G. 140, Elizabeth 146, 229, 146, Jane 30, Jane 89, Nancy 193, Peggy 135, Polly B. 205
SHARPE, Margaret N. 40
SHAW, Amanda 113, Elizabeth 118, Mahala 17, Martha Caroline 131, Mary 100, Mary Ann 118, Mary Jane 133, Pamelia 100, Rebecah 52, Sophia 73, Susan 246
SHELBURN, Ann P. 2
SHELBURNE, Elizabeth 256, Mary S. 61, Sally 222
SHELL, Amanda 84, Mary 184, Parmelia 281
SHELTON, Amanda Jane 25, America 25 Caroline 202, Lucinda L. 86, Margaret 8, Martha 153, Mary Ann 102, Polly 80, Priscilla 84
SHEPHERD, Polly 166, Sarah 278
SHEPMAN, Peggy 122
SHEPPARD, Marthy 57, Phebe 246
SHERMAN, Caroline 51
SHERRIN, Catharine 154, Elizabeth 294, Nancy 280
SHERWOOD, Martha 111
SHIELDS, Unity 118
SHINES, Ann Maria 15
SPINN, Ann Maria 15
SHOARES, Polly 104
SHOOK, Elizabeth 176
SHORES, Peggy 104
SHORT, Cyntha 225, Elizabeth 260, Lilly Ann 252, Molinda Ann 37, Mary M. 21, Milly 103, Polly 263, Rebecca 21, Sally 11, Sally L. 47
SHUMATE, Barbara 295, Barbary 275 Betsy 172, Jane 230, Marthusa 146 Sally 20
SHUTE, Elizabeth 65, Gracy 57
SILLS, Nancy 127
SIMMONS, Hicksy 66, Mary 214, Mary Abigail 180, Milly 253, Nancy 169, Temperance 94
SIMON, Lydia 187
SIMPKINS, Rachel 221, Ibby 265, Betsey 168
SIMPSON, Eliza An 246, Orpeth 23, Rebecca 121
SIMS, Ann H. 288, Mary D. 271, Polly 213, Sarah 272
SINDER (SINCLER) Mary 4
SINGLETARY, Mahala 284
SINGLETERY, Sally 151
SINGLETON, Lucy 272

SIRES, Mary Ann 30, Sarah 231
SKELLEY, Catharine 13
SKELLY, Sally 13, Sarah E. 227
SKELLINGTON, Clarissa 115,
SKILLINGTON, Cynthia 184, Elizabeth 241
SKINNER, Drucilla 7
SLATER, Ann 150, Sarah 28
SLAUGHTER, Cornelia 235
SLEDGE, Lucy 105, Martha Ann 291, Mary Ann 61, Sally 242
SLICKER, Patsey 188
SLOAN, Margaret 183, Nancy 157, Polly 256
SLOANE, Rachel 285
SLONE, Amanda 50
SMALL, Sally 116
SMITH, Amelia Ann 293, Ann C. 177 Ann Hickman 263, Ann P. 117, Anna 39, Barbary 210, Catharine S. 12, Charity 288, Eliza 239, Elizabeth 200, 110, 109, 211, 266, 70, Elizabeth A. 85, Elizabeth P. 29, Ellinor 30, Elvira H.H. 100, Fanny 52, Frances 125, Frances A. 99, Hannah 130, Jane 71, Jane A. 245, Jane E. 50, Judith 56, Kitty 30, Loretta 209 Louise 7, Lucinda 172, Marilda 84, Martha H. 243, 85, Mary 77, 107, 90, 145, 267, Mary E. 50, Mary H. 255, Mary Jane 206, Nancy 239, 132, 266, Narcissa 206, Peggy 176, Rachel 239, Sally 169 145, Sarah A. 254, Sarah E. 270, Sarah K. 240, Scina 211, Mrs. Sidney 93, Susan 208, Susan D. 210, Susan S. 276, Thania 210
SMITHSON, Catherine K. 241, Charlotte 241, Dolly 143, Eliza 241 Elizabeth 259, Louisa 244, Martha 263, 100, 155, 155, Mary Jane 155, Minerva 236, Nancy 263 Parmelia 98, Sally 226, Sarah 244, 235
SNEED, Bethenia 198, Bethunia 194 Catharine 70, Martha 239, Mary 245, Sarah 284
SNELLGROVE, Elizabeth 242
SNOW, Mary 232
SOMMERVILLE, Emily 220
SOUTH, Elizabeth 8
SOUTHALL, Eliza 121, Julia Ann 238 Mary 90, Nancy Ann 190, Rebecca 116, Sarah Jane 105
SOWELLS, Livinia 69
SPARKMAN, Celia 290, Clary 293

SPARKMAN, Delila 236, Delamy 245, Elizabeth 266, Margaret 210, Mary 3, Polly 269, Winey 293
SPEED, Sarah A. 250
SPENCE, Jane 96
SPENCER, Betsey 14, Frankey 149, Louisa 173, Mary Jane 133
SPROTT, Jane 50, Parraller 157, Rachel 249
SQUIRE, Sarah 184
STACKS, Elizabeth 128
STAGGS, Catharine 204, Dolley 274 Eliza 45, Milly 45, Nancy 67, Narcissa 64, Patsey 67, Polly 276
STANDLEY, Ancy 218, Hannah 47, Winny 4
STANFIELD, Allebury 153, Elizabeth 114, Jane 67, Martisha 113, Mary 182, 205, Milly 290, Nancy 248, Polly 290
STANLEY, Eliza 38, Elizabeth 218, 65, Emily 57, Mary 161, 64, Polly 43, Nancy 212, Sally 188, Sarah Jane 198
STAR, Polly 177
STARKS, Elizabeth 10
STARNES, Camilla 244, Catharine 182 Mary 182, 281, Parthenia 262
STATEN, Sally 11
STEELE, Mary 248, Nancy 286
STEPHENS, Anne 211, Ann M.D. 64, Catherine 31, Charlotte 215, Elisabeth 9, 292, Eliza Mary 212 Emily 198, Ferrely 30, Mary Ann 238, Mary M. 210, Minerva 255, Nancy 36, 228, Polly 233, Rosanna 54, Sarah 39
STEPHENSON, Dorchas 26, Eliza Ann 249, Jemima 249, Mary A. 60, Nancy 172, Peggy 163, Susan 121 Almira 291
STEVENS, Narcissa 272, Mary D. 171, Mary M. 220, Sally 267, Sarah Ann 123
STEVENSON, Sarah F. 192
STEWART, Esther 170, Jane 43, Nelly 233, Sally 216
STILL, Ann 283, Elizabeth 151, Louisa 141, Lucy Ann 171, Martha 174, 88, Martha Ann 22
STOBUCK, Margaret 210
STOCKETT, Alamannah 293, Lucy 237 Susan 203, Sophia 106, Susan 31
STODDART, Sally 118
STOKES, Betsey 222, Eliza 183, Lucinda 121, Philadelphia 253, Thursey 256

STONE, Agnes P. 141, Elizabeth 76,
E. H. 65, Jane 53, Mary 224,
Nancy 230, Parthenia 116, Rebecca 225, Sally 106, Virginia 134
STOVALL, Elizabeth 83
STRATRAM, Hannah 91
STREET, Sally M. 201
STRICKLAND, Celia A. 148, Tilpha 113
STRICKLIN, Polly 215
STRIPLAN, Ann 230
STUART, Eliza 115
STURDIVANT, Sally 277
SUDBERRY, Ann 225, Elizabeth 256, 200, Mary P. 33, Sarah C. 31
SULLIVAN, Betsey 77, Mary 239, Rebecca 185
SUMNER, Mary 214, Polly 251
SUMNERS, Sarah 48
SUTTON, Martha E. 281, Martha Virginia 281, Sarah 121
SWANSEY, Nancy 6
SWANSON, Adelicia 173, Amelia Ann 57, Martha E. 243, Mary 183, Nancy 103
SWEENEY, Louisa 211
SWISHER, Ann 282, Anna Houston 112 Cynthia 132, Nancy 271

TAILOR, Nancy 109
TAIT, Mary 58
TALIAFERO, Ann M. 234, Lucy 143, Mary A. 252, Verlinda 36
TALLIAFERRO, Harriett 127
TALLY, Henritta 13, Martha Ann 139
TALLEY, Parmelia 164, Patsey 77
TANKSLEY, Emily 171
TANNER, Julia A. 97, Lucy H. 117, Martha C. 157, Virginia H. 97
TAPLEY, Mary 186
TARKINGTON, Amelia 263, Betsey 216 Charity 21, Eliza 94, Keziah 85 Louisa 234, Milly 251, Polly 79 Tilpha 200, Zylpha 118
TARPLEY, Jane 113, Lucy 239, Nancy 214
TATE, Priscilla G. 106
TATUM, Ann M. 30, Celia 226, Mary 250, Peggy 250, Sally 231
TAYLOR, Anna 93, Betsey 184, 223, 146, Claressa 110, Eleanor (Nelly) 285, Eliza 280, Elizabeth 107, 172, 109, 223, 204, Ellendar 44, Fanny 102, Frances 31, 203, Grizzle 149, Julia 237 Lany 128, Martha 152, 261, 97,

TAYLOR, Martha H. 244, Mary Ann 233, Nancy 15, 287, 255, Polly 290, Rebecca 49, Rosey 243, Sally 48 Sarah 152, Selinda 28, Tabby 22
TEMPLE, Elizabeth 146, Martha Ann 13, Mary 202, Matilda 213, Nancy 139, Sarah Jane 53, Susan T. 196
TERRELL, Elizabeth 20, Harriet 262 Martha 117, Mary 144, Sarah 280
TERRILL, Anna 120
TERRY, Ann 283, Anna 257, Christian 258, Elizabeth 25, Lucy 207, Nancy 52
THACKEY, Ann 3
THEWEATT, Sally 98
THOMAS, Catharine 220, Eliza 153, Ellan 79, Louisa 121, Lucy 221, Martha 192, Nancy 162, Potcia 212 Polly 212, Portia E. 121, Rebecca J. 109, Ruth 91, Sally 197, Sarah W. 141
THOMASON, Caroline A. 98, Eliza H. A. 25
THOMPSON, Adeline 271, Agnes 154, Eliza Ann 130, Elizabeth 8, 35, 137, 94, 10, Jane 62, 89, 104, 32, Margaret 267, 69, Mariah 105, Martha A. R. 201, Mary 12, Mickey 90, Minerva Eliza Ann 166, Nancy 95, Polly 268, Rachel 282, Rebecca 18, Sarah 186, Susan C. 206, Susan W. 238
THOMPKINS, Sally 119
THORNBOROUGH, Martha 180
THORNBROUGH, Eliza E. 153, Louisa E. 153
THWEATT, Catherine 99, Elizabeth 210, 54, Frances D. 258, Mary 231 Nancy 166, 15, Rebecca 159
THURMAN, Ann 96, Macharina 18
TIFFANY, Osee 170, Sally 68
TIGNOR, Mary 89, Puina 151
TILLETT, Mary Ann 62, Nancy 294
TILMAN, Elizabeth 197, Frances 197
TILLMAN, Martha 211, 197, Mary 115
TIMMONS, Kerziah 78
TINDALE, Caledonia 170
TINDALL, Elizabeth 248, Sarah Jane 87
TINER, Brunnetta 215
TINSLEY, Elizabeth 65, Polly P. 163
TISDALE, Elizabeth 226, Nancy 79, 247, Susan 212
TOMBLIN, Nancy 187
TOMLINSON, Louisa 206, Martha 139 Sarah 186
TOMPKINS, Barsheba 69, Elizabeth 262 Rachel 35

TOOMBS, Frances 285
TOOMS, Susannah 163
TOON, Fanny 127, Kathron 230, Narcissa 13
TOONE, Milly 7, Sarah 57
TOWNLIN, Elizabeth 34
TOWNSON, Dosia 260, Jane 84
TRAIL, Mary 260
TRANTHAM, Elizabeth 110
TREMBLE, Nancy 226
TRENCHAM, Sealey 208
TRENTHAM, Sealey 207
TRIMBLE, Amanda 82, Elizabeth 194
TROTTER, Martha 16
TROUT, Nancy 254
TRUETT, Matilda 24, Sally 128
TUCKER, Annis 35, Edy B. 269, Eliza 241, Elizabeth 159, 258, Emeline 223, Fanny 252, Holly 28, Julia Ann 275, Malinda 269, Martha 77, 217, Mary 146, Matilda 252, Nancy 56, Rebecca 77, 56, 78, Sally 54, 77, Sarah 261, 29, Tennessee 9
TULL, Mary Elizabeth 56
TULLOSS, Ann M. 6, Mary 207, 208, 194
TUNING, Eliza 36
TURBEVILLE, Milly 150
TURMAN, Matilda 10
TURNAGE, Obedience 34
TURNER, Elizabeth 163, Frances 135, Isabella (Elizabeth) 233, Jane 199, Lucinda 149, Martha 226, Parmelia 105, Parthenia 193, Polly 197, Sally 20
TUTER (TEETER), Eliza 230
TWEATT, Elizabeth 24
TYNER, Sally 256

UNDERHILL, Naomy 193
UNDERWOOD, Cena 119, Elizabeth 234, Nancy 47
UPSHIRE, Charity 6
UTLEY, Nancy 272

VANNATTA, Maria 127, Nancy 120
VAN PELT, Lucinda 21
VAUGHAN, Amanda 227, Celia 238, Elizabeth A. 131, Elvira K. 4, Hannah D. 276, Jane 34, Judith 111, June (Jane) 209, Mary Jane 230, 192, Nancy 133, 287, 217, 124, Sarah 207, Sarah Ann 150, Susan A. 260
VAUGHN, Elizabeth A. 34, Mary 262, Milly 239, Susan 216

VAUGHT, Eliza Jane 296
VAUGHTER, Martha 217
VAULT, Martha 201, 283
VENABLE, Hannah 111, Jenny 94, Martha 92, 259
VINIBLE, Rebecca 74
VENATTA, Catharine 33
VERNON, Elly 227, Ellenor 89, Marion 82, Matilda 241, Mary 264, Nancy 112
VESTAL, Elizabeth 246, Martha 143
VINEGARDEN, Elizabeth 66
VINIBLE, Rebecca 74
VOWELL, Martha 147

WADDEL, Caty 249
WADDELL, Jane 75
WADDEY, Virginia 181
WADDILL, Susan 144
WADE, Betsey 168, Clarissa 24, Jane 68, Jenny 255, Mary 260, 160, Rebecca 125, Susan 239
WAKEFIELD, Cynthia 51, Elizabeth 296, Lucinda 246, Margaret 92, Mary 92, Nancy 92, Rebecca 119
WALKE, Polly 38
WALKER, Ann 207, Charity 172, Delilah Jane 92, Edy 107, Elizabeth 265, 44, 24, 4, Jane 278, 100, Judy 32, Lucinda 47, Mahala 257, Martha 27, Mary 206, 268, 267, Milly 257, Nancy 11, Nancy Jane 104, Peggy 131, Phebe Ann 184, Polly 93, Rebecca 156, Sarah Elizabeth 259, Sarah Rosanna 290, Susan 119, 7, 177, 230, Susanna 213
WALL, Catherine 48, Catharine 241, Christenia 270, Christener 27, Lucy 71, Mary 264, 35, Minerva Ann Tennessee 8, Nancy 68, 19, 190, 128
WALLACE, Martha 78, Rachel 259, Sarah 262, 223
WALLER, Almira 53, Betsey 247, Jane Elizabeth 106, Jane 113, Mary 113, Nancy 75, Nancy Ann 40, Sara Ann 240, Sarah F. 68
WALTERS, Elizabeth 247, Polly 249
WALTHALL, Jane 214
WALTON, Catharine 264, Eliza 58, Elizabeth 158, Kiziah 236, Lockey 44, Lucy 74, Martha 235, 294, 295, 273, Mary 131, Mildred 259, Susan 167
WARREN, America 86, Deborah 243, Eliza 84, Elizabeth 195, 291,

WARREN, Eve 249, Frances 249
  Jane 215, Lucinda 118, Martha
  Jane 32, Mary 269, Mary Jane 173
  Milly 179, Miranda 205, Nancy
  205, 124, 37, Sarah 26, 134,
  289, 241
WARMOTH, J. N. 111
WARSON, Elizabeth 45
WATERS, Elizabeth 182, Keziah 146
  Martha Ann 217, Peggy 37
WATKINS, Betsey 262, 10, Elizabeth
  153, Fanny 135, Martha 153, Mary
  248, Milly 180, Rebecca 246
WATSON, Eliza 256, Jane 28, Laetitia 67, Marion 29, Nancy 159
WEATHERS, Mary 86, Winafred 137
WEAVER, Didimoah 65
WEBB, Catharine 90, Elizabeth 129,
  79, 276, Fanny 234, Martha 197,
  Mary 160, 133, 117, Mildred 234,
  Patsey 44, Rachel 198, Rebecca
  139, Selica 286
WEBBER, Tabetha 13
WEBSTER, Nancy 156
WELCH, Betsey 140, Franky 171
WELBURN, Arabella 289
WELLBORN, Eliza Adaline 158
WELLS, Caroline 52, Catherine 223,
  Elizabeth 294, Frances Jane 252,
  Lucinda 202, Margaret 42, Martha
  Virginia 77, Mary 280, 268,
  Matilda 51, 235, Montgomery 141,
  Patsey 135, Polly 75, Sarah 194,
  26, Susan Ann 284, Tempy 235,
  Viny 64
WEST, Elizabeth 67, 55, Malinda
  Jane 188, Margaret 243, Susannah 277, Violet K.M. 103
WESTBROOK, Hannah 206
WESTBROOKS, Jane 71, Nancy 248
WHAILEY, Elizabeth 59
WHALEY, Mary E.T. 121
WHALY, Mary Anne 3
WHEELER, Frances J. 102, Jane 223,
  Mary Ann 102
WHITBY, Elizabeth 49, Martha 211,
  133, Mary E. 167, Polly 161, 235,
  Sarah 179
WHITE, Adeline 151, Ann 287, Anna
  54, Arrazine 293, Eleanor 56, 33,
  Catharine 262, Cynthia 136, Dicey
  Adelia 64, Eliza 206, Elisabeth
  255, Elizabeth 160, 278, Elizabeth Ann 106, Fanny Ann 251,
  Finetta (Tinetta) P. 219, Frances
  50, Isabella 55, Jane 71, 59,
  Janette 233, Julia 67, Lettie 236

WHITE, Lourana 50, Lovey 75,
  Lucinda 270, Mahala Ann 278,
  Margaret 238, Margaret Ann 100,
  Martha 258, 95, 282, Mary 11,
  172, 136, Mary Ann 71, Mary J.
  142, Matilda 96, Mildredge Ann
  103, Nancy 197, 288, 54, Nanny 13,
  Naoma 118, Pamelia 157, Patsey
  209, Peana 154, Penelope 219,
  Peny E. 150, Phebe Ann 280, Polly
  209, 50, 212, 129, Rachel 258,
  Rebecca 258, Ritty 189, Ruth 54,
  Sally 144, 31, 8, 38, Sarah 291,
  Sarah Ann H. 34, Susan 95
WHITLHEAD, Eliza Ann 262, Lucinda
  58
WHITFIELD, Eliza 202, Lucy 63,
  Martha Ann 48, Nancy 289, Rebecca
  5, Sarah 193, Theodocia 53, 51,
  Virginia 53
WHITLEY, Mary 37, Nancy 229
WHITLOCK, Dice 232, Ruth 288
WHITSITT, Martha 43, 44
WHITTENTON, Elizabeth 135
WHITUS, Sarah Jane 45
WHITWORTH, Martha 187, Rebecca 220
WIGGINS, Mary 27
WIGGS, Rebecca 269
WILBANKS, Polly 139
WILBURN, Elizabeth 176, Mary 45,
  Parmelia 34
WILD, Franky 276
WILDS, Elizabeth 226
WILEY, Jane 46, Sarah 8, Susan 41
WILIE, Elizabeth 131
WILKES, Mary Teresa 36
WILKINS, Eliza 134, Elizabeth 177,
  Elizabeth 41, Joanna 167, Nancy
  145, Polly 154, Rebecca 7, Sally
  38, Sarah 79, Susan 296
WILKINSON, Alley 45, Martha 280,
  Mary 138, Matilda 37, Polly 46,
  Sarah 19, Terressa 242
WILKS, Celicia 43, Jane 265
WILLETT, Charlotte 52, Hannah 161,
  Sarah 273
WILLIAMS, Ann 287, Caroline 51,
  Charlotte 39, Eliza 107, Elizabeth 76, 9, 292, 289, 197, 118,
  Frances 55, 116, Henrietta 3, 77,
  Jane 86, Jean 284, Kizzy 134,
  Louisa 277, Margaret 174, Martha
  283, 149, 220, Mary 174, 115, Mary
  A.E. 130, Mary Ann 115, Melissa
  Ann 23, Milley 32, Nancy 227, 73,
  228, 237, 214, Parler 166, Phebe
  2, Polly 93, 254, Rebecca 67, 3,

WILLIAMS, Sally 193, 31, Sarah 207 19, Sarah Ann 252, Secy 142, Sicily 173, Susan 134, 293,
WILLIAMSON, Emily 208, Jane 215, Lucinda 148, Margaret Jane 243, Martha 61, Martha Ann 63, Minerva 280, Nancy 191, 137, Priscilla 235, Rebecca 210, Rhoda 180, Sally 82, Susan 96
WILLIE (WYLIE), Nancy 154
WILLS, Martha 164, Palina 22
WILSON, Adeline 183, Almyra 44, Ann 250, Asanath 120, Betsey 220 177, Catharine 68, 183, 263, Charity 242, Eleanor 40, Eliza 197, 288, Elizabeth 233, 16, 234, 260, 198, Elvy 260, Emeline 287, Emily 238, Fanny 159, Jamie 280, Jane 243, 217, 15, 37 Jenny 286, 98, Leah 128, Malinda 286, Malvina 203, Margaret 160, Margaret Ann 203, Margaret M. 244, Margaret W. 176, Maria 284 Mary 160, 235, 283, 287, 121, 118, 260, 95, 48, 261, 287, Matilda 146, Melissa Ann 234, Narcissa 142, Patsey 269, Polly 265, 115, 242, Peggy 288, Rebecca 44, 114, 288, Rexina 287, Rispas 222, Rizpah 120, Sally 270, Sarah 271, 284, Sarah Norfleet 282, Scinthia 286, Susannah 228
WINDAWS, Catherine 108
WINDROW, Maranda 188
WING, Mary 129
WINROW, Lamisa 11, Sally 45
WINSETT, Anne 215, Irena 254, Letsey 130, Lucinda 36, Rilley 217, Sarah 172, Sency 21
WINSLOW, Eliza 63, Polly 222, Sally 82
WINSTED, Elixabeth 81
WINSTEAD, Mary 246, Patsey 182
WIRTHINGTON, Seally 245
WISENOR, Harriette 167, Nancy 264 Sarah 113
WISNER, Peggy 33, Sally 245
WITHERINGTON, Sarah 133, Selah 80
WITHERSPOON, Harriet 281, Polly 229
WITT, Eliza Ann 2, Agnes 140
WOMACK, Judith B. 18, Mary 222, Sarah 150
WOOD, America 27, Betsey 69, Caroline 117, Elizabeth 152, 159, 96, 205, Fanny 232, Frances 126,

WOOD, Frances 126, 159, Jean 91, Keziah 200, Malinda 105, Margaret 253, Mary 233, 204, Mary Ann 84, 232, Mary E. 71, 160, Nancy 27, Sally 148, 290, 294, Sarah 273, 181, Sarah 149, Susannah 119
WOODS, Edline 248, Mary Ann 220, Polly 129, Rhoda 266
WOODRUFF, Mary Jane 36, Susan 125
WOODSON, Margaret 164
WOOLF, Elizabeth 109
WOLDRIDGE, Elizabeth 275, Susan 195
WOOLDRIDGE, Mary 36, Narcissa 21, Susan 73
WOOTEN, Delila 230, Mary 242, Eleanor 204, Nancy 122, Patsey 184
WORD, Judith 142, Louisa 84, Margaret 278
WORLEY, Anna 279, Ruth 251
WRAY, Elizabeth 55, Louisa 249, Mary 243, 170, Mary Ann 166,
WRENN, Martha 229
WRIGHT, Ann 225, Betsey 161, Elizabeth 183, Jane 182, Lucinda 104, Polly 259, Priscilla 79, Sarah Jane 16
WYNNE, Amanda 102, Martha 194

YARBROUGH, Elizabeth Ann 59, Marcaney 277, Rebekah 20, Vinia 164
YATES, Diana 2, Dianna 242, Eleanor 43, Polly 192
YEARGAIN, Mary 240
YEARGAN, Rebica 15
YEARGIN, Sarah 107, Susan 143
YORK, Elizabeth 117, Jane 53, Mary 51, Nancy 108
YOUNG, Amanda Jane 208, Betsey 188, Lucy 51, Lucy Jane 196, Martha 71, 190, Mary 281, 253, 99, 264, Mary Ann 226, Mildred 78, Nancy 234, Narcissa Jane 122, Sally 136, Sarah 159, Sarah 196, Sarah Ann 99, Tempe 197
YOUNGER, Elizabeth 284, Lucy Ann 296, Mary 166, 267, Patsey 90, Sarah 208

ZACHRY, Caty 101
Zacry, Amanda 15

www.ingramcontent.com/pod-product-compliance
Lightning Source LLC
Chambersburg PA
CBHW020055020526
44112CB00031B/184